1999 SUPPLEMENT TO
HEALTH LAW

CASES, MATERIALS AND PROBLEMS

Third Edition

By

Barry R. Furrow
Professor of Law and Director, Health Law Institute
Widener University

Thomas L. Greaney
Professor of Law and Professor of Health Administration
St. Louis University

Sandra H. Johnson
Professor of Law, Professor of Health Administration and
Professor of Law in Internal Medicine
St. Louis University

Timothy S. Jost
Newton D. Baker, Baker & Hostetler Professor
of Law and Professor of Health Services
Management and Policy
The Ohio State University
and Visiting Professor
Washington and Lee University

Robert L. Schwartz
Professor of Law and Professor of Pediatrics
University of New Mexico

AMERICAN CASEBOOK SERIES®

WEST GROUP

ST. PAUL, MINN., 1999

Table of Contents

Table of Cases

The principal cases are in bold type. Cases cited or discussed in the text are roman type. References are to pages. Cases cited in principal cases and within other quoted materials are not included.

*

1999 SUPPLEMENT TO
HEALTH LAW
CASES, MATERIALS AND PROBLEMS
Third Edition

*

Chapter 1

DEFINING EVALUATING AND DIS-
TRIBUTING HEALTH CARE:
AN INTRODUCTION

Add, on page 48, at the end of note 1:

An excellent discussion of current issues of health care quality improvement can be found in Volume 76 of The Milbank Quarterly (No.4 1998), entitled Improving the Quality of Health Care.

Add, on page 50, before Part IV:

ROBERT H. BROOK, CAREN J. KAMBERG, AND ELIZABETH A. McGLYNN, HEALTH SYSTEM REFORM AND QUALITY

276 JAMA 476 (1996)

The U.S. health care delivery system is changing rapidly, dominated mainly by the shift from fee-for-service to managed care medicine. What are the implications for the practice of medicine as a result of the shift from patient-based to population-based medicine? As resources directed to health care are reduced, how will the trade-off between cost and quality be altered? Will quality even remain on the agenda as health system reform proceeds?

* * *

EIGHT ISSUES RELATED TO THE COST QUALITY TRADE–OFF

1. As the shift to managed care continues in response to cost pressures, will efforts focus solely on how to reduce expenditures, or will maintaining and even improving quality remain on the agenda? The principal concern at the employer and insurance company level has been the cost of health care. As health care delivery is transformed to a predominately managed care system, how can we ensure that quality of care remains part of the debate?

2. How will the delivery of care change as a result of the shift from patient-based to population-based medicine? The emergence of managed care as the predominant health care delivery mode has resulted in a fundamental change in the paradigm of medical care. Previously, a physician's primary responsibility was to do everything possible for the patient who visited his or

her office. Today, some physicians are responsible for a population of patients and for a budget that needs to be spent wisely. In other words, the physician in a managed care setting is responsible for the health of an entire enrolled population, not just those patients who actively use the health care system. This raises a number of questions: How do physicians make trade-offs between patients competing for limited resources? How much physician time should be invested in dealing with people who do not return to see a physician, or who never see a physician, as opposed to those who use the medical care system voluntarily? What strategies should be undertaken by the physician to track the patient population in terms of mental, physical, and social functioning? Should patients be required to be active participants in evaluating both their health care system and the effectiveness of the services that they receive (e.g., provide written information on their physical functioning after receiving a new pair of knees, or provide information that will be used to determine if their physician provided an appropriate physical examination)?

3.   How will a potential reduction in contact time affect the quality of the physician-patient encounter? Since the amount of time afforded these contacts is being reduced, improving the productivity of such encounters becomes even more important. However, several questions surround this issue of productivity. For example, how can the information needed by the physician to make clinical decisions be transmitted quickly and inexpensively? How will we produce outcomes consistent with patient expectations if reduced time with the patient means we do not have an opportunity to assess patient values, or explain the implications of different treatment options? Exactly what level and mix of clinical training is needed to provide the most efficient and effective care to patients?

4.   Will cost containment be a clinically rational process? Will we, like the Dutch and Swedes, set clinically based priorities defining which services should be provided (e.g., services for patients who cannot care for their basic needs due to physical or mental problems vs. services to further life expectancy or control pain)? Or will care be cut without reference to its potential health benefits?

5.   Are we prepared as a society to take actions needed to improve the medical marketplace? Will we accept even minimal regulation of health plans? Will we require the public to provide or allow access to information necessary to assess both the quality and effectiveness of care?

6.   How much excess supply of health professionals is required to ensure that the level of quality of care is maintained? If we train only enough cardiac surgeons to meet specific demands, what happens if some fraction of them provide care below acceptable standards and the performance of these surgeons can not be improved? Will the quest for efficiency eliminate a surplus of physicians, so that competition is reduced to a level that sacrifices quality? If all hospital beds are full, and it takes years to build a new hospital, is there any external motive for a hospital to improve its quality?

7.   What role does public information have in helping ensure that medical care provides the best value to all patients? Until recently, patients have not had access to data about the quality or cost of a particular type of care prior to receiving that care. This has changed somewhat with the public

release of 2 forms of information. First, data about provider outcomes and cost have been released by several state and private agencies. Second, procedure-specific guidelines are beginning to be published by government and private organizations. Both of these forms of information are meant to help patients with their medical care decisions. However, several questions still remain. Are the publicly available data on quality of care valid enough to be used by consumers in making healthcare choices? Are case-mix adjusters adequate to protect against gaming and misuse of data in ways that might actually reduce quality? What method of presenting information is most likely to facilitate consumer use? Indeed, will patients use this information to help them achieve the best value for their medical care dollars?

8.   What will be the effect on society as the currently disadvantaged populations learn, through the public release of information, that they are receiving inferior care? Both access to care and technical quality of care is inferior for disadvantaged populations. For example, socioeconomically disadvantaged persons have a higher chance of dying than non-disadvantaged patients when they are hospitalized with a condition that responds positively to medical care (e.g., myocardial infarction). In this time of cost containment, is society prepared to make high-quality resources available to all persons?

* * *

II.   RATIONING OF SCARCE HUMAN ORGANS

Insert at page 59, after Problem, "Establishing Criteria for Rationing Human Organs":

On April 2, 1998 the Secretary of HHS set forth the proposal for the final rule governing the operation of the OPTN. 63 FR 16296. The intention of the new rule was to improve the effectiveness and equity of the nation's organ transplantation system. HHS took this action in response to a GAO report which criticized the current method of allocation and distribution of the nation's organ supply. Organ Procurement Organizations–Alternatives Being Developed To More Accurately Assess Performance, GAO/HEHS 98–26 (11/26/97).

HHS's proposal came under attack by UNOS in a formal statement that addressed the new rule and its possible negative consequences. One major issue in the proposed rule is its shift to a single criterion for allocation. The HHS would require that organ allocation, among patients for whom the organ is a "match", be decided by medical urgency alone. Waiting time would be the "tie-breaker" among patients in the same category. UNOS argued that this policy change would result in sicker and fewer patients receiving transplants. The severe shortage of livers, for example, means there would almost always be an extremely sick patient on the active waiting list of a large area. These patients present a greater likelihood of failure of a transplant and an emergency retransplant. Therefore, such a policy would cause most patients to have to wait until they are extremely sick before having a significant chance to receive a transplant. Patients would lose their current 30% chance of receiving a transplant before becoming so sick as to require hospitalization. Furthermore, under this policy change, the overall survival rate in the entire patient population would decrease by 9.3%. Average waiting times for status 2b and 3 patients would double.

A second major issue is abandonment of local and regional distribution. In the HHS rule, neither place of residence nor place of listing would be a major determinant of access to a transplant. UNOS argued that this allocation scheme essentially created a single national list. Regardless of where the organ is procured, the patient with the highest status level and waiting time would receive the organ. The HHS policy assumes that technology for preservation of organs has advanced to accommodate the increased time delay between procurement and transplantation.

Other topics discussed in UNOS's statement against the proposed rule are the critical shortage of organs in every OPO, organ preservation, decreased donation and smaller centers closing, and the impact on minorities and economically disadvantaged, to name a few. For a detailed discussion of this issue, access UNOS's website by typing "United Network for Organ Sharing" into the internet search engine and go to Response to HHS Concerns about UNOS Statements Regarding the Regulations.

As a result of this heated debate, Congress passed PL 105–277 on 10/21/98 which set a one-year moratorium on the effective date for HHS's new rule regarding the nation's organ transplantation system and its operation. Other Congressional action in this area includes a final rule requiring hospitals to take action to increase organ donation by reporting every death, educating staff and providing data to the OPTN. 42 CFR § 482.5. In further efforts to increase donation, HHS began a program entitled Partners for the National Organ and Tissue Donation Initiative. 63 FR 49702–01.

Some states have entered the competition for available organs as a reaction to a move toward a national listing system. See e.g., Louisiana Statute "Anatomical Gift Act" (LA R.S. 17:2353) which states in part:

* * *

[I]n the event an anatomical gift is made in the state of Louisiana of any vascular organ for transplantation purposes, if the donor does not name a specific donee and the organ is deemed suitable for transplantation to an individual, the vascular organ shall be donated to the Louisiana-designated organ procurement organization. Said organization shall use its best efforts to determine if there is a suitable recipient in the state.

* * *

[T]he Louisiana-designated organ procurement organization may only transfer a vascular organ to an out-of-state organ procurement organization or suitable out-of-state recipient for transplantation if either:

(a) A suitable recipient in the state of Louisiana cannot be found in a reasonable amount of time.

(b) The Louisiana-designated organ procurement organization has a reciprocal agreement with the out-of-state procurement organization . . . .

* * *

Should organ transplantation be governed by federal or state law? Does it depend on the particular issue?

On page 67, after the Problem, "Organ Donation From an Adolescent":

JACOBSEN v. MARIN GENERAL HOSPITAL

United States District Court, N.D. California, 1997.
963 F.Supp. 866.

PATEL, District Judge.

Plaintiffs Karen and Hardy Jacobsen (collectively, "plaintiffs") brought this action against defendants Marin General Hospital ("Hospital"), California Transplant Donor Network, Inc. ("Network") and Marin County Coroner's Office ("Coroner") alleging various claims under California law arising from the harvesting of organs from the body of their son, Martin Jacobsen ("Martin"). This case is before the court pursuant to the court's diversity jurisdiction. 28 U.S.C. § 1332. Now before the court are separate motions to dismiss submitted by all three defendants in this action. * * *

Plaintiffs are citizens and residents of the Kingdom of Denmark and the parents of Martin Jacobsen, also a Danish citizen. Martin was visiting the United States as a tourist when he was found unconscious and suffering from head trauma in the early morning hours of October 4, 1995 * * * in Sausalito, California. The parties do not know how this occurred. Martin was taken to defendant Hospital and admitted at 4:05 a.m. on October 4. At this time, Dr. Morris, the attending physician, presumed he was homeless and indicated that no identification had been made. At 8:25 a.m., defendant Network contacted defendant Coroner requesting organ donation; Coroner denied this request. At 9:00 a.m. on October 4, a search began for Martin's next of kin or other persons authorized to make an anatomical gift.

At 9:30 a.m. on October 4, photos were taken by the Marin County Sheriff's Office ("sheriff") and the Coroner, where a blue card stating "Jacobsen, M" and "10/4/95" was displayed with the body. * * * At 12:25 p.m., another request for organ donation was made, but Dr. Morris indicated that Martin was not brain dead at that time. At 2:00 p.m., Network called the Sheriff who revealed that the patient had been identified by the FBI as Martin Jacobsen from New York City. * * *

The following day, on October 5, 1995 at 9:00 a.m., Network spoke with the Sheriff who stated that he felt "9/10" sure that the patient was Martin Jacobsen. At 9:40 a.m., Dr. Ramirez made a clinical determination of brain death. At 3:00 p.m., another determination of brain death was made by Dr. Nisam who stated in his report that the patient was being maintained pending identification of next of kin and that an extensive forty hour search by the Sheriff, Coroner, and FBI to find any family member or identification of the patient had been unsuccessful. His report also indicated that the body was "officially released" to Network for organ donation.

On October 6, 1995 around 9:00 a.m., the Sheriff reported to Network that they were unable to locate the identification of "this John Doe." At 10:13 a.m., Network requested authorization from Coroner to recover the organs of "John Doe." Coroner consented. Martin's kidney, liver, pancreas and heart were removed and the harvesting was completed at 2:16 a.m. on October 7, 1995.

Neither Martin nor plaintiffs would have consented to the maintenance of Martin's body or the removal of his organs for the purposes of making an anatomical gift. Plaintiffs filed their original complaint on October 4, 1996 and an amended complaint on January 22, 1997. Defendants Hospital, Network and Coroner subsequently filed separate motions to dismiss pursuant to Federal Rule of Civil Procedure 12(b)(6).

A motion to dismiss for failure to state a claim will be denied unless it appears that the plaintiff can prove no set of facts which would entitle him or her to relief. [   ] All material allegations in the complaint will be taken as true and construed in the light most favorable to the plaintiff. [   ]

* * *

Plaintiffs' various claims are rooted in the sequence of events culminating in the harvesting of Martin's organs in October 1995. They argue that defendants mutilated his body by maintaining it for harvesting, which was done without their consent. In their first amended complaint, plaintiffs bring the following * * * separate causes of action against all three defendants: (1) negligent search; (2) negligence in procuring injury-producing conduct of another; (3) intentional mutilation of a corpse and infliction of emotional distress; (4) negligent mutilation of a corpse and infliction of emotional distress... * * *

In response, defendants argue that they were complying with the provisions of the Uniform Anatomical Gift Act, adopted by the California legislature in 1988, when they maintained Martin's body and harvested organs from it. Accordingly, they argue that plaintiffs do not state any claims in their first amended complaint for which relief may be granted.

I.   The Uniform Anatomical Gift Act

Although all fifty states have adopted the Uniform Anatomical Gift Act (the "Gift Act") in some form, there is very little case law interpreting its provisions. [   ] The Gift Act is intended to "make uniform the law with respect to [organ donation] among states enacting it" and is codified in California in the Health and Safety Code. Cal. Health & Safety Code § 7156.5. * * * If the next of kin, as defined in [the statute] cannot be located to provide consent, the coroner or hospital, whichever entity has custody of the body at the time the consent is given, may authorize the anatomical gift so long as several criteria are met, including a reasonable "search" for persons listed in section 7151(a). [   ]

* * *

The court will now consider the substance of plaintiffs' remaining claims against all of the defendants... * * *. * * *

NEGLIGENT SEARCH CLAIM

Plaintiffs argue that the defendants acted negligently in searching for persons authorized to provide consent for an anatomical gift. The Gift Act authorizes a coroner, medical examiner, hospital, or local public health official to release and permit removal of a body part where that institution has custody of a body and after a "reasonable effort has been made to locate and inform" next of kin of their option to make, or object to, an anatomical gift. [   ] The court must determine whether the actions taken to locate plaintiffs, as described in the complaint, were reasonable under the requirements of the Gift Act.

Neither the parties nor the court has identified California cases interpreting what constitutes a "reasonable" search for next of kin under the Gift Act. Nevertheless, the Gift Act itself provides the court with some guidance. Where a coroner has custody of a body, the Gift Act states that "a reasonable effort [to locate next of kin] shall be deemed to have been made when a search for the persons has been underway for at least 12 hours." [   ] (emphasis added). Similarly, where a hospital has custody of a person who is still alive but expected to die, a reasonable search "may be initiated in anticipation of death, but ... the determination [to release a body for an anatomical gift] may not be made until the search has been underway for at least 12 hours." [   ] (emphasis added).

[T]his search shall include a check of local police missing persons records, examination of personal effects, and the questioning of any persons visiting the decedent before his or her death or in the hospital, accompanying the decedent's body, or reporting the death, in order to obtain information that might lead to the location of [next of kin]. [   ] These provisions suggest that when the legislature adopted the Gift Act, the legislature considered and accepted that some searches for next of kin would be unsuccessful, and that where the next of kin could not be located in twelve hours, other institutions would be empowered to release a body in order to fulfill the underlying purposes of the Gift Act. In adopting the Gift Act, the California legislature likely recognized that "[t]ime is usually of the essence in securing donated organs at the time of the donor's death." [   ]

By adopting a twelve hour search period and stating that a reasonable search "shall be deemed to have been made" once this amount of time has passed, it is clear that the California legislature contemplated (1) a relatively short period of time in which to conduct a search for next of kin and (2) the possibility that such a search might be unsuccessful. Therefore, the court must consider what actions could have reasonably been taken in a twelve hour period to determine whether a reasonable search for plaintiffs was conducted.

In plaintiffs' complaint, they state that a search for next of kin began at 9:00 a.m. on October 4 and continued until October 6 between 9:00 and 10:13 a.m., when Coroner released the body for harvesting. Martin had no identification on his person when he was found and brought to the hospital. As alleged in the complaint, the search for plaintiffs lasted about forty-eight hours, but was ultimately unsuccessful. The complaint discloses that the Sheriff was notified and involved in the search efforts, that five hours after the search had begun the FBI identified the body as belonging to Martin Jacobsen from New York City, and that a doctor's report described an extensive forty hour search conducted by the Sheriff, the Coroner and the FBI.

Plaintiffs argue that defendants search was negligent because they should have known he was from Denmark when they found a ring inscribed with Danish writing on Martin's finger and a Danish poem in his pocket. These facts do not establish that the search was unreasonable. It is quite possible that the hospital and police did not know that the language was Danish. Moreover, even if they could identify the language, these items alone do not immediately suggest nor create the inference that Martin was a Danish citizen. [ ] Accordingly, the search for plaintiffs was not negligent simply because defendants did not assume, on the basis of these items, that Martin was from Denmark. * * *

Plaintiffs also argue that the search was negligent because the Sheriff knew that Martin was a tourist and that based on this information, they should have checked the records of the Immigration and Naturalization Service ("INS") during their search for next of kin. The fact that the INS records were not checked during the search does not establish that it was unreasonable. The court notes that a person's status as a tourist in the San Francisco area does not immediately suggest that the person is from a foreign country. Many tourists from all over the United States and the world visit this area. Accordingly, the Sheriff's failure to check INS records upon discovering that Martin was a tourist provides little to support plaintiffs' negligent search claim.

Plaintiffs' description of the search suggests that all reasonable acts were taken to locate plaintiffs and obtain their consent prior to releasing Martin's body for harvesting. The complaint describes a search lasting over forty hours and involving the efforts of the Marin County Sheriff as well as the FBI; such a search is "reasonable" as contemplated by the legislature in adopting the Gift Act. Before Martin's body was released, defendants Hospital and Coroner complied with the Gift Act's provisions and conducted a reasonable, although ultimately unsuccessful, search to locate plaintiffs and obtain their consent.* Accordingly, the court finds that plaintiffs have failed to state a claim for negligent search against defendants Hospital and Coroner.

As for defendant Network, under the provisions of the Gift Act, Network had no legal duty to search for Martin's next of kin or obtain their consent for an anatomical gift ... [ ] Plaintiffs urge the court to impose this duty on Network based on unspecified "common law" duties for which plaintiffs have provided no authority. The court has found no California cases supporting plaintiffs' position and declines the opportunity to create such a duty here. Accordingly, the court finds that plaintiffs have not stated a claim against Network for negligent search. * * *

Plaintiffs' remaining claims for negligence in procuring injury-producing injury, joint enterprise and negligent and intentional infliction of emotional distress are based on plaintiffs' allegation that defendants mutilated Martin's body by maintaining it prior to harvesting and actually harvesting organs from it. Plaintiffs' contend that all three defendants acted in concert to mutilate the body of their son and obtain organs for transplantation, thereby causing them injury.

Defendants' behavior, as described in plaintiffs' complaint, is consistent with the provisions of the Gift Act. As discussed above, defendants' search for Martin's next of kin complied with the provisions of the Gift Act and constituted a reasonable search. Defendants also acted in compliance with

* The court notes that defendant Hospital had no legal duty under the provisions of the Gift Act to conduct a search for plaintiffs because defendant Coroner was the entity that ultimately gave the final consent and release of the body for harvesting. [ ] However, the Gift Act contemplates that a hospital might be re-quired to conduct a reasonable search where it has custody of a body prior to its release. [ ] Here, plaintiffs' complaint clearly states that defendant Coroner released the body; accordingly, only defendant Coroner had a duty to search for next of kin prior to releasing the body. * * *

other sections of the Gift Act. For example, hospitals are required to "cooperate in the implementation of the anatomical gift or release and removal of a part." [ ] The Gift Act also states that "[e]ach hospital in this state, after consultation with other hospitals and procurement organizations, shall establish agreements or affiliations for coordination of procurement and use of human bodies and parts." [ ] When identifying potential organ and tissue donors, hospitals must comply with laws requiring that the coroner be notified of all reportable deaths. [ ] * * * Furthermore, hospitals may contact organ and tissue procurement organizations when a potential donor is identified and ask them to assist in locating the potential donor's next of kin as required. [ ]

These provisions suggest that defendants acted in compliance with the Gift Act when they maintained Martin's body and harvested organs from it. Defendants were required, under the provisions of the Gift Act, to cooperate with one another to maintain the body and its organs for transplantation purposes. In accordance with the Gift Act and the Death Act, defendants maintained Martin's body and did not release it for harvesting until after there had been a determination of brain death that was confirmed by another physician. Plaintiffs have not alleged any facts showing that defendants violated the provisions of the Gift Act or acted contrary to the purposes for which it was enacted by the California legislature. Defendants' efforts to comply with the provisions of the Gift Act may not serve as a basis for tort liability. Therefore, plaintiffs can prove no set of facts entitling them to relief on any of their remaining claims. [ ] Accordingly, plaintiffs' remaining state claims against all three defendants must be dismissed.

Questions

How far does the good faith immunity provision of the UAGA extend? If hospital personnel knowingly or recklessly mislead family donors and frustrate the donor's actual and expressed wishes, does immunity apply? See Perry v. Saint Francis Hospital, 886 F.Supp. 1551 (D.Kan.1995), holding the hospital liable. What is the definition of good faith? Does an honest belief, the absence of malice and the absence of design to defraud or to seek an unconscionable advantage constitute good faith? See Lyon v. United States, 843 F.Supp. 531 (D.Minn.1994). If there is ambiguity in the organ consent form is the hospital acting in good faith in removing organs within the ambiguous gift? See Rahman v. Mayo Clinic, 578 N.W.2d 802 (Minn.App.1998).

Chapter 3

LIABILITY OF HEALTH CARE PROFESSIONALS

Add at page 154, a new note 5:

5. Courts expect the standard of care to be compliance with available technology at the time the diagnosis or treatment was offered to the patient. See, e.g., Klisch v. Meritcare Medical Group, Inc., 134 F.3d 1356 (C.A. 8th Cir. 1998), where the patient sued for negligent performance of surgery. The Court of Appeals held that: (1) a jury instruction that the jury should consider the state of medical technology at time of allegedly negligent surgery was appropriate; (2) under Minnesota law, the jury in a medical malpractice action should weigh information available to physicians at the time of treatment and without benefit of hindsight.

Add at page 158, following note 2a:

The Physicians Desk Reference is allowed by most courts as some evidence of the standard of care, if an expert witness relies on it. See, e.g., Morlino v. Medical Center, 706 A.2d 721 (N.J.1998), where a pregnant patient whose fetus died after she took an antibiotic brought action against prescribing physician, medical center, and obstetrician. The court held that Physicians' Desk Reference (PDR) entries alone did not establish standard of care, but the trier of fact can consider package inserts and parallel PDR references when they are supported by expert testimony. "When supported by expert testimony, PDR entries and package inserts may provide useful information of the standard of care. Physicians frequently rely on the PDR when making decisions concerning the administration and dosage of drugs."

Add at page 159, the following new note 2d:

d. evidentiary uses of clinical practice guidelines. Clinical practice guidelines, so long as they are developed by an expert witness as a testamentary anchor, will be allowed in evidence to help establish the standard of care. They can also be used to impeach the opinion of an expert witness. In Roper v. Blumenfeld, 706 A.2d 1151, 1156 (N.J.Super.A.D.1998), the defendant used 1992 Parameters of Care for Oral and Maxillofacial Surgery: A Guide of Practice, Monitoring and Evaluation in order to cross examine plaintiff's expert and to examine his expert. As used to impeach, it was permissible to counter the doctor's opinion that because plaintiff was injured during defendant's failed attempt at extraction, defendant must have deviated from the standard of care because the injury is not a medically accepted risk of the procedures he performed. "As to this claim, the article is quite relevant for it lists as a known risk and complication of 'erupted' teeth '[o]ral-facial neurologic dysfunction.' "

Add at page 162, a new Section B.1. Keeping Up With Technology:

The Internet enables a doctor to stay current through bulletin boards, physician-directed online services, and both commercial and government-sponsored Websites. Doctors are increasingly expected to seek and use the data. Medical knowledge about evidence-based medicine has accumulated at a staggering rate. Between 1966 and 1995, the number of clinical research articles based on randomized clinical trials jumped from about 100 per year to 10,000 annually. Mark R. Chassin, Is Health Care Ready for Six Sigma Quality? 76 the Milbank Quarterly 565, 574 (1998). Web-based databases have proliferated to sort and promote access by physicians to the newest clinical practice guidelines and other medical developments. The goal has to help physicians handle the information overload in an efficient and user-friendly way.

The National Guideline Clearinghouse, http://www.guideline.gov, offers free access by physicians and others to the current clinical practice guidelines, with instantaneous searches of the database. A search produces all guidelines on a given subject, along with an appropriateness analysis of each guideline. The Clearinghouse provides a standardized abstract of each guideline, and grades the scientific basis of its recommendations and the development process for each. Full text or links to sites with the guidelines are provided. Readers are given synopses to produce a side-by-side comparison of guidelines, outlining where those agree and disagree, and physicians can access electronic mail groups to discuss development and implementation. These guidelines must pass certain entry criteria to be included: they must be current, contain systematically developed statements to guide physician decisions, have been produced by a medical or other professional group, government agency, health care organization or other private or public organization; and they must show that they were developed through systematic search of peer-reviewed scientific evidence. The benefits: easy search features, database comprehensiveness and Internet location make this the most powerful tool to date. Various appropriateness tests have been developed to evaluate guidelines. See Paul G Shekelle and David L. Schriger, Evaluating the Use of the Appropriateness Method in the Agency for Health Care Policy and Research Clinical Practice Guideline Development Process, 31 Health Services Research (1996)

Other Internet based services are available on a commercial basis. One example is MDConsult, a commercial database available by subscription that makes available hundreds of medical textbooks and treatises, as well as easy access to clinical practice guidelines. Subscribership in such commercial sites, designed to be user-friendly, has grown geometrically over the past two years, as physicians look for easy research access to data about patient problems. A survey by MDConsult of physician subscribers found that physicians were accessing the website for a fast and easy way to check the literature while treating patients, allowing for immediate answers; to keep up and to expand a physician's knowledge base about particular conditions. Physicians felt that the immediacy of access to a comprehensive website improved their informational base and therefore their quality of practice.

Medscape is another commercial site that provides a full range of online resources for physicians. It offers a journal scan on the newest research findings, free access to abstracts on MEDLINE, access to drug searching through First DataBank, the largest Web-based drug and disease database, access to clinical practice guidelines, treatment updates, full text articles in many journals, and a clinical management series n the form of interactive e-med texts. A subscriber can also set up an email account to get specific information sent on a regular basis on specific topics. These commercial services in particular offer a busy physician quick and painless access, to both journals and guidelines, as well as to new literature and comments by experts.

The location of current information on the Internet facilitates its ease of access to physicians, and its link to other commercial sites makes it easy to connect to, no matter what portal a physician uses to access medical information databases on the Web. Failure to access such data bases is likely to become an important piece of evidence in a malpractice suit, since it is evidence that a physician has failed to stay current in his or her field of practice.

Computer technologies pose other liability risks for physicians. As patient records are computerized, it becomes easier to gain access to a full patient history. Patient records can be easily stored on CDROM or other media, so that access is virtually instantaneous. Patient drug records and possible interactions can therefore be researched effortlessly. For a physician to fail to make such a search and miss a possible problem or drug interaction leads to liability. Another liability risk created by reliance on computer record keeping is the failure to protect such computerized patient records. Computer storage raises issues of security, privacy and integrity of computer records. Breaches of security and unauthorized access to patient information can lead to a range of tort suits, from invasion of privacy to negligence in record maintenance. A physician or institution also has a duty to detect and cripple viruses. Physicians who fail to properly protect patient and other files from corruption may be as negligent as physicians who fail to keep proper paper records.

III. OTHER THEORIES

Add at page 196, at the end of note 5, the following paragraphs:

Courts have generally been reluctant to find a hospital or physician negligent for failing to advise patients that they were eligible for government funding. See, e.g., Mraz v. Taft, 619 N.E.2d 483 (Ohio App. 8th Dist. 1993)(neither hospital nor nursing home had any duty to advise husband that he qualified for Medicaid). Nor is a physician liable for the financial consequences of a misdiagnosis, for example a patient's cancellation of a life insurance policy upon being erroneously informed that he did not have cancer. See Blacher v. Garlett, 857 P.2d 566, 568 (Colo.C.A., Div.III 1993).

A physician may be required to know state law. In Stecker v. First Commercial Trust Company, 962 S.W.2d 792 (Ark.1998), the administrator of a child's estate sued doctor for medical negligence and failure to report suspected child abuse as required under Arkansas statute. Evidence that the child's life could have been saved if doctor had reported potential abuse presented question for jury on issue of proximate cause for purposes of medical malpractice claim.

IV. DEFENSES TO A MALPRACTICE SUIT

Add at page 218, note 3:

The failure of a patient to follow a treating physician's warnings about behavior can also be considered by the jury under contributory negligence instructions. In Cobo v. Raba, 495 S.E.2d 362 (N.C.1998), a physician who suffered from depression was treated by the defendant Dr. Raba. Dr. Cobo refused drug treatment for chronic depression, refused to allow the defendant to take notes, and insisted on psychoanalysis as the only mode of treatment. During this period he engaged regularly in unprotected homosexual intercourse with prostitutes, in spite of regular admonitions by the defendant as to the risks, including unprotected sex with a drug-addicted prostitute in a San Francisco bathhouse; he abused alcohol and drugs, and when he became HIV-positive, he substantially delayed his treatment. The court held that the plaintiff's conduct was "clearly active and related directly to his physical complaint," and the jury should be allowed to evaluate it through a contributory negligence instruction.

Add at page 219, note 5:

A patient's lack of compliance with treatment instructions may be submitted to the jury under comparative negligence statutes for comparison with the malpractice of the treating physician. In Cox v. Lesko, 953 P.2d 1033 (Kan.1998), the physician performed shoulder surgery for traumatic posterior subluxation in the left shoulder. The plaintiff then missed most of her physical therapy sessions over several months, which were aimed to strengthen her muscles and increase her shoulder's range of motion. Her condition failed to improve. Plaintiff's lack of compliance with therapy instructions was properly submitted to the jury under the comparative negligence statute as fault to be compared with the malpractice of the physician who performed the surgery.

Add at page 220, before the Problem, The Eyes Have It:

F. ERISA Preemption

ERISA preemption, discussed in the casebook at pages 298 et seq. and page 808 et seq., has been held to preempt common law malpractice actions against managed care organizations, although a variety of exceptions are emerging. Whether ERISA preempts an action against treating physicians for their malpractice is a different issue. The following case provides a first look at this issue.

NEALY v. U.S. HEALTHCARE HMO

93 N.Y.2d 209.
Court of Appeals, N.Y., 1999.

KAYE, Chief Judge:

The novel question presented by this appeal is whether the Employee Retirement Income Security Act (ERISA) preempts plaintiff's medical malpractice, breach of contract and breach of fiduciary duty claims against a primary care physician who allegedly delayed in submitting a specialist's referral form for approval by a health maintenance organization (HMO) governed by ERISA. Concluding that ERISA does not preempt plaintiff's claims, we reverse the Appellate Division's dismissal order and reinstate the complaint against the doctor.

In January 1992, plaintiff's husband, Glenn Nealy, then 37 years old, was diagnosed with coronary arteriosclerosis and a coronary artery lesion. As a result, Mr. Nealy took disability leave from his job at Photocircuits Corporation and was treated for his condition by a cardiologist, Dr. Stephen Green. His treatment, which included an angioplasty performed by Dr. Green in March 1992, was in large part covered by Blue Cross/Massachusetts Mutual, the carrier selected by Photocircuits to provide employee medical insurance. Around the time of Mr. Nealy's angioplasty, Photocircuits replaced its carrier with a choice of three HMOs, including U.S. Healthcare, and informed its employees that coverage would become effective April 1, 1992. Mr. Nealy promptly enrolled in the U.S. Healthcare Versatile Plus HMO, which allowed its members to see non-participating physicians, and paid his first monthly premium.

On April 2, and again on April 3, Mr. Nealy visited the offices of defendant, Dr. Ralph Yung, whom he had selected as his primary care provider under the U.S. Healthcare HMO.[1] He experienced renewed chest pain and also required follow-up care as a result of the angioplasty. On his first visit, Mr. Nealy was denied an appointment because he had not yet received a U.S. Healthcare identification number. The next day, he spoke with a U.S. Healthcare representative who told him that a copy of his enrollment form could be presented in lieu of an identification number, and he made a second attempt to visit Dr. Yung. Again he was turned away—this time because his enrollment form bore the wrong primary physician number.

On April 10, 1992—having received his U.S. Healthcare identification card the previous day—Mr. Nealy was examined by Dr. Yung. During that visit, Dr. Yung took a patient history that noted a history of angina and angioplasty, performed a routine new-patient physical examination, and renewed all the medications that had been prescribed by Dr. Green. At Dr. Yung's request, Mr. Nealy returned on April 13 to provide blood and urine samples for laboratory analysis. When Dr. Yung informed him during one or both of these visits that he should see a cardiologist, Mr. Nealy requested a referral to Dr. Green, who was not a participating U.S. Healthcare provider. Dr. Yung allegedly assured his patient that he would submit a request to U.S. Healthcare to approve an out-of-plan referral and do what he could to secure approval of the request. It was not until approximately April 20, however, that Dr. Yung completed a non-participating provider request form and submitted it for approval to U.S. Healthcare.[2]

---

1. Dr. Yung disputes plaintiff's allegation that Mr. Nealy visited his offices on April 2 and 3, admitting only that he first saw Mr. Nealy on or about April 10.

2. The parties dispute whether the non-participating referral form—instead of a "Versatile" form—was submitted to U.S. Health-

care at Mr. Nealy's request or the result of Dr. Yung's error. A "Versatile" referral would have allowed treatment by a non-participating doctor but required Mr. Nealy to pay a $250 deductible. Plaintiff maintains that Mr. Nealy never expressed a desire to avoid payment of the deductible and was motivated only by a

On May 4th, Mr. Nealy received a copy of a letter from U.S. Healthcare addressed to Dr. Yung denying the request for a referral to Dr. Green. The reason given was that U.S. Healthcare had a participating provider in the area. After the referral to Dr. Green was denied, Mr. Nealy decided to accept a referral to Dr. Carl Spivak, a participating U.S. Healthcare cardiologist. He obtained the referral to Dr. Spivak on May 18 and promptly made an appointment for the next day. Tragically, however, on May 18 Mr. Nealy suffered a massive myocardial infarction and died.

Seeking to recover damages for her husband's death, plaintiff commenced this action in Supreme Court asserting breach of contract, breach of fiduciary duty, wrongful death, negligence and other claims against defendants Dr. Yung, Dr. Richard H. Bernstein (Vice President and Director of U.S. Healthcare), U.S. Healthcare and two subsidiaries. Plaintiff also asserted medical malpractice claims against Dr. Yung and Dr. Bernstein. Dr. Bernstein and U.S. Healthcare successfully sought removal of the case to Federal court, where the claims were dismissed on the ground that they were preempted by ERISA (844 F.Supp. 966 [SDNY]), and no appeal was taken to determine the correctness of that decision. Because Dr. Yung—who had not yet been served with the summons and complaint—did not take part in the removal motion, the Federal court remanded the case against him, as the sole remaining defendant, to Supreme Court.

After service of process and discovery, Dr. Yung moved for summary judgment seeking dismissal of the complaint, alleging that ERISA preempted plaintiff's claims against him as well. Supreme Court denied the motion. The Appellate Division, however, reversed and dismissed the complaint, concluding that ERISA preempted plaintiff's claims. We disagree and now reinstate plaintiff's complaint against Dr. Yung.

Discussion

Concerned with employee pension plan abuses and mismanagement, Congress in 1974 enacted ERISA, a comprehensive statute "designed to promote the interests of employees and their beneficiaries in employee benefit plans" (Aetna Life Ins. v. Borges, 869 F.2d 142, 144 [2d Cir], cert. denied 493 U.S. 811, 110 S.Ct. 57, 107 L.Ed.2d 25; see also, 29 USC §§ 1001, 1001a, 1001b). ERISA subjects employee benefit plans to participation, funding and vesting requirements as well as rules regarding reporting, disclosure and fiduciary responsibility [ ]. By imposing these requirements, Congress sought "to insure against the possibility that the employee's expectation of * * * benefit[s] would be defeated through poor management by the plan administrator" (Massachusetts v. Morash, 490 U.S. 107, 115, 109 S.Ct. 1668, 104 L.Ed.2d 98). In aid of its goal of protecting plan participants and their beneficiaries, ERISA facilitates the development of a uniform national law governing employee benefit plans, and a standard system to guide the processing of claims and disbursement of benefits (New York State Conference of Blue Cross & Blue Shield Plans v. Travelers Ins. Co., 514 U.S. 645, 656–657, 115 S.Ct. 1671, 131 L.Ed.2d 695 [Travelers]).

desire to see his cardiologist as soon as possible. Dr. Yung claims that Mr. Nealy did not want to pay the deductible, which is why the non-participating referral form was submitted.

ERISA's preemption provision is central to achievement of its statutory purposes. The provision reads that ERISA "shall supersede any and all State laws insofar as they * * * relate to any employee benefit plan" covered by ERISA, and it applies to both State statutes and common law (§ 514[a], 29 USC § 1144[a]; id., at § 514[c][1], 29 USC § 1144[c][1]; Pilot Life Ins. Co. v. Dedeaux, 481 U.S. 41, 46, 107 S.Ct. 1549, 95 L.Ed.2d 39). Although the language of the preemption clause is "deliberately expansive," there is a presumption that Congress does not intend to supplant State law, and a claim traditionally within the domain of State law will not be superseded by Federal law "unless that was the clear and manifest purpose of Congress" (Travelers, 514 US, at 654–655).

The issue before us is whether ERISA's preemption clause bars plaintiff's medical malpractice, breach of contract and breach of fiduciary duty claims against her husband's primary care physician, Dr. Yung. All of these claims fall within the traditional domain of State regulation. Dr. Yung, therefore, bears the "considerable burden" of overcoming the presumption that Congress did not intend to preempt them [   ]. In an attempt to surmount that formidable hurdle, Dr. Yung alleges that ERISA preempts these claims because they "relate to" the administration of the U.S. Healthcare HMO. The Appellate Division agreed, holding that he was protected by ERISA preemption because he had acted in a "purely administrative" capacity, and not as an "actual provider of medical care" (___ A.D.2d ___, ___). We conclude that plaintiff's claims against Dr. Yung do not "relate to" an employee benefit plan.

The simple statutory words "relate to" have been the subject of significant scholarly comment and litigation, including considerable attention from the United States Supreme Court [   ] On the one hand, virtually any State law may be said to "relate to" an employee benefit plan, for "universally, relations stop nowhere" (Travelers, supra, 514 US, at 655). On the other hand, application of the preemption clause to "the furthest stretch of its indeterminancy" would render Congress' words of limitation a "mere sham" and nullify the presumption against preemption (id.). Plainly, there is tension between the "deliberately expansive" language of the preemption clause—which, applied literally, would operate to shield benefit plans—and ERISA's goal of protecting employees from abuses at the hands of such entities.

After many years of broadly interpreting ERISA's preemption clause, in 1995 the United States Supreme Court adopted a more pragmatic approach, noting that its prior efforts to define "relate to" did not always afford "much help drawing the line" (Travelers, 514 US, at 655–656). Whereas the Court had previously explained that a law "relates to" an employee benefit plan if it has a connection with or makes reference to such a plan, in Travelers the Court acknowledged that even that definition of the phrase failed to provide adequate guidance (id., at 656). Thus, the Court concluded, in determining whether a State law relates to an employee benefit plan, it is often necessary to "go beyond the unhelpful text and the frustrating difficulty of defining its key term, and look instead to the objectives of the ERISA statute as a guide to the scope of the state law that Congress understood would survive" (Travelers, 514 US, at 656; see also, DeBuono, supra, 117 S.Ct., at 1751 [where there is no clear "connection with or reference to" an ERISA benefit plan, consideration must be given to the objectives of ERISA to determine whether the presumption against preemption has been overcome]).

In Travelers itself, the Supreme Court concluded that a State statute imposing surcharges on hospital bills paid by certain employee benefit plans, but exempting Blue Cross/Blue Shield plans, was not preempted by ERISA. Arguing for preemption, the commercial insurers asserted that the surcharges had an indirect economic effect on choices made by insurance buyers, including ERISA plans, and as such, the State statute had a "connection with" those plans. The Supreme Court, however, held that the indirect economic influence of the surcharges did not interfere with the congressional goal of uniform standards of plan administration. The statute did not "bind plan administrators to any particular choice and thus function as a regulation of an ERISA plan itself," nor did it "preclude uniform administrative practice or the provision of a uniform interstate benefit package" (514 US, at 659–660). The effect of the law bore only on "the costs of benefits and the relative costs of competing insurance to provide them," and the law was therefore not preempted by ERISA [   ]

Here, plaintiff alleges that Dr. Yung, as a direct provider of medical services, violated the duties and standard of care owed to his patient by improperly assessing the nature and extent of his condition and by failing to take reasonable steps to provide for his timely treatment by a specialist. Viewed pragmatically, those claims are not preempted by ERISA. Plaintiff's allegations of negligent medical care do not "relate to" the administration of an ERISA plan merely because they refer to Dr. Yung's delay in submitting the U.S. Healthcare form seeking a referral to Dr. Green. Plaintiff does not allege that Dr. Yung is responsible for delay caused by U.S. Healthcare's decision-making process with respect to coverage or benefits. Her claim against Dr. Yung is that he failed to take timely action to treat her husband.

Provision of medical treatment under an HMO or other managed care plan often requires reference to that plan's administrative procedures or requirements. In this case, for example, under the terms of the U.S. Healthcare HMO plan, Mr. Nealy's primary care physician was required to complete and submit a referral form in order to obtain treatment by a specialist for his patient. That alone, however, does not transform Dr. Yung into an ERISA plan administrator, or plaintiff's State law action charging violations of a physician's duty of care into claims that "relate to" ERISA plan administration. While plaintiff's claims make reference to U.S. Healthcare's administrative framework, any effect those claims may have on an employee benefit plan is "too tenuous, remote or peripheral" to warrant a finding that they "relate to" such a plan (Shaw, supra, 463 US, at 100 n. 21).

Moreover, considering the objectives of the ERISA statute, it is clear that Congress did not intend to preempt claims such as those now before us. Plaintiff's claims do not bind an employee plan to any particular choice of benefits, do not dictate the administration of such a plan and do not interfere with a uniform administrative scheme [   ]. Indeed, plaintiff does not challenge any administrative determination relating to an employee benefit plan or the extent of rights and benefits under such a plan. In short, there is nothing about plaintiff's claims that "conflicts with the provisions of ERISA or operates to frustrate its [objectives]" (Boggs, supra, 117 S.Ct., at 1760). To the contrary, plaintiff's claims are consistent with ERISA's "principal object": the protection of plan participants and beneficiaries (id., at 1762).

Finally, the Appellate Division would have dismissed plaintiff's complaint on the independent ground that she failed to demonstrate that any deviation from professional standards was a proximate cause of Mr. Nealy's demise. At this juncture in the litigation, however, we cannot agree with that conclusion as a matter of law.

Add, at page 224, before section 2, the following paragraph:

For the physician who knows that his patients see alternative practitioners, or who offers such treatments as an option, what are his or her liabilities? Joint and several liability is likely to hook the physician firmly if injury is the end result of a continuum of care that includes alternative practitioners. For example, in Samuelson v. McMurtry, 962 S.W.2d 473 (Tenn.1998), the plaintiff was treated by physicians and a chiropractor. His problems began with a boil under his arm, treated by Dr. Holland. The next day he returned to the hospital with a fever and inflammation around the boil and was treated by Dr. McMurty. 8 days later, he went to the hospital emergency room with complaints of back pain. The next day he twice returned to the emergency room. On the first visit he was seen by Dr. Holland but on the second visit he was discouraged by hospital personnel from seeing a physician. The next day, he went to see Dr. Totty, a chiropractor, with complaints of intense back and chest pain and he was treated twice that day by Dr. Totty. The next day he died of pneumonia, "which had not been diagnosed by any of the health care providers." He could have been treated within 6–12 hours of his death. This case presents an apportionment of fault issue, since Dr. Totty was severed as a defendant. The court held that it was an error to sever the claim against him. The general rule will bind all practitioners who treat a patient for the same ailment:

> There can be little doubt that the participation of all potentially responsible persons as parties in the original action would have resulted in a fuller and fairer presentation of the relevant evidence and would have enabled the jury to make a more informed and complete determination of liability.

VI. DAMAGE INNOVATIONS

Add, at page 236, before Problem, "The Toxic Dentist," a new Section C. Punitive Damages

In the normal malpractice case, damages typically include special damages, such as costs of treating a condition and loss of earning capacity; and general damages, primarily pain and suffering. Punitive damages are extremely rare. See Chapter 6, Section III.D. for a discussion of such punitive damages in informed consent cases. Impatience and inattention to a patient's condition can however lead to punitive damage awards in egregious cases. In Dempsey v. Phelps, 700 So.2d 1340 (Ala.1997), the parents of a two year old child sued, after the child was treated for a clubfoot condition caused by spina bifida and got an infection after surgery, ultimately losing his big toe. The central issue was whether the physician's conduct rose to the level of wantonness, meriting punitive damages. After the surgery, Dr. Dempsey told the mother to bring the boy back a month later, even though postoperative wound healing infections are a common complication that need to be monitored more frequently. The mother testified that "on the top of the foot all the toes were purple and blue and red on the side some. And the top of the foot had kind of a mushy looking place on it that it was draining. It had some drainage on it there and it was—a little black around the edges and it was red. It was just 'real inflamed looking' ". The boy also had diarrhea and fever and wouldn't eat. Dr. Dempsey's response to Mrs. Phelps was that these were common conditions, nothing to worry about, and he did nothing for the fever or anything else. She came back the next day and Dr. Dempsey wouldn't even see the boy at first, and then he said it was just cast blisters, even though, in the mother's words, "[i]t was starting to smell." She came back again the next day and he was very annoyed, and failed to take the boy's temperature, check his lungs or do anything else. The jury awarded $125,000 punitive damage award, on top of other damages, in light of Dr. Dempsey's failures to properly follow-up the child's care.

Chapter 4

LIABILITY OF HEALTH CARE INSTITUTIONS

Add, at page 240, the following in section B.1, after the second paragraph:

Physicians can be held vicariously liable for the actions of medical students and residents on the support staff, as well as nurses and allied health professionals. In Brown v. Flowe, 496 S.E.2d 830 (N.C.App.1998), the defendant was a member of the faculty of the East Carolina University School of Medicine, with clinical privileges. The treating doctor was a fourth year resident at the hospital, without clinical privileges. The defendant controlled her "manner of performance" during surgery, advising her to apply steady pressure to insert a trocar into the decedent's abdomen, leading to her death. The court held that the faculty physician was vicariously liable, following the Hospital Bylaw requirement that "only a licensed physician with clinical privileges shall be directly responsible for a patient's diagnosis and treatment". The Affiliation Agreement provided that medical students and house shall "shall be responsibly involved in patient care under the supervision of the Dean and the faculty of the School of Medicine." See also Hebert v. LaRocca, 704 So.2d 331, 338 (La.App. 3 Cir.1997) (held that a physician in fellowship training "is to follow the instruction and direction of the teaching physician, is to perform those tasks assigned to him and to do so under the direct supervision and control of the teaching physician, and is to report anything which appears improper or out of the ordinary to the teaching physician.")

Add at page 295, a new note 3:

3. The issue of institutional and physician obligations to disclose payment incentive systems are discussed in Part 3, infra, and in Chapter 6, Part 5. Recent writing on the subject includes Paul R. Sugarman and Valerie A. Yarashus, Admissibility of Managed Care Financial Incentives in Medical Malpractice Cases, 34 Tort & Ins.L.J. 735; Stephen R. Latham, Regulation of Managed Care Incentive Payments to Physicians, 22 Am.J.L. & Med. 399 (1996); Henry T. Greely, Direct Financial Incentives in Managed Care: Unanswered Questions, 6 Health Matrix 53(1996); R.Adams Dudley et al., The Impact of Financial Incentives on Quality of Health Care, 76 The Milbank Quarterly 649 (1998).

Add, at page 298, a new Section 4. Corporate Negligence

4. *Corporate Negligence*

SHANNON v. McNULTY

718 A.2d 828.
Superior Court of Pa., 1998.

Orie Melvin, Judge:

Mario L. Shannon and his wife, Sheena Evans Shannon, in their own right and as co-administrators of the Estate of Evan Jon Shannon, appeal from an order entered in the Court of Common Pleas of Allegheny County denying their motion to remove a compulsory nonsuit. This appeal concerns the Shannons' claims of vicarious and corporate liability against HealthAmerica stemming from the premature delivery and subsequent death of their son. We reverse the order refusing to remove the compulsory nonsuit and remand for trial.

This medical malpractice action arises from the pre-natal care provided by appellees, Larry P. McNulty, M.D. and HealthAmerica, to Mrs. Shannon. The Shannons claimed Dr. McNulty was negligent for failing to timely diagnose and treat signs of pre-term labor, and HealthAmerica was vicariously liable for the negligence of its nursing staff in failing to respond to Mrs. Shannon's complaints by timely referring her to an appropriate physician or hospital for diagnosis and treatment of her pre-term labor. The Shannons also alleged HealthAmerica was corporately liable for its negligent supervision of Dr. McNulty's care and its lack of appropriate procedures and protocols when dispensing telephonic medical advice to subscribers.

The case went to trial before a jury, and at the close of the plaintiffs' case HealthAmerica moved for a compulsory nonsuit. The trial court denied the motion. HealthAmerica then proceeded to put on its case by calling two of its triage nurses. At the conclusion of the testimony of the second nurse the court recessed for the day. The following morning the court, sua sponte, reconsidered HealthAmerica's motion for compulsory nonsuit, entertained argument thereon, and granted the nonsuit. The Shannons filed timely post trial motions seeking to have the nonsuit removed. After denial of such motions, this appeal followed.

On appeal the Shannons present two questions for this Court to review:

1. [DID] THE TRIAL COURT [ERR] IN GRANTING A COMPULSORY NONSUIT IN FAVOR OF [APPELLEE], HEALTHAMERICA, AND AGAINST THE [APPELLANTS] [IN THAT APPELLANTS] MADE OUT A PRIMA FACIE CASE AGAINST HEALTHAMERICA FOR BOTH COMMON LAW VICARIOUS LIABILITY REGARDING THE ACTIONS OF HEALTHAMERICA'S TRIAGE NURSES AND EMPLOYEES, AND DIRECT CORPORATE LIABILITY.

2. [DID] THE TRIAL COURT [ERR] IN GRANTING A COMPULSORY NONSUIT AFTER [APPELLEE] HEALTHAMERICA PRESENTED EVIDENCE IN ITS CASE IN CHIEF.

(Appellants' Brief at 2). Initially, we note that the scope of review in an appeal from the denial of a motion to remove a compulsory nonsuit is limited to determining whether the trial court abused its discretion or committed an error of law. [   ] * * *

Generally, in a medical malpractice case the plaintiff must establish: (1) a duty owed by the health care provider to the patient; (2) a breach of that duty; (3) the breach was the proximate cause of, or a substantial factor in, bringing about the harm suffered by the patient; and (4) damages suffered by the patient that were a direct result of that harm. [   ] Moreover, except where it is obvious, the plaintiff must present expert testimony that the health care provider's conduct deviated from an accepted standard of care and such deviation was the proximate cause of the harm suffered.

The theory of corporate liability as it relates to hospitals was first adopted in this Commonwealth in the case of Thompson v. Nason Hospital, 527 Pa. 330, 591 A.2d 703 (Pa.1991). Our supreme court upheld a direct theory of liability against the hospital, stating:

> Corporate negligence is a doctrine under which the hospital is liable if it fails to uphold the proper standard of care owed the patient, which is to ensure the patient's safety and well-being while at the hospital. This theory of liability creates a nondelegable duty which the hospital owes directly to a patient. Therefore, an injured party does not have to rely on and establish the negligence of a third party. Id. at 707. (footnote omitted) The court then set forth four general areas of corporate liability:

> (1) A duty to use reasonable care in the maintenance of safe and adequate facilities and equipment;

> (2) A duty to select and retain only competent physicians;

> (3) A duty to oversee all persons who practice medicine within its walls as to patient care;

> (4) A duty to formulate, adopt and enforce adequate rules and policies to ensure quality care for patients. Id. The court further stated that "we adopt as a theory of hospital liability the doctrine of corporate negligence or corporate liability under which the hospital is liable if it fails to uphold the proper standard of care owed its patient." Id. at 708.

The evidence introduced by the Shannons may be summarized in relevant part as follows. Mrs. Shannon testified during the trial of this case that she was a subscriber of the HealthAmerica HMO when this child was conceived. It was Mrs. Shannon's first pregnancy. When she advised HealthAmerica she was pregnant in June 1992, they gave her a list of six doctors from which she could select an OB/GYN. She chose Dr. McNulty from the list. [   ] Her HealthAmerica membership card instructed her to contact either her physician or HealthAmerica in the event she had any medical questions or emergent medical conditions. The card contained the HealthAmerica emergency phone number, which was manned by registered nurses. [   ] She testified it was confusing trying to figure out when to call Dr. McNulty and when to call HealthAmerica because she was receiving treatment from both for various medical conditions related to her pregnancy, including asthma and reflux. [   ]

She saw Dr. McNulty monthly but also called the HealthAmerica phone line a number of times for advice and to schedule appointments with their in-house doctors. [   ] She called Dr. McNulty on October 2, 1992 with complaints of abdominal pain. The doctor saw her on October 5, 1992 and examined her for five minutes. He told Mrs. Shannon her abdominal pain was the result of a fibroid uterus, he prescribed rest and took her off of work for one week. He did no testing to confirm his diagnosis and did not advise her of the symptoms of pre-term labor. [   ]

She next called Dr. McNulty's office twice on October 7 and again on October 8 and October 9, 1992, because her abdominal pain was continuing, she had back pain, was constipated and she could not sleep. She asked Dr. McNulty during the October 8th call if she could be in pre-term labor because her symptoms were similar to those described in a reference book she had on labor. [   ] She told Dr. McNulty her pains were irregular and about ten minutes apart, but she had never been in labor so she did not know what it felt like. He told her he had just checked her on October 5th, and she was not in labor.[   ] The October 9th call was at least her fourth call to Dr. McNulty about her abdominal pain, and she testified that Dr. McNulty was becoming impatient with her. [   ]

On October 10th, she called HealthAmerica's emergency phone line and told them about her severe irregular abdominal pain, back pain, that her pain was worse at night, that she thought she may be in pre-term labor, and about her prior calls to Dr. McNulty. The triage nurse advised her to call Dr. McNulty again. [   ] Mrs. Shannon did not immediately call Dr. McNulty because she did not feel there was anything new she could tell him to get him to pay attention to her condition. She called the HealthAmerica triage line again on October 11, 1992, said her symptoms were getting worse and Dr. McNulty was not responding. The triage nurse again advised her to call Dr. McNulty. [   ] Mrs. Shannon called Dr. McNulty and told him about her worsening symptoms, her legs beginning to go numb, and she thought that she was in pre-term labor. He was again short with her and angry and insisted that she was not in pre-term labor.[   ]

On October 12, 1992, she again called the HealthAmerica phone service and told the nurse about her symptoms, severe back pain and back spasms, legs going numb, more regular abdominal pain, and Dr. McNulty was not responding to her complaints. One of HealthAmerica's in-house orthopedic physicians spoke with her on the phone and directed her to go to West Penn Hospital to get her back examined. [   ] She followed the doctor's advice and drove an hour from her house to West Penn, passing three hospitals on the way. At West Penn she was processed as having a back complaint because those were HealthAmerica's instructions, but she was taken to the obstetrics wing as a formality because she was over five (5) months pregnant. She delivered a one and one-half pound baby that night. He survived only two days and then died due to his severe prematurity. [   ]

The Shannons' expert, Stanley M. Warner, M.D., testified he had experience in a setting where patients would call triage nurses. Dr. Warner opined that HealthAmerica, through its triage nurses, deviated from the standard of care following the phone calls to the triage line on October 10, 11 and 12, 1992, by not immediately referring Mrs. Shannon to a physician or hospital for a cervical exam and fetal stress test. As with Dr. McNulty, these precautions would have led to her labor being detected and increased the baby's chance of survival. [   ] Dr. Warner further testified on cross examination that Mrs. Shannon turned to HealthAmerica's triage nurses for medical advice on these three occasions when she communicated her symptoms. She did not receive appropriate advice, and further, if HealthAmerica's triage nurses intended for the referrals back to Dr. McNulty to be their solution, they had a duty to follow up Mrs. Shannon's calls by calling Dr. McNulty to insure Mrs. Shannon was actually receiving the proper care from him.[   ]

CORPORATE LIABILITY

In granting the nonsuit the trial court concluded the Shannons failed to present sufficient evidence to establish negligence on the part of HealthAmerica under either a corporate or vicarious liability theory. After first questioning the applicability of corporate liability to an HMO such as HealthAmerica, the trial court offered the following rationale with respect to the inadequacy of the evidence of corporate negligence:

> First, only two of the four duties set forth in Thompson, supra, could conceivably apply to a health maintenance organization such as Health-America.... There was no discussion, for example, of how HealthAmerica selected participating physicians or the criteria used in monitoring the physicians' performance. Similarly, Plaintiffs produced no evidence regarding the formulation, adoption or enforcement of rules or policies by HealthAmerica in carrying out its duty to provide adequate care to its subscribers. In the absence of such evidence, it is apparent that Plaintiffs failed to meet their burden of establishing the necessary elements to maintain a cause of action for corporate negligence, thereby justifying the granting of a compulsory nonsuit.

(Trial Court Opinion dated July 2, 1997 at pages 6–7). Without addressing the trial court's conclusion that a lack of evidence regarding the formulation, adoption or enforcement of rules or policies by HealthAmerica defeats the Shannons' claim of corporate negligence, we find the third duty is applicable. In assessing whether the Shannons evidence was sufficient to allow the case to go the jury on the theory of corporate liability pursuant to this third duty, we find Welsh v. Bulger, 548 Pa. 504, 698 A.2d 581 (Pa.1997) to be instructive.

* * *

[The court's discussion of Welsh v. Bulger is omitted.]

Similarly, in the present case Dr. Warner, on direct examination, offered the following opinion when asked whether or not HealthAmerica deviated from the standard of care:

> I believe they did deviate from the standard of care. I believe on each occasion of the calls on October 10th, 11th, and October 12th, that Mrs. Shannon should have been referred to the hospital, and the hospital notified that this woman was probably in preterm labor and needed to be handled immediately. They did have the alternative of calling for a physician, if they wanted to, for him to agree with it, but basically she needed to be evaluated in a placd [sic] where there was a fetal monitor

and somebody to do a pelvic examination to see what was happening with her.

[   ]. When asked whether this deviation increased the risk of harm Dr. Warner stated that "it did increase the risk of harm to the baby, and definitely decreased the chance of [the baby] being born healthy." Id., at 147.

Dr. Warner further testified in response to a series of hypothetical questions as follows:

Q. I want you to assume that on Saturday, October 10th, that Mrs. Shannon calls Health America and she talks to a triage nurse, and she relates to the triage nurse she is experiencing severe abdominal pain. I want you to assume that she is told, the triage nurse who answered the phone, that she has related these symptoms to Dr. McNulty, and she related Dr. McNulty's response, or lack of response, to her complaints of abdominal pain. I want you to assume that the triage nurse's advice is simply to call the doctor back again. Now, under those facts do you have an opinion, within a reasonable degree medical certainty, whether or not Health America deviated from the standard of care?

A. I do.

Q. What is that opinion?

A. I believe they deviated from the standard of care, the nurse.

Q. We're talking now with respect to October 10th.

A. Yes, sir. The nurse at that time would have a responsibility to know these are signs and symptoms of preterm labor, and to make sure she gets care in a facility where the ability to have fetal monitoring and cervix examination are. She should call up Dr. McNulty and ask him to make arraignments [sic] for that, or she can send the patient directly to the hospital. She should, in any event, make sure that happens in a very timely fashion. In other words, do it right away, you don't delay in doing this. You want to get her there before it's too late, before the cervix dilates too far, before it's too late to inhibit labor.

* * *

Q. I want you to assume, Dr. Warner, that on October 11, 1992, Mrs. Shannon called Health America again, and again relayed her complaints of either abdominal pain, back pain or side pain. Once again she also relayed her history of what I just told you, and she relayed what Dr. McNulty had done and what he hadn't done up to October 11th, and that the advice from Health America was the same, call Dr. McNulty back again. Now, under that factual scenario do you have an opinion, within a reasonable degree of medical certainty, whether or not Health America deviate from the standard of care on October 11, 1992?

A. I do have an opinion.

Q. And what is that?

A. That they deviated from the standard of care on October 11, 1992, as well. This woman was obviously searching for help. She was worried, and nobody was responding to her. She needed to be brought into the hospital and monitored and examined, and Dr. McNulty did not provide for it. She tlaked [sic] to Health America, who is one of her medical providers, and they at least had to get her into the hospital on an emergency condition, seen right away and monitored and examined right away, and if they called ahead to the emergency room to let them know that, then the emergency room is conditioned to respond, they know they have to respond rapidly to this preterm labor situation before they lose the chance to stop the labor.

Q.   Moving down to October 12th, I want you to assume that Sheena Shannon called Health America on October 12, 1992, and relayed the same history. That is, the history now of back pain. I want you to assume that the nurse at Health America asked Sheena whether or not she had experienced any type of trauma over the course of the past year. Although she was also informed of her pregnancy and her gestational status, the nurse under this assumption was told that she had been in two automobile accidents, and the triage nurse then called an internist. The internist under this assumption called Sheena and told Sheena to go to the hospital, West Penn Hospital, for an orthopedic consult. I want you also to assume under this scenario that no provision was made by Health America to this hospital. Now, under that scenario did Health America deviate from the standard of care?

A.   Yes, they did deviate from the standard of care. Again she should have been sent to the emergency room right away, and the emergency room notified there was a possibility that she was in preterm labor, regardless of the fact she had prior car accidents. Once again, you can't differentiate back pain caused by preterm labor from other sources of back pain without going through a Physical examination and measurements [sic] that you need to determine whether or not she was in labor or not. So, she had to go in and be seen right away. Her call was at 12:42, as I understand, or about 12:30, I think I saw in one place.

Q.   That's right, 12:42.

A.   And she was five centimeters at 4:00 a.m., approximately. Since the first part of labor moves rather slowly, especially in a first baby, an hour or two could have made a significant difference. There's a good probability that if they had seen her at 2:00 a.m. she would still be at four centimeters or less, and they could have inhibited labor even on that night if they had gotten her in quickly enough.

Id. at 158–162.

Viewing the evidence in the light most favorable to the Shannons as the non-moving party, our examination of the instant record leads us to the conclusion that the Shannons presented sufficient evidence to establish a prima facie case of corporate liability pursuant to the third duty set forth in Thompson, supra. However, due to the different entities involved, this determination does not end our inquiry. The Welsh case involved a suit against a hospital and thus Thompson was clearly applicable. Instantly, HealthAmerica, noting this Court's decision not to extend corporate liability under the facts in McClellan v. Health Maintenance Organization of Pennsylvania, 413 Pa.Super. 128, 604 A.2d 1053 (Pa.Super.1992), argues that the Thompson duties are inapplicable to a health maintenance organization. We disagree.

In adopting the doctrine of corporate liability the Thompson court recognized "the corporate hospital's role in the total health care of its patients." Thompson, at 708. Likewise, we recognize the central role played by HMOs in the total health care of its subscribers. A great deal of today's healthcare is channeled through HMOs with the subscribers being given little or no say so in the stewardship of their care. Specifically, while these providers do not practice medicine, they do involve themselves daily in decisions affecting their subscriber's medical care. These decisions may, among others, limit the length of hospital stays, restrict the use of specialists, prohibit or limit post hospital care, restrict access to therapy, or prevent rendering of emergency room care. While all of these efforts are for the laudatory purpose of containing health care costs, when decisions are made to limit a subscriber's access to treatment, that decision must pass the test of medical reasonableness. To hold otherwise would be to deny the true effect of the provider's actions, namely, dictating and directing the subscriber's medical care.

Where the HMO is providing health care services rather than merely providing money to pay for services their conduct should be subject to scrutiny. We see no reason why the duties applicable to hospitals should not be equally applied to an HMO when that HMO is performing the same or similar functions as a hospital. When a benefits provider, be it an insurer or a managed care organization, interjects itself into the rendering of medical decisions affecting a subscriber's care it must do so in a medically reasonable manner. Here, HealthAmerica provided a phone service for emergent care staffed by triage nurses. Hence, it was under a duty to oversee that the dispensing of advice by those nurses would be performed in a medically reasonable manner. Accordingly, we now make explicit that which was implicit in McClellan and find that HMOs may, under the right circumstances, be held corporately liable for a breach of any of the Thompson duties which causes harm to its subscribers.

[The court also held that HealthAmerica was vicariously liable for the negligent rendering of services by its triage nurses, under Section 323 of the Restatement (Second) of Torts.]

Add at page 300, before Pappas:

MOSCOVITCH v. DANBURY HOSPITAL

25 F.Supp.2d 74.
District Court, Connecticut, 1998.

Droney, District Judge.

The plaintiff, Stewart Moscovitch, individually and as administrator of Nitai Moscovitch's estate, brought this action in the Connecticut Superior Court against the defendants Danbury Hospital, Vitam Center, Inc. ("Vitam") and Physicians Health Services, Inc. ("PHS"). The defendant PHS removed the case to this Court pursuant to 28 U.S.C. §§ 1441(a) and (b) (1994), asserting that the complaint contains claims arising under federal law to recover benefits due under a health care plan governed by the Employee Retirement Income Security Act of 1974 ("ERISA"), 29 U.S.C. §§ 1001–1461 (1994 & Supp.II.1996).

The plaintiff and the defendants Danbury Hospital and Vitam filed motions to remand this action to state court, arguing that it does not set forth a federal claim under ERISA and that, as a result, this court does not have original jurisdiction to hear this case. For the reasons set forth below, the motions to remand are granted.

I. BACKGROUND

The plaintiff's employer, Silicon Valley Group Lithography, Inc. ("Silicon Valley"), had an employee benefits plan which offered health benefits to eligible employees and their dependents through a group medical plan administered by PHS. The plaintiff, through his employment with Silicon Valley, enrolled in the PHS medical plan. The parties agree that the medical plan administered by PHS is an "employee welfare benefit plan" governed by ERISA. See 29 U.S.C. §§ 1002(1) and 1003(a). Under the terms of the medical plan, PHS provided health insurance coverage for the plaintiff's adolescent son, Nitai Moscovitch (the "decedent"), who was admitted to Danbury Hospital on July 24, 1995, after twice attempting to commit suicide. The decedent was transferred from Danbury Hospital to Vitam on July 31, 1995, for continued treatment. On the day of his arrival at Vitam, the decedent committed suicide. The plaintiff filed this action in the Connecticut Superior Court on July 18, 1997.

A. The Original Complaint

The original complaint in the Connecticut Superior Court contained six counts. The plaintiff, in his capacity as administrator of the decedent's estate, claimed that Danbury Hospital and Vitam were negligent in their care and treatment of the decedent, and also violated Connecticut General Statutes ("Conn.Gen.Stat.") sections 17a–541 and 17a–542 of the Connecticut patients' bill of rights. (Complaint, Counts 1, 3). The plaintiff also claimed that the actions of Danbury Hospital and Vitam deprived him of the services, companionship and society of his son. (Complaint, Counts 2, 4).

The claims against PHS, brought by the plaintiff in his capacity as administrator of the decedent's estate, were found in Count Five and Count Six. Count Five alleged that PHS, directly and through its agent Vitam, was negligent and failed to provide the decedent with the appropriate standard of care and treatment in violation of the decedent's rights under Conn.Gen.Stat. sections 17a–541 and 17a–542.

Count Six alleged that PHS is a "provider of health insurance benefits for the plaintiff's decedent" and violated the Connecticut Unfair Trade Practices Act ("CUTPA"), Conn.Gen.Stat. section 42–110a et seq. (1995), when it deprived the decedent of appropriate mental health insurance benefits because of cost containment considerations. Specifically, Count Six stated that although PHS initially authorized the admission of the decedent to Danbury Hospital for treatment of his depressive disorder and attempted suicide, it terminated the inpatient treatment at Danbury Hospital and required the decedent to transfer to Vitam. Count Six also alleged that Vitam was a facility inappropriate for the decedent because it was only prepared to treat adolescents with substance abuse problems, not persons with the type or magnitude of the problems of the decedent.

B.   The Removal and Motions to Remand

On August 15, 1997, PHS filed a notice of removal of the plaintiff's complaint from the Connecticut Superior Court to this court. In its removal petition, PHS asserted that removal was proper because this court has original jurisdiction over the claims against PHS pursuant to 28 U.S.C. § 1331 (1994). See 28 U.S.C. § 1441(a) and (b) (civil action filed in state court may be removed to federal district court if the district court has original subject matter jurisdiction). PHS contended that the complaint arose under federal law because it stated a claim under ERISA § 502(a) by seeking to recover benefits due under an ERISA plan. In support of its removal of the plaintiff's complaint, PHS also relied on the decision in Metropolitan Life v. Taylor, 481 U.S. 58, 107 S.Ct. 1542, 95 L.Ed.2d 55 (1987).

On September 5, 1997, the plaintiff filed a motion to remand this action to the Connecticut Superior Court. The plaintiff's motion challenges the removal on the grounds that PHS failed to obtain the consent of its co-defendants before removing the case and also disputes PHS's contention that the complaint raises a federal question. Specifically, the plaintiff states that he is not making a claim to recover benefits, enforce rights or clarify rights to future benefits under an ERISA plan, nor making a claim which relates to the quantity of the benefits the decedent received. The plaintiff contends that his claims against PHS relate solely to the quality of the medical care the decedent received, and are beyond the scope of ERISA.

On September 25, 1997, Danbury Hospital filed its motion to remand this case to the Connecticut Superior Court. Danbury Hospital, like the plaintiff, argues that the removal by PHS is not permitted since the complaint does not raise a federal question under ERISA. Finally, on May 5, 1998, Vitam requested permission to join in the motions to remand of the plaintiff and Danbury Hospital and adopt their arguments.

C.   The Amended Complaint

On the same day the plaintiff filed his motion to remand, he also filed a motion to amend his complaint in this court. The motion was granted and the amended complaint was filed on September 29, 1997.

The amended complaint is brought in five counts. As in the original complaint, Counts One and Three allege that Danbury Hospital and Vitam, respectively, were negligent in their care and treatment of the decedent and violated the decedent's rights under Conn.Gen.Stat. sections 17a–541 and 17a–542. Count One was also revised to allege that PHS and Vitam were the agents of Danbury Hospital and Count Three was revised to allege that PHS and Danbury Hospital were the agents of Vitam. The result of these amendments is that the plaintiff now attributes the alleged negligence of all three defendants to Danbury Hospital and Vitam. Counts Two and Four are identical to the loss of consortium claims made by the plaintiff in the original complaint.

The most significant difference between the original complaint and the amended complaint is the elimination of Count Six, which, as previously stated, charged PHS with a CUTPA violation for denying the decedent health benefits he was due under the plaintiff's medical plan. In addition, Count Five, like Counts One and Three, has been amended to allege that the actions of Danbury Hospital and Vitam are attributable to PHS under the theory they were the actual or apparent servants, agents or employees of PHS.

Count Five also includes twenty-nine new allegations of negligent conduct related to the quality of the care and treatment the decedent received from PHS and its agents.

II.   DISCUSSION

The motions to remand raise several difficult and complex issues. In deciding whether the plaintiff's original complaint was properly removed, the court must first consider whether PHS was required to obtain the consent of Danbury Hospital and Vitam before removal. If PHS did not need the consent of its co-defendants before removing this case, the court must then examine the "well-pleaded complaint rule" and its interpretation in Metropolitan Life v. Taylor, supra, to determine whether the complaint provides this court with jurisdiction under ERISA. In that analysis, the court must also decide whether it is proper to consider the amended complaint. The court will also address the difference between the jurisdictional mandate of complete preemption under ERISA § 502(a) and the defense of conflict preemption under ERISA § 514(a).

A.   Consent for Removal

* * *

[The court held that PHS did not require the consent of its co-defendants to remove the case.]

B.   Removal

1.   The Well–Pleaded Complaint Rule

For the purposes of determining removal jurisdiction, a district court's assessment of whether a complaint raises a federal question is generally governed by the "well-pleaded complaint rule," which requires that the court consider only the allegations in the complaint, not the matters raised in defense by the defendant.[   ]

There is, however, one corollary to the well-pleaded complaint rule recognized in the Metropolitan Life decision which provides that "Congress may so completely preempt a particular area that any civil complaint raising this select group of claims is necessarily federal in character." Metropolitan Life, 481 U.S. at 63–64, 107 S.Ct. 1542; [ ] The Supreme Court has determined that § 502(a)(1)(B) of ERISA's civil enforcement provisions, 29 U.S.C. § 1132(a)(1)(B),[3] is one of the few areas of law which falls within the complete preemption exception to the well-pleaded complaint rule. Metropolitan Life, 481 U.S. at 64–65, 107 S.Ct. 1542. In the ERISA context, "Congress has clearly manifested an intent to make causes of action within the scope of the civil enforcement provisions of § 502(a) removable to federal court." Id. at

---

3.   Section 502(a)(1)(B) provides:

A civil action may be brought—

(1) by a participant or beneficiary—

* * *

(B) to recover benefits due to him under the terms of his plan, to enforce his rights under the terms of the plan, or to clarify his rights to future benefits under the terms of the plan.

66, 107 S.Ct. 1542. In other words, "if [a plaintiff's] state law claim is within the scope of § 502(a) it is completely preempted regardless of how he has characterized it." Jass v. Prudential Health Care Plan, Inc., 88 F.3d 1482, 1488 (7th Cir.1996) [   ]. The issue in this case, therefore, is whether the plaintiff's claims fall within the complete preemption ambit of ERISA § 502(a).

2. Which Complaint Controls?

Before addressing the issue of complete preemption under ERISA § 502(a), the court must decide which complaint to consider because the plaintiff amended his complaint and substantially altered his allegations against PHS after the motion to remand was filed. In the context of removal, "[i]t is a fundamental principle of law that whether subject matter jurisdiction exists is a question answered by looking to the complaint as it existed at the time the petition for removal was filed." Collins v. Dartmouth Plan, Inc., 646 F.Supp. 244, 245 (D.Conn.1986) (citation omitted). Ordinarily, a plaintiff cannot defeat removal by amending the complaint to omit the basis for federal jurisdiction. [   ]

* * *

Here, the plaintiff's amended complaint was designed, at least in part, to remove any potential basis for federal jurisdiction in this case. The plaintiff's efforts were the apparent result of PHS's removal petition, which sought to recharacterize the plaintiff's state law negligence and CUTPA claims against PHS as ERISA claims. However, this case does not present a situation where the plaintiff chose a state forum, yet still intentionally elected to press a federal claim. It does not appear that the plaintiff intended his original claims against PHS to be federal in character and he did not seek relief under a federal statute. This, of course, does not mean that the plaintiff's claims against PHS cannot be removed to federal court; it just indicates that the plaintiff's attempt to amend his complaint is not the type of forum manipulation which concerned the court in Boelens. Moreover, the plaintiff has amended his complaint early in the litigation, prior to the filing of a responsive pleading, the initiation of discovery or the entry of a scheduling order.

Under these circumstances, it is appropriate to consider the amended complaint to determine whether the plaintiff's claims are preempted by ERISA § 502(a). [   ] Accordingly, this court will consider the allegations of the amended complaint in deciding the motions to remand.

3. ERISA § 502(a)

The amended complaint filed by the plaintiff eliminated the CUTPA claim against PHS for its failure to provide continuing coverage for the decedent's inpatient care at Danbury Hospital. PHS maintains, however, that Count Five of the amended complaint, which contains allegations of negligence against PHS, still falls within the scope of ERISA § 502(a). As noted earlier, ERISA § 502(a) completely preempts any state law claim brought by a plaintiff "to recover benefits due to him under the terms of his plan, to enforce his rights under the terms of the plan, or to clarify his rights to future benefits under the terms of the plan." 29 U.S.C. 1132(a)(1)(B). The plaintiff's claims against PHS, as set forth in Count Five of the amended complaint, fall outside the scope of ERISA § 502(a) because they are in the nature of claims for medical negligence, not claims for the improper denial of plan benefits.

The allegations of Count Five which PHS argues bring the plaintiff's claims within the scope of ERISA § 502(a) are: PHS improperly terminated the decedent's treatment at Danbury Hospital; improperly transferred plaintiff's decedent to Vitam; refused to provide psychiatric services at another inpatient facility which would have been more appropriate for the decedent's condition; improperly determined that plaintiff's decedent should be transferred to a drug treatment program; failed to provide the decedent and his family with alternative treatment options at other facilities; and failed to provide inpatient care to the decedent at Danbury Hospital.

Viewing these allegations in context with the other allegations of Count Five, however, it is clear that the plaintiff is challenging the appropriateness of the medical and psychiatric decisions of PHS concerning the care given to the decedent. Count Five does not assert that PHS was making wrong decisions about whether certain care would be covered by its plan, but instead challenges the decisions made by PHS with respect to the quality and appropriate level of care and treatment for the decedent. For example, Count Five alleges that PHS failed to properly diagnose and assess the decedent's psychiatric condition, failed to properly monitor, care and treat him, failed to properly oversee his treatment, and failed to prescribe and administer appropriate medication. Such claims do not fall within the scope of ERISA § 502(a).

This determination is consistent with the reasoning of Dukes v. U.S. Healthcare, 57 F.3d 350 (3d Cir.1995) and Rice v. Panchal, 65 F.3d 637 (7th Cir.1995). In Dukes, the Third Circuit was presented with the consolidated appeals of two district court decisions which denied the plaintiffs' motions to remand and granted the defendants' motions to dismiss. The district courts had held that they lacked removal jurisdiction over the plaintiffs' complaints because they did not fall within the scope of ERISA § 502(a). In reversing the district court decisions, the Third Circuit stated:

> Nothing in the complaints indicates that the plaintiffs are complaining about their ERISA welfare plans' failure to provide benefits due under the plan. Dukes does not allege, for example, that the Germantown Hospital refused to perform blood studies on Darryl because the ERISA plan refused to pay for those studies. Similarly, the Viscontis do not contend that Serena's death was due to their welfare plan's refusal to pay for or otherwise provide for medical services. Instead of claiming that the welfare plans in any way withheld some quantum of plan benefits due, the plaintiffs in both cases complain about the low quality of the medical treatment that they actually received and argue that the U.S. Healthcare HMO should be held liable under agency and negligence principles.

Dukes, 57 F.3d at 356–57.

The claims against PHS in this case are similar to the claims against the defendants in Dukes. The plaintiff here, like the plaintiffs in Dukes, challenges the quality of the medical treatment the decedent allegedly received from PHS and its agents Danbury Hospital and Vitam. Consistent with the holding in Dukes, this court finds that a claim about the quality of a benefit received is not a claim under ERISA § 502(a) to recover benefits due under the terms of a plan. Id. at 357.

This determination is supported by the text of ERISA § 502(a), which does not provide for the civil enforcement of claims related to the quality of benefits received. As the Third Circuit stated, "the legislative history, structure, or purpose of ERISA [do not] suggest that Congress viewed § 502(a)(1)(B) as creating a remedy for a participant injured by medical malpractice." Dukes, 57 F.3d at 357. Indeed,

> nothing in the legislative history suggest[s] that § 502 was intended as a part of a federal scheme to control the quality of the benefits received by plan participants. Quality control of benefits, such as health care benefits provided here, is a field traditionally occupied by state regulation and we interpret the silence of Congress as reflecting an intent that it remain as such.[   ]

In Rice, supra, the Seventh Circuit reversed the district court decision to dismiss the plaintiff's claims against his plan administrator and instructed the district court to remand the case to state court because the claims did not raise a federal question under ERISA. The Rice court determined that the plaintiff's complaint had been improperly removed since the claims were not completely preempted under ERISA § 502(a). Similar to the plaintiff's claims in Dukes and the plaintiff's claims here against PHS, the plaintiff in Rice sued the plan administrator for the medical malpractice of a plan doctor under the state common law theory of respondeat superior and did not allege that the plan administrator had denied the plaintiff benefits due under an ERISA plan. Such a claim was found to be the type that " '[b]eyond the simple need to refer to the ... [Plan], the ... [Plan] is irrelevant to the dispute....' " Rice, 65 F.3d at 645 (quoting Livadas v. Bradshaw, 512 U.S. 107, 125, 114 S.Ct. 2068, 129 L.Ed.2d 93 (1994)).

Remanding the instant action to the state court is also consistent with the Second Circuit decision in Lupo v. Human Affairs Int'l 28 F.3d 269 (2d.Cir.1994). In Lupo, the plaintiff alleged professional malpractice and related state law claims against an ERISA plan provider for the misconduct of one of its employees, a psychotherapist who had treated the plaintiff. The district court had dismissed the plaintiff's claims on the basis that they were preempted by ERISA. The Second Circuit reversed and ordered the case remanded to the state court and stated that the district court did not have jurisdiction over the plaintiff's claims because "none of these claims bears any resemblance to those described in [ERISA § 502(a)]." Lupo, 28 F.3d at 272.

To allow removal of the plaintiff's claims in this case would also undermine the purposes of the well-pleaded complaint rule. While a court "[must] not allow [a plaintiff] to avoid § 502(a)'s complete preemption exception by casting a claim that is clearly within the boundaries of § 502(a) as a state law action ... [the court] [can]not oblige [the plaintiff] to further delineate those boundaries by recasting his complaint sua sponte as one that rests on the federal common law of ERISA." Rice, 65 F.3d at 646 [   ].

Thus, while Congress intended federal courts to develop a common law of rights and obligations under the plan, the well-pleaded complaint rule prevents [this court] from forcing [the plaintiff] from participating in that process. This court, like a defendant, cannot recharacterize a plaintiff's claim in order to create federal question jurisdiction, for if [it] did so, then the plaintiff would be the master of nothing and the well-pleaded complaint rule would be undermined. Rice, 65 F.3d at 646 (citation omitted).

The court notes that PHS, in its objection to the motion to remand, characterizes itself as merely an "administrator of plan benefits" for the group health plan of plaintiff's employer and not an entity involved in the quality of care that was given the decedent. (Defendant PHS's Objection to Motions to Remand, p. 2, 8). However, Count Five of the amended complaint alleges that PHS made wrongful quality of care and treatment decisions and was itself negligent. The status of PHS as a plan administrator, rather than a health maintenance organization or care provider does not, by itself, shield PHS from state law or cause ERISA § 502(a) preemption. See e.g., Rice, 65 F.3d at 645.

The court also recognizes that it is often difficult to determine when an entity such as PHS is arranging, supervising, or providing the medical treatment of a plan participant—which would be outside the scope of ERISA § 502(a)—or merely making benefit determinations—which would be within the scope of ERISA § 502(a). [   ] This determination is especially difficult at this stage of the proceedings when the record is so limited. The court, however, guided by the well-pleaded complaint rule, must allow the plaintiff to make his case in the manner and forum of his choice if it is not preempted by federal law. Here, the amended complaint challenges the medical care decisions of PHS. It will be the plaintiff's burden to show that PHS crossed the line into making such treatment decisions, but he may attempt to do so under state law in state court because PHS has not met its burden of establishing removal jurisdiction. [   ]

The court concludes that the plaintiff's allegations against PHS assert claims for medical malpractice which do not fall within the scope of ERISA § 502(a). The complaint, therefore, is remanded to the Connecticut Superior Court.

4.   ERISA § 514(a)

Finally, the difference between complete preemption under ERISA § 502(a) and conflict preemption under ERISA § 514(a) is important to note.[4] Complete preemption under ERISA § 502(a) is an exception to the well-pleaded complaint rule that has jurisdictional consequences since it recharacterizes state law claims as claims arising under federal law. See Metropolitan Life Ins. Co., 481 U.S. at 64–67, 107 S.Ct.1542; Rice, 65 F.3d at 641. Conflict preemption under ERISA § 514(a), however, does not recharacterize claims as arising under federal law. Rather, preemption under ERISA § 514(a) serves as a defense to a state law claim.[   ]

The court's decision to remand this case to the Connecticut Superior Court is based on an analysis of ERISA § 502(a) and the complete preemption exception to the well-pleaded complaint rule. This decision does not address ERISA § 514(a) and the defense of conflict preemption to state law claims.

---

4.   Section 514(a) of ERISA provides in pertinent part: "Except as provided in subsection (b) of this section, the provisions of [ERISA] shall supersede any and all State laws insofar as they may now or hereafter relate to any employee benefit plan described in section 1003(a) of this title and not exempt under section 1003(b) of this title." 29 U.S.C. § 1144(a).

III. CONCLUSION

For the foregoing reasons the motions to remand filed by the plaintiff and the defendants Danbury Hospital and Vitam are GRANTED.

Replace, at page 300, the Pappas decision of the Pennsylvania Superior Court with the decision of the Pennsylvania Supreme Court, as follows:

PAPPAS v. ASBEL

724 A.2d 889.
Supreme Court of Pennsylvania, 1998.

CAPPY, Justice.

This is an appeal from the order of the Superior Court reversing the trial court's entry of summary judgment in favor of third-party defendant United States Healthcare Systems of Pennsylvania, Inc. ("U.S. Healthcare"). The issue on which this court granted allocatur is whether the Employee Retirement Income Security Act of 1974 ("ERISA"), 29 U.S.C. 1001, et seq., preempts the state tort law claims brought against U.S. Healthcare. For reasons which differ from those relied upon by the Superior Court, we find that ERISA does not preempt these claims. We therefore affirm the order of the Superior Court.

At 11:00 a.m. on May 21, 1991, Basile Pappas ("Pappas") was admitted to Haverford Community Hospital ("Haverford") through its emergency room complaining of paralysis and numbness in his extremities. At the time of his admission, Pappas was an insured of HMO–PA, a health maintenance organization operated by U.S. Healthcare.

Dr. Stephen Dickter, the emergency room physician, concluded that Pappas was suffering from an epidural abscess which was pressing on Pappas' spinal column. Dr. Dickter consulted with a neurologist and a neurosurgeon; the physicians concurred that Pappas' condition constituted a neurological emergency. Given the circumstances, Dr. Dickter felt that it was in Pappas' best interests to receive treatment at a university hospital.

Dr. Dickter made arrangements to transfer Pappas to Jefferson University Hospital ("Jefferson") for further treatment. At approximately 12:40 p.m. when the ambulance arrived, Dr. Dickter was alerted to the fact that U.S. Healthcare was denying authorization for treatment at Jefferson. Ten minutes later, Dr. Dickter contacted U.S. Healthcare to obtain authorization for the transfer to Jefferson. At 1:15 p.m., U.S. Healthcare responded to Dr. Dickter's inquiry and advised him that authorization for treatment at Jefferson was still being denied, but that Pappas could be transferred to either Hahnemann University ("Hahnemann"), Temple University or Medical College of Pennsylvania ("MCP").

Dr. Dickter immediately contacted Hahnemann. That facility advised Haverford at approximately 2:20 p.m. that it would not have information on its ability to receive Pappas for at least another half hour. MCP was then reached and within minutes it agreed to accept Pappas; Pappas was ultimately transported there at 3:30 p.m. Pappas now suffers from permanent quadriplegia resulting from compression of his spine by the abscess.

Pappas and his wife filed suit against Dr. David Asbel, his primary care physician, and Haverford. They claimed that Dr. Asbel had committed medical malpractice and that Haverford was negligent in causing an inordinate delay in transferring him to a facility equipped and immediately available to handle his neurological emergency.

Haverford then filed a third party complaint against U.S. Healthcare, joining it as a party defendant for its refusal to authorize the transfer of Pappas to a hospital selected by the Haverford physicians. Dr. Asbel also filed a cross-claim against U.S. Healthcare seeking contribution and indemnity.

U.S. Healthcare filed a motion for summary judgment on all of the third party claims, alleging that the third party claims are preempted by § 1144(a) of ERISA. The trial court granted the motion. The Superior Court on appeal, however, determined that ERISA did not preempt the state law claims. This court subsequently granted U.S. Healthcare's Petition for Allowance of Appeal in order to determine whether these third party claims fall within the scope of those state actions which are preempted by ERISA.

* * *

Our analysis begins with a review of the basic principles of preemption law. The Supremacy Clause of the United States Constitution provides that the laws of the federal government "shall be the supreme Law of the Land; ... any Thing in the Constitution or Laws of any state to the Contrary notwithstanding." U.S. Const., art. VI, cl. 2. It is this clause which gives to the United States Congress power to preempt state law.

In determining whether state law is preempted by a federal law, a reviewing court is cautioned that such a review "start[s] with the assumption that the historic police powers of the States [are] not to be superseded by ... Federal Act unless it [is] the clear and manifest purpose of Congress." Cipollone v. Liggett Group, 505 U.S. 504, 516, 112 S.Ct. 2608, 2617, 120 L.Ed.2d 407, 422 (1992) (citations omitted). Thus, Congress' intent is the "ultimate touchstone" in this analysis. Id.

A state law can be preempted in one of three ways. The first is where the United States Congress enacts a provision expressly preempting state law. [ ] Even where there is no explicit preemption provision, preemption will still be found where Congress has legislated the field so comprehensively that it has implicitly communicated the intent to occupy a given field to the exclusion of state law. [ ] Finally, a state law will be preempted where a state law actually conflicts with federal law. [ ]

It is this first method of preemption which is at issue in this matter. The express preemption provision in question states that "the provisions of this subchapter ... shall supersede any and all State laws[5] insofar as they may now or hereafter relate to any employee benefit plan...." 29 U.S.C. § 1144(a).

None of the parties in this matter dispute that the United States Supreme Court has yet to speak directly to the issue of whether negligence

5. "State law" was defined by Congress as including "all laws, decisions, rule, regulations, or other State action having the effect of law." 29 U.S.C. § 1144(c)(1). It is uncontested that a decision handed down by a state court, which would enter the common law of that state, is a "state law" as defined by ERISA.

claims against a health maintenance organization "relate to" an ERISA plan. U.S. Healthcare, however, cites to several United States Supreme Court cases from the 1980's and early 1990's as support for its contention that these claims should be preempted by ERISA.

* * *

[The court then discussed Pilot Life Ins. Co. v. Dedeaux, where the court applied a broad interpretation of preemption. It noted that New York State Conference of Blue Cross & Blue Shield Plans v. Travelers Ins. Co. subsequently narrowly this reading of the preemption clause, stating that "[p]reemption does not occur ... if the state law has only a tenuous, remote, or peripheral connection with covered plans, as in the cases with many laws of general applicability." Id. at 661, 115 S.Ct. at 1680, 131 L.Ed.2d at 708–709 (citation omitted). The earlier Supreme Court jurisprudence on preemption has therefore been thrown into doubt by the later caselaw discussed by the Court.]

* * *

Thus, although U.S. Healthcare is correct when it states that U.S. Supreme Court decisions from the 1980's and early 1990's support its position that the preemption provision is to be read broadly, Travelers and its progeny have thrown the expansive holdings of those earlier cases into question. We thus believe that it would be improper to adopt U.S. Healthcare's position that we must reflexively interpret the preemption provision in the broadest possible manner. Instead, we believe that the proper course of action is to follow the reasoning contained within the Travelers line of cases, even though we recognize that the Court's earlier cases have not been expressly overruled.

Based upon our interpretation of the Travelers line of cases, we conclude that negligence claims against a health maintenance organization do not "relate to" an ERISA plan. As noted by Travelers, Congress did not intend to preempt state laws which govern the provision of safe medical care. [ ] Claims that an HMO was negligent when it provided contractually-guaranteed medical benefits in such a dilatory fashion that the patient was injured indisputably are intertwined with the provision of safe medical care. We believe that it would be highly questionable for us to find that these claims were preempted when the United States Supreme Court has stated that there was no intent on the part of Congress to preempt state laws concerning the regulation of the provision of safe medical care.

Furthermore, we believe that negligence laws have "only a tenuous, remote, or peripheral connection with [ERISA] covered plans, as in the cases with many laws of general applicability," Travelers, 514 U.S. at 661, 115 S.Ct. at 1680, 131 L.Ed.2d at 708–709, and therefore are not preempted. We acknowledge that by allowing negligence claims, there will be a financial impact on HMOs. Yet, that is not enough to countermand the conclusion that these claims are not preempted. As noted by the De Buono Court, an incidental increase in the costs imposed on an ERISA plan will not mandate a finding of preemption.[ ]

For the foregoing reasons, we conclude that ERISA does not preempt the claims in question.

Chapter 5

REFORMING THE TORT SYSTEM FOR MEDICAL INJURIES

Add, at page 357, a new section V. Reforming ERISA:

As managed care organizations have expanded to cover a majority of Americans with health insurance, the tort reform issue has become not whether the tort system itself should be reformed, but whether ERISA preemption should be limited by legislation or judicial action so that more consumers can sue managed care organizations for their medical injuries. As the cases in the previous chapter have revealed, injured plaintiffs are often denied access to state courts as a result of ERISA preemption. Congress considered reform of ERISA during 1998 but no legislation was passed.

The following case provides a powerful critique of the current system and its frustrations.

ANDREWS–CLARKE v. TRAVELERS INSURANCE COMPANY

984 F.Supp. 49.
District Court of Massachusetts, 1997.

YOUNG, District Judge.

Surveys show many people think the insurance industry's drive to cut costs has reduced dramatically the overall quality of health care, limiting not only their access to the best doctors and hospitals but also putting such time and financial strain on physicians that they can't possibly provide first-rate treatment....

Hospital officials acknowledged that the cuts on hospital budgets have been steep and swift, occurring mostly because health insurers have scaled back the amount they reimburse hospitals to care for patients. As a result, hospitals are under pressure to send patients home sooner and sicker.

Here's what's happening; support for training doctors is dwindling, and research is under great financial pressure. The quality of delivered health care services is being squeezed, inexorably, by insurers who insist on paying less and less, because that's what their corporate clients insist on; financial incentives are being provided to reward "doing less"; fewer Americans have access to health insurance institutions. Dr. Lowell E. Schnipper, M.D.

Here's what happened in this case. Richard J. Clarke and his wife, Diane Andrews–Clarke, lived in Haverhill, Massachusetts, with their four young children, Deanna, Lacey, Carly, and Justin. Diane Andrews–Clarke, an employee of AT & T, maintained a family health insurance policy with Travelers Insurance Co. through her AT & T employee benefit plan. Her husband and children were named beneficiaries of that policy.

Richard Clarke drank to excess. On April 22, 1994, Dr. Smita Patel admitted Richard Clarke to St. Joseph Hospital in Nashua, New Hampshire, for alcohol detoxification and medical evaluation. St. Joseph Hospital contacted Greenspring, the utilization review provider that must pre-approve treatment under the terms of Clarke's health plan, regarding Clarke's admission. Greenspring authorized only a five day hospital stay for detoxification. Despite the fact that the Travelers' insurance policy held by Andrews–Clarke specifically stated that each insured beneficiary is entitled to at least one thirty day inpatient rehabilitation program per year, Greenspring refused to approve Clarke's enrollment in a thirty day inpatient alcohol rehabilitation program.

After this five day hospital stay, Clarke was discharged from St. Joseph Hospital with a diagnosis of alcohol dependence, alcohol withdrawal symptoms, elevated liver function, and low hemoglobin. He remained alcohol-free for twenty-five days, but then resumed drinking. On September 12, 1994, he voluntarily admitted himself to Baldpate Hospital in Georgetown, Massachusetts, seeking help to stop drinking. Although aware both of Clarke's medical condition and the clear terms of the Travelers' insurance policy, Greenspring refused to authorize more than eight days of inpatient treatment. Baldpate discharged Clarke on September 20, 1994.

Less than twenty-four hours later, Clarke drank a substantial amount of alcohol, ingested cocaine, swallowed a handful of prescription drugs, and attempted to commit suicide by locking himself in the garage with the car engine running. His wife saved his life, breaking through the garage door to find him slumped on the floor. She shut off the car engine and dialed 911. Although Clarke had no detectable pulse or respiration when the ambulance arrived, the paramedics were able to revive him. Clarke was then flown to Henrietta Goodall Hospital in Sanford, Maine, where he was placed in a hyperbaric chamber and successfully treated for carbon monoxide poisoning.

By now, it was tragically apparent to everyone but Travelers and its agent, Greenspring, that Clarke was a danger to himself and perhaps others. After conducting a commitment hearing, the Haverhill District Court so found, and ordered Clark committed to a thirty-day detoxification and rehabilitation program. The court referred the issue of Clarke's placement to the Court Clinic, which in turn sought Greenspring's approval for an insured admission to a private hospital. When Greenspring—despite the fact that enrollment in a thirty-day inpatient detoxification program is a defined benefit of the Travelers insurance policy—incredibly refused to authorize such a private admission, the court ordered Clarke committed to the Southeastern Correctional Center at Bridgewater for his detoxification and rehabilitation.

Clarke's life now spiralled inexorably down and out of control. While a patient at Bridgewater, he was forcibly raped and sodomized by another inmate in his unit. He received little in the way of therapy or treatment. After his release from Bridgewater on October 25, 1994, he made his way back to Haverhill where his wife and four minor children still lived. Diane Andrews–Clarke told Clarke that he could return to the marital home only if he remained sober. Unable to do so without hospitalization, Clarke began a three-week drinking binge.

After an episode of heavy drinking on November 10, 1994, Clarke was placed in protective custody by the Pelham, New Hampshire, police. Later that day, he was admitted to the Southern New Hampshire Medical Center in full respiratory arrest, with a blood alcohol level of .380 and a head injury. Southern New Hampshire Medical Center made no effort to treat Clarke's alcoholism and did not seek to obtain a detoxification admission at any other facility. Clarke spent the night sleeping on a stretcher because it was too cold to discharge him and there were no beds available in area shelters. He was released the next morning.

Upon leaving Southern New Hampshire Medical Center, Clarke purchased a six-pack of Meisterbrau beer, which he immediately began to consume. At 3:06 a.m. on November 12, 1994, the Pelham, New Hampshire, police discovered Clarke's body in a parked car, with a garden hose extending from the tailpipe to the passenger compartment. Clarke, age forty-one, sat lifeless in the front seat, clasping a sixteen ounce beer can in his right hand. He was pronounced dead at the scene.

Subsequent to Clarke's death, Diane Andrews–Clarke commenced this action against Travelers and Greenspring in the Superior Court of the Commonwealth of Massachusetts sitting in and for the County of Essex, individually and as administratrix of Clarke's estate and as next friend of their four minor children. Andrews–Clarke asserts that her husband's death was the direct and foreseeable result of the improper refusal of Travelers and its agent Greenspring to authorize appropriate medical and psychiatric treatment during Clarke's repeated hospitalizations for alcoholism in 1994. She brought claims against them for breach of contract, medical malpractice, wrongful death, loss of parental and spousal consortium, intentional and negligent infliction of emotional distress, and specific violations of the Massachusetts consumer protection laws.

Travelers and Greenspring promptly removed her case to this Court and then, just as promptly, asked this Court to throw her out without hearing the merits of her claim.

This, of course, is ridiculous. The tragic events set forth in Diane Andrews-Clarke's Complaint cry out for relief. Clarke was the named beneficiary of a health insurance policy offered through an employee benefit plan. That policy expressly provided coverage for certain medical and psychiatric treatments, including enrollment in a thirty-day inpatient alcohol detoxification and rehabilitation program. Doctors at several hospitals, and even the courts of the Commonwealth of Massachusetts, determined that Clarke was in need of such treatment, but the insurer and its agent, the utilization review provider, repeatedly and arbitrarily refused to authorize it. As a consequence of their failure to pre-approve—whether willful, or the result of negligent medical decisions made during the course of utilization review—Clarke never received the treatment he so desperately required, suffered horribly, and ultimately died needlessly at age forty-one.

Under traditional notions of justice, the harms alleged—if true—should entitle Diane Andrews–Clarke to some legal remedy on behalf of herself and her children against Travelers and Greenspring. Consider just one of her claims—breach of contract. This cause of action—that contractual promises can be enforced in the courts—pre-dates Magna Carta. It is the very bedrock of our notion of individual autonomy and property rights. It was among the first precepts of the common law to be recognized in the courts of the Commonwealth and has been zealously guarded by the state judiciary from that day to this. Our entire capitalist structure depends on it.

Nevertheless, this Court had no choice but to pluck Diane Andrews–Clarke's case out of the state court in which she sought redress (and where relief to other litigants is available) and then, at the behest of Travelers and Greenspring, to slam the courthouse doors in her face and leave her without any remedy.

This case, thus, becomes yet another illustration of the glaring need for Congress to amend ERISA to account for the changing realities of the modern health care system. Enacted to safeguard the interests of employees and their beneficiaries, ERISA has evolved into a shield of immunity that protects health insurers, utilization review providers, and other managed care entities from potential liability for the consequences of their wrongful denial of health benefits.

All of Diane Andrews–Clarke's cognizable state law causes of action arise out of the alleged improper processing of Clarke's claims for benefits under an ERISA employee benefit plan, and are therefore preempted.[24] At the same time, however, it is undisputed that ERISA's civil enforcement provision does not authorize recovery for wrongful death, personal injury, or other consequential damages caused by the improper refusal of an insurer or utilization review provider to authorize treatment.[26] Thus, the practical impact of ERISA

---

24. Section 514(a) of ERISA, 29 U.S.C. § 1144(a); [ ] Not every state law claim that is preempted by section 514(a) of ERISA, 29 U.S.C. § 1144(a), is subject to removal to federal court under the complete preemption exception to the well-pleaded complaint rule. [ ] In the case at bar, however, it is unnecessary for this Court to reach the issue of complete preemption because there is no question as to the propriety of the Defendants' removal to this Court pursuant to 28 U.S.C. § 1441. At the time of removal, Diane Andrews–Clarke was asserting federal claims under the Emergency Medical Treatment and Active Labor Act ("EMTALA"), 42 U.S.C. § 1395dd, in addition to the state law claims now at issue. Although she has since amended her Complaint so as to abandon the EMTALA claims, "an amendment to a complaint after removal designed to eliminate the federal claim will not defeat federal jurisdiction." Ching v. Mitre Corp., 921 F.2d 11, 13 (1st Cir.1990) (citations omitted). Nevertheless, this Court notes that, even if Andrews–Clarke had never asserted the federal EMTALA claims, removal to this Court would have been justified on the basis of the complete preemption doctrine. As all of her common law claims arise out of denial of benefits under an

ERISA plan, they fall squarely within the scope of ERISA's civil enforcement provision, section 502(a), 29 U.S.C. § 1132(a)(1)(B), and thus are subject to complete preemption. Pilot Life, 481 U.S. at 52, 107 S.Ct. at 1555–56.

26. [ ] Diane Andrews–Clarke does not seek "to recover benefits due to [Clarke] under the terms of [the] plan, to enforce [Clarke's] rights under the terms of the plan, or to clarify [Clarke's] rights to future benefits under the terms of the plan," pursuant to 29 U.S.C. § 1132(a)(1)(B). Similarly, due to Clarke's tragic death, any kind of injunctive relief pursuant to section 1132(a)(3) to enforce Clarke's rights under the plan is no longer viable. Finally, and most importantly, it is well settled that a claim for compensatory or consequential damages does not fall under the purview of "other equitable relief" available to an ERISA plan participant or beneficiary under Section 1132(a)(3). [ ] ERISA also authorizes a plan participant or beneficiary to seek appropriate relief under 29 U.S.C. § 1109(a) pertaining to a breach of fiduciary duty, see 29 U.S.C. § 1132(a)(2), but any extra-contractual damages recovered pursuant to that provision inure to the plan itself rather than to the individ-

in this case is to immunize Travelers and Greenspring from any potential liability for the consequences of their denial of benefits.[27]

ERISA is a "comprehensive statute designed to promote the interests of employees and their beneficiaries in employee benefit plans." It is therefore deeply troubling that, in the health insurance context, ERISA has evolved into a shield of immunity which thwarts the legitimate claims of the very people it was designed to protect.[29] What went wrong?

ERISA—The Legal "Pac Man"

Several commentators place the blame on the Supreme Court's historically broad construction of ERISA's key preemption provision. Indeed, the proper boundaries of ERISA preemption have been the subject of considerable debate. Until recently, the Supreme Court focused almost exclusively upon the "deliberately expansive" language of section 514(a) in interpreting its scope:

The key to § 514(a) is found in the words "relate to." Congress used those words in their broad sense, rejecting more limited pre-emption language that would have made the clause "applicable only to state laws relating to the specific subjects covered by ERISA." ... A law "relates to" an employee benefit plan, in the normal sense of the phrase, if it has a connection with or reference to such a plan.

In New York State Conference of Blue Cross & Blue Shield Plans v. Travelers Ins. Co., 514 U.S. 645, 115 S.Ct. 1671, 131 L.Ed.2d 695 (1995), however, the Supreme Court abruptly abandoned this strict textualist inter-

ual beneficiary. [ ] Despite arguments to the contrary, it is widely recognized that the absence of a comparable remedy under ERISA does not alter the analysis concerning preemption of the state law claims.[ ]

27. Several recent cases have held that when the doctors who actually treated the plan beneficiary are actual or ostensible agents of the plan (as is often the case in a staff-model HMO) a malpractice claim against the plan based upon a theory of vicarious liability is not preempted by ERISA. [ ] In the case, at bar, however, the malpractice claims against Travelers and Greenspring are premised upon a theory of direct rather than vicarious liability. Diane Andrews–Clarke does not allege that the doctors who treated Clarke at St. Joseph Hospital, Southern New Hampshire Medical Center, or Baldpate Hospital were actual or ostensible agents of Travelers or Greenspring, or that Travelers or Greenspring directed Clarke to seek treatment at these hospitals, but rather wishes to recover for negligent medical decisions made during the utilization review process. As a general matter, this Court further notes that the vicarious liability crack in the shield of ERISA preemption is one of narrow applicability. Unlike fully integrated staff-model HMOs, which hire physicians as employees, the majority of managed care plans contract with independent groups or networks of physicians. [ ] A beneficiary cannot assert a malpractice claim against such a plan premised

upon a theory of vicarious liability unless she can demonstrate that the plan held out the treating physician as its employee. [ ] This showing will become increasingly difficult as managed care plans begin to realize that a clear communication to its enrollees that the plan does not directly furnish medical treatment is all that is necessary to avoid liability.

29. This Court further notes that although ERISA regulates both employee pension plans and employee welfare benefit plans—including those that provide, "through the purchase of insurance or otherwise, ... medical, surgical, or hospital care or benefits," 29 U.S.C. 1002(1)(A)—the primary impetus for its passage was to stop certain abuses involving employee pension plans. See H.R.Rep. No. 807, 93d Cong., 2d Sess. 8 (1974), reprinted in 1 § 74 U.S.C.C.A.N. 4670, 4676–77. In contrast to the sweeping requirements that ERISA imposes upon employee pension plans, ERISA itself has little to do with the regulation of health finance; it simply imposes fiduciary and reporting obligations on private employee benefit plans. ERISA does not require employers to provide health insurance or any other benefit; it does not regulate what employers can charge for benefits; it does not prevent employers from eliminating benefits (except pensions). Catherine L. Fisk, The Last Article About the Language of ERISA Preemption? A Case Study of the Failure of Textualism, 33 Harv. J. on Legis. 35, 36–37 & n. 5 (1996).

pretation in favor of a more pragmatic approach. Acknowledging that if the term "relate to" were "taken to extend to the furthest stretch of its indeterminacy," ERISA preemption would be boundless, the Travelers court held that, to determine if the "starting presumption that Congress does not intend to supplant state law," has been overcome in a particular case, we must go beyond the unhelpful text and the frustrating difficulty of defining its key term ["relates to"], and look instead to the objectives of the ERISA statute as a guide to the scope of the state law that Congress understood would survive.

The most catastrophic consequences of overbroad interpretation of "relates to" preemption would thus appear to be waning. In three decisions since Travelers, the Supreme Court has further reinforced this more constrictive reading of section 514(a). Still, once the Supreme Court has spoken, it rarely backtracks. The Travelers court made clear that its prior ruling in Pilot Life remains good law.

Nevertheless, in the view of this Court, the outcome in this case is not the result of an overbroad reading of "relates to" preemption. Unlike the hospital surcharge statute at issue in Travelers, which had only an indirect economic influence on plan administration, here Diane Andrews–Clarke's claims go right to the heart of the benefit determination process. To permit these claims to go forward would contravene the intent of Congress to "ensure that plans and plan sponsors would be subject to a uniform body of benefits law ... [and] minimize the administrative and financial burden of complying with conflicting directives among States or between States and the Federal Government." As the Fifth Circuit noted in Corcoran, "it would be incompatible with the language, structure, and purpose of [ERISA] to allow [state] tort suits against entities so integrally connected with a plan."

This Court acknowledges that, in adopting ERISA's preemption provision, Congress intended to relieve employers and ERISA plans from the burdens of compliance with conflicting state laws not as an end in and of itself, but rather as a means to promote the principal object of ERISA as a whole—"to protect plan participants and beneficiaries." At the time of its enactment, however, ERISA did provide an adequate remedy for the wrongful denial of health benefits. The present gap in remedies is therefore attributable not to an overbroad application of ERISA's preemption clause, but rather to the failure of Congress to amend ERISA's civil enforcement provision to keep pace with the changing realities of the health care system.

When Congress passed ERISA in 1974, traditional fee-for-service insurance plans dominated the American health care industry. Under this model of health care delivery, a plan beneficiary who was ill or injured would visit the doctor of her choice, receive treatment, and then send the bill to her health insurer. If the insurer improperly refused to pay, the beneficiary could be made whole by commencing suit to recover the cost of the treatment pursuant to ERISA.

Today, in contrast, 75% of insured American workers and their beneficiaries receive their health care through some type of "managed care" plan. As a strategy to control costs, most managed care plans perform utilization review prior or concurrent to a proposed course of treatment to determine if it is medically necessary. "By its very nature, a system of prospective decision-making influences the beneficiary's choice among treatment options to a far greater degree than does the theoretical risk of disallowance of a claim facing a beneficiary in a retrospective [fee-for-service] system ... [T]he perception among insurers that prospective determinations result in lower health care costs is premised on the likelihood that a beneficiary, faced with the knowledge of specifically what the plan will or will not pay for, will choose the treatment option recommended by the plan in order to avoid risking total or partial disallowance of benefits." Accordingly, in the managed care context, the wrongful denial of benefits by an insurer—whether intentional, or the result of negligent medical decisions made during the utilization review process—will sometimes result in the beneficiary never receiving the treatment that she requires, and thus can lead to damages far beyond the out-of-pocket cost of the treatment at issue.

ERISA's civil enforcement provision, however, does not authorize recovery for wrongful death, personal injury, or other consequential damages caused by an improper refusal of an insurer or utilization review provider to authorize treatment. ERISA permits a beneficiary to seek an injunction ordering an insurer to authorize the disputed treatment, but such action is often impractical, either because of time constraints or—as was the case here—the incapacity of the beneficiary brought on by his medical condition. Thus, if a beneficiary never receives treatment because of the insurer's failure to pre-approve, ERISA leaves him without any meaningful remedy.

Faced by the absurd result here, some members of Congress—and a host of commentators—have suggested that courts should nevertheless imply such a remedy in order to uphold ERISA's overriding objective of promoting the interests of plan participants and beneficiaries. The Supreme Court, however, has long demonstrated an "unwillingness to infer causes of action in the ERISA context." This Court can neither simply disregard its sworn oath to comply with the opinions of the Supreme Court, nor can it "legislate by judicial decree nor apply a statute, such as ERISA, other than as drafted by Congress." Thus, the task of reforming ERISA "so that it may continue to serve its noble purpose of safeguarding the interests of employees" falls squarely upon the shoulders of Congress.

THE LARGER ISSUES

Perhaps even more disturbing than the perverse outcome generated by ERISA in this particular case is the fact that, in the current health care system, the misconduct alleged by Diane Andrews–Clarke may not be atypical. As discussed above, 75% of insured Americans now receive their health care through some type of "managed care" plan. Although the advent of managed care has eliminated many of the excesses that plagued the traditional fee-for-service system and has, at least temporarily, stabilized the growth of health care costs, it has also spawned a whole new set of potential abuses. In contrast to the old system, in which doctors had incentives to provide too much care, under managed care, the incentives are to provide as little treatment as possible. Indeed, there is a growing body of anecdotal evidence that managed care plans often deny necessary, and even life-saving medical treatment in the name of cutting costs.

Congress, the states, and even the health care industry have recognized the need for reform. In 1997 alone, state legislatures across the country have introduced approximately 1,000 bills regulating managed care, 182 of which have already been enacted into law. At both the federal and state levels, considerable emphasis has been placed on legislating quality standards for individual treatments and procedures. In response to public outcry concerning "drive-through deliveries," Congress enacted the Newborns' and Mothers' Health Care Protection Act of 1996 which requires all health plans to provide coverage for a minimum hospital stay of 48 hours after childbirth. In addition, Congress is presently considering bills that would force health plans to provide coverage for 1) certain emergency medical services, 2) minimum hospital stays for mastectomies and lumpectomies, 3) reconstructive breast surgery, 4) annual mammography screenings for women over the age of 40; and 5) gynecological services. Numerous states have already passed or are considering legislation similar to some or all of these proposals.[68]

68. See Freudenheim, Pioneering State For Managed Care Considers Change, at D8; Carol Jouzaitis, States Crack Down on HMOs' Abuse of Power: Laws Give Decisions Back to Physicians, Chi. Trib., Apr. 15, 1996, at 1. The Massachusetts legislature, for example, is presently considering, inter alia, bills that would require health insurance plans 1) that provide medical and surgical benefits to cover a minimum of 48 hours of inpatient care following a mastectomy and a minimum of 24 hours of inpatient care following a lumpectomy, see H.B. 3835, S.B. 679, Massachusetts 181st General Court (1997); 2) that cover mastectomies to also provide coverage for breast reconstruction surgery, see S.B. 665, Massachusetts 181st General Court (1997); and 3) to cover certain emergency medical services, see H.B. 2702, Massachusetts 181st General Court (1997). ERISA's "savings clause," 29 U.S.C. § 1144(b)(2)(A), excludes from ERISA preemption any state law which regulates insurance. Accordingly, state statutes requiring all insurance policies, including those purchased by ERISA plans, to provide certain minimum, benefits, are not preempted by ERISA. ERISA's "deemer clause," 29 U.S.C. § 1144(b)(2)(B), however, provides that an employee benefit plan does not constitute an insurer for purposes of the savings clause. An ERISA plan may therefore opt out of the these state regulations by self-insuring rather than purchasing insurance. Metropolitan Life Ins. Co., 471 U.S. at 747, 105 S.Ct. at 2392–93; see also Rutter, Democratizing HMO Regulations, 30 U. Mich. J.L. Reform at 188 (noting that state "mandated benefits" laws "create a powerful incentive for businesses to cancel their HMO contracts and self-fund their employee health plans instead"). Recent studies indicate that over 65% of employers self-insure. Troy Paredes, Stop–Loss Insurance, State Regulation, and ERISA: Defining the Scope of Federal Preemption, 34 Harv. J. on Legis. 233, 234 (1997). As early as 1993, this Court noted the dramatic shift to industry self-insurance as a means to avoid state insurance regulation. Pariseau, 822 F.Supp. at 846 n. 5 ("[W]hatever Congress may have originally intended . . . ,

entrepreneurial choice has significantly reduced the class of workers for whom the benefits of state insurance regulation are available. Today, while ERISA blankets the benefit plan landscape, its advantages have come at the cost of state insurance regulation for those who might heretofore have benefitted from such consumer oriented concerns."). Thus, only Congress has the authority to require all ERISA plans, including those that self-insure, to furnish particular benefits. There are several ways that an employer may structure an employee welfare benefit plan: For example, an employer may fully self-insure, or self-fund, its plan either by setting aside funds to satisfy potential claims against the plan or by simply paying benefits to plan participants out of the company's general accounts. In either case, the employer-sponsor retains the risk of providing health care. Alternatively, an employer may fully insure its plan by purchasing health and accident insurance on behalf of plan participants from a third-party insurer. Employers, however, are increasingly turning to a third option, which combines features of both models just described. Under this third option, referred to as a "stop-loss plan," an employer self-funds but purchases a form of reinsurance known as stop-loss insurance to insure itself against the risk that claims against its plan will exceed a certain specified level.

Over the last decade, employers have increasingly chosen to self-fund their welfare plans. The most recent studies indicate that over 65% of employers self-insure, and that about half of the nation's workforce is covered under a self-insured plan. In 1992, nearly 90% of Fortune 500 companies and 78% of employers with 1000 or more employees self-funded their welfare plans.

When employers self-fund, however, they expose themselves to a substantial risk of loss. As a result, few employers today fully self-fund their welfare plans. Instead, even employers that choose not to purchase basic health and accident insurance on behalf of their participants usually purchase stop-loss insurance to limit their exposure to risk and consequent

As matter of public policy, such piecemeal reforms are inadequate because they target the symptoms while ignoring the underlying pathology—the incentives for undercare which now pervade America's health care system. Persons who suffer from medical conditions that affect only a small or historically underrepresented portion of the population are left unprotected. Furthermore, although certain procedures such as mastectomy and child birth seem to lend themselves to uniform regulation, innumerable other medical conditions require more idiosyncratic treatment protocols. Attempts to draw bright-line rules regarding what levels of treatment are "medically necessary" for such conditions will ultimately "impede even proper denials" of treatment, and thus needlessly drive up health care costs.[72]

Rather than seeking directly to regulate managed care procedure-by-procedure, the more efficient approach is to allow insurers and utilization review providers to make benefit determinations on a case-by-case basis, but hold them legally accountable for the consequences of their decisions. By ensuring that bad medical judgments made during the utilization review process do not "end up being cost-free to the plans that rely on [utilization review] to contain medical costs," plan administrators will have more incentive to "seek out those [utilization review providers] that can deliver both high quality services and reasonable prices."

Some have argued that exposing managed care plans to the threat of direct liability will result in over-deterrence, and therefore undermine legitimate cost containment efforts. Congress, certainly sensitive to these concerns, of course has the power to cap the amount of damages that beneficiaries can recover against insurers and utilization providers, or to take other steps to

---

liability. The most recent data show that over 70% of otherwise self-funded plans are covered by some form of stop-loss insurance. Indeed 96% of employers with fewer than 1000 employees purchase stop-loss protection. Not only is the number of plans with stop-loss coverage substantial, but that number is increasing. [As discussed above], ERISA creates a distinction between fully insured plans and fully self-funded plans for federal preemption of state regulation governing welfare plans, ERISA preempts states from regulating fully self-funded plans but permits states to regulate fully insured plans indirectly by regulating their insurer. Paredes, Stop–Loss Insurance, State Regulation, and ERISA, 34 Harv. J. on Legis. at 234–35 (footnotes omitted). The question of whether ERISA also permits states to regulate a stop-loss plan's stop-loss insurer has yet to be answered by the courts. See id. at 235.

72. Corcoran, 965 F.2d at 1338; see also Jack K. Kilcullen, Groping for the Reins: ERISA, HMO Malpractice, and Enterprise Liability, 22 Am. J.L. & Med. 7, 49 (1996) ("[T]he cost of safety should be internalized to the plan and not, as under ERISA, externalized to the injured patient."); Jeanne Kassler M.D., Bitter Medicine: Greed and Chaos in American Health Care 88–92 (1994) (due to the lack of accountability in the current system, utilization review "firms make their money by cutting insurers' expenses, appropriately or other-

wise"). This Court notes that, even without the threat of liability, market forces do provide some incentive for managed care plans to provide quality care. The efficacy of such quality-based competition is limited, however, because it is "notoriously difficult for medical consumers to estimate the quality of care." Latham, Regulation of Managed Care Incentive Payments, 22 Am. J.L. & Med. at 412. "Although there is a great deal of effort being devoted to the development of objective measures of quality of care, this work is still in its clinical infancy." Id. This problem is exacerbated by the fact that 70% of all medical costs are incurred by only 10% of the general population. Kassler, Bitter Medicine at 29. Since the tangible effects of improper denials of care are felt most strongly by such a small minority of the enrollees, managed care plans are "tempted to compete for customers primarily by offering them the [immediately] tangible benefit of lower plan costs rather than by depending on customers to recognize high quality." Latham, Regulation of Managed Care Incentive Payments, 22 Am. J.L. & Med. at 412; see also Rutter, Democratizing HMO Regulation, 30 U. Mich. J.L. Reform, at 148–49 (noting that the "same HMO that eagerly provides cheap prescription drugs and brochures on cardiovascular health may deny expensive but vital care to its patients when they are sickest and most vulnerable").

limit industry liability. Under any criterion, however, the shield of near absolute immunity now provided by ERISA simply cannot be justified.

This Court takes judicial notice that Congress is now considering two bills which would remove the shield of de facto immunity that ERISA provides for managed care insurers and utilization review providers. The Managed Care Plan Accountability Act of 1997 would amend ERISA's civil enforcement provision, 29 U.S.C. § 1132(c), to provide a federal remedy to any ERISA plan participant or beneficiary who is wrongfully denied benefits under a managed care plan pursuant to a "clinically or medically inappropriate decision or determination resulting from the application of any cost containment technique ... [or] any utilization review directed at cost containment."[76] The Patient Access to Responsible Care Act of 1997, in contrast, would make ERISA's preemption provision, section 514(a), inapplicable to "any State cause of action to recover damages for personal injury or wrongful death against any person that provides insurance or administrative services to or for an employee welfare benefit plan maintained to provide health care benefits." [77]Although both of these bills are still in the early stages of the legislative process, Congress is at least aware of the current gap in remedies.[78]

The very reason that most "people seek health insurance is to have some medical security in a crisis." For the more than 50% of American workers who receive their health insurance through an ERISA-governed plan, however, such security is sorely lacking because of the de facto immunity that the law now confers upon insurers and utilization review providers associated with such plans. Unfortunately, to date, "ERISA [has proven] an excellent example of the classic observation that it is a great deal more difficult for Congress to correct flawed statutes than it is to enact them in the first place.... because interests coalesce around the advantageous aspects of the status quo." Although the alleged conduct of Travelers and Greenspring in this case is extraordinarily troubling, even more disturbing to this Court is the failure of Congress to amend a statute that, due to the changing realities of the modern health care system, has gone conspicuously awry from its original intent.

76. H.R. 1749, 105th Cong. § 2(a) (1997). The proposed amendment would allow the participant or beneficiary to recover any actual damages caused by the wrongful denial of benefits, including compensatory and consequential damages, with each specified defendant to be held jointly and severally liable, and would also grant courts the discretion to award punitive damages. H.R. 1749, 105th Cong. § 2(a) (1997).

77. S. 644, H.R. 1415, 105th Cong. (1997). By deferring to the states to define the proper scope of liability for insurers and utilization review providers, the latter proposal potentially would subject ERISA plans to the cost of compliance with conflicting standards of care. This Court takes judicial notice of still another bill now before Congress which would require plans to establish an expedited appeals process for benefit determinations made during the course of utilization review, with the possibility of further external appeals to an independent review organization certified under state law. Health Insurance Bill of Rights Act of 1997, S.

373, 105th Cong. § 2785 (1997). Unlike the other bills discussed herein, however, this proposal would not afford an adequate remedy to persons who, due to time constraints (even with the expedited process in place) or incapacity brought on by illness, are unable to take advantage of such grievance procedures. Congress might, however, find it desirable to combine the two forms of legislation.

78. Such legislation faces an uphill battle, however. See Anders, Health Against Wealth, at 210–226 (characterizing the managed care industry as having the "best lobbyists in America" and describing how these lobbyists have managed to defeat managed care reform proposals that seemed to enjoy widespread support amongst patient advocates and physicians); Fisk, The Last Article about the Language of ERISA Preemption?, 33 Harv. J. on Legis. at 99 (noting that, particularly at the federal level, "significant health care reform may be blocked ... by a well-organized and well-financed business and insurance lobby").

Does anyone care?

Do you?

Note

For an interesting proposal to amend ERISA to improve provider incentives for quality care, see Bryan A. Liang, Patient Injury Incentives in Law, 17 Yale Law & Pol. Rev. 1(1998).

Chapter 6

THE PROFESSIONAL–PATIENT RELATIONSHIP

Add, at the bottom of page 358:

The threshold duty continues to evolve in the setting of independent or workplace physician examinations of employees or potential insureds. In Webb v. T.D., 951 P.2d 1008 (Mont.1997), the court articulated a compound duty on physicians retained by third parties to do independent medical examinations:

> 1. to exercise ordinary care to discover those conditions which pose an imminent danger to the examinee's physical or mental well-being and take reasonable steps to communicate to the examinee the presence of any such condition;

> 2. to exercise ordinary care to assure that when he or she advises an examinee about her condition following an independent examination, the advice comports with the standard of care for the health care provider's profession.

II. CONFIDENTIALITY AND DISCLOSURE IN THE PHYSICIAN–PATIENT RELATIONSHIP

Add, at page 379, following Humphers v. First Interstate Bank of Oregon:

BIDDLE V. WARREN GENERAL HOSPITAL

1998 WL 156997.
Ohio Court of Appeals, 1998.

Presiding Judge Donald R. Ford

Appellants, Cheryl A. Biddle, individually and as surviving spouse and heir at law of Robert A. Biddle, deceased, and Gary Ball, bring this appeal from a judgment entry of the Trumbull County Court of Common Pleas granting the motions for summary judgment of appellees, Warren General Hospital ("WGH"), Kevin Andrews, Elliott, Heller, Maas, Moro & Magill Co., L.P.A., and Robert L. Heller.

In June 1993, WGH, through its Chief Financial Officer, Mark Tierney, and without the approval of the WGH Board of Directors, hired the law firm to screen some of WGH's records in search of those patients who might be eligible for Supplemental Security Income ("SSI") reimbursement of medical expenses. A procedure was established in which a courier for the law firm was sent to retrieve patient registration forms from WGH. The patient registration forms included the patient's address, birth date, employment information, and, most significantly, an "admitting diagnosis." Heller, a partner with the law firm, was responsible for screening the patient forms in search of those patients who were eligible for SSI benefits.

The law firm would then contact those patients regarding the possibility of having their financial obligation for medical treatment paid by SSI. Melanie Sutton ("Sutton") and Sharyn Jacisin, then employees of the law firm, were responsible for contacting those eligible patients. Heller instructed each of them to inform the patient that she was calling in behalf of WGH and that the patient might be eligible for Social Security benefits that may help in paying his or her medical bill. Under the agreement between WGH and the law firm, WGH would pay a contingency fee to the law firm from those amounts received by the hospital.

On May 12, 1994, Sutton learned that the law firm intended to terminate her employment. Apparently, as an act of prospective retaliation, she photocopied several of the registration forms of WGH's patients in the law firm's possession. She sent copies of these registration forms to WFMJ–TV, Inc. in Youngstown, Ohio. Those documents became the focus of an investigative report by Janet Rogers, which alleged breach of patient confidentiality at WGH. Appellant, Cheryl A. Biddle, and her husband, Robert A. Biddle, patients whose diagnoses were given to the law firm and then forwarded to WFMJ–TV by Sutton, voluntarily participated in this televised news report.

As a result of this purported breach of confidentiality, appellants filed their original complaint on June 10, 1995, alleging the following claims against both WGH and the law firm: (1) invasion of privacy; (2) intentional infliction of emotional distress; and (3) negligence. Appellants filed claims against WGH predicated upon breach of an implied contract of confidentiality and statutory violations concerning patient confidentiality. Finally, appellants alleged that the law firm had engaged in improper solicitation of clients, giving rise to civil liability.

I. BREACH OF CONFIDENTIALITY BY WGH

Applying these principles to the present case, we next determine whether summary judgment on appellants' claims was appropriate. This case presents issues that focus on the nature of the relationship between physician and patient and, to a lesser degree, between attorney and client. Preliminarily, we would like to clarify that this matter involves the duty of a physician and a hospital to maintain confidential patient information, not the physician-patient privilege. The physician-patient privilege prevents a doctor from testifying regarding any communication made between the physician and patient relating to the patient's treatment.[] The physician-patient privilege is not coextensive with the duty to maintain confidences, which applies to the non-testimonial disclosure of confidential information by a physician.

Therefore, the duty of confidentiality, which applies with equal vigor to hospitals and physicians, protects patients from a significantly broader scope of disclosures than the physician-patient privilege.[] One court has explained the importance of confidentiality as follows:

"When a physician discloses confidential information without authority, he invades two distinct interests of the patient: (1) the patient's interest in the security of the confidential relationship and his corresponding expectation of secrecy; and (2) the patient's specific interest in avoiding whatever injuries will result from circulation of the information. [Note], Alan B. Vickery, Breach of Confidence: An Emerging Tort, 82 Colum.L.Rev. 1426, 1434 (1982). Invasion of the first interest will most likely result in the patient refusing to disclose confidential information in the future, even when it is important to do so. Invasion of the second interest could result in a variety of injuries to the patient:

"The more intimate or embarrassing the information, the more damaging the disclosure will probably be. The [patient] may suffer ridicule, loss of business or professional reputation, or deterioration of personal relationships. Though injury often flows from widespread publication of disclosed information, the greatest injury may well be caused by disclosure to a single person, such as an employer or a spouse. [Id.]" Bullion v. Gadaleto (W.D.Va.1995), 872 F.Supp. 303, 306.

The duty of confidentiality is derived from several sources, the first of which is the statutory physician-patient privilege, R.C. 2317.02(B). Second, the Hippocratic Oath, although rather brief, focuses significantly on confidentiality and states, in part "[w]hat I may see or hear in the course of the treatment or even outside of the treatment in regard to the life of men, which on no account one must spread abroad, I will keep to myself holding such things shameful to be spoken about." Third, an Ohio physician's certificate to practice medicine may be revoked or suspended for the willful betrayal of a professional confidence. [] Fourth, the relationship between physician and patient is fiduciary in nature. [] Accordingly, except to the extent that a physician's duty of confidentiality is derived from the statutory physician-patient privilege, this case involves only the physician's duty of confidentiality, not the physician-patient privilege.

* * * [A]ppellants have alleged in the nineteenth paragraph of their complaint that WGH "conducted a systematic, planned and concerted practice of the release of confidential patient information without prior authorization to do so, thus violating the patient [sic] confidentiality." Accordingly, appellants adequately pleaded the tortious breach of confidentiality claim.

Therefore, due to the importance of the duty to maintain confidences, and to clarify the law on this subject, we expressly recognize the tort of breach of confidentiality in Ohio. We further hold that in order to establish a cause of action for breach of confidentiality, a plaintiff must demonstrate an "unconsented, unprivileged disclosure to a third party of nonpublic information that the defendant has learned within a confidential relationship." Id. at 1455. * * * []

* * *

Before determining whether a tortious breach of patient confidentiality occurred in the present case, some explanation of the elements of the cause of action will be helpful. First, we decline to define which other relationships are "confidential" under this test, except to hold that a physician-patient relationship is confidential. Second, although this is not intended to be an exhaustive list, for purposes of this cause of action, a physician's disclosure is "privileged" in those instances when public policy and the Revised Code mandate disclosure such as: (1) diagnosis of occupational diseases[]; (2) contagious or infectious diseases[]; (3) suspected child abuse[]; and (4) certain evidence of serious criminal conduct[].

* * *

WGH's primary argument in support of its contention that it did not breach patient confidentiality is that appellants consented to the release of the registration forms to the law firm. This argument fails for two reasons. First, the purported waiver was not properly before the trial court. When considering a motion for summary judgment, a court can consider only "the pleadings, depositions, answers to interrogatories, written admissions, affidavits, transcripts of evidence in the pending case, and written stipulations of fact[.]" Civ.R. 56(C). * * *

* * *

Second, even if the purported "Authorization For Release of Information" was properly before the court, that document would not provide the necessary consent to make summary judgment appropriate with respect to this element. The form states:

> Authorization is hereby granted Warren General Hospital, its medical staff and medical associates to obtain and release to my insurance company and/or third party payor such information, including medical records, as may be necessary for the completion of my hospitalization claims. I understand that the information released may contain documentation concerning treatment for alcohol and/or drug abuse, a psychiatric condition, or HIV test results, an AIDS diagnosis, or AIDS-related condition. (Emphasis added.)

By its express terms, this release only permits the disclosure of medical records to the patient's insurance company or to a third party payor, such as a governmental entity. The form does not directly or indirectly permit the disclosure of confidential medical information to WGH's law firm(s). Consequently, WGH has failed to carry its burden of showing that there is no issue of material fact with respect to the existence and/or scope of consent. Accordingly, appellants have raised a genuine issue of material fact on each of the elements of the tort of breach of confidentiality.

Appellees contend that they did not breach the duty of confidentiality because WGH provided the registration forms to the law firm, where they were to be kept confidential. However, the elements of the tort of breach of confidentiality only require the disclosure of confidential information to any third party, which includes a law firm for the hospital. If hospitals wish to engage in this type of procedure in the future, liability can be avoided by obtaining clear patient consent for this type of informational release.

Additionally, the law firm argues that WGH had "a qualified privilege to surrender the patient registration forms to the law firm. Likewise, the law firm had a qualified privilege to receive them and review them as it did." A qualified privilege is a defense to a defamation action "in which the interest that the defendant is seeking to vindicate is conditioned upon publication in a reasonable manner and for a proper purpose." Hahn v. Kotten (1975), 43 Ohio St.2d 237, 243, 331 N.E.2d 713.

This language indicates that a qualified privilege addresses the malice element in a defamation action. In the instant case, whether the disclosure was made with malice is irrelevant. Instead, any harm to appellants resulted from the disclosure of presumably truthful information relating to their medical conditions. Accordingly, in our view, the application of a qualified privilege is inappropriate in a case that does not involve defamation; thus, qualified privilege is inapplicable to the case at bar.

Assuming, arguendo, that the privilege could be applied in this case, we conclude that the public policy protecting the confidential nature of the physician-patient relationship is more compelling than the public policy permitting certain disclosures to be protected by a qualified privilege. Therefore, the release of these medical documents was not subject to a qualified privilege. Accordingly, the trial court erred in granting appellees' motions for summary judgment with respect to WGH's breach of patient confidentiality.

II. INDUCEMENT OF BREACH OF CONFIDENTIALITY

Although appellants do not allege a cause of action against the law firm for breach of confidentiality, they assert that the law firm induced WGH to breach its duty of confidentiality. As mentioned before, the relationship between a physician and a patient is fiduciary in nature. Hammonds at 802. In Hammonds, the court held that a third party who induces the breach of a fiduciary's duty of loyalty, or participates in such breach, is liable to the injured party. Id. at 803.

We are persuaded by the test pronounced by the Supreme Court of Massachusetts, which provides that a patient may recover in tort from a party who induces a physician to disclose confidential information about the patient when the following elements are proven:

> (1) [T]he defendant knew or reasonably should have known of the existence of the physician-patient relationship; (2) the defendant intended to induce the physician to disclose information about the patient or the defendant reasonably should have anticipated that his actions would induce the physician to disclose such information; and (3) the defendant did not reasonably believe that the physician could disclose that information to the defendant without violating the duty of confidentiality that the physician owed the patient. Alberts at 121. []

Applying these factors to appellants' claim against the law firm, we conclude that there is a genuine issue of material fact concerning whether the law firm induced WGH to disclose confidential patient information. First, due to the nature of the relationship between the law firm and WGH, it is immediately apparent that the law firm was aware of the physician-patient relationship. Second, there is a factual question as to whether the law firm should have reasonably anticipated that its actions would have induced WGH to release confidential patient information. In his deposition, Heller testified that at the original meeting regarding the arrangement between WGH and the law firm, he "proposed" that the "law firm attempt to be a collection agency for [WGH] in getting individuals whose medical bills weren't paid, potentially eligible for SSI * * *.'' Heller further stated that he informed WGH's representatives at the meeting that in order to perform this service, he needed to know each patient's "medical condition." Consequently, there is an issue of fact on the question of whether the law firm induced WGH to release such information.

The final issue with respect to the inducement claim is whether the law firm reasonably believed that WGH could disclose the admitting diagnoses without breaching physician-patient confidentiality. The law firm argues that there was no breach of confidentiality here since the registration forms were protected by the law firm's duty of confidentiality to its client, WGH. DR 4–101(B)(1). However, in our view, the determination of whether such a belief was reasonable is a question of fact since the law firm did not raise the issue of confidentiality during the planning and negotiation of the arrangement, and the law firm's attorneys should have had a heightened awareness of the extreme importance of maintaining confidentiality. Accordingly, appellants have raised a genuine issue of material fact on the claim of inducement of breach of confidentiality against the law firm.

In summary, we hold that summary judgment was improper with respect to appellants' claim against WGH for tortious breach of patient confidentiality. Further, we conclude that appellants have asserted a cognizable claim against the law firm for inducing WGH to breach patient confidentiality.

[The Court then rejected appellants' claims for invasion of privacy, intentional infliction of emotional distress, and negligence. They concluded that an action of implied breach of the duty of confidentiality, a contracts-based action, was better subsumed under the tort-based action for express breach of confidentiality].

Add, at page 388, at the end of note 6:

Duties to warn patients of medical risks may arise out of medical knowledge of how diseases are communicated. In Tenuto v. Lederle Laboratories, 687 N.E.2d 1300 (N.Y.1997), Dr. Schwartz gave a second dose of oral poliomyelitis vaccine manufactured by Lederle to a five month old girl. He did not ask the girl's father Mr. Tenuto whether he had previously been vaccinated against polio, nor did he advise the parents of the risk for contact polio and precautions to avoid exposure, particularly in light of surgical wound from surgery that Mr. Tenuto was about to undergo. It was a rare but predictable risk that live viruses in an infant recipient's gastrointestinal tract may grow and revert to virulent form. When these wild viruses are excreted from the infant's bowel in feces or from the mouth in saliva, contact with feces or saliva may result in infection and in vulnerable adults in paralytic polio. These risks, known since 1961, were found since 1977 in the package inserts and the PDR.

The court held that plaintiffs fell within a determinate and identified class of immediate family members whose relationships to the "person acted upon have traditionally been recognized as a means of extending and yet limiting the scope of liability for injuries caused by a party's negligent acts or omissions."

Moreover, existence of a special relationship sufficient to supply the predicate for extending the duty to warn and advise plaintiffs of their peril and the need to employ precautions is especially pointed where, as here, the physician is a pediatrician engaged by the parents to provide medical services to their infant, and whose services, by necessity, require advising the patient's parents. Thus, the special relationship factor is triangulated here, involving interconnections of reliance running directly between plaintiffs and Dr. Schwartz, and indirectly from their status and responsibility as the primary caretakers of his infant patient.

. . . it would be inferable that in administering the vaccine and advising plaintiffs, as parents of his infant patient, Dr. Schwartz knew or should have known that his comprehensive services necessarily brought into play the protection of the health of plaintiffs, who relied upon his professional expertise in providing advice and other forms of medical services.

What about a day care teacher, an au pair caring for the infant, a visiting grandmother? Is warning the parents sufficient? Is this duty, like the duty imposed on the physician in Bradshaw, supra at n. 2, self-limiting?

III. INFORMED CONSENT: THE PHYSICIAN'S OBLIGATION

Add at page 408 a new note 4e:

e. Doing nothing as an option. In a health care environment of managed care, conservative practice is the goal and doing nothing and "watchful waiting" are desirable clinical approaches to patient care. In Wecker v. Amend, 918 P.2d 658 (C.A. Kansas 1996), the plaintiff contended that Dr. Amend failed to obtain her informed consent before performing laser surgery on her cervix. She had a human papilloma virus wart on her cervix. Since this might be precancerous, Dr. Amend recommended laser surgery to remove it. She watched a video about laser surgery, which stated that "Laser surgery involves the same risks as with any surgical procedure. There is a small risk of excessive bleeding and possible infection, but those cases are not common and can be treated". Following the surgery, she suffered excessive bleeding and he had to perform a total hysterectomy to control the bleeding. She underwent further surgeries and injections to control her pain. She argue that he failed to inform her of alternatives including the option of no treatment at all.

One expert testified that it was reasonable to do nothing and see if the wart disappeared. In the court's words,

. . . how can a patient give an informed consent to treatment for a condition if the patient is not informed that the condition might resolve itself without any treatment at all? The court held that the jury must be instructed that a physician has a duty to advise a patient of the option of choosing no treatment at all. (Italics mine)

Add, at page 417, note 1:

Consumer advocates have lobbied with success for disclosure of hospital and physician performance data in a variety of formats, including report cards and other rankings. Studies of the effects of disclosure of such data have not been encouraging. See for example Eric C. Schneider, Arnold M. Epstein, Use of Public Performance Reports: A Survey of Patients Undergoing Cardiac Surgery, 279 J.A.M.A. 1638, 1642(1998). The authors concluded that ". . . public reporting of mortality outcomes in Pennsylvania has had virtually no direct impact on patients' selection of hospitals or surgeons. Nevertheless, a substantial number of patients expressed interest in data on mortality outcomes and claimed that they would use such reports in their decision making ... [w]ithout a tailored and intensive program for dissemination and patient education, efforts to aid patient decision making with performance reports are unlikely to succeed." See also Judith H. Hibbard, Paul Slovic, and Jacquelyn J. Jewett, Informing Consumer Decisions in Health Care: Implications from Decision–Making Research, 75 Milbank Q. 395, 411–412 (1997)(finding little congruence between current report card strategies and decision-making research.); Stephen T. Mennemeyer, Michael A. Morrisey, and Leslie Z. Howard, Death and Reputation: How Consumers Acted Upon HCFA Mortality Information, 34 Inquiry 117 (1997) (quality measures aimed at the public must be very simply designed and described; complex measures are largely ignored).

Add, at page 419, note 5:

Disclosure of a provider's HIV status to a patient, particularly prior to invasive surgery, is often required. In Doe v. Noe No.1, 690 N.E.2d 1012 (Ill.App. 1 Dist.1997), the court followed Maryland's approach in Faya v. Almaraz, (620 A.2d 327 1993), finding that a physician should disclose his or her HIV-positive status to a patient who is going to submit to an invasive surgery.

Add, at page 419, after note 6, a new note 7:

7. The perils of 3rd party disclosure. Disclosure of HIV-positive status to third parties, where the patients have not faced risks of exposure, can lead to liability by the party disclosing this status information. In Tolman v. Doe, 988 F.Supp. 582 (D.C.E.D.Va. 1997), the HIV-positive physician sued another physician in state court, alleging causes of action including defamation and intentional infliction of emotional distress based on a letter by defendant to plaintiff's patients informing them that plaintiff had Acquired Immune Deficiency Syndrome (AIDS) and that defendant would not want plaintiff as his cardiologist.

The plaintiff Dr.Tolman was a physician. He was also gay. He has not kept this fact secret from family, close friends, or acquaintances. In 1994, he learned that he had AIDS. Dr. Tolman was in compliance with the Center for Disease Control ("CDC") guidelines while treating patients and, specifically, performing cardiology procedures. Recommendations For Preventing Transmission Of Human Immunodeficiency Virus and Hepatitis B Virus To Patients During Exposure–Prone Invasive Procedures MMWR, Vol. 40/No. RR–8 ("CDC Rec."), at 1.

Defendant Dr. Doe was a physician who practiced with Dr. Tolman until 1996, when he left to take a position out of state. In September or October of 1995, Dr. Doe learned that Dr. Tolman had AIDS. Dr. Doe stated that his "personal opinion" is to disagree with the CDC's determination that a physician with AIDS who complies with the CDC's guidelines may safely perform the procedures that Dr. Tolman was performing. In May 1996 Dr. Doe had a conversation with a patient, during which the patient expressly asked Dr. Doe if Dr. Tolman had AIDS. The patient also asked what Dr. Doe recommended regarding the patient's continued treatment by Dr. Tolman. Dr. Doe told the patient that Dr. Tolman had AIDS and that he (Dr. Doe) would not want a physician with AIDS treating him if he were a patient.

In December 1996, Dr. Doe wrote a letter to between ten and fifteen patients. The letter stated in relevant part:

I would like to tell you that I left the program for personal reasons and because my personal career at . . . was not going anywhere, and also because I could not work any more with Dr. Tolman, especially when I learned that he had AIDS and continues to perform invasive procedres [sic] on the [cardiology] patients.

(Unfortunately, he never told me any thing about it himself, maybe because he did not want me to know that he was homosexual.)

I don't realy [sic] know what to tell you regarding your heart transplant care after you learn this fact. Howevr [sic], I will leave this to your personal judgment. I personally will not want somebody with AIDS to be my physcian [sic], let alone being my [cardiologist]. You may want to think of an alternative that will beter [sic] serve you.

The court held that the plaintiff, for purposes of a motion for summary judgment, had established that a defamatory publication was false. The letter reasonably implied that Dr. Tolman was unfit to practice as a physician, specifically to perform invasive procedures, and that he was placing his patients at an inappropriate risk by continuing these procedures while having contracted AIDS. The court noted the CDC report described the procedures done by the plaintiffs as not "exposure prone" procedures. The court further found that the "CDC has determined that physicians with AIDS, such as Dr. Tolman, are fit to practice medicine and to perform the procedures at issue." He was also in compliance with CDC guidelines in treating patients.

The evidence offered by Defendant consists of the type of speculative inferences, glancing statistics, and unsupported conclusions that Abbott warns against. Indeed, Doe's effort to rebut the consensus of public health officials is much weaker than the effort that was rejected on summary judgment by the Abbott trial court and affirmed on appeal. No reasonable jury could disagree that Defendant's insinuations that Plaintiff was unfit to be a physician, and more specifically, to perform the procedures in question, were false.

Add at page 427, the following Note 5:

5. One study suggests that the defendants' approach in Arato can create problems. Physician failures to help cancer patients understand their survival odds may lead patients to overestimate their odds of survival, and may influence their preference for medical therapies that are highly toxic and unproductive, in light of the prognosis of a short life expectancy. This describes the facts of Arato. See Jane C. Weeks et al., Relationship Between Cancer Patients' Predictions of Prognosis and Their Treatment Preferences, 279 J.A.M.A. 1709 (1998).

Add at page 440, the following new case and notes:

NEADE v. PORTES

303 Ill.App.3d 799, 710 N.E.2d 418.
Appellate Court of Illinois, 1999.

Thomas, Justice.

Plaintiff, Therese Neade, as the administrator of the estate of her deceased husband, Anthony Neade, appeals the circuit court's judgment dismissing portions of count I and all of count II of her amended complaint against defendants Steven Portes, M.D., and Primary Care Family Center,

S.C. (Primary Care). At the times alleged in plaintiff's complaint, Dr. Portes was president of Primary Care. Count I alleged that defendants committed medical negligence, which caused the death of Anthony Neade. Count II alleged that Dr. Portes breached his fiduciary duty to Anthony Neade by failing to disclose that he had a contract with Neade's Health Maintenance Organization (HMO) that created an incentive to minimize diagnostic tests and specialist referrals. On appeal, plaintiff contends that the trial court erred in striking the allegations from count I of her amended complaint because those allegations adequately alleged a breach of the applicable standard of care. Plaintiff also contends that the trial court erred in dismissing count II of the amended complaint because that count stated a cause of action for breach of fiduciary duty.

I. FACTS

Plaintiff's amended complaint alleged the following. Anthony Neade was approximately 37 years old in 1990 when he began to show the classic symptoms of coronary artery blockage, including chest pain radiating into his arm and shortness of breath. As a result, Neade was hospitalized from August 10 to 13, 1990. In addition to his physical symptoms, Neade had a family history of heart disease, was overweight, suffered from hypertension, smoked, and had a high cholesterol count. While in the hospital, Neade underwent various tests, including a thallium stress test. Dr. Thomas Engel (a defendant below but not a party to this appeal) interpreted the result as normal and discharged Neade with a diagnosis of hiatal hernia and/or esophagitis. Count III of plaintiff's amended complaint, which is not at issue in this appeal, alleged that Dr. Engel misinterpreted the thallium stress test and EKG data results. However, even if the test results were properly interpreted, plaintiff alleged that Dr. Portes knew that 20% of normal or negative thallium stress test results are false negatives.

Following his discharge from the hospital, Neade continued to experience chest pain and, therefore, saw Dr. Portes on August 17, August 28, and September 24, 1990. Dr. Portes did not examine Neade during these visits but, relying on the thallium stress test and EKG data, assured Neade that his chest pain was not cardiac related.

In October 1990, Neade again went to Primary Care complaining of stabbing chest pain. Dr. Portes asked his associate, Dr. George Huang, to examine Neade. Primary Care employed Dr. Huang part time, and he had no hospital privileges. After examining Neade, Dr. Huang recommended that he undergo an angiogram, a test that is more specific for coronary artery disease than the thallium stress test. Because Dr. Portes was Neade's primary care physician, however, Dr. Portes had to authorize any hospitalization or additional tests. Without examining Neade, Dr. Portes told Dr. Huang that the pain was not cardiac related and refused to authorize Neade's hospitalization for an angiogram.

In June 1991, Neade again returned to Primary Care, complaining of chest pain radiating up the right side of his neck and sweating when the pain was great. At Dr. Portes's request, Dr. Seymour Schlager, another part-time employee of Primary Care, saw Neade. Dr. Schlager also recommended hospitalization for an angiogram, but Dr. Portes again refused to authorize hospitalization. Without examining Neade and relying on the thallium stress test, Dr. Portes advised Dr. Schlager that Neade's chest pain was not cardiac related.

Count I of plaintiff's amended complaint alleged that Dr. Portes's reliance on the thallium stress test and the EKG and his failure to authorize an angiogram constituted medical negligence. Further, as a proximate result of defendants' medical negligence, Neade suffered a massive myocardial infarction caused by coronary artery blockage on September 16, 1991. Neade died nine days later.

The allegations that were stricken from count I of plaintiff's amended complaint alleged that Dr. Portes, as president of Primary Care, negotiated and entered into contracts with various entities, including Chicago HMO. That contract provided a capitation fee for subscribers of Chicago HMO who utilized defendants' services, as well as a "Medical Incentive Fund," which was to be used for various purposes, including certain tests and referrals to medical specialists. The contract further provided that any monies left in the Medical Incentive Fund at the end of the 12–month contract period would be split 60–40 between defendants and Chicago HMO. Neade's health care insurance was through Chicago HMO. Therefore, if Neade received an angiogram and a referral to a specialist, those fees would be paid from the Medical Incentive Fund administered by defendants.

Count II of plaintiff's amended complaint alleged that a fiduciary relationship existed between Dr. Portes and Neade pursuant to which Dr. Portes had a duty to act in good faith and in the best interest of Neade. Plaintiff alleged that Dr. Portes breached his fiduciary duty by refusing to authorize further testing of Neade, refusing to allow specialists to examine Neade, failing to disclose to Neade defendants' financial relationship with Chicago HMO, including the Medical Incentive Fund, and entering into a contract with Chicago HMO which put defendants' financial well-being in direct conflict with Neade's physical well-being. Plaintiff claimed that as a proximate result of defendants' breach of fiduciary duty, Neade suffered a massive myocardial infarction and died.

Dr. Portes and Primary Care moved to strike from count I the allegations regarding the Medical Incentive Fund and to dismiss Count II entirely. Defendants argued that any financial motive was irrelevant to whether Dr. Portes violated the applicable standard of care in treating Neade. Defendants also argued that there was no cause of action against a physician for breach of fiduciary duty. The trial court granted defendants' motion as to both counts with prejudice.

Plaintiff then filed a motion to reconsider, attaching to the motion plaintiff's affidavit and excerpts of the deposition of Dr. Jay Schapira. Dr. Schapira testified that the applicable standard of care, as well as ethical considerations, required a doctor to divulge his financial interest in withholding care so that a patient could make an informed decision concerning the quality of care he is receiving and concerning the doctor's true motivation in treating him. Plaintiff's affidavit stated that had she known of Dr. Portes's financial interest in refusing to authorize additional treatment for decedent, she would have sought a second opinion. Plaintiff also filed a proposed "supplement" to the complaint incorporating these additional allegations.

Defendants filed a motion, which the trial court denied, to strike the deposition excerpt and affidavit from plaintiff's motion to reconsider. However, after considering those materials, the court denied the motion to reconsider. Plaintiff timely appealed.

II. JURISDICTION

* * *

[The court's analysis of jurisdiction is omitted.]

III. STANDARD OF REVIEW

[The court's discussion of the standard of review is omitted.]

IV. BREACH OF FIDUCIARY DUTY

* * *

* * *

Defendants then claim that there is no case law to support plaintiff's argument that Dr. Portes had a fiduciary duty to disclose his contractual compensation relationship with Chicago HMO. Defendants are correct that there is no Illinois case law addressing this issue. In fact, in our review of other jurisdictions, we have found no cases that address the specific issue raised in this case. However, given the changing nature of health care in this country, courts most likely will be faced with increasing issues concerning managed care and its effect on the physician-patient relationship. Cost containment measures in the health care industry have come under increasing scrutiny in recent years. Traditionally, the entity responsible for paying for health care was separate from the person or organization that delivered the health care. [] More and more, however, the financing and the delivery of health care have been integrated, requiring physicians to be both a care giver and a cost manager.[] Under managed health care plans similar to the plan through which Neade was insured, a patient must choose a primary care physician who serves as a "gatekeeper," deciding whether the patient requires laboratory tests, inpatient hospitalization, or a referral to a specialist.[] Further, in risk/bonus arrangements like the Medical Incentive Fund here, the gatekeeper is paid a bonus for controlling referrals, which arguably creates an incentive for the gatekeeper to limit the use of high-end health services. []

As one commentator has noted, most HMO enrollees do not know that their physicians have financial deterrents to providing more expensive health care to their patients. 83 Geo. L.J. at 1837. Thus, in order to make proper choices concerning health care, "the mechanisms that govern the restrictions on treatment need to be disclosed to the patient." 83 Geo. L.J. at 1837. In this case, plaintiff contends that the obligation to disclose financial incentive arrangement should be placed on the gatekeeper physician pursuant to his fiduciary duty and that a failure to do so constitutes a breach of fiduciary duty.

As noted, in reviewing case law from other jurisdictions, we have found no cases that have addressed whether a physician has a fiduciary duty to disclose the financial incentive arrangement he has with an HMO, although we have found federal case law holding, under analogous fact patterns, that a patient has a cause of action against his HMO for failing to disclose the financial incentive scheme that it has with its physicians. Herdrich v. Pegram, 154 F.3d 362 (7th Cir.1998); Shea v. Esensten, 107 F.3d 625 (8th Cir.1997).

* * *

[The court's discussion of Shea is omitted.]

The foregoing cases, thus, recognize that patients should be informed of financial arrangements that may negatively impact their health care. In this case, as noted, we must determine whether the burden of disclosing such relationships can be placed on a physician pursuant to his fiduciary duty. While many jurisdictions, including our own, recognize that there is a fiduciary relationship between a physician and his patient, there is no consensus concerning whether a plaintiff can bring a cause of action against his physician for breach of fiduciary duty. For example, the Supreme Court of California has held that a physician has a fiduciary relationship with his patient and that a patient can state a cause of action for breach of a physician's fiduciary duty to disclose facts material to the patient's consent. Moore v. Regents of the University of California, 51 Cal.3d 120, 793 P.2d 479, 271 Cal.Rptr. 146 (1990). In Moore, the plaintiff, who suffered from hairy-cell leukemia, alleged that the defendants, by virtue of the physician-patient relationship, conducted research on his cells and planned to benefit financially by their exclusive access to plaintiff's cells without disclosing the extent of their research and economic interests. 51 Cal.3d at 128, 793 P.2d at 483, 271 Cal.Rptr. at 150. The court concluded that a physician must disclose personal interests, whether research or economic, unrelated to the patient's health that may affect the physician's professional judgment. Moore, 51 Cal.3d at 129, 793 P.2d at 483, 271 Cal.Rptr. at 150. Further, a physician's failure to disclose such interests may give rise to a cause of action for breach of fiduciary duty or for performing medical procedures without informed consent. Moore, 51 Cal.3d at 129, 793 P.2d at 483, 271 Cal.Rptr. at 150.

In reaching its conclusion, the Moore court noted that "a reasonable patient would want to know whether a physician has an economic interest that might affect the physician's professional judgment." 51 Cal.3d at 129, 793 P.2d at 483, 271 Cal.Rptr. at 150. The court also noted that the desire to protect patients from a possible conflict of interest is reflected in legislative enactments prohibiting a physician from charging or referring a patient to an organization in which the physician has an interest without first disclosing that interest. Moore, 51 Cal.3d at 129–30, 793 P.2d at 483–84, 271 Cal.Rptr. at 150–51. Cf. Bowlin v. Duke University, 108 N.C.App. 145, 423 S.E.2d 320 (1992) (in claim for constructive fraud against physician arising out of breach of fiduciary duty, court recognized that plaintiff had established existence of relationship of trust and confidence with her physician but held that plaintiff had not stated claim absent allegations showing breach of fiduciary duty).

In contrast, the court of appeals of Minnesota has held that a trial court properly dismissed the plaintiffs' claim for breach of fiduciary duty arising from their physician's failure to disclose a "kickback" scheme, whereby the distributor of Protropin, a synthetic growth hormone drug, made payments to the physician to induce him to refer patients for Protropin-related services and supplies. D.A.B. v. Brown, 570 N.W.2d 168, 169 (Minn.App.1997). The court held that the complaint sounded in malpractice and that the allegations concerning the kickback scheme presented a classic informed consent issue. D.A.B., 570 N.W.2d at 171. The court concluded:

> "While we agree that a physician's advice about treatment options should be free from self-serving financial considerations, any cause of action based on that conduct necessarily flows from the therapeutic relationship. Any breach of fiduciary duty that may have occurred during the doctor's prescription of medication to his patients arose while the doctor was examining, diagnosing, treating, or caring for his patients. Thus, the complained-of acts constitute an integral part of the process of rendering medical treatment." D.A.B., 570 N.W.2d at 172.

In so holding, the court acknowledged that it had recognized causes of action against attorneys for breach of fiduciary duty in addition to legal malpractice claims but declined to recognize a separate cause of action against physicians. D.A.B., 570 N.W.2d at 172.

Similarly, the Colorado Court of Appeals has held that a trial court properly denied the plaintiffs' request to add a claim for breach of fiduciary duty to their complaint against their physician where the breach-of-fiduciary-duty claim would have been duplicative of their negligence claims. Spoor v. Serota, 852 P.2d 1292 (Colo.App.1992); see also Awai v. Kotin, 872 P.2d 1332 (Colo.App.1993) (claim for breach of fiduciary duty against psychologist properly dismissed where factual allegations supporting claim were same factual allegations that supported claim of negligence and, thus, were duplicative). Using similar reasoning, the New Mexico Court of Appeals held that a breach-of-fiduciary-duty claim, based upon allegations that a chiropractor and his corporation designed treatment programs to the detriment of patients in order to generate income, did not state a cause of action separate from the plaintiff's fraud claim, and, therefore, the plaintiff could not recover under both causes of action. Garcia v. Coffman, 124 N.M. 12, 946 P.2d 216 (N.M.App.1997). Finally, the Supreme Court of Arizona has declined to find a breach of trust action arising from an undisclosed risk of surgery where the plaintiff had an adequate remedy through a medical malpractice action should any undisclosed risk occur. Hales v. Pittman, 118 Ariz. 305, 576 P.2d 493 (1978).

In those cases holding that a plaintiff could not state a claim for breach of fiduciary duty apart from a claim for medical negligence, the courts found that the breach-of-fiduciary-duty claims merely were duplicative of the medical negligence claims and, thus, would constitute a second recovery under one set of facts. In this case, defendants also claim that plaintiff's breach-of-fiduciary-duty count is in essence a medical negligence claim and thus is duplicative and should be stricken. While we are mindful that in many cases a cause of action for breach of fiduciary duty against a physician will be duplicative of a medical negligence claim, we also recognize, as did the court in Moore, that in some instances a plaintiff may be able to plead a cause of action for breach of fiduciary duty separate from medical negligence. We find support for our conclusion in legislative enactments, in the current opinions of the American Medical Association (AMA), and in cases holding that a plaintiff can plead separate causes of action against his attorney for legal negligence and for breach of fiduciary duty.

Illinois courts have recognized that a fiduciary relationship exists between a physician and his patient. Petrillo v. Syntex Laboratories, Inc., 148 Ill.App.3d 581, 587–88 (1986). In addition, our legislature, like the California legislature, has recognized a potential conflict of interest where a physician or health care worker refers a patient for health services to an entity in which he has an investment interest. 225 ILCS 47/5 (West 1996). Thus, the Health Care Worker Self–Referral Act (225 ILCS 47/1 et seq. (West 1996)) prohibits a health care worker from referring a patient for health services to an entity in which he is an investor and in which he does not provide direct services, unless the health care worker discloses his investment interest to the patient. 225 ILCS 47/20(b)(7) (West 1996). Further, if the health care worker's financial interest is incompatible with the referred patient's interests, the health care worker is required to make alternative arrangements for the patient's care. 225 ILCS 47/20(b)(10) (West 1996). It follows, then, that there is a potential conflict of interest, which the physician should disclose, where, incompatibly with the patient's interest, he has a financial interest in minimizing referrals or tests.

We find further support for requiring physicians to disclose any financial arrangements with insurers in Current Opinions of the Council on Ethical and Judicial Affairs of the American Medical Association (Current Opinions) (1996–1997 edition). Section 8.132 of Current Opinions provides:

"Physicians must not deny their patients access to appropriate medical services based upon the promise of personal financial reward, or the avoidance of financial penalties. Because patients must have the necessary information to make informed decisions about their care, physicians have an obligation to assure the disclosure of medically appropriate treatment alternatives, regardless of cost.

Physicians must assure disclosure of any financial inducements that may tend to limit the diagnostic and therapeutic alternatives that are offered to patients or that may tend to limit patients' overall access to care. Physicians may satisfy this obligation by assuring that the managed care plan makes adequate disclosure to patients enrolled in the plan." (Emphasis added.) Current Opinions, § 8.132 (1996–97).

Plaintiff's expert, Dr. Jay Schapira, testified at his deposition that Current Opinions addresses the fact that there could be a conflict of interest in a physician's motivation, and when that possibility exists, the physician must disclose it to the patient. Dr. Schapira explained that the standard of care requires a physician to divulge his financial interests in withholding care to a patient so that the patient can make an informed decision about the quality of care he is receiving and the physician's motivation in taking care of him, considering the trust situation between a physician and patient. Defendants argue, however, that a violation of the AMA's medical ethics does not amount to a breach of the legal standard of care. While we agree that a violation of the AMA's medical ethics does not in itself amount to a breach of the legal standard of care, such a violation certainly is relevant to determining whether a physician has breached his standard of care and certainly can form the basis of an expert's opinion that a physician has breached the standard of care. As the Appellate Court, First District, has observed, "the ethics of the medical profession constitute more than just a set of regulations affecting members of a particular profession; they also grant the public, specifically a patient seeking a physician's help, an affirmative right to rely on his physician to faithfully execute those ethical obligations." (Emphasis in original.) Petrillo, 148 Ill.App.3d at 592. Thus, it would be antithetical to hold that the ethical obligations of a physician require him to disclose financial inducements that might tend to limit the diagnostic and therapeutic alternatives available to a patient and also, in determining whether a patient's physician has acted within the standard of care, to hold that a patient has no right to rely on his physician to faithfully execute his ethical obligation.

Our conclusion that a plaintiff may be able to plead a cause of action for breach of fiduciary duty separate from a claim for medical negligence finds further support in Illinois cases that have held that a plaintiff can allege claims for both legal malpractice and for breach of fiduciary duty against his attorney.[] Such claims, however, are not without limitation and not every claim for legal negligence also sets forth a claim for breach of fiduciary duty. [] Thus, where the allegations in a claim for breach of fiduciary duty are virtually identical to those set forth in a claim for legal negligence, it has been held that a cause of action for breach of fiduciary duty has not been properly pleaded and should be dismissed as duplicative.[] This result is similar to that reached by other jurisdictions that have held that a plaintiff could not state a claim for breach of fiduciary duty against his physician where that claim was duplicative of another claim in his cause of action.

Turning to the facts of this case, then, we must examine the specific allegations in plaintiff's medical negligence claim and her breach-of-fiduciary-duty claim to determine whether plaintiff has pleaded separate causes of action. Plaintiff's medical negligence claim against defendants alleged that defendants breached the standard of care in that they (1) failed to provide appropriate care and treatment for Neade after he demonstrated signs and symptoms of coronary artery blockage; (2) failed to properly monitor Neade's condition; (3) unreasonably continued to rely on the results of the thallium stress test and EKG despite Neade's continuing symptoms; (4) failed to personally review the thallium stress test and EKG; (5) failed to take into account Neade's personal factors in combination with his symptoms; (6) failed to make an adequate differential diagnosis; (7) failed to eliminate the differential diagnosis of hiatal hernia or esophagitis; and (8) failed to order or allow an angiogram after Drs. Huang and Schlager recommended the test. As a result of defendants' negligence, Neade suffered a massive myocardial infarction and subsequently died.

Plaintiff's breach-of-fiduciary-duty claim alleged that a fiduciary relationship existed between defendant Dr. Portes and Neade whereby Neade placed trust and confidence in Dr. Portes to act in Neade's best interests and that, pursuant thereto, Dr. Portes had a duty to act in good faith and in the best interests of Neade. Plaintiff claimed that defendant Dr. Portes breached that duty by (1) refusing to order or allow further testing of Neade; (2) refusing to order or allow other specialists to examine or evaluate Neade; (3) failing to disclose the financial relationship that defendants had with Neade's health insurance carrier and that defendants would receive 60% of any monies not expended for the benefit of patients; (4) negotiated and entered into a contract with Chicago HMO that placed defendants' financial well-being in direct conflict with Neade's physical well-being; (5) failed to allow tests because those tests would reduce monies available to defendants; (6) refused to allow an angiogram because such test would reduce monies available to defendants; and (7) negotiated and entered into a contract with Chicago HMO that contained provisions that did not promote the quality of care of a patient such as Neade. Plaintiff further alleged that, as a direct and proximate result of defendant Dr. Portes's breach of fiduciary duty, Neade suffered a massive myocardial infarction and died.

We find that the foregoing allegations allege two separate and distinct causes of action. The claim for medical negligence is premised upon defendant Dr. Portes's allegedly improper reliance on the thallium stress test and EKG in deciding that further tests to rule out coronary artery blockage were not necessary, despite the recommendations of two other physicians. The breach-of-fiduciary-duty-claim is based upon defendant Dr. Portes's failure to disclose to Neade that he had a financial incentive to refrain from ordering any tests or referring Neade to a specialist to determine the cause of his symptoms. In an affidavit attached to plaintiff's motion to reconsider, plaintiff alleged that, had Dr. Portes disclosed his financial relationship with the HMO, she would have questioned him regarding his refusal to approve the recommended angiogram and would have recommended that her husband obtain a second opinion or consult another primary physician.

In so holding, we do not intend to open the floodgates of litigation, and we caution that not every claim for medical negligence will also set forth a claim for breach of fiduciary duty. In this case, however, we find that plaintiff's claim for breach of fiduciary duty is not duplicative of her medical negligence claim. It is conceivable that a trier of fact could find both that Dr. Portes was within the standard of care and therefore not negligent in relying on the thallium stress test and the EKG in deciding that an angiogram was not necessary and also that Dr. Portes did breach his fiduciary duty in not disclosing his financial incentive arrangement and, as a proximate result thereof, Neade did not obtain a second opinion, suffered a massive coronary infarction, and died.

Notes and Questions

1. What problems would be created by a duty to disclose payment incentives? Is a physician tacitly admitting that her clinical judgment is significantly affected by how she is paid? How does this compare to the effect of fee-for-service reimbursement? If a health plan uses a complex mix of salary-holdbacks, feedback, and bonuses, how much information should a patient be told? How much does a patient want to know?

2. Courts continue to struggle with arguments for a new cause of action based on breaches of fiduciary duties. In D.A.B. v. Brown, 570 N.W.2d 168 (C.A.Minn. 1997), Doctor Brown prescribed Protropin, a synthetic growth hormone, to more than 200 patients from 1986 to 1994. Protropin treatment can cost between $20,000 and $30,000 per year. He was sued by a class of patients, along with the drug manufacturer and drug distributor, for breach of fiduciary duty, conspiracy, common law fraud, negligent misrepresentation, and violation of Minnesota Prevention of Consumer Fraud Act. As part of a guilty plea to a federal prosecution, the distributor admitted that it had paid the doctor to

induce him to refer patients for Protropin related services and supplies. Minnesota law prohibits physician compensation for referral of patients or prescription of drugs, but the law has no private remedy. The plaintiff argued, quoting Mark Rodwin, among others, that a physician's fiduciary duty was to act in the patient's best interests, without conflicts of interest.

The court was reluctant to create a new theory, finding that traditional malpractice tests and informed consent doctrine should encompass an injuries suffered.

The doctor's duty to disclose the kickback scheme presents a classic informed consent issue ... To hold otherwise would permit avoidance of every statute defining the physician/patient relationship. Indeed, it is difficult to imagine any medical malpractice claim that would not be pleaded as a breach of fiduciary duty claim in order to bypass legislative procedures aimed at implementing common law. [] We decline to create a new cause of action simply to permit the putative class to avoid showing injury or to circumvent the legislatively mandated statute of limitations.

The plaintiffs argued a Moore line of cases, that a new tort is needed, based on breach of a fiduciary duty by a physician who receives kickbacks for prescribing a manufacturer's and distributor's products. Under such a claim, a different statute of limitations applies, and the injury is presumed, with the fiduciary required to "disgorge itself of all profits gained as a result of the breach." The plaintiffs had argued an analogy to Shea v. Esensten, 107 F.3d 625 (8th Cir.1997) (holding that HMO had fiduciary duty under ERISA to disclose its incentive structure to plan participant.). The court rejected this argument. "While we agree that a physician's advice about treatment options should be free from self-serving financial considerations, any cause of action based on that conduct necessarily flows from the therapeutic relationship. Any breach of fiduciary duty that may have occurred during the doctor's prescription of medication to his patients arose while the doctor was examining, diagnosing, treating, or caring for his patients. Thus, the complained-of acts constitute an integral part of the process of rendering medical treatment."

Chapter 7

PROFESSIONAL RELATIONSHIPS IN HEALTH CARE ENTERPRISES

Insert at page 467, before Notes and Questions, the following:

VOLCJAK v. WASHINGTON COUNTY HOSPITAL ASSOCIATION

Court of Special Appeals of Maryland, 1999.
124 Md.App. 481, 723 A.2d 463.

ADKINS, JUDGE.

Appellant, Edward E. Volcjak (Volcjak), sued Washington County Hospital Association (WCHA or hospital) in the Circuit Court for Washington County because the hospital terminated his clinical privileges in anesthesiology without providing him a hearing when it entered an exclusive contract with a group of anesthesiologists. Volcjak also sued the group that obtained the exclusive contract, Blue Ridge Anesthesia Associates, LLC (Blue Ridge). The court granted summary judgment in favor of the hospital on Volcjak's contract . . . claim[ ].

* * *

FACTUAL AND LEGAL BACKGROUND

Volcjak held clinical privileges in anesthesiology at WCHA from 1974 until termination of those privileges by WCHA in 1996. The catalyst for the hospital's decision to terminate Volcjak was a severely critical report of the division of anesthesiology at WCHA issued by the United States Department of Health and Human Services, Health Care Financing Administration (HCFA). At the time HCFA conducted its survey and issued its report [outlining alleged breaches in clinical practice standards in the WCHA Anesthesiology Division,] Volcjak was Chief of the WCHA Anesthesiology Division.

* * *

On April 11, 1995, the president and CEO of the hospital prepared a document entitled "Plan of Action." In the Plan of Action, the president indicated that the Executive Committee of the WCHA Board had authorized him to take steps to institute an exclusive arrangement for anesthesia services at the hospital.

* * *

Volcjak's most recent two-year term of privileges was scheduled to expire in October of 1995. By letter of September 29, 1995, WCHA informed Volcjak that he was granted reappointment to the Medical Staff and granted clinical privileges in anesthesiology, but subject to one significant new condition:

> Your reappointment and clinical privileges are further conditioned by the business decision of the Board of Trustees to grant a person or group ("Provider") the exclusive rights to manage and provide anesthesia services at the Hospital. The Hospital is actively seeking such a Provider and expects to enter into a written contract with them in the near future. When such a contract is finalized, your clinical privileges and membership will be terminated unless you are selected as the exclusive Provider or you contract with or become employed by the Provider.

On November 1, 1995, Volcjak's attorney ... wrote to WCHA, requesting a hearing concerning the hospital's letter of September 29. ... assert[ing] that the September 29 letter constituted a recommended adverse action under ... the Medical Staff Bylaws, thus entitling Volcjak to a hearing. ... No hearing was thereafter granted by WCHA to Volcjak.

* * *

Hospital Contract With Blue Ridge and Termination of Volcjak's Privileges

On November 3, 1995, WCHA wrote to Volcjak advising him that the Board had decided to pursue an exclusive contract with Capital Anesthesia, Inc. (the corporate predecessor to Blue Ridge, hereinafter, Capital), and had begun contract negotiations with that group on October 27. On November 2, 1995, a letter was mailed to Volcjak by Dr. Dan Lawson, on behalf of Capital advising that at the request of WCHA, Capital would be conducting interviews of the anesthesiologists currently privileged at WCHA with a view towards future employment with Capital.

* * *

On January 25, 1996, WCHA entered into a contract with Blue Ridge, a limited liability company formed by the principals of Capital, to provide, on an exclusive basis, all services for anesthesiology at the hospital. In that contract, the WCHA agreed to indemnify Blue Ridge from all claims filed by any anesthesiologist having clinical privileges at the hospital prior to the contract. Immediately following the hospital's promise to indemnify Blue Ridge, the contract continued as follows:

> To reduce the possibility of suits by anesthesiologists ... [Blue Ridge] agrees to evaluate those providers rendering Anesthesia Services at the Hospital and to consider them for long term employment or contract by using at least the following criteria: Education, experience, clinical skills and malpractice claims history.

On February 7, 1996, WCHA, by letter, advised Volcjak that the hospital had entered into an exclusive contract with Blue Ridge for the provision of anesthesia services at WCHA, and that:

Unless you make arrangements with Blue Ridge to provide services as its employee or contractor, your membership and privileges will be terminated shortly, in which case you will be notified in early March of the effective date of termination.

* * *

Volcjak called Dr. Lawson and spoke to him on February 28. Lawson advised Volcjak that Capital was no longer taking applications for anesthesiologists.

* * *

Volcjak again requested a hearing on the "hospital's threatened action to cancel . . . his privileges," this time by letter dated March 21, to the WCHA Chief of Staff. This request was denied, and WCHA, through its attorneys, confirmed . . . that Volcjak's privileges had automatically expired when he failed to contract with Blue Ridge.

WCHA Medical Staff Bylaws

The Medical Staff Bylaws of WHCA, governing relations between the hospital and its doctors, address when a physician shall be entitled to a hearing . . . [stating], in part:

Except as otherwise specified in these Bylaws, any one or more of the following actions or recommended actions shall be deemed actual or potential adverse action and constitute grounds for a hearing:

* * *

(c) denial of Medical Staff reappointment;

(d) demotion to lower Medical Staff category or membership status;

* * *

(f) revocation of Medical Staff membership;

* * *

(h) involuntary reduction of current Clinical Privileges . . .;

* * *

(j) termination of all Clinical Privileges . . .

* * *

(l) denial of reinstatement after leave of absence. . . .

A physician member is entitled . . . to notice of the recommendation made or action proposed to be taken, and notice of his right to a hearing. The member has thirty days following receipt of notice of the action or recommendation to request a hearing.

* * *

DISCUSSION

I.

Breach of Contract Count Against the Hospital

Appellant, in his breach of contract claim against the hospital, asserts that WCHA breached his contractual rights under the Medical Staff Bylaws by refusing to give him a hearing when it decided to terminate his privileges. Both Volcjak and the hospital agree that the WCHA Charter and Bylaws, and the Medical Staff Bylaws constitute a contract between them. See Anne Arundel Gen. Hosp., Inc. v. O'Brien, 49 Md.App. 362, 370, 432 A.2d 483 (1981). The hospital contends that the Bylaws do not apply when WCHA terminates privileges of a medical staff member as the result of a decision to enter into an exclusive contract, and that the Bylaws require the hospital to afford the physician a hearing only when it formally accuses the physician of professional misconduct. WCHA bases its position upon what it views as a reasonable reading of the Bylaws themselves, as well as case law interpreting similar bylaws in other cases.

* * *

Discussion of Cases Interpreting Similar Bylaws

WCHA would have us read the decision of this Court in O'Brien as controlling precedent requiring that we disregard the plain language of the Bylaws. In that case, the plaintiff physicians whose privileges were terminated claimed entitlement to a hearing, pursuant to a Medical Staff bylaw provision requiring a hearing before a committee of the Medical Staff when any physician "receives notice from the . . . Administrator that his appointment or status as a member of the staff or the exercise of his clinical privileges will be adversely affected. . . . " Id. at 370 n. 3, 432 A.2d 483. We held that Anne Arundel General Hospital (AAGH) was not required, pursuant to its bylaws, to hold a hearing regarding the termination of privileges of AAGH's radiologists when their exclusive contract to provide radiological services to AAGH expired, and they were unable to reach an agreement as to the terms and conditions of a new exclusive contract. See id. at 378, 432 A.2d 483.

* * *

There are several important differences between O'Brien and the present case. First, the plaintiffs in O'Brien had obtained privileges at AAGH only pursuant to the terms of their exclusive contract to provide radiological services that contained explicit provisions for what would occur when the contract expired.

* * *

By contrast, Volcjak never entered into an exclusive contract with the hospital, and never signed a provision stating that his privileges would automatically terminate on a certain date without notice or action by WCHA. . . . Rather, the contract that he had with the hospital, the corporate and Medical Staff Bylaws, provided that he would be given a hearing if there was any adverse action regarding his privileges.

WCHA urges that the automatic termination of privileges provision in the plaintiffs' contract in O'Brien was not critical to our decision. Rather, it urges us to interpret O'Brien broadly as holding that a bylaw provision for a hearing will never apply when a hospital makes what it characterizes as a "business decision" to enter an exclusive contract for services within a particular medical speciality [sic] or sub-speciality [sic].

The United States District Court for Maryland, applying Maryland law, declined to give O'Brien the broad meaning ascribed by WCHA in a case similar to the one sub judice, decided in 1996. See Strauss, 916 F.Supp. at 541. In Strauss, the defendant hospital made a decision that it also characterized as a "business decision" to enter an exclusive contract and terminate the privileges of all radiation oncologists, including Strauss, unless they were able to contract with the new exclusive provider. See id. at 535 ... The hospital, like WCHA in this case, relied upon O'Brien for the proposition that it had no obligation to give the plaintiffs the hearing provided by the bylaws upon termination of the plaintiffs' privileges because the hearing was "required only when a physician's privileges are being restricted or revoked due to specific allegations of professional incompetence or neglect which must be reported to federal and state regulatory agencies." Id. at 538. It asserted that the plaintiffs' privileges were terminated after the Board of Trustees made a " 'reasonable management decision' to solve the problems in the Division of Radiation Oncology by bringing in new leadership and closing the medical staff of the Division." Id.

* * *

[T]he Strauss Court held that the physicians whose privileges had been terminated were entitled to have a hearing because "a doctor faced with charges of this kind must be given a due process opportunity to defend himself." Id. (quoting O'Brien, 49 Md.App. at 371, 432 A.2d 483). The district court explicitly pointed out that a hearing was proper under O'Brien even when a hospital's decision to enter the exclusive contract had the dual purpose of 1) disciplining physicians for failing in their duties, and 2) making a business decision. See id. at 541 n. 17.

Like Strauss, this case also involves allegations that impinge upon the professional qualifications of the plaintiff. . . . While WCHA characterized its decision to enter an exclusive contract as a "business decision," the undisputed facts show that allegations of inadequate "quality of care" involving Volcjak and the other anesthesiologists made in the HCFA report were the primary or exclusive reason for such a decision. Contrary to WCHA's assertion that a hearing would serve no purpose because Volcjak's termination was merely a business decision, it is these allegations that frame the issues to be decided at the hearing.

* * *

We have no doubt that the hospital, under its Corporate Bylaws and Medical Staff Bylaws had the right to make a business decision to enter an exclusive contract for anesthesiology services and not to reappoint Volcjak to the medical staff. See O'Brien, 49 Md.App. at 378, 432 A.2d 483. But the Bylaws provide Volcjak with due process through internal procedural protections as the hospital completes the decision-making process, and these protections were allegedly not followed by WCHA. Under the Bylaws, Volcjak was entitled to a hearing by a Committee of the Medical Staff at some point during the continuum of actions that comprised the adverse action.

* * *

The results of the hearing could have influenced the president or Board in several ways. One, they may have decided that Volcjak was highly qualified as a physician, but could not perform the necessary leadership role.... A hearing could have a substantive impact upon the course of events for other reasons as well. The results of a hearing may have influenced Blue Ridge to proceed in the manner in which it treated Volcjak.

* * *

In summary, the hospital took an adverse action with respect to Volcjak's privileges in the course of resolving the problems raised by the HCFA report. Volcjak timely requested a hearing, twice, after receipt of the letters announcing this adverse action. The hospital's denial of a hearing constituted a denial of the procedural protections contained in the Medical Staff Bylaws, which are part of Volcjak's contract with the hospital.... For these reasons, we conclude that the trial court erred when it granted WCHA's motion for summary judgment[.]

Questions

In termination actions like those in Mateo–Woodburn and Volcjak, the issue of the reasons for termination is central. Usually, a hospital would want to have reasons for terminating privileges or establishing an exclusive contract or switching exclusive providers. Those reasons almost necessarily will be subject to inferences about quality. Is it better for hospitals not to give reasons? How do you reconcile Volcjak and Mateo–Woodburn?

Insert at page 468, a new note following Note 4:

In late 1997, the UFCW Local 56 sought NLRB certification to be a bargaining representative for 400 New Jersey "primary care and specialty physicians" employed by a for-profit HMO. The physicians stated that they hoped such representation would help them regain control of patient care decisions. If the NLRB determined that the physicians were independent contractors rather than employees, certification would be denied. See Collective Bargaining: UFCW Files Petition to Represent Doctors on N. J. HMO Provider Panel, BNA Health Care Policy Report, 5 HCP d37 (Nov. 3, 1997). Although a local preliminary determination found the physicians to be independent contractors, a Washington board found enough merit to warrant a full hearing on the matter, stating that such characterization is not always "clear cut." See Representation: Divided NLRB Orders Full Hearing on UFCW Petition for HMO Physicians, BNA Health L. Rep., 7 BHLR 1454 (Sept. 17, 1998). What argument could be made for independent contractor status of the physicians? For employee status?

Insert at page 472, a new note following Note 2:

Some states have enacted statutes prohibiting HMOs from deselecting providers without fair notice and hearing. Of the statute excerpted below, which would be more helpful to a physician like Dr. Harper? What would be an explanation for the varying scope of state statutes that address HMO deselection? Why do you think the National Association of Insurance Commissioners ("NAIC") has not drafted a uniform deselection provision for states to adopt? What provisions would you include in a federal law? Are these statutes a move in the right direction, or do they make it impossible for managed care? Why?

The Texas Health Maintenance Organization Act provides:

Art 20A.18A. Physician and Provider Contracts

* * *

(b) Before terminating a contract with a physician or provider, the health maintenance organization shall provide a written explanation to the physician or provider of the reasons for termination. On request and before the effective date of the termination, but within a period not to exceed 60 days, a physician or provider shall be entitled to a review of the health maintenance organization's proposed termination by an advisory review panel, except in a case in which there is imminent harm to patient health or an action by a state medical or dental board, other medical or dental licensing board, or other licensing board or other government agency, that effectively impairs the physician's or provider's ability to practice medicine, dentistry, or another profession, or in a case of fraud or malfeasance. The advisory review panel shall be composed of physicians and providers, including at least one representative in the physician's or provider's specialty or a similar specialty, if available, appointed to serve on the standing quality assurance committee or utilization review committee of the health maintenance organization. The decision of the advisory review panel must be considered but is not binding on the health maintenance organization. The health maintenance organization shall provide to the affected physician or provider, on request, a copy of the recommendation of the advisory review panel and the health maintenance organization's determination.

Tex.Ins. Code Ann. art. 20A.18A (West 1997).

Similarly, Rhode Island provides:

23–17.13–3 Certification of health plans.

* * *

(10) Plans shall not be allowed to include clauses in physician or other provider contracts that allow for the plan to terminate the contract "without cause"; provided, however, cause shall include lack of need due to economic considerations.

(11) There shall be due process for non-institutional providers for all adverse decisions resulting in a change of privileges of a credentialed non-institutional provider. The details of the health plan's due process shall be included in the plan's provider contracts.

(a) A health plan is deemed to have met the adequate notice and hearing requirement of this section with respect to a non-institutional provider if the following conditions are met (or are waived voluntarily by the non-institutional provider):

(i) The provider shall be notified of the proposed actions and the reasons for the proposed action.

(ii) The provider shall be given the opportunity to contest the proposed action.

(iii) The health plan has developed an internal appeals process that has reasonable time limits for the resolution of such internal appeal.

R.I. Gen. Laws § 23–17.13–3 (1997).

Insert on page 473, at the end of Note 4, the following:

A recent California case has looked at the discontinuity between staff privileges/exclusive contracting cases and the managed care plan cases. See Potvin v. Metropolitan Life Insurance Co., 63 Cal. Rptr.2d 202 (Cal.App.1997) (Potvin considered a physician's contract containing a "without cause" termination provision which stated that the agreement could be terminated by either party at any time, with or without cause, by giving thirty days prior written notice). The case followed Delta Dental in holding that a health care plan termination must meet the common law standard of fundamental fairness and must provide minimum procedures prior to a no-cause termination. The court also stated that the termination must not be arbitrary, but does not apply that standard as the case was appealed on a motion for summary judgment. The defendant health plan relied upon California staff privileges cases similar to Mateo–Woodburn to argue that no procedure is required when the physician has agreed by contract to such a term. The court rejected the defendant's argument by observing first that each of the cases relied upon by the defendant had been decided prior to Delta Dental. The court also noted that one of the cases relied upon by the defendant was "very limited in its holding," as it applied only to a physician who had an exclusive contract to provide services. The court does not explain why this distinction is important. The case offered by the defendant had also relied upon Mateo–Woodburn's rationale that procedures are not required for the termination of staff privileges where the decision is incidental to reorganization and "quasi-legislative." The Potvin decision does not comment on this aspect of the case, though it does quote it. Potvin may presage a reconsideration of the staff privileges/exclusive contract cases. The California Supreme Court has since accepted the case for review; but as of the date this note was written, there was still no decision. See 941 P.2d 1121, 67 Cal.Rptr.2d 1 (1997).

Insert on page 474, at the end of Note 7, the following:

Courts continue to differ in deciding whether ERISA preempts state law regarding physician contracting in managed care. See BPS Clinical Laboratories v. Blue Cross and Blue Shield of Michigan, 217 Mich.App. 687, 552 N.W.2d 919 (Mich.App.1996)(repudiating the earlier 1994 BPS decision that found ERISA preemption, due to the 1995 Supreme Court decision in of Travelers (see Chapter 13, page 808)); Napoletano v. CIGNA Healthcare, 680 A.2d 127 (Conn.1996), cert. denied, 520 U.S. 1103 (1997)(finding that the doctors' claims did not "relate to" administration of the health care plan as required for ERISA preemption, but instead required CIGNA to enforce the "general criteria for its selection or termination of health care providers" that they had already established and were maintaining). But see Prudential Insurance Co. v. National Park Med. Center, 964 F.Supp. 1285 (E.D.Ark.1997), aff'd in pertinent part, 154 F.3d 812 (8th Cir. 1998)(holding that Arkansas' Patient Protection Act was preempted because it made reference to ERISA). See generally Joanne P. Hopkins & Mark A. Kadzielski, Credentialing and "Deselection" of Providers in Healthcare Delivery Systems, 31 J. Health & Hosp. L. 1 (Spring 1997).

Insert on page 479, at the end of Note 4, the following:

In 1998, the Minnesota Association of Nurse Anesthetists filed a new claim against Unity Hospital alleging, in part, violations of federal antitrust laws and the Minnesota whistleblower statute. See Minnesota Ass'n of Nurse Anesthetists v. Unity Hosp., 5 F. Supp.2d 694 (D.Minn.1998). The court granted summary judgment in favor of Unity regarding the federal antitrust allegations and dismissed the state whistleblower claim without prejudice, declining to exercise supplemental jurisdiction.

Insert at page 482, at the end of Note 2, the following:

In 1997, the Kaiser Northern California region nurses took action against the HMO's inattention to the union's patient care concerns by calling six separate strikes. Prior to a seventh strike, Kaiser agreed to allow eighteen union selected nurses to serve as "quality liaisons." These liaisons between labor and management will use existing committees to resolve problems encountered when nurses experience quality concerns in patient care. The agreement also allows the liaisons to bring in outside regulatory agencies and the public to assist in resolving issues. See Health Care Employees: CAN Members Ratify Contract with Kaiser in Northern California, Daily Labor Report, Apr. 27, 1998 (80 DLR A–11, 1998); Peter Kilborn, Today's Nurses: More Work, Less Interaction with Patients, The Journal Record, April 15, 1998, (1998 WL 11960571). What do you think of this "ombudsman" approach? Do you think it will be effective?

Replace at page 483, the Providence Hospital citation and comment in Note 5 with the following:

Subsequent to Health Care and Retirement, the circuits have been split as to what constitutes "supervisory duties" so as to deny protection by the NLRA. Recently, the Sixth Circuit (quoting Manor West) held that "it is the existence of disciplinary authority that counts [as supervision under 29 U.S.C.A. § 152(11)], and not the frequency of its exercise." See Grancare, Inc. v. National Labor Relations Board, 137 F.3d 372 (6th Cir. 1998) (holding that RN and LPN charge nurses were supervisors due to proof of an authority to discipline, a substantial lack of on-site supervisory personnel, and authority of the duties of others work activity). The Fourth Circuit found that the regulation of nursing assistant tasks, authority to run the facility in the absence of other personnel, and authority to call for an evacuation when warranted substantiated a supervisory role under § 152(11). See Beverly Enterprises, Virginia, Inc. v. National Labor Relations Board, 165 F.3d 290 (4th Cir. 1999). However, the D.C. Circuit held that the supervisory authority relied on in Manor West is not always tantamount to establishing supervisory status, especially when the authority is "more imagined than real." See Beverly Enterprises–Massachusetts, Inc. v. National Labor Relations Board, 165 F.3d 960 (D.C.Cir.) (finding the presence of overseeing shift supervisors and a failure of charge nurses to exercise disciplinary authority created a "paper authority" that was not meaningful in practice). What criteria would you use to evaluate supervisory status? Wouldn't a charge nurse always be in some supervisory capacity, just by the nature of the position?

Insert at page 484, at the end of Note 7, the following:

In late 1997, the UFCW Local 56 sought NLRB certification to be a bargaining representative for 400 New Jersey "primary care and specialty physicians" employed by a for-profit HMO. The physicians stated that they hoped such representation would help them regain control of patient care decisions. However, if the NLRB determined that the physicians were independent contractors rather than employees, certification would be denied. See Collective Bargaining: UFCW Files Petition to Represent Doctors on N. J. HMO Provider Panel, BNA Health Care Policy Report, 5 HCP d37 (Nov. 3, 1997). Although a local preliminary determination found the physicians to be independent contractors, a Washington board found enough merit to warrant a full hearing on the matter, stating that such characterization is not always "clear cut." See Representation: Divided NLRB Orders Full Hearing on UFCW Petition for HMO Physicians, BNA Health L. Rep., 7 BHLR 1454 (Sept. 17, 1998). Would physicians employed by an HMO be considered supervisors under the NLRA? If they are considered supervisors, what effect would that determination have upon their bargaining rights?

Insert on page 490, at the end of Note 2, the following:

In Estate of Mauro v. Borgess Medical Center, 137 F.3d 398 (6th Cir.1998), the Sixth Circuit affirmed the 1995 Michigan district court's summary judgment in Mauro, finding that the HIV positive surgical technician did pose a direct threat to the health and safety of others that could not be eliminated by reasonable accommodation, and thus was not "otherwise qualified" under the ADA or Rehab Act. However, a strong dissent in the case argues that Mauro's documented job activities did not constitute "exposure-prone" procedures as defined by the CDC, thus creating an issue of material fact.

Insert on pages 491–92, at the end of Note 8, the following:

Doe v. St. Joseph's Hospital has been overruled by Alexander v. Rush North Shore Medical Center, 101 F.3d 487 (7th Cir.1996)(holding that a physician with staff privileges at a hospital may not bring a Title VII action alleging the hospital's revocation of staff privileges constituted unlawful discrimination absent proof of an employment relationship with the hospital). In Alexander, the Seventh Circuit applied a five-part test to decide whether the doctor's relationship with the hospital was that of an independent contractor or an employee. The test consisted of the following guidelines: (1) the extent of the employer's control and supervision over the worker, including scheduling and performance of work; (2) the kind of occupation and nature of skill required, including whether skills are obtained in the workplace; (3) the responsibility for costs of operation, such as equipment, supplies, fees, licenses, workplace, and maintenance of operations; (4) the method and form of payment and benefits; and (5) the length of job commitment and/or expectations.

Insert at page 492, a new note following Note 9:

The recent Supreme Court decision in Bragdon v. Abbott, 524 U.S. 624 (1998), included elsewhere in this Supplement, should be noted in this section as it will be of significant importance in future ADA employment cases. Keep in mind that the Court's definition of disability applies both to claims of discriminatory health care services and to claims of discrimination in employment, so that physicians can be either defendants or plaintiffs in ADA cases.

Chapter 8

THE STRUCTURE OF THE HEALTH CARE ENTERPRISE

Insert on page 507, before Notes and Questions:

IN RE CAREMARK INTERNATIONAL INC. DERIVATIVE LITIGATION

Court of Chancery of Delaware, 1996.
698 A.2d 959.

ALLEN, Chancellor.

Pending is a motion ... to approve as fair and reasonable a proposed settlement of a consolidated derivative action on behalf of Caremark International, Inc. ("Caremark"). The suit involves claims that the members of Caremark's board of directors (the "Board") breached their fiduciary duty of care to Caremark in connection with alleged violations by Caremark employees of federal and state laws and regulations applicable to health care providers. As a result of the alleged violations, Caremark was subject to an extensive four year investigation by the United States Department of Health and Human Services and the Department of Justice. In 1994 Caremark was charged in an indictment with multiple felonies. It thereafter entered into a number of agreements with the Department of Justice and others. Those agreements included a plea agreement in which Caremark pleaded guilty to a single felony of mail fraud and agreed to pay civil and criminal fines. Subsequently, Caremark agreed to make reimbursements to various private and public parties. In all, the payments that Caremark has been required to make total approximately $250 million.

This suit was filed in 1994, purporting to seek on behalf of the company recovery of these losses from the individual defendants who constitute the board of directors of Caremark. The parties now propose that it be settled.

* * *

The ultimate issue then is whether the proposed settlement appears to be fair to the corporation and its absent shareholders.

* * *

Legally, evaluation of the central claim made entails consideration of the legal standard governing a board of directors' obligation to supervise or monitor corporate performance. For the reasons set forth below I conclude, in light of the discovery record, that there is a very low probability that it would be determined that the directors of Caremark breached any duty to appropriately monitor and supervise the enterprise. Indeed the record tends to show an active consideration by Caremark management and its Board of the Caremark structures and programs that ultimately led to the company's indictment and to the large financial losses incurred in the settlement of those claims. It does not tend to show knowing or intentional violation of law. Neither the fact that the Board, although advised by lawyers and accountants, did not accurately predict the severe consequences to the company that would ultimately follow from the deployment by the company of the strategies and practices that ultimately led to this liability, nor the scale of the liability, gives rise to an inference of breach of any duty imposed by corporation law upon the directors of Caremark.

[As part of its patient care business, which accounted for the majority of its revenues, Caremark provided alternative site health care services, including infusion therapy, growth hormone therapy, HIV/AIDS-related treatments and hemophilia therapy. Caremark's managed care services included prescription drug programs and the operation of multi-specialty group practices and it employed over 7,000 employees in ninety branch operations. It had a decentralized management structure but began to centralize operations in 1991 to increase supervision over branch operations. Caremark had taken a number of steps to assure compliance with the antikickback provisions of the Medicare fraud and abuse law discussed in Chapter 9. As early as 1989, Caremark's predecessor issued an internal "Guide to Contractual Relationships" ("Guide"), which was reviewed and updated, annually, to govern its employees in entering into contracts with physicians and hospitals. Caremark claimed there was uncertainty concerning the interpretation of federal anti-kickback laws because of the scarcity of court decisions and the "limited guidance" afforded by HHS "safe harbor" regulations. After the federal government had commenced its investigation, Caremark announced that it would no longer pay management fees to physicians for services to Medicare and Medicaid patients and required its regional officers to approve each contractual relationship it entered into with a physician. Caremark established an internal audit plan designed to assure compliance with business and ethics policies. Although a report by Price Waterhouse, its outside auditor, concluded that there were no material weaknesses in Caremark's control structure, the Board's ethics committee adopted a new internal audit charter requiring a comprehensive review of compliance policies and the compilation of an employee ethics handbook concerning such policies, and took various other steps throughout 1993 and 1994 to assure compliance with its policies.

In August and September, 1994, two federal grand juries indicted Caremark and individuals for violations of the anti-kickback laws charging among other things that Caremark had made payments to a physician under "the guise of research grants . . . and consulting agreements" so he would prescribe Protropin, a Caremark-manufactured drug. Plaintiffs filed this derivative suit claiming Caremark directors breached their duty of care by failing adequately to supervise Caremark employees or institute corrective measures thereby exposing the company to liability. In September, 1994, Caremark publicly announced that as of January 1, 1995, it would terminate all remaining financial relationships with physicians in its home infusion, hemophilia, and growth hormone lines of business.]

B.   Directors' Duties To Monitor Corporate Operations

The complaint charges the director defendants with breach of their duty of attention or care in connection with the on-going operation of the corporation's business. The claim is that the directors allowed a situation to develop and continue which exposed the corporation to enormous legal liability and that in so doing they violated a duty to be active monitors of corporate performance. The complaint thus does not charge either director self-dealing or the more difficult loyalty-type problems arising from cases of suspect director motivation, such as entrenchment or sale of control contexts. The theory here advanced is possibly the most difficult theory in corporation law upon which a plaintiff might hope to win a judgment. The good policy reasons why it is so difficult to charge directors with responsibility for corporate losses for an alleged breach of care, where there is no conflict of interest or no facts suggesting suspect motivation involved, were recently described in Gagliardi v. TriFoods Int'l, Inc., Del.Ch., 683 A.2d 1049, 1051 (1996).

1.   Potential liability for directoral decisions: Director liability for a breach of the duty to exercise appropriate attention may, in theory, arise in two distinct contexts. First, such liability may be said to follow from a board decision that results in a loss because that decision was ill advised or "negligent". Second, liability to the corporation for a loss may be said to arise from an unconsidered failure of the board to act in circumstances in which due attention would, arguably, have prevented the loss. The first class of cases will typically be subject to review under the director-protective business judgment rule, assuming the decision made was the product of a process that was either deliberately considered in good faith or was otherwise rational. What should be understood, but may not widely be understood by courts or commentators who are not often required to face such questions, is that compliance with a director's duty of care can never appropriately be judicially determined by reference to the content of the board decision that leads to a corporate loss, apart from consideration of the good faith or rationality of the process employed. That is, whether a judge or jury considering the matter after the fact, believes a decision substantively wrong, or degrees of wrong extending through "stupid" to "egregious" or "irrational", provides no ground for director liability, so long as the court determines that the process employed was either rational or employed in a good faith effort to advance corporate interests. To employ a different rule—one that permitted an "objective" evaluation of the decision—would expose directors to substantive second guessing by ill-equipped judges or juries, which would, in the long-run, be injurious to investor interests.[79] Thus, the business judgment rule is process oriented and informed by a deep respect for all good faith board decisions.

---

79.   The vocabulary of negligence while often employed, is not well-suited to judicial review of board attentiveness, especially if one attempts to look to the substance of the decision as any evidence of possible "negligence." Where review of board functioning is involved, courts leave behind as a relevant point of reference the decisions of the hypothetical "reason-able person", who typically supplies the test for negligence liability. It is doubtful that we want business men and women to be encouraged to make decisions as hypothetical persons of ordinary judgment and prudence might. The corporate form gets its utility in large part from its ability to allow diversified investors to accept greater investment risk. If those in

2. Liability for failure to monitor: The second class of cases in which director liability for inattention is theoretically possible entail circumstances in which a loss eventuates not from a decision but, from unconsidered inaction. Most of the decisions that a corporation, acting through its human agents, makes are, of course, not the subject of director attention. Legally, the board itself will be required only to authorize the most significant corporate acts or transactions: mergers, changes in capital structure, fundamental changes in business, appointment and compensation of the CEO, etc. As the facts of this case graphically demonstrate, ordinary business decisions that are made by officers and employees deeper in the interior of the organization can, however, vitally affect the welfare of the corporation and its ability to achieve its various strategic and financial goals.

Modernly this question has been given special importance by an increasing tendency, especially under federal law, to employ the criminal law to assure corporate compliance with external legal requirements, including environmental, financial, employee and product safety as well as assorted other health and safety regulations. In 1991, pursuant to the Sentencing Reform Act of 1984, the United States Sentencing Commission adopted Organizational Sentencing Guidelines which impact importantly on the prospective effect these criminal sanctions might have on business corporations. The Guidelines set forth a uniform sentencing structure for organizations to be sentenced for violation of federal criminal statutes and provide for penalties that equal or often massively exceed those previously imposed on corporations. The Guidelines offer powerful incentives for corporations today to have in place compliance programs to detect violations of law, promptly to report violations to appropriate public officials when discovered, and to take prompt, voluntary remedial efforts.

* * *

[I]t would, in my opinion, be a mistake to conclude that our Supreme Court's [prior statements regarding directors' duty to monitor] means that corporate boards may satisfy their obligation to be reasonably informed concerning the corporation, without assuring themselves that information and reporting systems exist in the organization that are reasonably designed to provide to senior management and to the board itself timely, accurate information sufficient to allow management and the board, each within its scope, to reach informed judgments concerning both the corporation's compliance with law and its business performance.

Obviously the level of detail that is appropriate for such an information system is a question of business judgment. And obviously too, no rationally designed information and reporting system will remove the possibility that the corporation will violate laws or regulations, or that senior officers or directors may nevertheless sometimes be misled or otherwise fail reasonably to detect acts material to the corporation's compliance with the law. But it is important that the board exercise a good faith judgment that the corporation's information and reporting system is in concept and design adequate to

charge of the corporation are to be adjudged personally liable for losses on the basis of a substantive judgment based upon what persons of ordinary or average judgment and average risk assessment talent regard as "prudent," "sensible" or even "rational", such persons will have a strong incentive at the margin to authorize less risky investment projects.

assure the board that appropriate information will come to its attention in a timely manner as a matter of ordinary operations, so that it may satisfy its responsibility.

Thus, I am of the view that a director's obligation includes a duty to attempt in good faith to assure that a corporate information and reporting system, which the board concludes is adequate, exists, and that failure to do so under some circumstances may, in theory at least, render a director liable for losses caused by non-compliance with applicable legal standards.[80] I now turn to an analysis of the claims asserted with this concept of the directors duty of care, as a duty satisfied in part by assurance of adequate information flows to the board, in mind.

III.   ANALYSIS OF THIRD AMENDED COMPLAINT AND SETTLEMENT
A.   The Claims

* * *

In order to show that the Caremark directors breached their duty of care by failing adequately to control Caremark's employees, plaintiffs would have to show either (1) that the directors knew or (2) should have known that violations of law were occurring and, in either event, (3) that the directors took no steps in a good faith effort to prevent or remedy that situation, and (4) that such failure proximately resulted in the losses complained of ...

1.   Knowing violation for statute: Concerning the possibility that the Caremark directors knew of violations of law, none of the documents submitted for review, nor any of the deposition transcripts appear to provide evidence of it. Certainly the Board understood that the company had entered into a variety of contracts with physicians, researchers, and health care providers and it was understood that some of these contracts were with persons who had prescribed treatments that Caremark participated in providing. The board was informed that the company's reimbursement for patient care was frequently from government funded sources and that such services were subject to the [anti-kickback law]. But the Board appears to have been informed by experts that the company's practices while contestable, were lawful. There is no evidence that reliance on such reports was not reasonable.

2.   Failure to monitor: Since it does appears that the Board was to some extent unaware of the activities that led to liability, I turn to a consideration of the other potential avenue to director liability that the pleadings take: director inattention or "negligence". Generally where a claim of directorial liability for corporate loss is predicated upon ignorance of liability creating activities within the corporation ... in my opinion only a sustained or systematic failure of the board to exercise oversight—such as an utter failure to attempt to assure a reasonable information and reporting system exits—will establish the lack of good faith that is a necessary condition to liability. Such a test of liability—lack of good faith as evidenced by sustained or systematic failure of a director to exercise reasonable oversight—is quite high. But, a

---

80. Any action seeking recovery for losses would logically entail a judicial determination of proximate cause, since, for reasons that I take to be obvious, it could never be assumed that an adequate information system would be a system that would prevent all losses. I need not touch upon the burden allocation with respect to a proximate cause issue in such a suit.

demanding test of liability in the oversight context is probably beneficial to corporate shareholders as a class, as it is in the board decision context, since it makes board service by qualified persons more likely, while continuing to act as a stimulus to good faith performance of duty by such directors.

Here the record supplies essentially no evidence that the director defendants were guilty of a sustained failure to exercise their oversight function. To the contrary, insofar as I am able to tell on this record, the corporation's information systems appear to have represented a good faith attempt to be informed of relevant facts. If the directors did not know the specifics of the activities that lead to the indictments, they cannot be faulted.

The liability that eventuated in this instance was huge. But the fact that it resulted from a violation of criminal law alone does not create a breach of fiduciary duty by directors. The record at this stage does not support the conclusion that the defendants either lacked good faith in the exercise of their monitoring responsibilities or conscientiously permitted a known violation of law by the corporation to occur. The claims asserted against them must be viewed at this stage as extremely weak.

B.   The Consideration For Release of Claim

The proposed settlement provides very modest benefits. Under the settlement agreement, plaintiffs have been given express assurances that Caremark will have a more centralized, active supervisory system in the future. Specifically, the settlement mandates duties to be performed by the newly named Compliance and Ethics Committee on an ongoing basis and increases the responsibility for monitoring compliance with the law at the lower levels of management. In adopting the resolutions required under the settlement, Caremark has further clarified its policies concerning the prohibition of providing remuneration for referrals. These appear to be positive consequences of the settlement of the claims brought by the plaintiffs, even if they are not highly significant. Nonetheless, given the weakness of the plaintiffs' claims the proposed settlement appears to be an adequate, reasonable, and beneficial outcome for all of the parties. Thus, the proposed settlement will be approved.

Insert at page 507, at the end of Note 2:

Does the standard established by the Chancellor in approving the settlement of the Caremark litigation give directors and senior officers of large, far-flung corporate enterprises sufficient incentives to assure that their employees comply with the law? What factors militate against imposing a simple negligence standard with regard to the duty to monitor? Are the interests of the Caremark shareholders advanced by this holding? What role, if any, should the public interest in assuring compliance with the anti-kickback law play in deciding a case of this type?

For the view that the decision in the Sibley Hospital case typified the tendency of courts to be more receptive to duty of care complaints where the transaction is tainted by duty-of-loyalty implications, see Evelyn Brody, The Limits of Charity Fiduciary Law, 57 Md. L. Rev. 1401, 1442–43, (1998)("One wonders whether Judge Gesell would have found any duty-of-care breach—or, more important, even granted standing to the plaintiff patients—had the funds been deposited at banks where the hospitals' directors were not also directors.''). On the fiduciary duties of boards in health care institutions generally, see Naomi Ono, Boards of Directors Under Fire: An Examination of Nonprofit Board Duties in the Health Care Environment, 7 Annals Health L. 107 (1998).

Insert at page 507, at the end of Note 3:

The obligation of fiduciaries to make full disclosures in self-dealing transactions is illustrated by Boston Children's Heart Foundation, Inc. v. Nadal–Ginard, 73 F.3d 429 (1st Cir. 1996). The case involved the activities of a physician, Dr. Nadal–Ginard, who was president and a member of the board of Boston Children's Heart Foundation ("BCHF"), a non-profit corporation established to conduct the clinical and research activities of the cardiology department at Boston Children's Hospital. The defendant was also chairman of the cardiology department at the hospital and a member of the faculty of Harvard Medical School. Conflicting interest problems arose in connection with Dr. Nadal–Ginard's activities on behalf of the Howard Hughes Medical Institute ("Institute"), which provided him substantial compensation for directing the activities of the Institute's Laboratory of Cellular and Molecular Cardiology at Boston Children's Hospital. In his capacity as president of BCHF, Dr. Nadal–Ginard was empowered to set his own salary and determine other compensation-related matters. In so doing, however, Dr. Nadal–Ginard failed to disclose that BCHF was paying him for much of the same work for which he was receiving substantial compensation from the Institute. The First Circuit concluded that Dr. Nadal–Girard's actions setting his own compensation at BCHF constituted self-dealing and required full disclosure of all material information regarding his salary and compensation determinations. Despite the fact that the BCHF by-laws granted Dr. Nadal–Ginard exclusive authority to set his own salary, the Court found that he had not acted in good faith by failing to make full disclosure. 73 F.3d at 434. It further held the information regarding his compensation arrangements with the Institute were material because had BCHF been armed with the information, it may have found he was over-compensated. In so holding, the First Circuit rejected the defendant's claim that no breach occurred because the salary was fair and reasonable, as the failure to act in good faith was sufficient to establish the breach regardless of the reasonableness of the salary. Id.

For an analysis of the implications of fiduciary duties and other legal obligations for placing physicians on hospital boards, see Michael Peregrine, Structuring Physician Membership on the Hospital Governing Board, 31 J. Health & Hosp. L. 133 (1998).

Insert at page 510, at the end of the second full paragraph:

The Missouri Court of Appeals upheld the trial court in the Missouri Blue Cross case, finding that the Blues' actions in transferring its managed care assets to a for-profit subsidiary constituted an abuse of its authority as a nonprofit health services corporation under state laws. Blue Cross and Blue Shield of Mo. v. Angoff et. al., ___ S.W.2d ___, 1998 WL 435697 (Mo.App. W.D.1998). Cf. Fair Care Foundation v. District of Columbia Dept. of Ins. & Sec. Regulation, 716 A.2d 987 (D.C. Cir.1998)(upholding agency determination that a business combination between two Blue Cross licensees did not constitute a conversion of the nonprofit District of Columbia licensee and afforded sufficient protection to entity's charitable assets). For an analysis of the legal and valuation issues posed when parties attempt to settle challenges to conversion cases, see Joel Ferber & JoAnna King, A Cure for the Blues: Resolving Nonprofit Blue Cross conversions, 32 J. Health L. 75 (1999). An excellent series of articles analyzing nonprofit conversions is found in 16 Health Affairs (March/April 1997).

Insert at p. 514, at the end of Note 1:

In cases involving hospital systems with multiple corporate entities, courts are usually reluctant to pierce the corporate veil even where the parent exercises extensive control over the subsidiary and its name is prominently displayed in the advertising, signs and literature of the subsidiary hospital. See, e.g., Humana, Inc. v. Kissun, 221 Ga. App. 64, 471 S.E. 2d 514 (1996); see also, Ritter v. BJC Barnes Jewish Christian Health Systems, 987 S.W.2d 377 (Mo.App. E.D.1999) (refusing to hold parent entity liable on agency, veil-piercing, vicarious liability or apparent authority theories despite extensive control over subsidiary hospital's operations).

Page 515–518, replace Morelli v. Ehsan with the following:

BERLIN v. SARAH BUSH LINCOLN HEALTH CENTER

Supreme Court of Illinois, 1997.
179 Ill.2d 1, 688 N.E.2d 106.

Justice NICKELS delivered the opinion of the court:

Plaintiff, Richard Berlin, Jr., M.D., filed a complaint for declaratory judgment and a motion for summary judgment seeking to have a restrictive covenant contained in an employment agreement with defendant, Sara Bush Lincoln Health Center (the Health Center), declared unenforceable. The circuit court of Coles County, finding the entire employment agreement unenforceable, granted summary judgment in favor of Dr. Berlin. The circuit court reasoned that the Health Center, as a nonprofit corporation employing a physician, was practicing medicine in violation of the prohibition on the corporate practice of medicine. A divided appellate court affirmed, and this court granted the Health Center's petition for leave to appeal.

The central issue involved in this appeal is whether the "corporate practice doctrine" prohibits corporations which are licensed hospitals from employing physicians to provide medical services. We find the doctrine inapplicable to licensed hospitals and accordingly reverse.

BACKGROUND

The facts are not in dispute. The Health Center is a nonprofit corporation duly licensed under the Hospital Licensing Act to operate a hospital. In December 1992, Dr. Berlin and the Health Center entered into a written agreement whereby the Health Center employed Dr. Berlin to practice medicine for the hospital for five years. The agreement provided that Dr. Berlin could terminate the employment relationship for any reason prior to the end of the five-year term by furnishing the Health Center with 180 days advance written notice of such termination. The agreement also contained a restrictive covenant which prohibited Dr. Berlin from competing with the hospital by providing health services within a 50–mile radius of the Health Center for two years after the end of the employment agreement.

On February 4, 1994, Dr. Berlin informed the Health Center by letter that he was resigning effective February 7, 1994, and accepting employment with the Carle Clinic Association. After his resignation, Dr. Berlin immediately began working at a Carle Clinic facility located approximately one mile from the Health Center. Shortly thereafter, the Health Center sought a preliminary injunction to prohibit Dr. Berlin from practicing at the Carle Clinic based on the restrictive covenant contained in the aforesaid employment agreement.

* * *

Hospital Employment of Physicians

The Health Center and its supporting amici curiae contend that no judicial determination exists which prohibits hospitals from employing physicians. In support of this contention, the Health Center argues that this court has acknowledged the legitimacy of such employment practices in past decisions. See, e.g., Gilbert v. Sycamore Municipal Hospital, 156 Ill.2d 511, 190 Ill.Dec. 758, 622 N.E.2d 788 (1993); Darling v. Charleston Community Memorial Hospital, 33 Ill.2d 326, 211 N.E.2d 253 (1965). In the alternative, the Health Center contends that if a judicial prohibition on hospital employment of physicians does exist, it should be overruled. In support of this contention, the Health Center argues that the public policies behind such a prohibition are inapplicable to licensed hospitals, particularly nonprofit hospitals.

The Health Center also contends that there is no statutory prohibition on the corporate employment of physicians. The Health Center notes that no statute has ever expressly stated that physicians cannot be employed by corporations. To the contrary, the Health Center argues that other legislative actions recognize that hospitals can indeed employ physicians. Citing Illinois' Emergency Medical Treatment Act and Osteopathic and Allopathic Healthcare Discrimination Act.

Dr. Berlin and supporting amici curiae contend that this court, in People ex rel. Kerner v. United Medical Service, Inc. adopted the corporate practice of medicine doctrine, which prohibits corporations from employing physicians. Dr. Berlin concludes that the Health Center, as a nonprofit corporation, is prohibited by the Kerner rule from entering into employment agreements with physicians.

Dr. Berlin also disputes the Health Center's contention that public policy supports creating an exception to the Kerner rule for hospitals. He argues that, because no legislative enactment subsequent to the Kerner case expressly grants hospitals the authority to employ physicians, the legislature has ratified the corporate practice of medicine doctrine as the public policy of Illinois. At this point, a review of the corporate practice of medicine doctrine is appropriate.

Corporate Practice of Medicine Doctrine

The corporate practice of medicine doctrine prohibits corporations from providing professional medical services. Although a few states have codified the doctrine, the prohibition is primarily inferred from state medical licensure acts, which regulate the profession of medicine and forbid its practice by unlicensed individuals. See A. Rosoff, The Business of Medicine: Problems with the Corporate Practice Doctrine, 17 Cumb. L.Rev. 485, 490 (1987). The rationale behind the doctrine is that a corporation cannot be licensed to practice medicine because only a human being can sustain the education, training, and character-screening which are prerequisites to receiving a professional license. Since a corporation cannot receive a medical license, it follows that a corporation cannot legally practice the profession.

The rationale of the doctrine concludes that the employment of physicians by corporations is illegal because the acts of the physicians are attributable to the corporate employer, which cannot obtain a medical license. The prohibition on the corporate employment of physicians is invariably supported by several public policy arguments which espouse the dangers of lay control over professional judgment, the division of the physician's loyalty between his patient and his profitmaking employer, and the commercialization of the profession.

Application of Doctrine in Illinois

This court first encountered the corporate practice doctrine in Dr. Allison, Dentist, Inc. v. Allison, 360 Ill. 638, 196 N.E. 799 (1935). In Allison, the plaintiff corporation owned and operated a dental practice. When defendant, a dentist formerly employed by plaintiff, opened a dental office across the street from plaintiff's location, plaintiff brought an action to enforce a restrictive covenant contained in defendant's employment contract. Defendant's motion to dismiss the action was granted on the grounds that plaintiff was practicing dentistry in violation of the Dental Practice Act. In affirming the judgment of the lower court, this court stated:

> "To practice a profession requires something more than the financial ability to hire competent persons to do the actual work. It can be done only by a duly qualified human being, and to qualify something more than mere knowledge or skill is essential. The qualifications include personal characteristics, such as honesty, guided by an upright conscience and a sense of loyalty to clients or patients, even to the extent of sacrificing pecuniary profit, if necessary. These requirements are spoken of generically as that good moral character which is a pre-requisite to the licensing of any professional man. No corporation can qualify." [The Court next discussed cases finding the corporate practice doctrine barred corporations from operating dental clinics employing dentists and prevented a medical clinic providing medical services through licensed physicians.]

* * *

Prior to the instant action, apparently no Illinois court has applied the corporate practice of medicine rule set out in People ex rel. Kerner v. United Medical Service, Inc., or specifically addressed the issue of whether licensed hospitals are prohibited from employing physicians. We therefore look to other jurisdictions with reference to the application of the corporate practice of medicine doctrine to hospitals.

Applicability of Doctrine to Hospitals in Other Jurisdictions

Although the corporate practice of medicine doctrine has long been recognized by a number of jurisdictions, the important role hospitals serve in the health care field has also been increasingly recognized. Accordingly, numerous jurisdictions have recognized either judicial or statutory exceptions to the corporate practice of medicine doctrine which allow hospitals to employ physicians and other health care professionals. See, e.g., Cal. Bus. & Prof.Code § 2400 (West 1990) (exception for charitable hospitals).... A review of this authority reveals that there are primarily three approaches utilized in determining that the corporate practice of medicine doctrine is inapplicable to hospitals.

First, some states refused to adopt the corporate practice of medicine doctrine altogether when initially interpreting their respective medical practice act. These states generally determined that a hospital corporation which employs a physician is not practicing medicine, but rather is merely making medical treatment available. See, e.g., State ex rel. Sager v. Lewin, 128 Mo.App. 149, 155, 106 S.W. 581, 583 (1907) ("[H]ospitals are maintained by private corporations, incorporated for the purpose of furnishing medical and surgical treatment to the sick and wounded. These corporations do not practice medicine but they receive patients and employ physicians and surgeons to give them treatment")....

Under the second approach, the courts of some jurisdictions determined that the corporate practice doctrine is inapplicable to nonprofit hospitals and health associations. These courts reasoned that the public policy arguments supporting the corporate practice doctrine do not apply to physicians employed by charitable institutions. See, e.g., Group Health Ass'n v. Moor, 24 F.Supp. 445, 446 (D.D.C.1938) (actions of nonprofit association which contracts with licensed physicians to provide medical treatment to its members in no way commercializes medicine and is not the practice of medicine), aff'd, 107 F.2d 239 (D.C.Cir.1939)....

In the third approach, the courts of several states have determined that the corporate practice doctrine is not applicable to hospitals which employ physicians because hospitals are authorized by other laws to provide medical treatment to patients....

We find the rationale of the latter two approaches persuasive. We decline to apply the corporate practice of medicine doctrine to licensed hospitals. The instant cause is distinguishable from Kerner, Allison, and Winberry. None of those cases specifically involved the employment of physicians by a hospital. More important, none of those cases involved a corporation licensed to provide health care services to the general public.

The corporate practice of medicine doctrine set forth in Kerner was not an interpretation of the plain language of the Medical Practice Act. The Medical Practice Act contains no express prohibition on the corporate employment of physicians.[81] Rather, the corporate practice of medicine doctrine was inferred from the general policies behind the Medical Practice Act. Such a

---

81. In contrast, the Dental Practice Act, applied by this court in [the dental clinic and Allison cases], expressly prohibited a corpora- tion from furnishing dentists and owning and operating a dental office.

prohibition is entirely appropriate to a general corporation possessing no licensed authority to offer medical services to the public, such as the appellant in Kerner. However, when a corporation has been sanctioned by the laws of this state to operate a hospital, such a prohibition is inapplicable.

The legislative enactments pertaining to hospitals provide ample support for this conclusion. For example, the Hospital Licensing Act defines "hospital" as:

"any institution, place, building, or agency, public or private, whether organized for profit or not, devoted primarily to the maintenance and operation of facilities for the diagnosis and treatment or care of * * * persons admitted for overnight stay or longer in order to obtain medical, including obstetric, psychiatric and nursing, care of illness, disease, injury, infirmity, or deformity." (Emphasis added.) 210 ILCS 85/3 (West Supp.1995).

In addition, the Hospital Lien Act provides "[e]very hospital rendering service in the treatment, care and maintenance, of such injured person" a lien upon a patient's personal injury cause of action. (Emphasis added.) Pub. Act 89–280, eff. January 1, 1996 (amending 770 ILCS 35/1 (West 1994)). Moreover, the Hospital Emergency Service Act (210 ILCS 80/0.01 et seq. (West 1994)) requires "[e]very hospital * * * which provides general medical and surgical hospital services "to also provide emergency services. (Emphasis added.) 210 ILCS 80/1 (West 1994)....

The foregoing statutes clearly authorize, and at times mandate, licensed hospital corporations to provide medical services. We believe that the authority to employ duly-licensed physicians for that purpose is reasonably implied from these legislative enactments. We further see no justification for distinguishing between nonprofit and for-profit hospitals in this regard. The authorities and duties of licensed hospitals are conferred equally upon both entities.

In addition, we find the public policy concerns which support the corporate practice doctrine inapplicable to a licensed hospital in the modern health care industry. The concern for lay control over professional judgment is alleviated in a licensed hospital, where generally a separate professional medical staff is responsible for the quality of medical services rendered in the facility.[82]

Furthermore, we believe that extensive changes in the health care industry since the time of the Kerner decision, including the emergence of corporate health maintenance organizations, have greatly altered the concern over the commercialization of health care. In addition, such concerns are relieved when a licensed hospital is the physician's employer. Hospitals have an independent duty to provide for the patient's health and welfare. [Citations to Darling and other cases omitted].

We find particularly appropriate the statement of the Kansas Supreme Court that "[i]t would be incongruous to conclude that the legislature

82. Moreover, in the instant case, the employment agreement expressly provided that the Health Center had no control or direction over Dr. Berlin's medical judgment and practice, other than that control exercised by the professional medical staff. Dr. Berlin has never contended that the Health Center's lay management attempted to control his practice of medicine.

intended a hospital to accomplish what it is licensed to do without utilizing physicians as independent contractors or employees. * * * To conclude that a hospital must do so without employing physicians is not only illogical but ignores reality." St. Francis Regional Med. Center v. Weiss, 254 Kan. 728, 745, 869 P.2d 606, 618 (1994). Accordingly, we conclude that a duly-licensed hospital possesses legislative authority to practice medicine by means of its staff of licensed physicians and is excepted from the operation of the corporate practice of medicine doctrine.

Consequently, the employment agreement between the Health Center and Dr. Berlin is not unenforceable merely because the Health Center is a corporate entity.

* * *

Justice HARRISON, dissenting:

In People ex rel. Kerner v. United Medical Service, Inc., this court held that a corporation cannot employ physicians and collect fees for their services because such conduct constitutes the practice of medicine and the practice of medicine by corporations is prohibited. The court based its conclusion on the Medical Practice Act, reasoning that under the statute, a license is required to practice medicine and

"[t]he legislative intent manifest from a view of the entire law is that only individuals may obtain a license thereunder. No corporation can meet the requirements of the statute essential to the issuance of a license." Kerner, 362 Ill. at 454, 200 N.E. 157.

More than 60 years have passed since Kerner was decided. If the legislature believed that our construction of the Act was erroneous or that the rule announced in Kerner should be changed, it could have amended the law to authorize the practice of medicine by entities other than individuals. With limited exceptions not applicable here, it has not done so. To the contrary, it has continued to adhere to the requirements that medicine can only be practiced by those who hold valid licenses from the state and that only individuals can obtain such licenses.... When it amends a statute but does not alter a previous interpretation by this court, we assume that the legislature intended for the amendment to have the same interpretation previously given ...

That the legislature has acquiesced in the judiciary's construction of the Medical Practice Act is especially clear given recent developments in the law. Under ...the Regulatory Agency Sunset Act, the Medical Practice Act was scheduled for repeal on December 31, 1997, unless the General Assembly enacted legislation providing for its continuation. On April 12, 1996, the appellate court filed its opinion in this case, holding under Kerner that the Medical Practice Act bars the corporate practice of medicine by hospitals. Subsequent to that decision, the General Assembly passed and the Governor signed new legislation extending the Medical Practice Act until January 1 of the year 2007. The new legislation made no substantive changes to the licensing requirements and included no provisions contrary to the appellate court's holding. Because the legislature is presumed to know the construction the statute has been given by the courts, its reenactment of the law can only be understood as an endorsement of the construction followed by the appellate court here. The corporate practice of medicine by hospitals is prohibited.

* * *

Hospitals do not fall within any of [the exceptions contained in the Medical Practice Act]. The majority argues that additional exceptions can be implied based on other statutes enacted by the General Assembly. It is a fundamental rule of statutory construction, however, that the enumeration of certain things in a statute implies the exclusion of all other things ...

Wholly aside from this problem, none of the other statutes invoked by my colleagues supports their position. The most that can be said of those statutes is that they authorize hospitals to operate facilities for the diagnosis and care of patients and to make emergency service available regardless of ability to pay. Hospitals may also employ physician's assistants, provided such assistants function under the supervision of a licensed physician. None of those endeavors, however, requires that hospitals have the power to employ physicians directly or to charge patients for the physicians' services. All may be accomplished by granting staff privileges to duly licensed private physicians, and the Hospital Licensing Act presumes that hospitals will staff their facilities in precisely that way....

In addition to creating special rules for HMOs, the General Assembly has also decided to allow physicians to employ various forms of business organizations in practicing their profession. Physicians may incorporate [as professional corporations or in other forms permitted under Illinois law and may operate limited liability companies]. ...Again, however, none of these provisions pertains to hospitals, and no inference can be drawn from any of them that the General Assembly intended to alter the prohibition against the corporate practice of medicine by hospitals.

For the foregoing reasons, I agree with the appellate court that the corporate practice doctrine prohibited defendant, Sarah Bush Lincoln Health Center, from entering into an employment agreement with Dr. Berlin. That agreement, including its restrictive covenant, was void and unenforceable....

Page 518, replace Notes 2 and 3 with the following:

2. Does the Court's analysis in Berlin provide any grounds for upsetting the corporate practice of medicine doctrine outside of the context of employment of physicians by hospitals? What arguments can be used to allow MSOs or other integrating entities to employ physicians? Are the majority's arguments based on legislative intent persuasive, or are they simply a way to rationalize overturning long-established precedent? Do changes in the nature of the practice of medicine justify courts amending the common law where the legislature has failed to act?

3. As noted above, commentators have been highly critical of the corporate practice of medicine doctrine. Can it be argued that the doctrine can help rectify the problems associated with risk sharing and managed care? Does it help restore the fiduciary ties between patient and physician that have been eroded by managed care? For an affirmative answer, see Andre Hampton, Resurrection of the Prohibition on the Corporate Practice of Medicine: Teaching Old Dogma New Tricks, 66 U. Cin. L. Rev. 489 (1998).

Page 525, add the following Note:

3. *Integration or Dis–Integration?* The assumption made by many policy-makers and health care analysts that market forces would propel providers inexorably toward more complete integration has proved inaccurate. The pace of integration has slowed with many IDSs proving unprofitable as they have failed to realize cost savings, improve quality, or increase volume or revenues as originally promised. Edric B. Engert & Douglas W. Emery, Integrated Delivery Systems: Non Fait Accompli, 7 Managed Care Q. 29 (1999). Among the many factors contributing to these financial difficulties is that IDSs have vastly overpaid for physician practices they have purchased. See Mary Chris Jaklevic, Dealing With Docs: Dropping Money–Losing Practices Can Be A Costly Decision, Modern Healthcare 42, March 1, 1999 at 42 (citing studies showing that hospital-sponsored primary care networks with 50–150 physicians lost an average of $83,290 per physician). More generally, analysts point out that IDSs have been unprepared to take on the insurance role and have not developed information and case management systems capable of dealing with the complexities of providing quality care, reducing unnecessary services and avoiding adverse selection. Engert & Emery at 34–36. At the same time, payors have not adopted capitation as a form of payment as readily as anticipated; discounted fee-for-service remains the dominant form of payment used by managed care systems. See C. J. Simon & David Emmons, Physician Earnings at Risk: an Examination of Capitated Contracts, 16 Health Affs. 120 (Spring,1997). Finally, greater demand for access and choice has led to less global capitation than anticipated and reliance on other payment methods that are less well-suited to IDS structures. Engert & Emery at 33. One notable casualty of the new market realities has been the physician practice management (PPM) industry. Industry analysts attribute PPMs' failure to reliance on acquisitions to boost revenues rather than investing in information systems, equipment and services to foster long-term performance and greater efficiency. Many of these publicly traded companies have seen their stock values plummet and at least one prominent company, FPA Medical Management, has filed for bankruptcy. Rhonda L. Rundle & Anita Sharpe, Physician–Management Firms Have Landed in Sick Bay, Wall St. J. July 31, 1998, at B4; Anita Sharpe, MedPartners Is Abandoning Physician–Management Business, Wall St. J., November 11, 1998, at A4.

A number of lawsuits have been filed charging PPMs a wide variety of state and federal laws including fee splitting, racketeering and securities statutes. See Alan S. Gassman & Scott P. Swope, Exposure of Officers and Directors of Practice Management Companies, 1 Health Care Fraud & Abuse Newsletter 27 (Dec. 1998).

What are the legal issues posed by unwinding an unsuccessful integrated system? A critical question for a corporation is whether to declare bankruptcy under Chapter 7 or Chapter 11 of the Bankruptcy Code or to attempt to negotiate the disposition and sale of assets and allocation of liabilities. Where multiple (and often antagonistic) parties own the IDS, there is a risk that at least one may attempt to block the unwinding or hold out so as to lessen the enterprise value of the IDS and impair returns to creditors. See Robert A. Klyman, Bankruptcy Opportunities and Pitfalls: Strategies for Restructuring and Unwinding Integrated Delivery Systems, 31 J. Health L. 163 (1998). In addition, IDS owners run the legal risks of fraudulent transfers, contract breaches and contingent liabilities. In these circumstances, the Bankruptcy Code may provide an effective tool for the unwinding the entity in a manner that will preserve the going concern value of the IDS's assets and avoid various legal entanglements. For a thoughtful review of the legal and strategic issues presented by a Chapter 11 filing in the health care context, see Klyman, supra.

Insert on page 547, at the end of Note 3, the following:

In the past, state Medicaid payment systems have reimbursed providers under a modified fee-for-service arrangement. However, more states are now contracting with HMOs to arrange services to the Medicaid population. Most of these HMOs do not provide the care directly, but rather arrange for care to be delivered by another provider. See generally Lawrence M. Brauer & Marvin Friedlander, IRS Exempt Organizations CPE Text for FY 1999: Chapter D, Exemption of Medicaid HMOs and Medicaid Service Organizations Under IRC 501(c)(3), 98 Tax Notes Today 156–18 (Aug. 13, 1998). How should the IRS view these HMOs for tax treatment? How are charitable purposes accomplished under this system? What argument for exemption can be made using Geisinger and Sound Health? What arguments can be made against exemption? Is this arrangement similar to providing insurance under § 501(m)(1) described below?

Replace on page 547, Note 4 with the following:

4. In an unreleased technical advice memorandum, the IRS revoked the § 501(c)(3) status of a health maintenance organization, finding that it essentially provided insurance under § 501(m)(1). See generally IRS Revokes HMO's Exempt Status for Essentially Providing Insurance, 98 Tax Notes Today 243–13 (Dec. 18, 1998). Under § 501(m)(1) an organization described in § 501(c)(3) or § 501(c)(4) shall be exempt "only if no substantial part of its activities consists of providing commercial-type insurance." The legislative history indicates that this provision was intended, in part, to bar continued § 501(c)(4) exemption for Blue Cross/Blue Shield organizations, which had enjoyed such status for many years despite being in many respects indistinguishable from commercial health insurers. See H.R. Rep. No. 99–426, 99th Cong. 1st Sess. 662—6 (1986); 1986–3 C.B. (Vol. 2) 662—6. Consequently, where an organization's activities resemble those of commercial insurers, generally, § 501(m) would serve to deny exemption under § 501(c)(4).

Using the "risk of economic loss" analysis used in the Memorandum below, how might the IRS rule if (a) the HMO pays its contracted physicians "capitated fees," paying the physicians the same fees regardless of the amount of health care services the HMO's enrollees require?; (b) the HMO pays its contracted physicians almost exclusively under a fee schedule that represents a meaningful discount from the physicians' usual and customary charges ("discounted fee-for-service") and also withholds from these payments a significant percent of the fees otherwise payable, pending compliance with periodic budget or utilization standards?; (c) the HMO pays its contracted physicians on a discounted fee-for-service basis and does not withhold from these payments a significant portion of the fees otherwise payable pending compliance with periodic budget or utilization standards, but the physicians are eligible to receive a bonus based on the achievement of a budget surplus?

INTERNAL REVENUE SERVICE NATIONAL OFFICE
TECHNICAL ADVICE MEMORANDUM

Dec. 14, 1998.

* * *

FACTS

[L, a § 501(c)(3) corporation, is a member of a nonprofit, multicorporate health care system ("M") and has been licensed as a qualified health maintenance organization ("HMO"). Under this HMO offered by L, enrollees are permitted to utilize physicians other than network physicians by paying a higher premium. L provides primary care and specialty care physician services through contracts with various physicians ("Participating Physician Services Agreement"). Under the Participating Physician Services Agreement, L compensates physicians on a fee-for-service basis by paying the greater of a capitated fee or 85 percent of the physician's usual and customary billed charges. The Agreement does not provide for L to withhold any portion of these fees. In some cases, in the event of budget surpluses, the physicians may be eligible to receive additional payments ("Participating Physician Settlement Payments"). However, in the event of budget deficit, the physicians have no financial obligations.]

SECTION 501(c)(3)

[The IRS finds that L does not satisfy the requirements for exemption under section 501(c)(3) of the Code because it (1) does not satisfy the "community benefit standard" and (2) does not satisfy the integral part doctrine.]

SECTION 501(m)

When individuals enroll in an HMO and pay the HMO fixed premiums, the HMO agrees that it will arrange for the provision of health care services to treat the enrollees' injuries and illnesses. Under this arrangement, enrollees protect themselves against the risk that they would suffer economic loss from having to pay for health care services that are necessary because of injuries or illnesses. By enrolling in an HMO, individuals shift the risk of this economic loss to the HMO. When the HMO enrolls a large number of such individuals, the HMO distributes this risk of loss among all of its enrollees. For HMOs that operate on a staff model basis, this risk is predominantly a normal business risk of an organization engaged in furnishing medical services on a fixed-price basis, rather than an insurance risk. . . . On the other hand, for HMOs that operate on other than a staff model basis, this arrangement constitutes a contract of insurance.

However, if a non-staff model HMO shifts a substantial portion of its risk of economic loss to its health care providers, it would no longer bear a substantial portion of the risk of economic loss that would result from having to provide health care services to its enrollees.

* * *

L is not a staff model HMO. Instead, L contracts with hospitals ... and with primary care and specialty physicians ... to provide medical services for its enrollees.... [T]he arrangement with L's enrollees to provide health care services in return for a fixed fee constitutes a contract of insurance[.]

* * *

As a result of this fee-for-service compensation arrangement with its participating physicians, L has shifted to these physicians only an incidental portion of its total economic risk of loss associated with its obligation to provide health care services to its enrollees.

* * *

Since the compensation L pays to its physician providers represents 52.4 percent of its total medical expenses, these services are substantial. Thus, by retaining a substantial portion of the risk of loss, L remains substantially engaged in providing health insurance to its enrollees.

Since this health insurance is the same type of health insurance as that which is offered by commercial insurance companies, it is "commercial-type" insurance under § 501(m)(1) of the Code.

* * *

[Therefore, L does not qualify for exemption either under § 501(c)(3) or § 501(c)(4).]

Insert at page 555, a new note following Note 6:

7.   Intermountain Health Care (yes, the same Intermountain Health Care) also operates Intermountain Health Care Health Plans, a tax-exempt managed care organization. Recently, Intermountain's competitors complained to the IRS that IHC Health Plans' exempt status gives them an unfair market advantage. In a preliminary ruling, the IRS stated that "ownership by a nonprofit health care provider does not justify exempt status for a managed care company." See Exempt Status of Utah's Largest HMO Threatened, 98 Tax Notes Today 247–H (Dec. 24, 1998). Should competitive market concerns be included in an IRS determination of exemption? Why not just exempt all entities run by tax-exempt organizations if a "charitable purpose" is furthered?

Replace on page 555, the Private Letter Ruling 9024085 with the following:

As tax exempt hospital systems seek to contain costs and compete for managed care contracts, whole hospital joint ventures between exempt hospitals and for-profit hospital corporations are growing steadily. However, given this increase in joint ventures, tax-exempt hospitals still lacked substantial guidance from the IRS. Finally, in March of 1998, the IRS released Revenue Ruling 98–15.

REVENUE RULING 98–15

1998–12 I.R.B. 6.

[In this Revenue Ruling, the IRS provides the following examples to illustrate whether an organization that operates an acute care hospital constitutes an organization whose principal purpose is providing charitable hospital care when it forms a limited liability company (LLC) with a for-profit corporation and then contributes its hospital and all of its related operating assets to the LLC, which then operates the hospital.]

Situation 1

A is a nonprofit corporation that owns and operates an acute care hospital. A has been recognized as exempt from federal income tax under § 501(a) as an organization described in § 501(c)(3) and as other than a private foundation as defined in § 509(a) because it is described in § 170(b)(1)(A)(iii). B is a for-profit corporation that owns and operates a number of hospitals.

A concludes that it could better serve its community if it obtained additional funding. B is interested in providing financing for A's hospital, provided it earns a reasonable rate of return. A and B form a limited liability company, C. A contributes all of its operating assets, including its hospital to C. B also contributes assets to C. In return, A and B receive ownership interests in C proportional and equal in value to their respective contributions.

C's Articles of Organization and Operating Agreement ("governing documents") provide that C is to be managed by a governing board consisting of three individuals chosen by A and two individuals chosen by B. A intends to appoint community leaders who have experience with hospital matters, but who are not on the hospital staff and do not otherwise engage in business transactions with the hospital.

The governing documents further provide that they may only be amended with the approval of both owners and that a majority of three board members must approve certain major decisions relating to C's operation including decisions relating to any of the following topics:

A. C's annual capital and operating budgets;

B. Distributions of C's earnings;

C. Selection of key executives;

D. Acquisition or disposition of health care facilities;

E. Contracts in excess of $x per year;

F. Changes to the types of services offered by the hospital; and

G. Renewal or termination of management agreements.

The governing documents require that C operate any hospital it owns in a manner that furthers charitable purposes by promoting health for a broad cross section of its community. The governing documents explicitly provide that the duty of the members of the governing board to operate C in a manner that furthers charitable purposes by promoting health for a broad cross section of the community overrides any duty they may have to operate C for the financial benefit of its owners. Accordingly, in the event of a conflict between operation in accordance with the community benefit standard and any duty to maximize profits, the members of the governing board are to satisfy the community benefit standard without regard to the consequences for maximizing profitability.

The governing documents further provide that all returns of capital and distributions of earnings made to owners of C shall be proportional to their ownership interests in C. The terms of the governing documents are legal, binding, and enforceable under applicable state law.

C enters into a management agreement with a management company that is unrelated to A or B to provide day-to-day management services to C. The management agreement is for a five-year period, and the agreement is renewable for additional five-year periods by mutual consent. The management company will be paid a management fee for its services based on C's gross revenues. The terms and conditions of the management agreement, including the fee structure and the contract term, are reasonable and comparable to what other management firms receive for similar services at similarly situated hospitals. C may terminate the agreement for cause.

None of the officers, directors, or key employees of A who were involved in making the decision to form C were promised employment or any other inducement by C or B and their related entities if the transaction were approved. None of A's officers, directors, or key employees have any interest, including any interest through attribution determined in accordance with the principles of § 318, in B or any of its related entities.

Pursuant to § 301.7701–3(b) of the Procedure and Administrative Regulations, C will be treated as a partnership for federal income tax purposes.

A intends to use any distributions it receives from C to fund grants to support activities that promote the health of A's community and to help the indigent obtain health care. Substantially all of A's grantmaking will be funded by distributions from C. A's projected grantmaking program and its participation as an owner of C will constitute A's only activities.

Situation 2

D is a nonprofit corporation that owns and operates an acute care hospital. D has been recognized as exempt from federal income tax under § 501(a) as an organization described in § 501(c)(3) and as other than a private foundation as defined in § 509(a) because it is described in § 170(b)(1)(iii). E is a for-profit hospital corporation that owns and operates a number of hospitals and provides management services to several hospitals that it does not own.

D concludes that it could better serve its community if it obtained additional funding. E is interested in providing financing for D's hospital, provided it earns a reasonable rate of return. D and E form a limited liability company, F. D contributes all of its operating assets, including its hospital to F. E also contributes assets to F. In return, D and E receive ownership interests proportional and equal in value to their respective contributions.

F's Articles of Organization and Operating Agreement ("governing documents") provide that F is to be managed by a governing board consisting of three individuals chosen by D and three individuals chosen by E. D intends to appoint community leaders who have experience with hospital matters, but who are not on the hospital staff and do not otherwise engage in business transactions with the hospital.

The governing documents further provide that they may only be amended with the approval of both owners and that a majority of board members must approve certain major decisions relating to F's operation, including decisions relating to any of the following topics:

A.   F's annual capital and operating budgets;

B.   Distributions of F's earnings over a required minimum level of distributions set forth in the Operating Agreement;

C.   Unusually large contracts; and

D.   Selection of key executives.

F's governing documents provide that F's purpose is to construct, develop, own, manage, operate, and take other action in connection with operating the health care facilities it owns and engage in other health care-related activities. The governing documents further provide that all returns of capital and distributions of earnings made to owners of F shall be proportional to their ownership interests in F.

F enters into a management agreement with a wholly-owned subsidiary of E to provide day-to-day management services to F. The management agreement is for a five-year period, and the agreement is renewable for additional five-year periods at the discretion of E's subsidiary. F may terminate the agreement only for cause. E's subsidiary will be paid a management fee for its services based on gross revenues. The terms and conditions of the management agreement, including the fee structure and the contract term other than the renewal terms, are reasonable and comparable to what other management firms receive for similar services at similarly situated hospitals.

As part of the agreement to form F, D agrees to approve the selection of two individuals to serve as F's chief executive officer and chief financial officer. These individuals have previously worked for E in hospital management and have business expertise. They will work with the management company to oversee F's day-to-day management. Their compensation is comparable to what comparable executives are paid at similarly situated hospitals.

Pursuant to § 301.7701–3(b). F will be treated as a partnership for federal tax income purposes.

D intends to use any distributions it receives from F to fund grants to support activities that promote the health of D's community and to help the indigent obtain health care. Substantially all of D's grantmaking will be funded by distributions from F. D's projected grantmaking program and its participation as an owner of F will constitute D's only activities.

ANALYSIS

For federal income tax purposes, the activities of a partnership are often considered to be the activities of the partners. Aggregate treatment is also consistent with the treatment of partnerships for purpose of the unrelated business income tax under § 512(c). In light of the aggregate principle discussed in Butler and reflected in § 512(c), the aggregate approach also applies for purposes of the operational test set forth in § 1.501(c)(3)–1(c). Thus, the activities of an LLC treated as a partnership for federal income tax purposes are considered to be the activities of a nonprofit organization that is an owner of the LLC when evaluating whether the nonprofit organization is operated exclusively for exempt purposes within the meaning of § 501(c)(3).

A § 501(c)(3) organization may form and participate in a partnership, including an LLC treated as a partnership for federal income tax purposes, and meet the operational test if participation in the partnership furthers a charitable purpose, and the partnership arrangement permits the exempt organization to act exclusively in furtherance of its exempt purpose and only incidentally for the benefit of the for-profit partners. Similarly, a § 501(c)(3) organization may enter into a management contract with a private party giving that party authority to conduct activities on behalf of the organization and direct the use of the organization's assets provided that the organization retains ultimate authority over the assets and activities being managed and the terms and conditions of the contract are reasonable, including reasonable compensation and a reasonable term. However, if a private party is allowed to control or use the non-profit organization's activities or assets for the benefit of the private party, and the benefit is not incidental to the accomplishment of exempt purposes, the organization will fail to be organized and operated exclusively for exempt purposes.

Situation 1

After A and B form C, and A contributes all of its operating assets to C, A's activities will consist of the health care services it provides through C and any grantmaking activities it can conduct using income distributed to C. A will receive an interest in C equal in value to the assets it contributes to C, and A's and B's returns from C will be proportional to their respective investments in C. The governing documents of C commit C to providing health care services for the benefit of the community as a whole and to give charitable purposes priority over maximizing profits for C's owners. Furthermore, through A's appointment of members of the community familiar with the hospital to C's board, the board's structure, which gives A's appointees voting control, and the specifically enumerated powers of the board over changes in activities, disposition of assets, and renewal of the management agreement. A can ensure that the assets it owns through C and the activities it conducts through C are used primarily to further exempt purposes. Thus, A can ensure that the benefit to B and other private parties, like the management company, will be incidental to the accomplishment of charitable purposes. Additionally, the terms and conditions of the management contract, including the terms for renewal and termination are reasonable. Finally, A's grants are intended to support education and research and give resources to help provide health care to the indigent. All of these facts and circumstances establish that, when A participates in forming C and contributes all of its operating assets to C, and C operates in accordance with its governing documents, A will be furthering charitable purposes and continue to be operated exclusively for exempt purposes.

Because A's grantmaking activity will be contingent upon receiving distributions from C, A's principal activity will continue to be the provision of hospital care. As long as A's principal activity remains the provision of hospital care. A will not be classified as a private foundation in accordance with § 509(a)(1) as an organization described in § 170(b)(1)(A)(iii).

Situation 2

When D and E form F, and D contributes its assets to F, D will be engaged in activities that consist of the health care services it provides through F and any grantmaking activities it can conduct using income distributed by F. However, unlike A, D will not be engaging primarily in activities that further an exempt purpose. "While the diagnosis and cure of disease are indeed purposes that may furnish the foundation for characterizing the activity as 'charitable,' something more is required." See Sound Health and Geisinger. In the absence of a binding obligation in F's governing documents for F to serve charitable purposes or otherwise provide its services to the community as a whole, F will be able to deny care to segments of the community, such as the indigent. Because D will share control of F with E, D will not be able to initiate programs within F to serve new health needs within the community without the agreement of at least one governing board member appointed by E. As a business enterprise, E will not necessarily give priority to the health needs of the community over the consequences for F's profits. The primary source of information for board members appointed by D will be the chief executives, who have a prior relationship with E and the management company, which is a subsidiary of E. The management company itself will have broad discretion over F's activities and assets that may not always be under the board's supervision. For example, the management company is permitted to enter into all but "unusually large" contracts without board approval. The management company may also unilaterally renew the management agreement. Based on all these facts and circumstances, D cannot establish that the activities it conducts through F further exempt purposes. "[I]n order for an organization to qualify for exemption under § 501(c)(3) the organization must 'establish' that it is neither organized nor operated for the 'benefit of private interests." Consequently, the benefit to E resulting from the activities D conducts through F will not be incidental to the furtherance of an exempt purpose. Thus, D will fail the operational test when it forms F, contributes its operating assets to F, and then serves as an owner to F.

HOLDING

A will continue to qualify as an organization described in § 501(c)(3) when it forms C and contributes all of its operating assets to C because A has established that A will be operating exclusively for a charitable purpose and only incidentally for the purpose of benefiting the private interests of B. Furthermore, A's principal activity will continue to be the provision of hospital care when C begins operations. Thus, A will be an organization described in § 170(b)(1)(A)(iii) and thus, will not be classified as a private foundation in accordance with § 509(a)(1), as long as hospital care remains its principal activity.

D will violate the requirements to be an organization described in § 501(c)(3) when it forms F and contributes all of its operating assets to F because D has failed to establish that it will be operated exclusively for exempt purposes.

Notes

1.   Why are management control issues important to the IRS analysis of whole hospital joint ventures? See Gregory A. Petroff, Whole Hospital Joint Ventures: The IRS Position On Control, 98 Tax Notes Today 138–89 (July 20, 1998). Some recommended changes for the hospital in Situation 2 to retain its § 501(c)(3) status include shortening the management term to five years, requiring a 24–hour emergency room at one or more of the LLC hospitals, and adopting a list of reserved powers similar to those in Situation 1. See Gerald M. Griffith, Revenue Ruling 98–15: Dimming the Future of All Nonprofit Joint Ventures?, 31 J. Health & Hosp. L., 71, 88 (June 1998). How do these relate to the criteria for tax exemption discussed earlier? What other changes would you recommend? Why?

2.   Although eagerly awaited, the guidance offered by Revenue Ruling 98–15 has met with criticism for what it does not address. See Robert C. Louthian, III, IRS Provides Whole Hospital Joint Venture Guidance in Revenue Ruling 98–15, 7 BNA Health L. Rep. 477 (March 19, 1998). Many feel that the ruling's "polar opposite" situations do not help to clarify the many gray areas experienced in joint ventures. What situations would still be left unanswered by the ruling? Perhaps in response to such criticism, the IRS recently released a professional education text containing articles highlighting various tax issues. See Exempt Organizations: Hospitals To Receive Scrutiny This Year in IRS Text Spotlighting Areas of Interest, 7 BNA Health L. Rep. 1307 (Aug. 13, 1998). Included in the IRS text is an article on Revenue Ruling 98–15, described as "required reading" and being an "important piece to complement the analysis of [98–15]." Id. The article lists questions that IRS agents should review when determining if a hospital joint venture furthers the exempt purpose of the not-for-profit entity while scrutinizing any nonincidental private benefit to the for-profit managers, and concludes that a hospital joint venture will pass scrutiny if the "charitable purposes supersede profit maximization purposes." If you were the IRS employee drafting questions for the list, what questions would you include? Why?

3.   The IRS has recently approved a "gainsharing" arrangement between a tax-exempt hospital and group of cardiologists on the hospital's staff. Under the gainsharing program agreement, the cardiologists design and implement cost-effective "process improvement initiatives" (such as care pathways) and any cost savings garnered under the improvement plans fund a "process improvement award pool." The cardiologists' performance with respect to the process improvement initiatives are evaluated annually under predetermined evaluation criteria. If the cardiologists satisfy the criteria, they are eligible to receive an award from the pool. Although passing IRS scrutiny, the arrangement still awaits the OIG's approval under the fraud and abuse laws (see Ch. 9 Sec. II). See James Wiehl, et al., Client Alert Explains Gainsharing Letter Rulings, 99 Tax Notes Today 42–82 (Mar. 4, 1999); IRS Approves Gainsharing Programs in Two Unreleased Private Letter Rulings, BNA Health L. Rep., 8 BHLR 295 (Feb. 25, 1999). How does this relate to GCM 39862?

Insert at page 563, after GCM 39862 and before Hermann Hospital, the following:

The following excerpt is from a 1996 IRS Revised Denial Letter denying tax-exempt status to Redlands Surgical Services (RSS), an entity formed for the sole purpose of participating in a joint venture. See Revised Denial Letter Issued to Redlands Surgical Services (Apr. 1, 1996), reprinted in Garland Carter, Full Text: Redlands Surgical Services Revised Denial Letter, Tax Notes Today 213–27 (Nov. 4, 1997). The decision is currently on appeal. Although this letter was drafted a year earlier than Rev. Rul. 98–15, supra, how are the two similar?

An explanation of the complicated nature of the proposed arrangement referenced in the IRS letter provides:

> RSS is a member corporation, with RHS Corp. as its sole member. RSS is also a partner . . . in the Redlands Ambulatory Surgery Center (RASC) Partnership and Inland Surgery Center Limited Partnership (ISC LP). RHS is a nonprofit public benefit corporation, . . . and is the parent corporation of tax-exempt Redlands Community Hospital. . . . Surgical Care Affiliates Inc. (SCAI) is a for-profit, publicly held corporation that owns and manages 40 ambulatory surgery centers in the United States. Redlands–SCA Surgery Centers Inc., . . . the for-profit partner in RASC partnership, is a wholly owned for-profit subsidiary of SCAI. SCA Management, another for-profit subsidiary of SCAI, entered into a management agreement with ISC LP to manage Inland Surgery Center, which operates an ambulatory surgical center. RASC Partnership entered into ISC LP as the general partner, along with 32 limited partners (physicians on the hospital's medical staff). See Joan Ronder Domike et al., IRS Disputes Authority Relied On By Redlands Surgical Services, 98 Tax Notes Today 153–76 (Aug. 10, 1998) (summarizing a IRS reply brief).

IRS REVISED DENIAL LETTER

April 1, 1996.

* * *

You were formed as a component part of the Redlands Hospital System, which includes the System's parent organization, RHS Corp.; Redlands Community Hospital; and the Redlands Community Hospital Foundation (a fund-raising entity). All the organizations mentioned in the previous sentence have been recognized as exempt under section 501(c)(3) of the Code and are public charities within the meaning of section 509(a)(1), (2), or (3). (The System's other entity, Redlands Health Services, is a for-profit subsidiary wholly owned by RHS Corp.)

You were created for the purpose of owning a partnership interest in the Redlands Ambulatory Surgery Center Partnership (hereinafter referred to as "Center"). Center is a general partnership between yourself and Redlands–SCA Surgery Centers, Inc., a wholly-owned for-profit subsidiary of Surgical Care Affiliates, Inc., a for-profit corporation. The information submitted states that you hold a 46 percent interest in this general partnership. This partnership, in turn, currently owns a 59 percent interest in and is the general partner of Inlands Surgery Center Limited Partnership (hereinafter referred to as "ISC"). Physicians on staff in the Redlands Hospital System have invested in ISC through the purchase of limited partnership interests. The information submitted states that these limited partners currently have a 41 percent interest in ISC.

* * *

The sole activity of ISC ... involves the operation of an ambulatory surgical center (hereinafter referred to as "Inlands") which serves the Redlands community. Located within two blocks of Redlands Community Hospital, it provides ambulatory surgical services to persons within the Redlands Hospital System service area.

* * *

Your representatives state that your investment in Inlands, through Center, came about because, in the late 1980s, Redlands Health System found that it needed to have access to an offsite ambulatory surgical care facility because potential patients desired to obtain minor surgery without having to become part of an acute-care hospital environment. Rather than constructing its own ambulatory surgery center, RHS Corp., the parent entity, decided to affiliate with Inlands, an established and successful ambulatory surgery center located near the hospital. This decision was based on financial resource limitations, inexperience in operating such a center and the fact that the Redlands community could not sustain two surgery centers, particularly two centers within two blocks of each other.

* * *

You are also instrumental in establishing and maintaining a close working relationship between Redlands Community Hospital and Inlands. This business arrangement has been profitable for all the parties involved and you pay your share of the profits to your related organizations.

* * *

Participation in the partnerships is your sole activity and appears to be undertaken for primarily financial gain. The minutes of your board of directors' meetings (and those of RHS Corp.) indicate that you were concerned almost exclusively about your share of the net income and profits of the Center and that you were pleased with the return on your investment which was characterized as "significant".

* * *

The submitted information establishes that you are a separately incorporated entity whose sole purpose is to enter into a general partnership with a for-profit corporation. This general partnership has, in turn, purchased an interest in an existing limited partnership. The limited partnership operates a for-profit ambulatory surgery center, Inlands.

[Y]ou are in a minority ownership position. You own 46 percent of the general partnership. The general partnership in turn owns 59 percent of Inlands. In short, you have less than a 30 percent ownership interest in Inlands. You have no meaningful control over the general partnership as the partnership agreement provides that partnership will be governed equally by the two partners through an equal number of managing directors.... Moreover, as discussed below, you have no real control over Inlands due to the authority exercised by SCA Management, a wholly-owned subsidiary of Surgical Care Affiliates, Inc. Your general partner in Center is another wholly-owned subsidiary of Surgical Care Affiliates, Inc. You have the liability of a general partner, but cannot exercise control; instead, for-profit interests do.

Inlands' day-to-day activities are directed by a for-profit management company, SCA Management. The contract with SCA Management is for a set 15 year period and renewable for two additional five year terms and can only be terminated by ISC in the event of a breach of the agreement by SCA Management. Therefore, day-to-day activities and many major decisions, including fee structure, are also controlled by for-profit interests, not by you. Instead, your sole activity regarding the activities of Inlands, other than to have provided capital to help purchase Inlands, is to provide quality assurance services to Inlands. This quality assurance is done in part through a medical advisory board. Center appoints one-half of the members of this board and the other half is appointed by the limited partners. All members of the medical advisory board must be physicians who are limited partner/investors in ISC. You have indicated that Inlands' operations are comparable to other ambulatory surgery centers as to operating with a profit and as to payor mix. In addition, it appears that the patients of the ambulatory surgery center can be patients of that facility, the referring private physicians or any other health care provider in the area.

* * *

Inlands remains a noncharitable, for-profit ambulatory surgical center, operated for the financial benefit of its investors. The primary beneficiaries from this activity are Inlands' investors and SCA Management. Accordingly, you are operating for the private benefit of others and this is a substantial non-exempt activity. Therefore, you do not qualify for recognition of exemption under section 501(c)(3) of the Code.

* * *

[The letter further analyzes that Inlands performs no charity care and does not satisfy the integral part test.]

* * *

Basically, all you have done is to invest in a for-profit entity, Inlands, and transfer the profits you earn from this investment to your parent, RHS Corp.; this is not sufficient to enable you to qualify for recognition of exemption under section 501(c)(3) of the Code.

Replace page 570, Note 3 with the following Note:

On April 21, 1997, the IRS released final Physician Recruitment Guidelines in Revenue Ruling 97–21. Although Rev. Rul. 97–21 closely follows the text of the Announcement 95–25 (1995–14 I.R.B. 11), it contains some changes and some additions. Compare the new Rev. Rul. 97–21 with Announcement 95–25. What changes do you find? What might be the rationale for the changes? Is this Revenue

Ruling consistent with the Hermann Hospital Closing Agreement? What recruitment incentives prohibited in Hermann Hospital are now acceptable under Rev. Rul. 97–21? See Gerald M. Griffith, IRS Guidance on Physician Recruitment: From the Seeds of Herman Hospital to the Proposed and Final Rulings and Beyond, 30 J. Health & Hosp. L., 75 (1997); Carolyn D. Wright, EO Experts Give Physician Recruitment Ruling High Marks, 97 Tax Notes Today 78–3 (Apr. 23, 1998).

REVENUE RULING 97–21

1997–18 I.R.B. 8.

* * *

Situation 1

Hospital A is located in County V, a rural area, and is the only hospital within a 100 mile radius. County V has been designated by the U.S. Public Health Service as a Health Professional Shortage Area for primary medical care professionals (a category that includes obstetricians and gynecologists). Physician M recently completed an ob/gyn residency and is not on Hospital A's medical staff. Hospital A recruits Physician M to establish and maintain a full-time private ob/gyn practice in its service area and become a member of its medical staff. Hospital A provides Physician M a recruitment incentive package pursuant to a written agreement negotiated at arm's-length. The agreement is in accordance with guidelines for physician recruitment that Hospital A's Board of Directors establishes, monitors, and reviews regularly to ensure that recruiting practices are consistent with Hospital A's exempt purposes. The agreement was approved by the committee appointed by Hospital A's Board of Directors to approve contracts with hospital medical staff. Hospital A does not provide any recruiting incentives to Physician M other than those set forth in the written agreement.

In accordance with the agreement, Hospital A pays Physician M a signing bonus, Physician M's professional liability insurance premium for a limited period, provides office space in a building owned by Hospital A for a limited number of years at a below market rent (after which the rental will be at fair market value), and guarantees Physician M's mortgage on a residence in County V. Hospital A also lends Physician M practice start-up financial assistance pursuant to an agreement that is properly documented and bears reasonable terms.

Situation 2

Hospital B is located in an economically depressed inner-city area of City W. Hospital B has conducted a community needs assessment that indicates both a shortage of pediatricians in Hospital B's service area and difficulties Medicaid patients are having obtaining pediatric services. Physician N is a pediatrician currently practicing outside of Hospital B's service area and is not on Hospital B's medical staff. Hospital B recruits Physician N to relocate to City W, establish and maintain a full-time pediatric practice in Hospital B's service area, become a member of Hospital B's medical staff, and treat a reasonable number of Medicaid patients. Hospital B offers Physician N a recruitment incentive package pursuant to a written agreement negotiated at arm's-length and approved by Hospital B's Board of Directors. Hospital B does not provide any recruiting incentives to Physician N other than those set forth in the written agreement.

Under the agreement, Hospital B reimburses Physician N for moving expenses as defined in § 217(b), reimburses Physician N for professional liability "tail" coverage for Physician N's former practice, and guarantees Physician N's private practice income for a limited number of years. The private practice income guarantee, which is properly documented, provides that Hospital B will make up the difference to the extent Physician N practices full-time in its service area and the private practice does not generate a certain level of net income (after reasonable expenses of the practice). The amount guaranteed falls within the range reflected in regional or national surveys regarding income earned by physicians in the same specialty.

Situation 3

Hospital C is located in an economically depressed inner city area of City X. Hospital C has conducted a community needs assessment that indicates indigent patients are having difficulty getting access to care because of a shortage of obstetricians in Hospital C's service area willing to treat Medicaid and charity care patients. Hospital C recruits Physician O, an obstetrician who is currently a member of Hospital C's medical staff, to provide these services and enters into a written agreement with Physician O. The agreement is in accordance with guidelines for physician recruitment that Hospital C's Board of Directors establishes, monitors, and reviews regularly to ensure that recruiting practices are consistent with Hospital C's exempt purpose. The agreement was approved by the officer designated by Hospital C's Board of Directors to enter into contracts with hospital medical staff. Hospital C does not provide any recruiting incentives to Physician O other than those set forth in the written agreement. Pursuant to the agreement, Hospital C agrees to reimburse Physician O for the cost of one year's professional liability insurance in return for an agreement by Physician O to treat a reasonable number of Medicaid and charity care patients for that year.

Situation 4

Hospital D is located in City Y, a medium to large size metropolitan area. Hospital D requires a minimum of four diagnostic radiologists to ensure adequate coverage and a high quality of care for its radiology department. Two of the four diagnostic radiologists currently providing coverage for Hospital D are relocating to other areas. Hospital D initiates a search for diagnostic radiologists and determines that one of the two most qualified candidates is Physician P.

Physician P currently is practicing in City Y as a member of the medical staff of Hospital E (which is also located in City Y). As a diagnostic radiologist, Physician P provides services for patients receiving care at Hospital E, but does not refer patients to Hospital E or any other hospital in City Y. Physician P is not on Hospital D's medical staff. Hospital D recruits Physician P to join its medical staff and to provide coverage for its radiology department. Hospital D offers Physician P a recruitment incentive package pursuant to a written agreement, negotiated at arm's-length and approved by Hospital D's

Board of Directors. Hospital D does not provide any recruiting incentives to Physician P other than those set forth in the written agreement.

Pursuant to the agreement, Hospital D guarantees Physician P's private practice income for the first few years that Physician P is a member of its medical staff and provides coverage for its radiology department. The private practice income guarantee, which is properly documented, provides that Hospital D will make up the difference to Physician P to the extent the private practice does not generate a certain level of net income (after reasonable expenses of the practice). The net income amount guaranteed falls within the range reflected in regional or national surveys regarding income earned by physicians in the same specialty.

Insert at page 570–71, at the end of Note 5, the following:

In July of 1998, the IRS released proposed regulations to 26 U.S.C. § 4958. See 63 Fed. Reg. 41,486 (1998). These proposed regulations clarify the scope of the statute through definitions, explanations, and examples.

Below are two examples in the proposed regulations that provide guidance on who would and who would not be considered a "disqualified person" under the statute. Do you note any differences between the examples and the statute? Do the examples add to the statutory definition of "disqualified person"? If so, how? How do the examples compare to the earlier IRS identification of "insiders" for private inurement purposes evident in the materials you have studied in this chapter?

[1.] A, an applicable tax-exempt organization for purposes of section 4958, owns and operates one acute care hospital. B is a for-profit corporation that owns and operates a number of hospitals. A and B form C, a limited liability company. In exchange for proportional ownership interests, A contributes its hospital, and B contributes other financial assets, to C. All of A's assets then consist of its membership interest in C. A continues to be operated for exempt purposes based almost exclusively on the activities it conducts through C. C enters into a management agreement with a management company, M, to provide day-to-day management services to C. M is generally subject to supervision by C's board, but M is given broad discretion to manage C's day-to-day operation. Under these facts and circumstances, M is in a position to exercise substantial influence over the affairs of A because it has day to day control over the hospital operated by C, A's ownership interest in C is its primary asset, and C's activities form the basis for A's continued exemption as an organization described in section 501(c)(3). Therefore, M is a disqualified person with respect to any transaction involving A, including any transaction that A conducts through C, that provides economic benefits to M directly or indirectly.

[2.] X is a radiologist employed by U, a large acute-care hospital that is an applicable tax-exempt organization for purposes of section 4958. X has no managerial authority over any part of U or its operations. X gives instructions to staff with respect to the radiology work X conducts, but X does not serve as supervisor to other U employees. X's total compensation package includes nontaxable retirement and welfare benefits and a specified amount of salary. X's compensation is greater than the amount of compensation referenced for a highly compensated employee . . . in the year benefits are provided. X is not related to any other disqualified person of U. X does not serve on U's governing body or as an officer of U. Although U participates in a provider-sponsored organization ... X does not have a material financial interest in that organization. Whether X is a disqualified person is determined by all relevant facts and circumstances. X did not found U, and although X makes a modest annual financial contribution to U, the amount of the contribution does not make X a substantial contributor.... X does not receive compensation based on revenues derived from activities of U that X controls, and has no authority to control or determine a significant portion of U's capital expenditures, operating budget, or compensation for employees. Under these facts and circumstances, X does not have substantial influence over the affairs of U, and therefore X is not a disqualified person with respect to any transaction involving U that provides economic benefits to X directly or indirectly.

63 Fed. Reg. 41,486, 41,499 (1998).

Although § 4958 places a tax on any "excess benefit" of a transaction over fair market value, the IRS allows a "rebuttable presumption" that the transaction is not an excess benefit transaction if three conditions are met at the time of contracting. Why would the IRS consider an arrangement to be at fair market value if these conditions are met? Would you add any more conditions? The proposed regulation § 53.4958–6 provides:

(a) In general. Payments under a compensation arrangement between an applicable tax-exempt organization and a disqualified person shall be presumed to be reasonable, and a transfer of property, right to use property, or any other benefit or privilege between an applicable tax-exempt organization and a disqualified person shall be presumed to be at fair market value, if the following conditions are satisfied—

(1) The compensation arrangement or terms of transfer are approved by the organization's governing body or a committee of the governing body composed entirely of individuals who do not have a conflict of interest with respect to the arrangement or transaction;

(2) The governing body, or committee thereof, obtained and relied upon appropriate data as to comparability prior to making its determination; and

(3) The governing body or committee adequately documented the basis for its determination concurrently with making that determination.

63 Fed. Reg. 41,486, 41,503–04 (1998).

Although the proposed regulations provide detailed explanations regarding "excess benefit," they reference private benefit and inurement. What does the IRS mean by "substantive statutory standards" in § 53.4958–7? Why would the IRS include § 53.4958–7?

§ 53.4958–7 Special rules.

(a) Substantive requirements for exemption still apply. The excise taxes imposed by section 4958 do not affect the substantive statutory standards for tax exemption under sections 501(c)(3) or (4). Organizations are described in those sections only if no part of their net earnings inure to the benefit of any private shareholder or individual.

63 Fed. Reg. 41,486, 41,505 (1998) (emphasis added).

Chapter 9

REGULATORY CONTROL OF PROVIDERS' FINANCIAL RELATIONSHIPS

Insert at page 583 immediately before Notes and Questions:

UNITED STATES v. KRIZEK

United States Court of Appeals, District of Columbia Circuit, 1997.
111 F.3d 934.

SENTELLE, CIRCUIT JUDGE.

This appeal arises from a civil suit brought by the government against a psychiatrist and his wife under the civil False Claims Act ("FCA"), and under the common law. The District Court found defendants liable for knowingly submitting false claims and entered judgment against defendants for $168,-105.39. The government appealed, and the defendants filed a cross-appeal. We hold that the District Court erred and remand for further proceedings.

[The Court held that the District Court erred in changing its benchmark for a preemptively false claim from 9 hours billed in any given day to 24 hours because it did not afford the government the opportunity to introduce additional evidence.]

* * *

The Krizeks cross-appeal on the grounds that the District Court erroneously treated each CPT code as a separate "claim" for purposes of computing civil penalties. The Krizeks assert that the claim, in this context, is the HCFA 1500 [form] even when the form contains a number of CPT codes.

The FCA defines "claim" to include any request or demand, whether under a contract or

> otherwise, for money or property which is made to a contractor, grantee, or other recipient if the United States Government provides any portion of the money or property which is requested or demanded, or if the Government will reimburse such contractor, grantee, or other recipient for any portion of the money or property which is requested or demanded.

31 U.S.C. § 3729(c). Whether a defendant has made one false claim or many is a fact-bound inquiry that focuses on the specific conduct of the defendant....

The gravamen of these cases is that the focus is on the conduct of the defendant. The Courts asks, "With what act did the defendant submit his demand or request and how many such acts were there?" In this case, the Special Master adopted a position that is inconsistent with this approach. He stated,

> The CPT code, not the HCFA 1500 form, is the source used to permit federal authorities to verify and account for discrete units of medical service provided, billed and paid for. In sum, the government has demanded a specific accounting unit to identify and verify the services provided, payments requested and amounts paid under the Medicare/Medicaid program. The CPT code, not the HCFA 1500 form, is that basic accounting unit.

The Special Master concluded that because the government used the CPT code in processing the claims, the CPT code, and not the HCFA 1500 in its entirety, must be the claim. This conclusion, which was later adopted by the District Court, misses the point. The question turns, not on how the government chooses to process the claim, but on how many times the defendants made a "request or demand." 31 U.S.C. § 3729(c). In this case, the Krizeks made a request or demand every time they submitted an HCFA 1500.

Our conclusion that the claim in this context is the HCFA 1500 form is supported by the structure of the form itself. The medical provider is asked to supply, along with the CPT codes, the date and place of service, a description of the procedures, a diagnosis code, and the charges. The charges are then totaled to produce one request or demand—line 27 asks for total charges, line 28 for amount paid, and line 29 for balance due. The CPT codes function in this context as a type of invoice used to explain how the defendant computed his request or demand.

The government contends that fairness or uniformity concerns support treating each CPT code as a separate claim, arguing that "[t]o count woodenly the number of HCFA 1500 forms submitted by the Krizeks would cede to medical practitioners full authority to control exposure to [FCA] simply by structuring their billings in a particular manner." Precisely so. It is conduct of the medical practitioner, not the disposition of the claims by the government, that creates FCA liability. Moreover, even if we considered fairness to be a relevant consideration in statutory construction, we would note that the government's definition of claim permitted it to seek an astronomical $81 million worth of damages for alleged actual damages of $245,392. We therefore remand for recalculation of the civil penalty.

* * *

[W]e turn now to the question whether, in considering the sample, the District Court applied the appropriate level of scienter. The FCA imposes liability on an individual who "knowingly presents" a "false or fraudulent claim." 31 U.S.C. § 3729(a). A person acts "knowingly" if he:

(1) has actual knowledge of the information;

(2) acts in deliberate ignorance of the truth or falsity of the information; or

(3) acts in reckless disregard of the truth or falsity of the information,

and no proof of specific intent to defraud is required.

31 U.S.C. § 3729(b). The Krizeks assert that the District Court impermissibly applied the FCA by permitting an aggravated form of gross negligence, "gross negligence-plus," to satisfy the Act's scienter requirement.

In Saba v. Compagnie Nationale Air France, 78 F.3d 664 (D.C.Cir.1996), we considered whether reckless disregard was the equivalent of willful misconduct for purposes of the Warsaw Convention. We noted that reckless disregard lies on a continuum between gross negligence and intentional harm. In some cases, recklessness serves as a proxy for forbidden intent. Such cases require a showing that the defendant engaged in an act known to cause or likely to cause the injury. Use of reckless disregard as a substitute for the forbidden intent prevents the defendant from "deliberately blind[ing] himself to the consequences of his tortuous action." Id. at 668. In another category of cases, we noted, reckless disregard is "simply a linear extension of gross negligence, a palpable failure to meet the appropriate standard of care." Id. In Saba, we determined that in the context of the Warsaw Convention, a showing of willful misconduct might be made by establishing reckless disregard such that the subjective intent of the defendant could be inferred.

The question, therefore, is whether "reckless disregard" in this context is properly equated with willful misconduct or with aggravated gross negligence. In determining that gross negligence-plus was sufficient, the District Court cited legislative history equating reckless disregard with gross negligence. A sponsor of the 1986 amendments to the FCA stated,

> Subsection 3 of Section 3729(c) uses the term "reckless disregard of the truth or falsity of the information" which is no different than and has the same meaning as a gross negligence standard that has been applied in other cases. While the Act was not intended to apply to mere negligence, it is intended to apply in situations that could be considered gross negligence where the submitted claims to the Government are prepared in such a sloppy or unsupervised fashion that resulted in overcharges to the Government. The Act is also intended not to permit artful defense counsel to require some form of intent as an essential ingredient of proof. This section is intended to reach the "ostrich-with-his-head-in-the-sand" problem where government contractors hide behind the fact they were not personally aware that such overcharges may have occurred. This is not a new standard but clarifies what has always been the standard of knowledge required.

132 Cong. Rec. H9382–03 (daily ed. Oct. 7, 1986) (statement of Rep. Berman).

While we are not inclined to view isolated statements in the legislative history as dispositive, we agree with the thrust of this statement that the best reading of the Act defines reckless disregard as an extension of gross negligence. Section 3729(b)(2) of the Act provides liability for false statements made with deliberate ignorance. If the reckless disregard standard of section 3729(b)(3) served merely as a substitute for willful misconduct—to prevent the defendant from "deliberately blind[ing] himself to the consequences of his tortuous action"—section (b)(3) would be redundant since section (b)(2) already covers such struthious conduct. Moreover, as the statute explicitly states that specific intent is not required, it is logical to conclude that reckless disregard in this context is not a "lesser form of intent,"[ ] but an extreme version of ordinary negligence.

We are unpersuaded by the Krizeks' citation to the rule of lenity to support their reading of the Act. Even assuming that the FCA is penal, the rule of lenity is invoked only when the statutory language is ambiguous. Because we find no ambiguity in the statute's scienter requirement, we hold that the rule of lenity is inapplicable.

We are also unpersuaded by the Krizeks' argument that their conduct did not rise to the level of reckless disregard. The District Court cited a number of factors supporting its conclusion: Mrs. Krizek completed the submissions with little or no factual basis; she made no effort to establish how much time Dr. Krizek spent with any particular patient; and Dr. Krizek "failed utterly" to review bills submitted on his behalf. Most tellingly, there were a number of days within the seven-patient sample when even the shoddiest record keeping would have revealed that false submissions were being made—those days on which the Krizeks' billing approached twenty-four hours in a single day. On August 31, 1985, for instance, the Krizeks requested reimbursement for patient treatment using the 90844 code thirty times and the 90843 code once, indicating patient treatment of over 22 hours. Outside the seven-patient sample the Krizeks billed for more than twenty-four hours in a single day on three separate occasions. These factors amply support the District Court's determination that the Krizeks acted with reckless disregard.

Finally, we note that Dr. Krizek is no less liable than his wife for these false submissions. As noted, an FCA violation may be established without reference to the subjective intent of the defendant. Dr. Krizek delegated to his wife authority to submit claims on his behalf. In failing "utterly" to review the false submissions, he acted with reckless disregard.

* * *

Insert the following on page 583 at the end of Note 1:

Does the opinion of the Court of Appeals in Krizek clarify the boundary between "reckless disregard" and willful misconduct? Between "reckless disregard" and gross negligence? What evidence did it rely upon to reach its conclusion that the Krizeks had run afoul of that standard? Can you explain at what point evidence of shoddy record keeping and submission of implausible claims would constitute "reckless disregard" under the False Claims Act?

Insert on page 583 at the end of Note 5:

After the Court of Appeals' determined that each 1500 Form constituted a "claim," the district court faced the question of how many of the multiple forms, which in total exceeded 24 hours, constituted separate "claims." Absent proof as to which specific claims were submitted beyond the 24–hour limit, the district court chose to count only the number of days (three) exceeding the 24–hour benchmark rather than the total number of claims exceeding that benchmark (eleven). United States v. Krizek, 7 F. Supp.2d 56 (D.D.C.1998). Judge Sporken voiced continued frustration with the government's case: "The Government's pursuit of Dr. Krizek is reminiscent of Inspector Javert's quest to capture Jean

Valjean in Victor Hugo's Les Miserables ... [T]here comes a point when a civilized society must say enough is enough." 5 F.2d at 60.

Insert on page 584, at the end of the page:

The combined effect of the Health Insurance Portability and Accountability Act of 1996 (HIPAA) and the Balanced Budget Act of 1997 (BBA) has been to vastly increase federal and state resources devoted to prosecuting false claims against the government. As noted in the text, these acts provided increased funding for federal government prosecutions, enhanced fraud and abuse data collection programs and new prosecutorial tools to pursue claims against providers. They have resulted in major new investigative initiatives and litigation and have produced significant governmental recoveries. In fiscal year 1998, the federal government secured 300 convictions under various claims for fraud and abuse and false claims, prosecuted over 1,000 civil suits, resulting in paybacks to the government, and secured 3000 exclusions from the Medicare and Medicaid program. Remarks of D. McCarty Thornton, Chief Counsel to the Inspector General, Department of Health and Human Services at the American Health Lawyers Association Institute on Medicare and Medicaid Payment Issues, Mar. 24–26, 1999. Government officials claim that these prosecutions are having an important "sentinel effect." That is, based on Medicare audits showing decreases in improper claims and declines in the average Medicare case mix, prosecutors assert that their efforts in prosecuting fraud and abuse are contributing to improved compliance and lower costs for federal programs. Id.

The Department of Justice and HCFA have undertaken a number of investigative initiatives targeting specific areas of concern. For example, the Physicians at Teaching Hospitals Audit Program (PATH) focused on Medicare and Medicaid requirements that attending physicians must be present and directly supervise the provision of services by residents in teaching hospitals. The program resulted in a number of important settlements against major teaching hospitals (the University of Pennsylvania settled for $30 million and Thomas Jefferson University for $12 million) and has also engendered litigation challenging whether the PATH audits reflect appropriate standards for teaching physician services and claiming coercion by the OIG in threatening to seek potentially devastating penalties to compel teaching hospitals into large settlements. See, e.g., Association of American Medical Colleges v. United States, 34 F.Supp.2d 1187 (C.D.Cal.1998). See also General Accounting Office, Medicare: Concerns With Physicians at Teaching Hospitals (PATH) Audits (July 23, 1998), (finding the government has legal cause to pursue these claims but questioning whether the hospitals' errors were as serious as publicly portrayed). Other major initiatives include the "Lab Scam" project investigating fraudulent laboratory test schemes which has resulted in $642 million in settlements and OIG's investigation of improper billing for non-physician out-patient services under prospective payment (the "DRG Payment Window" investigation.) See Federal Resources Are Stacking up to Tackle Health Care Fraud, Mod. Health Care, March 9, 1998 at 32; OIG Report No. A–03–94–0021, Medicare & Medicaid Guide (CCH) ¶ 43, 631 (Aug. 29, 1995). The government has also focused its attention on certain providers whose practices have raised red flags. See, e.g., Office of Inspector General, Special Fraud Alert: Fraud and Abuse in Nursing Home Arrangements With Hospices, 63 Fed. Reg. 10, 415 (1998); Special Fraud Alert on Physician Liability for Certifications in the Provision of Medical Equipment and Supplies and Home Health Services, 64 Fed. Reg. 1813 (1999); Fraud Alert: Providers Target Medicare Patients in Nursing Facilities, 61 Fed. Reg. 30, 623 (1996). Recently, the OIG has raised the possibility of applying the False Claims Act to abuses in the managed care area, targeting such practices as HMOs illegally enrolling Medicare beneficiaries, knowingly submitting incorrect enrollment data, illegally delaying referrals of patients for care, and improperly denying care. See Laurie McGinley & David S. Cloud, U.S. Takes Aim at HMO Fraud in Medicare and Medicaid, Wall St. J., Oct. 19, 1998, at A28.

Insert at page 588 at the end of Note 4:

Qui Tam actions in the health care area continue to proliferate, as total filed cases rose from 17 in 1992 to over 300 in 1998. The Department of Justice's current intervention rate is 22%. See Thornton, supra. Qui Tam actions accounted for over half of the total False Claims Act recoveries in 1997. Qui Tam Statistics, False Claims Act and Qui Tam Quarterly Review (Jan. 1998). In United States ex rel. Thompson v. Columbia/HCA Healthcare Corp., 125 F.3d 899 (5th Cir. 1997), a widely-noted qui tam case, a physician in Corpus Christi, Texas (who proceeded with the action after the government declined to intervene) asserted that defendants' violations of the Stark law and Medicare self-referral laws, false certifications and claims for services not medically necessary were actionable under the False Claims Act. The Fifth Circuit held that claims for service in violation of the antikickback statute and Stark laws "do not necessarily constitute false or fraudulent claims under the False Claims Act." However, on remand the District Court judge found Thompson's arguments persuasive that "the FCA reaches all fraudulent attempts to cause the government to pay out money" and therefore concluded that violations of Stark and antikickback laws can form the basis of an FCA action. United States ex rel. James Thompson v. Columbia/HCA Healthcare Corp., 20 F.Supp.2d 1017 (S.D.Tex.1998).

Insert at page 593 after the first full paragraph:

New legislative proposals for enhancing fraud and abuse prosecutions are being advanced. Vice President Gore recently announced a new initiative that would expand the subpoena power of the attorney general; provide new powers to seek injunctions to stop criminal kickback schemes while they are under investigation; allow civil and criminal enforcement authorities to share information; establish new civil money penalties of at least $25,000 and up to $50,000 for individuals or entities involved in those schemes; and make violators of the antikickback laws responsible for damages of triple the total compensation offered in return for federal health care program business. Roundup: Gore Announces Legislative Proposals to Improve Criminal, Civil Fraud Efforts, 8 Health L. Rep. (BNA) 532 (Apr. 1, 1999)

Insert at page 604 immediately before the Notes and Questions:

UNITED STATES v. STARKS

United States Court of Appeals, Eleventh Circuit, 1998.
157 F.3d 833.

BIRCH, CIRCUIT JUDGE:

Defendants Angela Starks and Andrew Siegel seek to overturn their convictions under the anti-kickback provision of the Social Security Act, 42 U.S.C. § 1320a–7b ("the Anti–Kickback statute"). Specifically, Starks and

Siegel argue that the district court erred by refusing to instruct the jury concerning the relevant mens rea. In addition, Starks and Siegel contend that the Anti–Kickback statute is unconstitutionally vague. We AFFIRM IN PART, REVERSE IN PART, and REMAND.

BACKGROUND

In 1992, Andrew Siegel was both the president and the sole shareholder of Future Steps, Inc., a corporation that developed and operated treatment programs for drug addiction. On April 22, 1992, Future Steps contracted with Florida CHS, Inc. to run a chemical dependency unit for pregnant women at Florida CHS's Metropolitan General Hospital ("the Hospital"). In return, Florida CHS promised to pay Future Steps a share of the Hospital's profits from the program. As a Medicaid provider, the Hospital performed medical services for indigent and disabled persons and received payment for these activities through Consultec, the fiscal intermediary for the Florida Medicaid program. Before executing the Future Steps–Florida CHS contract, Siegel initialed each page of the agreement, which included a provision explicitly forbidding Future Steps from making any payment for patient referrals in violation of the Anti-Kickback statute.

At the time Siegel signed this contract, Angela Starks and Barbara Henry had just become community health aides in the employ of the State of Florida Department of Health and Rehabilitative Services ("HRS"). Although Starks and Henry were employees of HRS, they actually worked in a federally-funded research project in Tampa, Florida known as "Project Support." As part of their duties, Starks and Henry advised pregnant women about possible treatment for drug abuse. Upon beginning their work at HRS, Starks and Henry learned from their supervisor both that they could not accept any outside employment that might pose a conflict of interest with their work at HRS and that they were obligated to report any outside employment to HRS.

During the spring of 1992, Future Steps had difficulty attracting patients. One of Future Steps's salaried "liaison workers," Robin Doud–Lacher, however, identified Project Support as a potential source of referrals because of its relationship with high-risk pregnant women. When Doud–Lacher's initial efforts to establish a referral relationship between Future Steps and Project Support failed, Siegel suggested to Doud–Lacher that she spend more time at Project Support, give diapers to Project Support, take Project Support workers to lunch, and otherwise build a relationship with Project Support's employees.

During one of her subsequent visits to Project Support, Doud–Lacher learned from Starks and Henry that cuts in federal spending threatened to reduce their work hours. When Starks and Henry asked if Doud–Loucher knew of other available work, she promised to inquire for them about opportunities at Future Steps.

After discussing Starks and Henry's interest with her immediate supervisor, Doud–Lacher spoke directly with Siegel about hiring the two women. Despite Starks and Henry's extant employment with HRS, Siegel told Doud–Loucher that he would pay Starks and Henry $250 for each patient they referred: $125 when a referred woman began inpatient drug treatment with Future Steps and $125 after each such woman had stayed in Future Steps's program for two weeks.[83] After accepting Siegel's terms, Starks and Henry did not report their referral arrangement to anyone at Project Support or HRS.

At the outset of their work for Future Steps, Starks and Henry received checks written on Future Steps's account and signed by Siegel. Before issuing these checks, Siegel verified that the referred patients had actually entered the Future Steps program; he did not, though, verify that the referrals were legal. Although the checks Siegel signed were coded variously as payments for aftercare, counseling, and marketing expenses, Siegel was actually only paying Starks and Henry for their referrals. In fact, Siegel did not at any time pay Starks and Henry for any of their time, effort, or business expenses, or for any covered Medicare service.

When Doud–Lacher left Future Steps, Siegel had Michael Ix, another liaison worker, assume responsibility for the Starks and Henry referral arrangement. Generally, either Starks or Henry would call Ix and ask him to pick up a referral directly from the Project Support clinic. When Ix arrived at Future Steps with the referred patient, Siegel would give Ix a check for Starks and Henry. Later, after Henry told Ix that she did not want anyone at Project Support to see her receiving checks from Future Steps, Ix agreed to deliver the checks to Starks and Henry either in the Project Support parking lot or at a restaurant. Between June 1992 and January 1993, Future Steps wrote checks payable to Starks totaling $2750 and to Henry totaling $1975.

At the end of 1992, Future Steps began paying Starks and Henry in cash. To make these payments, Ix would withdraw cash from his personal bank account and meet Starks and Henry either at a restaurant or at a twelve-step program; Siegel and Future Steps would then reimburse Ix. On one occasion, Siegel accomplished this reimbursement by meeting Ix in a restaurant restroom and giving him $600. In total, Ix paid Starks and Henry approximately $1000 to $1200 in cash.

Beyond the impropriety of Starks and Henry's acceptance of referral payments from Siegel, the referral arrangement directly affected Starks and Henry's counseling of the pregnant women who relied on them and Project Support for help. At trial, several of Future Steps's clients testified that Starks and Henry threatened that HRS would take away their babies if they did not receive treatment for their drug addictions; in some instances, Starks and Henry threatened women with the loss of their babies if they did not go specifically to Future Steps. According to these women's testimony, Starks and Henry informed them only about Future Steps's program (eschewing discussion of alternative treatments), and most waited with Starks and Henry at the Project Support clinic until someone from Future Steps arrived to take them to the Hospital. Starks and Henry's physician supervisor also testified that she told the two HRS employees to be more evenhanded in their advice to Project Support's patients, after the number of women going to Future Steps from Project Support increased substantially.

---

83. Although Starks and Henry had suggested limiting their referrals to patients living outside the area surrounding Project Support and/or restricting their recruiting for Future Steps to their non-HRS hours, Siegel imposed no bounds on the nature of their referral efforts.

In total, Starks and Henry referred eighteen women from Project Support to Future Steps. From these referrals, the Hospital received $323,023.04 in Medicaid payments.

On July 29, 1994, a federal grand jury indicted Siegel, Starks, Henry, and Doud–Lacher on five counts related to the referrals. Count One charged all four defendants with conspiring against the United States, in violation of 18 U.S.C. § 371, by offering to pay remuneration for referral of Medicare patients, in violation of 42 U.S.C. § 1320a–7b(b)(2)(A), and by soliciting and receiving such referral payments, in violation of 42 U.S.C. § 1320a–7b(b)(1)(A). Counts Two and Three charged Siegel and Doud–Loucher with paying remuneration to Starks and Henry to induce referrals of Medicaid patients, in violation of 42 U.S.C. § 1320a–7b(b)(2)(A). Finally, Count Four charged Starks and Count Five charged Henry with soliciting and receiving referral payments, in violation of 42 U.S.C. § 1320a–7b(b)(1)(A).

DISCUSSION

On appeal, defendants Starks and Siegel renew two contentions from their trial. First, they claim that the district court committed reversible error when it refused to instruct the jury that, because of the Anti–Kickback statute's mens rea requirement, Starks and Siegel had to have known that their referral arrangement violated the Anti–Kickback statute in order to be convicted. Second, Starks and Siegel argue that the Social Security Act's prohibition on paid referrals, when considered together with the Act's safe harbor provision, 42 U.S.C. § 1320a–7b(b)(3) ("the Safe Harbor provision"), is unconstitutionally vague. We address each of these arguments before turning to the government's cross-appeals concerning Siegel's sentence.

I. STARKS AND SIEGEL'S APPEALS

A. THE "WILLFULLY" INSTRUCTION

Starks and Siegel argue that the district court erred in its instruction concerning the mens rea required under the Anti–Kickback statute. According to 42 U.S.C. § 1320a–7b(b), it is illegal for a person to "knowingly and willfully solicit[ ] or receive[ ] any remuneration" for referrals for services covered by the federal government. At trial, the district court gave our circuit's pattern instruction regarding the term "willfully":

> The word willfully, as that term is used from time to time in these instructions, means the act was committed voluntarily and purposely, with the specific intent to do something the law forbids, that is with a bad purpose, either to disobey or disregard the law.

In reviewing the district court's charge, we determine whether the court's instructions as a whole sufficiently informed the jurors so that they understood the issues and were not misled. [ ]

In support of their claim, Starks and Siegel rely heavily on United States v. Sanchez–Corcino, 85 F.3d 549 (11th Cir.1996), and Ratzlaf v. United States, 510 U.S. 135, 114 S.Ct. 655, 126 L.Ed.2d 615 (1994). Since we heard oral argument on this case, however, the Supreme Court has issued an opinion in Bryan v. United States, ___ U.S. ___, 118 S.Ct. 1939, 141 L.Ed.2d 197 (1998), that clearly refutes Starks and Siegel's position.

In Sanchez–Corcino, a panel of this court held that the term "willfully" in 18 U.S.C. § 922(a)(1)(D) (requiring license for firearms), meant that the government had to prove that a defendant "acted with knowledge of the [§ 922(a)(1)(D)] licensing requirement." Id. at 553, 554 ("[k]nowledge of the general illegality of one's conduct is not the same as knowledge that one is violating a specific rule"). In Bryan, though, the Supreme Court explicitly rejected our decision in Sanchez–Corcino. See Bryan, __ U.S. at __, 118 S.Ct. at 1946. According to the Bryan Court, a jury may find a defendant guilty of violating a statute employing the word "willfully" if it believes "that the defendant acted with an evil-meaning mind, that is to say, that he acted with knowledge that his conduct was unlawful." Id. at __, 118 S.Ct. at 1946. Further, the Supreme Court distinguished tax or financial cases, such as Ratzlaf, that "involved highly technical statutes that presented the danger of ensnaring individuals engaged in apparently innocent conduct." Id.[84] Because "the jury found that [the defendant] knew that his conduct was unlawful," the Bryan Court wrote, "[t]he danger of convicting individuals engaged in apparently innocent activity that motivated our decisions in the tax cases and Ratzlaf is not present here." Id. (footnote omitted). Thus, the Court held that "the willfulness requirement of [the firearms statute] does not carve out an exemption to the traditional rule that ignorance of the law is no excuse; knowledge that conduct is unlawful is all that is required." Id.[85]

Analogously, the Anti–Kickback statute does not constitute a special exception. Section 1320a–7b is not a highly technical tax or financial regulation that poses a danger of ensnaring persons engaged in apparently innocent conduct. Indeed, the giving or taking of kickbacks for medical referrals is hardly the sort of activity a person might expect to be legal; compared to the licensing provisions that the Bryan Court considered, such kickbacks are more clearly malum in se, rather than malum prohibitum. Thus, we see no error in the district court's refusal to give Starks and Siegel's requested instruction.[86]

B. VAGUENESS

Starks and Siegel also argue that the Anti–Kickback statute is unconstitutionally vague because people of ordinary intelligence in either of their positions could not have ascertained from a reading of its Safe Harbor provision that their conduct was illegal.[87] Under the Safe Harbor provision,

84. In Ratzlaf, the Court reviewed a gambler's conviction for illegally structuring his banking transactions so as to avoid technical reporting requirements.

85. The Bryan Court thus upheld a jury instruction strikingly similar to the district court's "willfully" charge in this case:

A person acts willfully if he acts intentionally and purposely and with the intent to do something the law forbids, that is, with the bad purpose to disobey or to disregard the law. Now, the person need not be aware of the specific law or rule that his conduct may be violating. But he must act with the intent to do something that the law forbids. [ ]

86. Starks and Siegel also claim that the evidence was not sufficient to prove that they acted "willfully." Given that the government

only had to show that they knew that they were acting unlawfully, however, this claim is unpersuasive. The government produced ample evidence, including the furtive methods by which Siegel remunerated Starks and Henry, from which the jury could reasonably have inferred that Starks and Siegel knew that they were breaking the law—even if they may not have known that they were specifically violating the Anti–Kickback statute.

87. Starks and Siegel offer a variety of arguments to the effect that persons working in the medical field cannot anticipate what is prohibited under the Anti–Kickback statute and what is protected by that statute's Safe Harbor provision. They do not, and cannot, challenge, however, the government's contention that, since this is not a First Amendment

the Anti–Kickback statute's prohibition on referral payments shall not apply to ... any amount paid by an employer to an employee (who has a bona fide employment relationship with such employer) for employment in the provision of covered items and services.... According to Starks and Siegel, this provision is vague because ordinary people in their position might reasonably have thought that Starks and Henry were "bona fide employees" who were exempt from the Anti–Kickback statute's prohibition on remuneration for referrals.

Starks and Siegel are correct that a criminal statute must define an offense with sufficient clarity to enable ordinary people to understand what conduct is prohibited. Both the particular facts of this case and the nature of the Anti–Kickback statute, however, undercut Starks and Siegel's vagueness argument. First, even if Starks and Siegel believed that they were bona fide employees, they were not providing "covered items or services." As the government has shown, Starks received payment from Siegel and Future Steps only for referrals and not for any legitimate service for which the Hospital received any Medicare reimbursement. At the same time, persons in either Siegel's or Starks's position could hardly have thought that either Starks or Henry was a bona fide employee; unlike all of Future Steps's other workers, Starks and Henry did not receive regular salary checks at the Hospital. Instead, they clandestinely received their checks (often bearing false category codes) or cash in parking lots and other places outside the Project Support clinic so as to avoid detection by other Project Support workers.

Furthermore, beyond these particular facts, we see no reason to view the Anti–Kickback statute as vague. In Village of Hoffman Estates v. The Flipside, 455 U.S. 489, 498–499, 102 S.Ct. 1186, 1193, 71 L.Ed.2d 362 (1982), the Supreme Court set out several factors for a court to consider in determining whether a statute is impermissibly vague, including whether the statute (1) involves only economic regulation, (2) provides only civil, rather than criminal, penalties, (3) contains a scienter requirement mitigating vagueness, and (4) threatens any constitutionally protected rights. As two of our sister circuits have already concluded, these factors militate against finding the Anti–Kickback statute unconstitutional. [ ] Indeed, the statute regulates only economic conduct,[88] and it does not chill any constitutional rights. Moreover, although the statute does provide for criminal penalties, it requires "knowing and willful" conduct, a mens rea standard that mitigates any otherwise inherent vagueness in the Anti–Kickback statutes's provisions. [ ] In sum, we agree with the district court that the Anti–Kickback statute gave Starks and Siegel fair warning that their conduct was illegal and that the statute therefore is not unconstitutionally vague.

* * *

case, we must evaluate their claim of vagueness only on an as-applied basis. [ ] Thus, we consider Starks and Siegel's claim in light of the facts of this individual case, looking only to the constitutionality of the Anti–Kickback statute as the government has applied it to Starks and Siegel. [ ]

88. In Hoffman Estates, the Court explained that "economic regulation is subject to a less strict vagueness test because its subject is often more narrow, and because businesses, which face economic demands to plan behavior carefully, can be expected to consult relevant legislation in advance of action." 455 U.S. at 498, 102 S.Ct. at 1193 (footnote omitted).

CONCLUSION

... With regard to Starks and Siegel's appeal, we hold that the district court did not err when it refused to give their requested instruction, and that the Anti–Kickback statute is not unconstitutionally vague as applied to Starks and Siegel. Therefore, we AFFIRM these parts of the district court's judgment. ...

Insert the following at page 605 at the end of Note 5:

The Supreme Court's decision in Bryan v. United States, 524 U.S. 184, 118 S.Ct. 1939 (1998), went a long way toward clarifying the general principles of intent applicable in criminal cases, but did not fully resolve the issue with respect to the Medicare and Medicaid Fraud and Abuse Statute. First, the Court made it clear that "willfully" will be construed in the criminal context to require proof of knowledge of some law or legal standard: "As a general matter, when used in the criminal context, a 'willful' act is one undertaken with a 'bad purpose.' " 118 S.Ct. at 1945. Proof of this standard, however, may be satisfied by showing that the defendant "acted with an evil-meaning mind," which the Court defined as acting "with knowledge that his conduct was unlawful." Id. At the same time, as noted in Stark, Bryan lowered the standard of proof necessary to satisfy its test by accepting an accused's knowledge of general illegality unless the relevant statute is "highly technical." See Sharon L. Davies, Willfulness Under the Anti–Kickback Rules–Lessons from Bryan v. United States, 10 Health Lawyer, 14 (July, 1998). In a vigorous dissent, Justice Scalia argued that the majority's approach in Bryan might allow convictions where the defendant's knowledge of the illegality of his conduct went to issues peripheral to the conduct with which he was charged. For example, the dissenters posited that the defendant in Bryan might be guilty of the offense of selling firearms without a license even if he did not know of the license requirement but was aware that some other aspect of his conduct, such as filing serial numbers off the guns, was prohibited. Id. at 118 S.Ct. At 1950. Might this allow criminal prosecution of providers unfamiliar with the anti-kickback law but aware of their culpability under a statute with only a highly attenuated relationship to the anti-kickback law? See Davies supra at 17.

What aspects of the anti-kickback law does the 11th Circuit rely upon in Starks in holding that specific knowledge of that statute is not required? Are you satisfied that this approach does not run a risk of "ensnaring persons engaged in apparently innocent conduct" under the test set out in Bryan? What evidence going to the defendant's intent was available to satisfy the government's burden of showing that the defendants knew they were acting unlawfully? Were the inferences drawn from the defendant's conduct sufficient in this case? See generally Sharon L. Davies, The Jurisprudence of Willfullness: An Evolving Theory of Excusable Ignorance, 48 Duke L. J. 341 (1998).

Insert the following immediately after Note 6 on page 605:

7. When might the actions of attorneys advising clients and preparing documents that result in violations of the anti-kickback laws result in criminal liability? In the first Medicare fraud trial of lawyers, two attorneys were charged with participating in a conspiracy to solicit and pay bribes of $2 million to two osteopaths in Kansas City, Missouri for referring nursing home patients to several hospitals. The district court dismissed all charges against the lawyers finding that no reasonable jury could find beyond a reasonable doubt that the defendant

lawyers willfully committed any of the criminal acts charged in the indictment. United States v. Anderson, No. 98–20030 (D. Kan., transcript filed Mar. 9, 1999). The judge stressed that the record revealed that the lawyers held a good faith belief that it was possible to structure the deal between the hospitals and the medical group legally and that they had advised their clients that if fair market value were paid for legitimate consulting services, the relationship would pass legal muster. It also observed that the record showed that the lawyers relied on their clients for information and were not engaged to monitor the activity of consultants. Furthermore, when potential compliance problems were brought to their attention, the attorneys urged their clients to make sure that fair market value for real services was being required. Id.

The court went on to observe that

[E]ven if patient referrals were devoutly hoped for and anticipated; even if the volume of patients could be large; even if the parties might never have come together but for [one hospital] having embarked on a long-range plan that depended on attracting nursing home patients, there is nothing in the evidence of the law that would have a priori precluded a legal relationship from being entered into under these circumstances. The state of the law was in flux and the lawyers adapted their advice to it as it changed.... The problem here is that a very simple concept, "payment for patients is illegal," became far from simple as Congress, the Executive Branch, and the Courts got more deeply involved.

Do these comments suggest a different view of the anti-kickback statute than that expressed by the 11th Circuit in Starks? The result for the providers charged in the conspiracy was quite different, however. The jury convicted two hospital executives and both doctors who received the kickbacks for violations of the Medicare fraud statute and for participating in a conspiracy to defraud the federal government. Relying heavily on incriminating documents and statements, the government was apparently able to persuade the jury, which was instructed under the Greber "one purpose" standard, that payments to the doctors were designed at least in part to induce referrals, notwithstanding evidence of legitimate patient care and improved continuity of care purposes surrounding the arrangement. See J. Duncan Moore, Jr., Kansas Referral Arrangement Verdict: Guilty Decision May Prompt Hospital Execs to Review Contractual Relationships, Set Up Legal Safeguards, Mod. Healthcare, Apr. 12, 1999 at 2.

Insert on page 608 after the first full paragraph:

The Office of Inspector General has indicated that it plans to promulgate eight new safe harbors to the anti-kickback laws concerning investments in group practices, referral agreements for specialty services between doctors, and investments in ambulatory surgical centers. Several of these safe harbors relate to facilities in physicians investments, physician recruitment by hospitals in underserved areas, subsidies for malpractice insurance for obstetrical care, and the sale of physician practices in medically underserved areas. Roundup: Gore Announces Legislative Proposals to Improve Criminal, Civil Fraud Efforts, 8 Health L. Rep. (BNA) (Apr. 1, 1999).

Insert on page 608 at the end of the page:

DEPARTMENT OF HEALTH AND HUMAN SERVICES OFFICE OF THE INSPECTOR GENERAL

Advisory Opinion No. 98–4, April 15, 1998.

Dear [Name Redacted]:

We are writing in response to your request for an advisory opinion, in which you ask whether a proposed management services contract between a medical practice management company and a physician practice, which provides that the management company will be reimbursed for its costs and paid a percentage of net practice revenues (the "Proposed Arrangement"), would constitute illegal remuneration as defined in the anti-kickback statute, § 1128B(b) of the Social Security Act (the "Act").

You have certified that all of the information you provided in your request, including all supplementary letters, is true and correct, and constitutes a complete description of the material facts regarding the Proposed Arrangement. In issuing this opinion, we have relied solely on the facts and information you presented to us. We have not undertaken any independent investigation of such information.

Based on the information provided, we conclude that the Proposed Arrangement may constitute prohibited remuneration under § 1128B(b) of the Act.

I. FACTUAL BACKGROUND

A. The Parties

Dr. X is a family practice physician who has incorporated as, and practices under the name of, Company A ("Company A"). Company A is proposing to enter into an agreement to establish a family practice and walk-in clinic with a corporation, Company B ("Company B"). Dr. X is the sole Requestor of this advisory opinion.

B. The Arrangement

Under the Proposed Arrangement, Company A will provide all physician services at the clinic. Company A may hire additional physicians and other medical personnel with the mutual agreement of Company B. Company A will pay all physician compensation and fringe benefits, including but not limited to, licensing fees, continuing education, and malpractice premiums.

Company B will find a suitable location for the clinic and furnish the initial capital for the office, furniture, and operating expenses. Once operational, Company B will provide or arrange for all operating services for the clinic, including accounting, billing, purchasing, direct marketing, and hiring of non-medical personnel and outside vendors.

Company B will also provide Company A with management and marketing services for the clinic, including the negotiation and oversight of health care contracts with various payors, including indemnity plans, managed care plans, and Federal health care programs.

In addition to Company B's activities on behalf of Company A, Company B will set up provider networks. These networks may include Company A and, if required by Company B, Company A has agreed that it will refer its patients to the providers in such networks.

In return for its services, Company B's payment will have three components. Company A will be required to make a capital payment equal to a percentage of the initial cost of each capital asset purchased for Company A per year for six years. Company B will also receive a fair market value payment for the operating services it provides and an at-cost payment for any operating services for which it contracts. Company B will receive a percentage of Company A's monthly net revenues for its management services.

If the percentage payment described above is not permitted by law, then the parties will establish a management fee reflecting the contemplated financial results of the arrangement or, if the parties cannot agree to a fixed amount, the parties will hire an accounting firm to determine an appropriate fixed fee (the "Alternative Proposed Arrangement").

II.   LEGAL ANALYSIS

A.   Anti–Kickback Statute

[The Advisory Opinion summarizes the provisions of the anti-kickback statute, § 1128(B)(b), and notes the holding in Greber that liability may be ascribed to both sides of an illegal arrangement where "one purpose" of the remuneration was to obtain money for referrals or induce further referrals.]

B.   Safe Harbor Regulations

In 1991, the Department of Health and Human Services (the "Department") published safe harbor regulations that define practices that are not subject to the anti-kickback statute because such practices would be unlikely to result in fraud or abuse. Failure to comply with a safe harbor provision does not make an arrangement per se illegal. For this Proposed Arrangement, the only safe harbor regulation potentially available is the personal services and management contracts safe harbor. See 42 C.F.R. § 1001.952(d).

The personal services and management contracts safe harbor provides protection for personal services contracts if all of the following six standards are met: (i) the agreement is set out in writing and signed by the parties; (ii) the agreement specifies the services to be performed; (iii) if the services are to be performed on a part-time basis, the schedule for performance is specified in the contract; (iv) the agreement is for not less than one year; (v) the aggregate amount of compensation is fixed in advance, based on fair market value in an arms-length transaction, and not determined in a manner that takes into account the volume or value of any referrals or business otherwise generated between the parties for which payment may be made by Medicare or a State health care program; and (vi) the services performed under the agreement do not involve the promotion of business that violates any Federal or State law.

We conclude that the Proposed Arrangement does not qualify for this safe harbor. In order for an agreement to be protected by this safe harbor, strict compliance with all six standards is necessary. In this case, the compensation is not an aggregate amount, fixed in advance, as the safe harbor requires. Accordingly, the safe harbor standards are not satisfied.

C. Percentage Compensation Arrangement

Because compliance with a safe harbor is not mandatory, the fact that the Proposed Arrangement does not fit within a safe harbor does not mean that the Proposed Arrangement is necessarily unlawful. Rather, we must analyze this Proposed Arrangement on a case-by-case basis.

Percentage compensation arrangements for marketing services may implicate the anti-kickback statute. In our preamble to the 1991 final safe harbor rules, 56 Fed. Reg. 35952 (July 29, 1991), we explained that the anti-kickback statute "on its face prohibits offering or acceptance of remuneration, inter alia, for the purposes of 'arranging for or recommending purchasing, leasing, or ordering any ... service or item' payable under Medicare or Medicaid. Thus, we believe that many marketing and advertising activities may involve at least technical violations of the statute." 56 Fed. Reg. at 35974.

This Proposed Arrangement is problematic for the following reasons.

• The Proposed Arrangement may include financial incentives to increase patient referrals. The compensation that Company B receives for its management services is a percentage of Company A's net revenue, including revenue from business derived from managed care contracts arranged by Company B. Such activities may potentially implicate the anti-kickback statute, because the compensation Company B will receive will be in part for marketing services. Where such compensation is based on a percentage, there is at least a potential technical violation of the anti-kickback statute. In addition, Company B will be establishing networks of specialist physicians to whom Company A may be required to refer in some circumstances. Further, Company B will presumably receive some compensation for its efforts in connection with the development and operation of these specialist networks. In these circumstances, any evaluation of the Proposed Arrangement requires information about the relevant financial relationships. However, Company B is not a requestor for this advisory opinion, and Company A does not have information regarding Company B's related business arrangements.

Accordingly, we have insufficient information to ascertain the level of risk of fraud or abuse presented by the Proposed Arrangement.[89]

• The Proposed Arrangement contains no safeguards against overutilization. In light of the proposed establishment of provider networks with required referral arrangements, there is a risk of potential overutilization. Under the Proposed Arrangement, we are unable to determine what, if any, controls will be implemented under managed care contracts negotiated for Company A by Company B. Without such controls, we can not be assured that items and services paid for by Federal health care programs will not be overutilized.

---

89. We are also precluded from reaching a conclusion about the Alternative proposed Arrangement. Such a determination would require us to evaluate whether the agreed upon fee is fixed at fair market value. We are prevented from making that determination by § 1128D(b)(3)(A) of the Act, which prohibits our opining on fair market value in an advisory opinion.

- The Proposed Arrangement may include financial incentives that increase the risk of abusive billing practices. Since Company B receives a percentage of Company A's revenue and will arrange for Company A's billing, Company B has an incentive to maximize Company A's revenue. This Office has a longstanding concern that percentage billing arrangements may increase the risk of upcoding and similar abusive billing practices.

III. CONCLUSION

The advisory opinion process permits the OIG to protect specific arrangements that "contain[ ] limitations, requirements, or controls, that give adequate assurances that Federal health care programs cannot be abused." See 62 Fed. Reg. 7350, 7351 (February 19, 1997). Based on the facts we have been presented, the Proposed Arrangement appears to contain no limitations, requirements, or controls that would minimize any fraud or abuse.

Therefore, since we cannot be confident that there is no more than a minimal risk of fraud or abuse, we must conclude that the Proposed Arrangement may involve prohibited remuneration under the anti-kickback statute and thus potentially be subject to sanction under the anti-kickback statute, § 1128B(b) of the Act. Any definitive conclusion regarding the existence of an anti-kickback violation requires a determination of the parties' intent, which determination is beyond the scope of the advisory opinion process.[90]

IV. LIMITATIONS

The limitations applicable to this opinion include the following:

- This advisory opinion is issued only to Dr. X, who is the Requestor of this opinion. This advisory opinion has no application, and cannot be relied upon, by any other individual or entity.
- This advisory opinion is applicable only to the statutory provision specifically noted above. No opinion is herein expressed or implied with respect to the application of any other Federal, state, or local statute, rule, regulation, ordinance, or other law that may be applicable to the Proposed Arrangement.
- This advisory opinion will not bind or obligate any agency other than the U.S. Department of Health and Human Services.

This opinion is also subject to any additional limitations set forth at 42 C.F.R. Part 1008.

Sincerely,

/s/

D. McCarty Thornton
Chief Counsel to the Inspector General

Notes

1. Trace the remunerations in the transaction described in Advisory Opinion 98–4. How does each run a risk of inducing referrals? Does the compensation for

90. Our conclusion regarding the risk of fraud or abuse in relation to the anti-kickback statute should not be construed to mean that a finding of fraud or abuse is an implied element necessary to establish a violation of the statute.

management services received by Company B create financial incentives to increase referrals? Would "safeguards against overutilization" mentioned in the Opinion have assuaged the Inspector's General's concerns? What risk does Company B's involvement in setting up networks pose? Are there steps which could be taken to avoid anti-kickback concerns?

2.   Can a meaningful determination on the riskiness of a proposed venture be made without information regarding the parties' intent? What specific questions should be posed to those requesting an advisory opinion to clarify the intent underlying a proposed transaction? Is it even possible to undertake such a proceeding in the context of the advisory opinion process? See generally Scott J. Kelly, The Health Insurance Portability and Accountability Act of 1996: A Medicare Fraud Advisory Opinion Mandates Sends the Inspector "Shopping for Hats," 59 Ohio St. L. J. 303 (1998); Timothy S. Jost and Sharon L. Davies, Medicare and Medicare Fraud and Abuse, § 3–17, at 159–60, 166.

Insert on page 616 immediately before the Problem, Group Practices

On January 9, 1998, HCFA published its long-awaited, proposed Stark II Rules. Medicare and Medicaid Programs: Physicians' Referrals to Health Care Entities With Which They Have Financial Relationships, 63 Fed. Reg. 1659 (1998) (proposed Jan. 9, 1998). These rules are extremely complex and detailed and have generated a large volume of comments submitted in response to the Federal Register notice, and there is no predicting when the Final Rules will be published. The rules provide detailed explanations and guidance on some of the minutiae of the Stark II statute and offer HCFA's interpretation of the intent of some of its provisions. See Albert Shay & Gary Francesconi, Proposed Stark II Rules: Clarification or More Confusion?, 312 J. Health & Hosp. L. 95 (1998). Among the more important aspects of the rules are the following.

The rules define a financial relationship to include any indirect ownership or investment interest "no matter how many levels removed from a direct interest." 63 Fed. Reg. at 1686. They also attempt to flesh out the scope of several of the "designated health services" and specifically exclude certain procedures that HCFA deems unlikely to incur risks of overutilization. See e.g., Id. at 1676. The Stark II rules also contain detailed provisions governing group practice arrangements including requisites for qualifying as a group practice, criteria for determining who is a group practice member, and the definition of the "full range of services" test and related issues. See Id. at 1687–90. In addition, the In-office Ancillary Services Exception to the ownership interest and compensation arrangement test is clarified somewhat as HCFA attempted to draw lines regarding the requirements of direct supervision and the location of provided services. Id. at 1684–85.

Probably the most noteworthy development contained in the proposed Stark II regulation is the announcement of three significant new general exceptions to otherwise prohibited compensation arrangements between physicians and health care entities. First, the rules announce a new "fair market value" exception which exempts arrangements between physicians or groups of physicians (even if they do not qualify as a group practice) and an entity, where the compensation or payment is based on the fair market value and not reflective of the volume or value of referrals. However, several conditions must be met. The agreement must: be in writing and cover only identifiable specified items or services; cover all the items or services provided between the parties; be effective for a specified time period (the period may be less than one year); provide for compensation that is set in advance; and be commercially reasonable to further the legitimate business purposes of the parties. This exception is notable because of its potential sweep. It may, for example, provide a catch-all that protects transactions that fail to meet the detailed specifics of other exceptions contained in the statute. A second proposed exception is a "de minimis" exception which would allow physicians to receive incidental compensation or benefits which are small in value ($50 per gift and $300 per year) and made available to other similarly situated providers, and are not based on the volume or value of referrals and not in the form of cash or cash equivalents. Finally, the Stark II regulations propose a "pass-through discount" exception which exempts discounts received by physicians, provided the discount is (1) passed-through in full to patients or their insurers and (2) does not "inure to the benefit of the referring physician." Id. at 1694.

As of April, 1998, HCFA had received nearly 4,000 comments on its proposed Stark II regulations. Providers have voiced criticisms that these rules interfere with the efficient delivery of health care, increase costs and micromanage doctors' offices. The law's author, Fortney ("Pete") Stark, has asked the Institute of Medicine for ideas on how the law can be improved and simplified. Medicare: Rep. Stark Asks Institute of Medicine to Form Working Group on Self–Referral Law, Health Care Daily (BNA), July 28, 1998.

Chapter 10

ANTITRUST

Insert new Note 4 on page 631:

4. The Justice Department and FTC continue to challenge formal and informal physician organizations whose purposes are to eliminate competitive bidding among members of their group or to reduce the influence of HMOs and PPOs in their markets. For example, the FTC entered into a consent decree with Montana Associated Physicians, Inc. (MAPI), an organization of 115 physicians practicing in over 30 independent physician practices and constituting 43% of all the physicians in Billings, Montana. In re Montana Associated Physicians, Inc. and Billings Physician Hospital Alliance, Inc., FTC Docket No. C–3704, 62 Fed. Reg. 11,201 (Mar. 11, 1997). According to the FTC's complaint, physicians formed MAPI to present a "united front" when dealing with managed care plans in an attempt to "resist competitive pressures to discount fees" and forestall entry of HMOs and PPOs into the area. Individual members of MAPI told HMOs that they would negotiate only through their organization and no individual MAPI member contracted with HMOs. Similarly, a number of investigations and cases have been brought involving "sham" networks of physicians and attempts to organize labor unions to engage in collective bargaining. See Casebook, pp. 650–674; Note on Physician Unions, infra this Supplement.

Delete note 3 on page 642.

Insert on page 642, at the end of Note 3:

CALIFORNIA DENTAL ASSOCIATION
Supreme Court of the United States, 1999.
119 S.Ct. 1604.

JUSTICE SOUTER delivered the opinion of the Court.

There are two issues in this case: whether the jurisdiction of the Federal Trade Commission extends to the California Dental Association (CDA), a nonprofit professional association, and whether a "quick look" sufficed to justify finding that certain advertising restrictions adopted by the CDA violated the antitrust laws. We hold that the Commission's jurisdiction under the Federal Trade Commission Act (FTC Act) extends to an association that, like the CDA, provides substantial economic benefit to its for-profit members, but that where, as here, any anticompetitive effects of given restraints are far from intuitively obvious, the rule of reason demands a more thorough enquiry into the consequences of those restraints than the Court of Appeals performed.

I

[Petitioner California Dental Association (CDA), a nonprofit association of local dental societies to which about three-quarters of the State's dentists belong, provides desirable insurance and preferential financing arrangements for its members, and engages in lobbying, litigation, marketing, and public relations for members' benefit. Members agree to abide by the CDA's Code of Ethics, which, inter alia, prohibits false or misleading advertising. The CDA has issued interpretive advisory opinions and guidelines relating to advertising. The FTC claimed that in applying its guidelines so as to restrict two types of truthful, nondeceptive advertising: price advertising, particularly discounted fees, and advertising relating to the quality of dental services, the CDA violated § 5 of the FTC Act. In its administrative proceedings, the Commission held that the advertising restrictions violated the Act under an abbreviated rule-of-reason analysis. In affirming, the Ninth Circuit sustained the Commission's jurisdiction and concluded that an abbreviated or "quick look" rule-of-reason analysis was proper in this case.]

The dentists who belong to the CDA ... to abide by a Code of Ethics (Code) including the following § 10:

> "Although any dentist may advertise, no dentist shall advertise or solicit patients in any form of communication in a manner that is false or misleading in any material respect. In order to properly serve the public, dentists should represent themselves in a manner that contributes to the esteem of the public. Dentists should not misrepresent their training and competence in any way that would be false or misleading in any material respect."

The CDA has issued a number of advisory opinions interpreting this section, and through separate advertising guidelines intended to help members comply with the Code and with state law the CDA has advised its dentists of disclosures they must make under state law when engaging in discount advertising.[1]

Responsibility for enforcing the Code rests in the first instance with the local dental societies, to which applicants for CDA membership must submit copies of their own advertisements and those of their employers or referral services to assure compliance with the Code. The local societies also actively seek information about potential Code violations by applicants or CDA members. Applicants who refuse to withdraw or revise objectionable advertisements may be denied membership; and members who, after a hearing, remain similarly recalcitrant are subject to censure, suspension, or expulsion from the CDA. []

* * *

1. The disclosures include:

"1. The dollar amount of the nondiscounted fee for the service[.]

"2. Either the dollar amount of the discount fee or the percentage of the discount for the specific service[.]

"3. The length of time that the discount will be offered[.]

"4. Verifiable fees[.]

"5. [The identity of] [s]pecific groups who qualify for the discount or any other terms and conditions or restrictions for qualifying for the discount." Id., at 724.

II

[The Court held that the Commission's jurisdiction extends to an association that, like the CDA, provides substantial economic benefit to its for-profit members. It interpreted the FTC Act, which gives the Commission authority over a "corporatio[n]," 15 U.S.C. § 45(a)(2), "organized to carry on business for its own profit or that of its members," § 44, to grant the FTC jurisdiction over nonprofit associations whose activities provide substantial economic benefits to their for-profit members rather than requiring that a supporting organization must devote itself entirely to its members' profits or of the entity's activities must go to raising the members' bottom lines. While the Act does not cover all membership organizations of profit-making corporations without more, the economic benefits conferred upon CDA's profit-seeking professionals plainly fall within the object of enhancing its members' "profit," which is the Act's jurisdictional touchstone.]

III

The Court of Appeals treated as distinct questions the sufficiency of the analysis of anticompetitive effects and the substantiality of the evidence supporting the Commission's conclusions. Because we decide that the Court of Appeals erred when it held as a matter of law that quick-look analysis was appropriate (with the consequence that the Commission's abbreviated analysis and conclusion were sustainable), we do not reach the question of the substantiality of the evidence supporting the Commission's conclusion.[2]

In National Collegiate Athletic Assn. v. Board of Regents of Univ. of Okla.[] we held that a "naked restraint on price and output requires some competitive justification even in the absence of a detailed market analysis." []. Elsewhere, we held that "no elaborate industry analysis is required to demonstrate the anticompetitive character of" horizontal agreements among competitors to refuse to discuss prices, National Soc. of Professional Engineers v. United States, [] or to withhold a particular desired service, FTC v. Indiana Federation of Dentists []. In each of these cases, which have formed the basis for what has come to be called abbreviated or "quick-look" analysis under the rule of reason, an observer with even a rudimentary understanding of economics could conclude that the arrangements in question would have an anticompetitive effect on customers and markets. . . . As in such cases, quick-look analysis carries the day when the great likelihood of anticompetitive effects can easily be ascertained. . . .

The case before us, however, fails to present a situation in which the likelihood of anticompetitive effects is comparably obvious. Even on Justice BREYER's view that bars on truthful and verifiable price and quality advertising are prima facie anticompetitive, and place the burden of procompetitive justification on those who agree to adopt them, the very issue at the threshold of this case is whether professional price and quality advertising is sufficiently verifiable in theory and in fact to fall within such a general rule. Ultimately our disagreement with Justice BREYER turns on our different responses to this issue. Whereas he accepts, as the Ninth Circuit seems to have done, that

---

2. We leave to the Court of Appeals the question whether on remand it can effectively assess the Commission's decision for substantial evidence on the record, or whether it must remand to the Commission for a more extensive rule-of-reason analysis on the basis of an enhanced record.

the restrictions here were like restrictions on advertisement of price and quality generally, it seems to us that the CDA's advertising restrictions might plausibly be thought to have a net procompetitive effect, or possibly no effect at all on competition. The restrictions on both discount and nondiscount advertising are, at least on their face, designed to avoid false or deceptive[3] in a market characterized by striking disparities between the information available to the professional and the patient.[4] Cf. Carr & Mathewson, The Economics of Law Firms: A Study in the Legal Organization of the Firm, 33 J. Law & Econ. 307, 309 (1990) (explaining that in a market for complex professional services, "inherent asymmetry of knowledge about the product" arises because "professionals supplying the good are knowledgeable [whereas] consumers demanding the good are uninformed"); Akerlof, The Market for "Lemons": Quality Uncertainty and the Market Mechanism, 84 Q.J. Econ. 488 (1970) (pointing out quality problems in market characterized by asymmetrical information). In a market for professional services, in which advertising is relatively rare and the comparability of service packages not easily established, the difficulty for customers or potential competitors to get and verify information about the price and availability of services magnifies the dangers to competition associated with misleading advertising. What is more, the quality of professional services tends to resist either calibration or monitoring by individual patients or clients, partly because of the specialized knowledge required to evaluate the services, and partly because of the difficulty in determining whether, and the degree to which, an outcome is attributable to the quality of services (like a poor job of tooth-filling) or to something else (like a very tough walnut). See Leland, Quacks, Lemons, and Licensing: A Theory of Minimum Quality Standards, 87 J. Pol. Econ. 1328, 1330 (1979); 1 B. Furrow, T. Greaney, S. Johnson, T. Jost, & R. Schwartz, Health Law § 3–1, p. 86 (1995) (describing the common view that "the lay public is incapable of adequately evaluating the quality of medical services"). Patients' attachments to particular professionals, the rationality of which is difficult to assess, complicate the picture even further. Cf. Evans, Professionals and the Production Function: Can Competition Policy Improve Efficiency in the Licensed Professions?, in Occupational Licensure and Regulation 235–236 (S. Rottenberg ed.1980) (describing long-term relationship between professional and client not as "a series of spot contracts" but rather as "a long-term agreement, often implicit, to deal with each other in a set of future unspecified or incompletely specified circumstances according to certain rules," and adding that "[i]t is not clear how or if these [implicit contracts] can be reconciled with the promotion of effective price competition in individual spot markets for particular services"). The existence of such significant challenges to informed decisionmaking by the customer for professional

3. That false or misleading advertising has an anticompetitive effect, as that term is customarily used, has been long established. Cf. FTC v. Algoma Lumber Co., 291 U.S. 67, 79–80, 54 S.Ct. 315, 78 L.Ed. 655 (1934) (finding a false advertisement to be unfair competition).

4. "The fact that a restraint operates upon a profession as distinguished from a business is, of course, relevant in determining whether that particular restraint violates the Sherman Act. It would be unrealistic to view the practice of professions as interchangeable with other business activities, and automatically to apply to the professions antitrust concepts which originated in other areas. The public service aspect, and other features of the professions, may require that a particular practice, which could properly be viewed as a violation of the Sherman Act in another context, be treated differently." Goldfarb v. Virginia State Bar, 421 U.S. 773, 788–789, n. 17, 95 S.Ct. 2004, 44 L.Ed.2d 572 (1975).

services immediately suggests that advertising restrictions arguably protecting patients from misleading or irrelevant advertising call for more than cursory treatment as obviously comparable to classic horizontal agreements to limit output or price competition.

[The Court of Appeals] brushe[d] over the professional context and describe[d] no anticompetitive effects. Assuming that the record in fact supports the conclusion that the CDA disclosure rules essentially bar advertisement of across-the-board discounts, it does not obviously follow that such a ban would have a net anticompetitive effect here. Whether advertisements that announced discounts for, say, first-time customers, would be less effective at conveying information relevant to competition if they listed the original and discounted prices for checkups, X-rays, and fillings, than they would be if they simply specified a percentage discount across the board, seems to us a question susceptible to empirical but not a priori analysis. . . . Put another way, the CDA's rule appears to reflect the prediction that any costs to competition associated with the elimination of across-the-board advertising will be outweighed by gains to consumer information (and hence competition) created by discount advertising that is exact, accurate, and more easily verifiable (at least by regulators). As a matter of economics this view may or may not be correct, but it is not implausible, and neither a court nor the Commission may initially dismiss it as presumptively wrong.[5]

* * *

The Court of Appeals was comparably tolerant in accepting the sufficiency of abbreviated rule-of-reason analysis as to the nonprice advertising restrictions. The court began with the argument that "[t]hese restrictions are in effect a form of output limitation, as they restrict the supply of information about individual dentists' services." Although this sentence does indeed appear as cited, it is puzzling, given that the relevant output for antitrust purposes here is presumably not information or advertising, but dental services themselves. The question is not whether the universe of possible advertisements has been limited (as assuredly it has), but whether the limitation on advertisements obviously tends to limit the total delivery of dental services. The court came closest to addressing this latter question when it went on to assert that limiting advertisements regarding quality and safety "prevents dentists from fully describing the package of services they offer," adding that "[t]he restrictions may also affect output more directly, as quality and comfort advertising may induce some customers to obtain non-emergency care when they might not otherwise do so," ibid. This suggestion about output is also puzzling. If quality advertising actually induces some

5. Justice BREYER suggests that our analysis is "of limited relevance," because "the basic question is whether this . . . theoretically redeeming virtue in fact offsets the restrictions' anticompetitive effects in this case." He thinks that the Commission and the Court of Appeals "adequately answered that question," but the absence of any empirical evidence on this point indicates that the question was not answered, merely avoided by implicit burden-shifting of the kind accepted by Justice BREYER. The point is that before a theoretical claim of anticompetitive effects can justify shifting to a defendant the burden to show empirical evidence of procompetitive effects, as quick-look analysis in effect requires, there must be some indication that the court making the decision has properly identified the theoretical basis for the anticompetitive effects and considered whether the effects actually are anticompetitive. Where, as here, the circumstances of the restriction are somewhat complex, assumption alone will not do.

patients to obtain more care than they would in its absence, then restricting such advertising would reduce the demand for dental services, not the supply; and it is of course the producers' supply of a good in relation to demand that is normally relevant in determining whether a producer-imposed output limitation has the anticompetitive effect of artificially raising prices.[6] ...

Although the Court of Appeals acknowledged the CDA's view that "claims about quality are inherently unverifiable and therefore misleading," it responded that this concern "does not justify banning all quality claims without regard to whether they are, in fact, false or misleading." As a result, the court said, "the restriction is a sufficiently naked restraint on output to justify quick look analysis." The court assumed, in these words, that some dental quality claims may escape justifiable censure, because they are both verifiable and true. But its implicit assumption fails to explain why it gave no weight to the countervailing, and at least equally plausible, suggestion that restricting difficult-to-verify claims about quality or patient comfort would have a procompetitive effect by preventing misleading or false claims that distort the market. It is, indeed, entirely possible to understand the CDA's restrictions on unverifiable quality and comfort advertising as nothing more than a procompetitive ban on puffery....

The point is not that the CDA's restrictions necessarily have the procompetitive effect claimed by the CDA; it is possible that banning quality claims might have no effect at all on competitiveness if, for example, many dentists made very much the same sort of claims. And it is also of course possible that the restrictions might in the final analysis be anticompetitive. The point, rather, is that the plausibility of competing claims about the effects of the professional advertising restrictions rules out the indulgently abbreviated review to which the Commission's order was treated. The obvious anticompetitive effect that triggers abbreviated analysis has not been shown.

In light of our focus on the adequacy of the Court of Appeals's analysis, Justice BREYER's thorough-going, de novo antitrust analysis contains much to impress on its own merits but little to demonstrate the sufficiency of the Court of Appeals's review. The obligation to give a more deliberate look than a quick one does not arise at the door of this Court and should not be satisfied here in the first instance. Had the Court of Appeals engaged in a painstaking discussion in a league with Justice BREYER's (compare his 14 pages with the Ninth Circuit's 8), and had it confronted the comparability of these restrictions to bars on clearly verifiable advertising, its reasoning might have sufficed to justify its conclusion. Certainly Justice BREYER's treatment of the antitrust issues here is no "quick look." Lingering is more like it, and indeed Justice BREYER, not surprisingly, stops short of endorsing the Court of Appeals's discussion as adequate to the task at hand.

---

6. Justice BREYER wonders if we "mea[n] this statement as an argument against the anticompetitive tendencies that flow from an agreement not to advertise service quality." But as the preceding sentence shows, we intend simply to question the logic of the Court of Appeals's suggestion that the restrictions are anticompetitive because they somehow "affect output," presumably with the intent to raise prices by limiting supply while demand remains constant. We do not mean to deny that an agreement not to advertise service quality might have anticompetitive effects. We merely mean that, absent further analysis of the kind Justice BREYER undertakes, it is not possible to conclude that the net effect of this particular restriction is anticompetitive.

Saying here that the Court of Appeals's conclusion at least required a more extended examination of the possible factual underpinnings than it received is not, of course, necessarily to call for the fullest market analysis. Although we have said that a challenge to a "naked restraint on price and output" need not be supported by "a detailed market analysis" in order to "requir[e] some competitive justification," . . . The truth is that our categories of analysis of anticompetitive effect are less fixed than terms like "per se," "quick look," and "rule of reason" tend to make them appear. We have recognized, for example, that "there is often no bright line separating per se from Rule of Reason analysis," since "considerable inquiry into market conditions" may be required before the application of any so-called "per se" condemnation is justified. As the circumstances here demonstrate, there is generally no categorical line to be drawn between restraints that give rise to an intuitively obvious inference of anticompetitive effect and those that call for more detailed treatment. What is required, rather, is an enquiry meet for the case, looking to the circumstances, details, and logic of a restraint. The object is to see whether the experience of the market has been so clear, or necessarily will be, that a confident conclusion about the principal tendency of a restriction will follow from a quick (or at least quicker) look, in place of a more sedulous one. And of course what we see may vary over time, if rule-of-reason analyses in case after case reach identical conclusions. For now, at least, a less quick look was required for the initial assessment of the tendency of these professional advertising restrictions. Because the Court of Appeals did not scrutinize the assumption of relative anticompetitive tendencies, we vacate the judgment and remand the case for a fuller consideration of the issue.

It is so ordered.

Justice BREYER, with whom Justice STEVENS, Justice KENNEDY, and Justice GINSBURG join, concurring in part and dissenting in part.

I agree with the Court that the Federal Trade Commission has jurisdiction over petitioner, and I join Parts I and II of its opinion. I also agree that in a "rule of reason" antitrust case "the quality of proof required should vary with the circumstances," that "[w]hat is required . . . is an enquiry meet for the case," and that the object is a "confident conclusion about the principal tendency of a restriction." But I do not agree that the Court has properly applied those unobjectionable principles here. In my view, a traditional application of the rule of reason to the facts as found by the Commission requires affirming the Commission—just as the Court of Appeals did below.

I

The Commission's conclusion is lawful if its "factual findings," insofar as they are supported by "substantial evidence," "make out a violation of Sherman Act § 1." [] To determine whether that is so, I would not simply ask whether the restraints at issue are anticompetitive overall. Rather, like the Court of Appeals (and the Commission), I would break that question down into four classical, subsidiary antitrust questions: (1) What is the specific restraint at issue? (2) What are its likely anticompetitive effects? (3) Are there offsetting procompetitive justifications? (4) Do the parties have sufficient market power to make a difference?

A

The most important question is the first: What are the specific restraints at issue? [] Those restraints do not include merely the agreement to which the California Dental Association's (Dental Association or Association) ethical rule literally refers, namely, a promise to refrain from advertising that is " 'false or misleading in any material respect.' [] Instead, the Commission found a set of restraints arising out of the way the Dental Association implemented this innocent-sounding ethical rule in practice, through advisory opinions, guidelines, enforcement policies, and review of membership applications. As implemented, the ethical rule reached beyond its nominal target, to prevent truthful and nondeceptive advertising. In particular, the Commission determined that the rule, in practice:

(1) "precluded advertising that characterized a dentist's fees as being low, reasonable, or affordable,"

(2) "precluded advertising . . . of across the board discounts," and

(3) "prohibit[ed] all quality claims."

Whether the Dental Association's basic rule as implemented actually restrained the truthful and nondeceptive advertising of low prices, across-the-board discounts, and quality service are questions of fact. The Administrative Law Judge (ALJ) and the Commission may have found those questions difficult ones. But both the ALJ and the Commission ultimately found against the Dental Association in respect to these facts. And the question for us—whether those agency findings are supported by substantial evidence, is not difficult.

The Court of Appeals referred explicitly to some of the evidence that it found adequate to support the Commission's conclusions. It pointed out, for example, that the Dental Association's "advisory opinions and guidelines indicate that . . . descriptions of prices as 'reasonable' or 'low' do not comply" with the Association's rule; that in "numerous cases" the Association "advised members of objections to special offers, senior citizen discounts, and new patient discounts, apparently without regard to their truth"; and that one advisory opinion "expressly states that claims as to the quality of services are inherently likely to be false or misleading," all "without any particular consideration of whether" such statements were "true or false." []

The Commission itself had before it far more evidence. It referred to instances in which the Association, without regard for the truthfulness of the statements at issue, recommended denial of membership to dentists wishing to advertise, for example, "reasonable fees quoted in advance," "major savings," or "making teeth cleaning . . . inexpensive." It referred to testimony that "across-the-board discount advertising in literal compliance with the requirements 'would probably take two pages in the telephone book' and '[n]obody is going to really advertise in that fashion.' " And it pointed to many instances in which the Dental Association suppressed such advertising claims as "we guarantee all dental work for 1 year," "latest in cosmetic dentistry," and "gentle dentistry in a caring environment."

* * *

B

Do each of the three restrictions mentioned have "the potential for genuine adverse effects on competition"? I should have thought that the anticompetitive tendencies of the three restrictions were obvious. An agreement not to advertise that a fee is reasonable, that service is inexpensive, or that a customer will receive a discount makes it more difficult for a dentist to inform customers that he charges a lower price. If the customer does not know about a lower price, he will find it more difficult to buy lower price service. That fact, in turn, makes it less likely that a dentist will obtain more customers by offering lower prices. And that likelihood means that dentists will prove less likely to offer lower prices. But why should I have to spell out the obvious? To restrain truthful advertising about lower prices is likely to restrict competition in respect to price—"the central nervous system of the economy." For present purposes, I need not decide whether the Commission was right in applying a per se rule. I need only assume a rule of reason applies, and note the serious anticompetitive tendencies of the price advertising restraints.

The restrictions on the advertising of service quality also have serious anticompetitive tendencies. This is not a case of "mere puffing," as the FTC recognized. The days of my youth, when the billboards near Emeryville, California, home of AAA baseball's Oakland Oaks, displayed the name of "Painless" Parker, Dentist, are long gone—along with the Oakland Oaks. But some parents may still want to know that a particular dentist makes a point of "gentle care." Others may want to know about 1–year dental work guarantees. To restrict that kind of service quality advertisement is to restrict competition over the quality of service itself, for, unless consumers know, they may not purchase, and dentists may not compete to supply that which will make little difference to the demand for their services. That, at any rate, is the theory of the Sherman Act. And it is rather late in the day for anyone to deny the significant anticompetitive tendencies of an agreement that restricts competition in any legitimate respect, let alone one that inhibits customers from learning about the quality of a dentist's service.

Nor did the Commission rely solely on the unobjectionable proposition that a restriction on the ability of dentists to advertise on quality is likely to limit their incentive to compete on quality. Rather, the Commission pointed to record evidence affirmatively establishing that quality-based competition is important to dental consumers in California. [The dissent goes on to summarize evidence that advertising concerning quality will bring in more patients and that restrictions adversely affected dentists who advertise.]

C

We must also ask whether, despite their anticompetitive tendencies, these restrictions might be justified by other procompetitive tendencies or redeeming virtues. [] This is a closer question—at least in theory. The Dental Association argues that the three relevant restrictions are inextricably tied to a legitimate Association effort to restrict false or misleading advertising. The Association, the argument goes, had to prevent dentists from engaging in the kind of truthful, nondeceptive advertising that it banned in order effectively to stop dentists from making unverifiable claims about price or service quality, which claims would mislead the consumer.

The problem with this or any similar argument is an empirical one. Notwithstanding its theoretical plausibility, the record does not bear out such a claim. The Commission, which is expert in the area of false and misleading advertising, was uncertain whether petitioner had even made the claim. It characterized petitioner's efficiencies argument as rooted in the (unproved) factual assertion that its ethical rule "challenges only advertising that is false or misleading." Regardless, the Court of Appeals wrote, in respect to the price restrictions, that "the record provides no evidence that the rule has in fact led to increased disclosure and transparency of dental pricing." With respect to quality advertising, the Commission stressed that the Association "offered no convincing argument, let alone evidence, that consumers of dental services have been, or are likely to be, harmed by the broad categories of advertising it restricts." Nor did the Court of Appeals think that the Association's unsubstantiated contention that "claims about quality are inherently unverifiable and therefore misleading" could "justify banning all quality claims without regard to whether they are, in fact, false or misleading."

With one exception, my own review of the record reveals no significant evidentiary support for the proposition that the Association's members must agree to ban truthful price and quality advertising in order to stop untruthful claims. The one exception is the obvious fact that one can stop untruthful advertising if one prohibits all advertising. But since the Association made virtually no effort to sift the false from the true, [] that fact does not make out a valid antitrust defense. []

In the usual Sherman Act § 1 case, the defendant bears the burden of establishing a procompetitive justification. [] And the Court of Appeals was correct when it concluded that no such justification had been established here.

D

I shall assume that the Commission must prove one additional circumstance, namely, that the Association's restraints would likely have made a real difference in the marketplace. The Commission, disagreeing with the ALJ on this single point, found that the Association did possess enough market power to make a difference. In at least one region of California, the mid-Peninsula, its members accounted for more than 90% of the marketplace; on average they accounted for 75%. In addition, entry by new dentists into the market place is fairly difficult. Dental education is expensive (leaving graduates of dental school with $50,000–$100,000 of debt), as is opening a new dentistry office (which costs $75,000–$100,000). And Dental Association members believe membership in the Association is important, valuable, and recognized as such by the public.

These facts, in the Court of Appeals' view, were sufficient to show "enough market power to harm competition through [the Association's] standard setting in the area of advertising." 128 F.3d, at 730. And that conclusion is correct. . . .

II

In the Court's view, the legal analysis conducted by the Court of Appeals was insufficient, and the Court remands the case for a more thorough application of the rule of reason. But in what way did the Court of Appeals fail? I find the Court's answers to this question unsatisfactory—when one divides the overall Sherman Act question into its traditional component parts and adheres to traditional judicial practice for allocating the burdens of persuasion in an antitrust case.

Did the Court of Appeals misconceive the anticompetitive tendencies of the restrictions?

[The majority] criticizes the Court of Appeals for failing to recognize that "the restrictions at issue here are very far from a total ban on price or discount advertising" and that "the particular restrictions on professional advertising could have different effects from those 'normally' found in the commercial world, even to the point of promoting competition...."

The problem with these statements is that the Court of Appeals did consider the relevant differences. It rejected the legal "treatment" customarily applied "to classic horizontal agreements to limit output or price competition"—i.e., the FTC's (alternative) per se approach. It did so because the Association's "policies do not, on their face, ban truthful nondeceptive ads"; instead, they "have been enforced in a way that restricts truthful advertising." [] ...

Did the Court of Appeals misunderstand the nature of an anticompetitive effect? The Court says:

"If quality advertising actually induces some patients to obtain more care than they would in its absence, then restricting such advertising would reduce the demand for dental services, not the supply; and ... the producers' supply ... is normally relevant in determining whether a ... limitation has the anticompetitive effect of artificially raising prices." Ante, at ___.

But if the Court means this statement as an argument against the anticompetitive tendencies that flow from an agreement not to advertise service quality, I believe it is the majority, and not the Court of Appeals, that is mistaken. An agreement not to advertise, say, "gentle care" is anticompetitive because it imposes an artificial barrier against each dentist's independent decision to advertise gentle care. That barrier, in turn, tends to inhibit those dentists who want to supply gentle care from getting together with those customers who want to buy gentle care. There is adequate reason to believe that tendency present in this case.

Did the Court of Appeals inadequately consider possible procompetitive justifications? The Court seems to think so ... The basic question is whether this, or some other, theoretically redeeming virtue in fact offsets the restrictions' anticompetitive effects in this case. Both court and Commission adequately answered that question.

The Commission found that the defendant did not make the necessary showing that a redeeming virtue existed in practice. ...

With respect to the restraint on advertising across-the-board discounts, the majority summarizes its concerns as follows: "Assuming that the record in fact supports the conclusion that the [Association's] disclosure rules essentially bar advertisement of [such] discounts, it does not obviously follow that such a ban would have a net anticompetitive effect here." I accept, rather than assume, the premise: The FTC found that the disclosure rules did bar advertisement of across-the-board discounts, and that finding is supported by substantial evidence. And I accept as literally true the conclusion that the Court says follows from that premise, namely, that "net anticompetitive effects" do not "obviously "follow from that premise. But obviousness is not the point. With respect to any of the three restraints found by the Commission, whether "net anticompetitive effects" follow is a matter of how the Commission, and, here, the Court of Appeals, have answered the questions I laid out at the beginning. Has the Commission shown that the restriction has anticompetitive tendencies? It has. Has the Association nonetheless shown offsetting virtues? It has not. Has the Commission shown market power sufficient for it to believe that the restrictions will likely make a real world difference? It has.

The upshot, in my view, is that the Court of Appeals, applying ordinary antitrust principles, reached an unexceptional conclusion. It is the same legal conclusion that this Court itself reached in Indiana Federation—a much closer case than this one. There the Court found that an agreement by dentists not to submit dental X rays to insurers violated the rule of reason. The anticompetitive tendency of that agreement was to reduce competition among dentists in respect to their willingness to submit X rays to insurers, []—a matter in respect to which consumers are relatively indifferent, as compared to advertising of price discounts and service quality, the matters at issue here. The redeeming virtue in Indiana Federation was the alleged undesirability of having insurers consider a range of matters when deciding whether treatment was justified—a virtue no less plausible, and no less proved, than the virtue offered here. The "power" of the dentists to enforce their agreement was no greater than that at issue here (control of 75% to 90% of the relevant markets). It is difficult to see how the two cases can be reconciled.

* * *

I would note that the form of analysis I have followed is not rigid; it admits of some variation according to the circumstances. The important point, however, is that its allocation of the burdens of persuasion reflects a gradual evolution within the courts over a period of many years. That evolution represents an effort carefully to blend the procompetitive objectives of the law of antitrust with administrative necessity. I hope that this case does not represent an abandonment of that basic, and important, form of analysis.

For these reasons, I respectfully dissent from Part III of the Court's opinion.

Insert on page 674 immediately above Notes and Questions:

U.S. DEPARTMENT OF JUSTICE, BUSINESS REVIEW LETTER RE: SANTA FE MANAGED CARE ORGANIZATION

February 12, 1997

* * *

This letter responds to your request on behalf of Santa Fe, New Mexico Managed Care Organization ("SFMCO") . . . seeking the issuance of a business review letter under the Department of Justice's Business Review Procedure. SFMCO will be a provider-controlled network organization that will offer hospital and physician services to health insurance plans and other third-party payers using capitation and global fee contracts as well as other types of contract arrangements. Based on the information you have provided and our interviews with a number of payers and providers knowledgeable about the market, the Department has no present intention to challenge under the antitrust laws the formation of SFMCO's proposed network.

[SFMCO will be organized as a nonprofit corporation; its members will be (1) St. Vincent's Hospital ("St. Vincent's"), a nonprofit hospital which is the only acute care hospital open to the general public within approximately 60 miles of Santa Fe, and (2) approximately 70–75 physician members. Both St Vincent's and the physician members will share substantial financial risk for SFMCO's operations].

* * *

SFMCO will also subcontract individually with non-member physicians to provide services as part of SFMCO's physician panel. The non-member participating physicians will not share financial risk with SFMCO's members. Any Santa Fe physician who is not a SFMCO member will be eligible to subcontract as a non-member participating physician.

Both SFMCO's members and its non-member participating physicians will participate in the network on a non-exclusive basis. There will be no restriction on their ability to compete with the SFMCO venture, and they will not be discouraged from joining other networks or contracting directly with health benefit plans. You state that SFMCO is intended to be a de jure and de facto non-exclusive network.

SFMCO's primary interest is in negotiating risk contracts with payers. SFMCO's By–Laws define "risk contracts" as agreements between SFMCO and third-party payers that include a 20 percent or greater payment withhold or capitated or percentage of premium payment arrangements or other risk payment methodology. In further describing these provisions, you cite and quote language from the Statements of Antitrust Enforcement Policy in Health Care, issued by the Department and the Federal Trade Commission in August 1996 (the "Policy Statements"). From this description, we understand, and assume for purposes of this business review, that in all SFMCO's risk contracts SFMCO's member physicians will share "substantial financial risk" as that term is described in the Policy Statements.

For contracts that do not involve substantial financial risk sharing, SFMCO will act as a "messenger" to facilitate contracting between third-party payers and SFMCO's individual member and non-member participating physicians. We understand from your letters and your telephone conversations with staff, and we assume for purposes of this letter, that all such messenger arrangements will carefully avoid agreements among competing network providers on prices and price-related terms, will not facilitate collective decision-making by network providers, and will satisfy the description of such messenger arrangements found in Statement 9 of the Policy Statements.

With three exceptions, SFMCO's member physicians together with any physician employees of St. Vincent's will not exceed 30 percent of the physicians with offices in the City of Santa Fe in any physician specialty. The exceptions, which are discussed below, are for (1) physician specialties in which all the SFMCO member physicians in the specialty are in a preexisting integrated practice group that has not been formed or expanded to avoid the 30 percent limitation, (2) family practitioners and internists who, you have told us, are good substitutes for each other in the Santa Fe area, and (3) pediatricians.

The non-member participating physicians will subcontract individually with SFMCO to provide physician services as part of SFMCO's provider panel. The subcontract will establish a capitated payment as compensation for non-member participating primary care physicians and a discounted fee-for-service schedule for all other non-member participating physicians. Unlike SFMCO's member physicians (whose compensation will be linked to SFMCO's overall financial performance through a formula that will make them liable for a share of SFMCO's deficits and eligible for a share of SFMCO's surplus), the non-member participating physicians' compensation will not depend on the overall economic performance of SFMCO.

SFMCO will bear, and not pass through to payers, the risk that its non-member participating physicians might deliver services inefficiently. No increases in fee schedules or capitation payments for non-member participating physicians will be automatically passed on to any payer; SFMCO, through its members, will absorb any such increases. In addition, no contract between SFMCO and a payer will be structured so that changes in SFMCO's payments to non-member participating physicians will automatically affect payments to SFMCO from the payer. Similarly, payments to non-member participating physicians will not depend on, or automatically vary in response to, the provisions of SFMCO's contracts with payers. You represent that SFMCO will be structured so that it will have the incentive to bargain down the compensation to be paid to non-member participating physicians.

No third-party payer will directly compensate a non-member participating physician for that physician's services pursuant to a contract with SFMCO. However, on behalf of SFMCO, a payer may administer payments to all physicians on SFMCO's provider panel, including non-member participating physicians. In all cases, the ultimate payment risk will remain with SFMCO.

We understand that non-member participating physicians will not participate in any discussion, negotiation, decision or agreement concerning fees or fee-related contract provisions for member physicians or each other....

Antitrust Analysis

As proposed, SFMCO appears to be an economically integrated joint venture designed with the stated purpose of producing significant efficiencies that should benefit third-party payers and their subscribers. To the extent that competitors will be participating in price or price-related agreements, they will share substantial financial risk in a manner that will create incentives to achieve efficiencies. In all situations not involving substantial financial risk sharing, SFMCO will utilize "messenger" arrangements that should avoid agreements on price and price-related terms if implemented carefully. Consequently, we have analyzed SFMCO's proposal under the rule of reason.

* * *

SFMCO will, with three exceptions, limit the sum of its members and the physician employees of St. Vincent's in any physician specialty to 30 percent of the physicians in that specialty with offices in the City of Santa Fe ... The first exception to the 30 percent limitation is for a preexisting integrated physician group not formed or expanded to avoid the 30 percent limitation. Where all SFMCO members in a specialty belong to such a preexisting group, the group's inclusion in SFMCO would not increase market concentration or power in that physician specialty.

The second exception is for family practitioners and internists. (We have assumed for purposes of this business review that you are correct in asserting that these physicians are good substitutes for each other in the Santa Fe area.) We understand that of the 50 internists and family practitioners in the Santa Fe area, 14 are expected to become SFMCO members and an additional four are employed by St. Vincent's. Thus, 36 percent of the internists and family practitioners will be SFMCO members or employees of the hospital. Nevertheless, we have concluded that the percentage is not so large that it is likely to cause anticompetitive effects under the circumstances and assumptions described in this letter.

The third exception to the 30 percent limitation is for pediatricians. There are a total of only 11 pediatricians in the area. Of these, two will become SFMCO members and an additional six are employed by St. Vincent's (some on a part-time basis). The two pediatricians that will become SFMCO members constitute a fully integrated group practice.

The two member pediatricians plus the six pediatrician employees of St. Vincent's are more than 70 percent of the pediatricians in the area. Although SFMCO points out that the six hospital-employed pediatricians (as well as the hospital-employed internists and family practitioners) will not be SFMCO members, the hospital will be a member and its interest in SFMCO could affect how and the extent to which it will make those physicians available either to payers contracting outside SFMCO or as SFMCO non-member participating physicians. However, you have pointed out that the SFMCO member pediatricians will be a small minority among the primary care physicians whose compensation will be paid out of a single fixed revenue pool. Since paying the pediatricians supra competitive amounts would reduce the revenues available to compensate the other physicians participating in the pool, those other physicians will have strong incentives to keep the pediatricians' compensation at competitive levels. This is more likely to be the case here since neither the six St. Vincent's pediatricians nor St. Vincent's itself will be involved in any of SFMCO's physician pricing discussions or decisions.

Nevertheless, we are concerned that managed care plans desiring to enter the market in Santa Fe could have difficulty obtaining sufficient pediatric care for their enrollees without SFMCO. Despite the presence in the market of family practitioners who do provide care to children, the availability of pediatrician services is important to the marketability of managed care plans. Thus, it is particularly important that both the member and non-member participating pediatricians in SFMCO will in fact participate non-exclusively as you have represented. The conclusion reached in this letter is based in significant part on this representation, and we caution that particular care must be taken to ensure that competition is not injured because of the concentration of pediatricians in SFMCO's provider panel.

Another matter of considerable concern is SFMCO's proposal to supplement its panel of physician members by subcontracting with additional physicians to offer payers a panel that could include virtually all of the physicians in Santa Fe. The Department has entered into final judgments that permitted such subcontracting arrangements where there appeared to be a demand for multi-specialty physician panels with high percentages of the physicians in the market, where the subcontract arrangements created divergence of economic interest between the subcontracting physicians and the member physicians so that the members had an incentive to control the network's costs from the physician subcontracts, and where market conditions otherwise indicated that the subcontract arrangements creating divergence of interest were sufficient to make exclusive behavior unlikely.[91]

SFMCO asserts that payers in the Santa Fe area desire physician panels that are as broad as possible and certainly more inclusive than 30 percent of the physicians in each physician specialty. SFMCO believes that managed care plans in the Santa Fe area need to offer as large a physician panel as possible in order to be attractive to payers. The information we have obtained from payers in the Santa Fe area is generally consistent with these representations, and we have assumed these representations to be correct for purposes of this business review letter.

SFMCO's proposed subcontracting arrangements also appear to be structured in a manner to create a divergence of economic interest between SFMCO's members and the subcontracting participating physicians that will reduce the likelihood of anticompetitive conduct. SFMCO will bear the ultimate responsibility for payment of compensation to the non-member participating physicians. Unlike the subcontracting physicians whose compensation will not depend on the overall economic performance of SFMCO, the compensation of SFMCO's members will be directly and substantially linked to how well SFMCO performs financially. Member physicians will be both liable for a share of SFMCO's deficits and eligible for a share of the venture's surplus. SFMCO members will have the incentive to bargain down the compensation to be paid to non-member participating physicians.

We have spoken to payers, employers, physicians, and others, and reviewed documents and other information provided by SFMCO. While our investigation indicates the existence of significant actual and potential competition to SFMCO, clearly SFMCO's proposal creates the potential for anticompetitive conduct with harmful effects on consumers. In some physician specialties, more than 30 percent of the physicians in the area will be joining SFMCO as members who will set fees and decide other competitively sensitive matters for the venture. In addition, the members will be subcontracting with

---

91. See, e.g., Competitive Impact Statements in United States v. Health Choice of Northwest Missouri, Inc., Case No. 95–6171–CV–SJ–6 (W.D. Mo.; filed Sept. 13, 1995), 60 Fed. Reg. 51808, 51815 (October 3, 1995); United States and State of Connecticut v. Health Care Partners, Inc., Case No. 395–CV–01946–RNC (D. Conn.; filed Sept. 13, 1995), 60 Fed. Reg. 52018, 52020 (Oct. 4, 1995).

most, if not all, of the remaining physicians in the area. If the members and non-member physicians in fact view their interests as congruent, they could easily assert market power with serious anticompetitive consequences.

However, SFMCO's provider-controlled network also has the potential for creating significant efficiencies by offering payers capitation and global fee arrangements that are not now generally available in the Santa Fe area. These benefits must be weighed against the potential for competitive harm. Taking this into account and under all the circumstances here, we are unable to say that SFMCO's plan will likely cause anticompetitive harm if it is implemented carefully as proposed.

We have also considered the possible effects of including St. Vincent's in the network, since it is the only acute care inpatient hospital in the area. The inclusion of St. Vincent's will not reduce competition among hospitals, and we have found no reason to conclude that its inclusion in the network is likely to cause anticompetitive vertical effects.

For these reasons, and based on the facts you have represented, the Department of Justice has no present intention of challenging the formation of SFMCO's proposed network. However, we strongly emphasize that if in practice its formation and operation causes anticompetitive harm, the Department remains free to bring whatever action or proceeding it subsequently comes to believe is required by the public interest. . . .

> Sincerely,
> Joel I. Klein
> Assistant Attorney General

Insert on page 674 at the end of Note 1:

Consider the Department of Justice's Business Review Letter in the Sante Fe Managed Care Organization matter. Specifically, which factors justified approval where safety zone thresholds were exceeded in certain specialties? Are you satisfied with the Department's explanation concerning its decision to permit SFMCO to include 70% of all pediatricians in the relevant market? Finally, note that the organization has the potential to include 100% of all physicians, as non-members may subcontract with the organization in the future. What assurances satisfied the Department of Justice that this arrangement would not enable SFMCO to push prices to anticompetitive levels?

Insert at the end of page 675 after Note 4:

Note on Physician Unions

Of the roughly 750,000 practicing doctors in the United States, only about 42,000 are members of labor unions, some 6,000 to 9,000 of whom are residents employed at hospitals. Recently, however, there has been a strong upsurge in interest in joining unions. Physicians have been attracted by promises that unions will enable them to "level the playing field" in contractual bargaining with managed care entities and may improve their ability to assure quality of care for their patients. See Robert L. Lowes, Strength in Numbers: Could Doctor Unions Really Be the Answer? 75 Med. Econ. 114 (1998); Steven Greenhouse, Angered by H.M.O.'s Treatment, More Doctors Are Joining Unions, N.Y. Times, Feb. 4, 1999.

Because many activities of unions, most notably collective bargaining over salaries or compensation, involve collective agreements by competitors, physician unions raise obvious antitrust problems. The critical issue facing these unions is whether they qualify for the labor exemption under the antitrust laws. This exemption has two parts: (1) a statutory exemption, found in Sections 6 and 20 of the Clayton Act and Section 4 of the Norris LaGuardia Act, which together combine to protect unions and their members carrying out their legitimate objectives and permits strikes and boycotts in the course of disputes "concerning terms and conditions of employment" and (2) a non-statutory exemption that harmonizes antitrust policy with the National Labor Relations Act of 1935 and extends antitrust immunity to certain concerted actions involving unions and employers. Both the statutory and non-statutory exemptions require the activity to arise out of a "labor dispute," which must involve a labor organization comprised only of employees, not independent contractors, and the promotion of legitimate labor interests as opposed to entrepreneurial or nonlabor interests unrelated to the employer-employee relationship. An additional qualification is that employees holding managerial or supervisory positions are not authorized to bargain collectively through labor organizations under the NRLA. NLRB v. Yeshiva University, 444 U.S. 672 (1980).

The upshot of this is that pursuant to the antitrust labor exemption physicians who are employees and occupy non-supervisory positions may collectively bargain through labor unions. Thus, unions have organized doctors who are employees of hospitals, HMOs and employer organizations. See casebook p. 484 and supra this supplement. Recently, however, independent doctors participating in managed care plans have sought to unionize claiming that they are in effect "employees" of such organizations because the latter exercises extensive control over their practices and have strong economic leverage over them. See Edward B. Hirshfeld, Physicians, Union and Antitrust, 32 J. Health L. 39 (1999).

The government has challenged several attempts to organize physician unions that did not meet the prevailing standard for an exemption under the antitrust laws. In FTC and the Commonwealth of Puerto Rico v. College of Physicians–Surgeons of Puerto Rico, 5 Trade Reg. Rep. (CCH) § 335 (D.P.R. Oct. 2, 1997), the FTC alleged that the College, a quasi-public organization consisting of all physicians in Puerto Rico, engaged in an illegal boycott when it held a 72–hour protest where members refused to provide services except on an emergency basis to protest health reform legislation that had a capitation rate that was too low in the view of members. The College agreed to a Consent Order with the FTC barring future boycotts and to payment of a $300,000 fine. See also, United States v. Federation of Physicians and Dentists, Inc., No. 98–475 (D. Del. Aug. 12, 1998) (civil action charging a physician union consisting of nearly all orthopedic surgeons in Delaware with organizing a boycott and jointly terminating contracts in order to resist fee reduction proposed by Blue Cross of Delaware with Blue Cross).

Legislative Proposals. At the time this Supplement was written, Congress was considering a proposal to grant health care professionals the same treatment afforded to bargaining unions under the NLRA. If enacted, the bill would legalize per se conduct such as collective negotiations by physicians on both price and non-price issues when undertaken in compliance with the legislation. Quality Health–Care Coalition Act of 1999, H.R. 1304 106th Cong. (1999). The principal sponsor of the bill, Representative Thomas Campbell, observed that it would allow health care professionals to form their own associations to bargain with HMOs and other insurers on an even playing field. This, he asserted, would inure to the benefit of consumers. "It's the best way I can see to let the market deal with the complaints so many health care professionals have raised with HMOs." Physicians: Judiciary Committee to Consider Bill Allowing Doctors to Bargain Collectively, Health Care Daily (BNA), July 24, 1998. Chairman Pitofsky of the Federal Trade Commission criticized the Campbell Bill in testimony to Congress as unnecessary to protect consumer interests in quality of care and as likely to discourage vigorous price and quality competition among managed care organizations that would benefit consumers. See Statement of Robert Pitofsky, Chairman, Federal Trade Commission, before the Committee of Judiciary, U.S. House of Representatives, concerning H.R. 4277 (July 29, 1998). How effective do you think the proposed exemption will be in assuring quality of care for consumers? At lessening managed care "abuses"? Do physicians have other means at their disposal to effectively advocate for patients' rights and high quality care? Is it likely in your view that physicians will use the exemption to negotiate in their self-interests, i.e., for higher fees and less restrictive managed care controls?

Insert on page 696, at the end of note 2:

May "unfair" business practices be challenged as business torts even though they may not constitute violations of the antitrust laws? In Brokerage Concepts, Inc. v. U.S. Healthcare, Inc., 140 F.3d 494 (3d Cir. 1998), the Court of Appeals overturned a jury verdict that found an antitrust violation in a case in which a prominent HMO allegedly coerced a self-insured pharmacy chain to switch third-party administrators (TPAs) which serviced the chain's employee health plan. The plaintiff claimed that the requirement that it use the defendant HMO's subsidiary as its TPA in order to remain a part of the HMO's pharmacy network constituted an illegal tying agreement or coerced reciprocal dealing under § 1 of the Sherman Act. The Third Circuit found no antitrust offense, questioning whether a sale transaction actually existed. Applying the Rule of Reason, it went on to hold that the HMO's lack of market power precluded a claim under the Sherman Act. Id. At the same time, however, the court allowed the plaintiff's claim for intentional interference with contractual or prospective contractual relations under state law to go to trial. A jury subsequently awarded the plaintiffs $105,000 on the tortuous interference charge and rejected the defense that the conduct was justified by a "business competitor's privilege." Under the charge to the jury, the latter defense would not apply where a defendant used "wrongful means" to advance its interest in competing for business (which the court defined as "taking away a competitor's business by applying economic pressure in an area that is unrelated to the field in which the parties compete"). See Contract Disputes: U.S. Healthcare's Competitor's Privilege Defense Fails to Sway Pennsylvania Jury, 8 Health L. Rptr. (BNA), Feb. 4, 1999. On the question of whether tort law should apply a different standard than antitrust law, see Marina Lao, Tortious Interference and the Federal Antitrust Law of Vertical Restraints, 83 Iowa L. Rev. 35 (1997).

Insert on page 711 at the end of Note 3:

The government's losing streak in hospital merger cases came to an end with the district court's decision in Federal Trade Commission and State of Missouri v. Tenet Healthcare Corporation, 17 F. Supp.2d 937 (E.D.Mo.1998). The key issue in the case was the geographic market and the district court, applying the Eighth Circuit's "dynamic" inquiry into where patients would travel for hospital services, accepted the government's contention that the market for inpatient acute care services supplied by the merging hospitals was local. Notably, the court relied heavily on the testimony of employers and third-party payers about their own likely responses to price increases and the responses of local citizens to options in the marketplace.

Insert on page 712 at the end of Note 4:

See also FTC v. Cardinal Health, Inc., 12 F. Supp.2d 34 (D.D.C.1998) in which a district court enjoined two mergers involving wholesale drug distributors. The court rejected defendants' argument that the relevant market should include self-distribution by large pharmaceutical chains that purchased and warehoused their own pharmaceuticals directly from manufacturers.

Insert on page 713 at the end of Note 5:

Managed Care Mergers The health insurance industry has witnessed a rapid succession of major mergers. In the years 1993 to 1998, a dozen health insurers were acquired by the six principal remaining companies: Aetna, Cigna, United Healthcare, Foundation Health Systems, Pacificare and Wellpoint Health Networks. The most recent and largest acquisition is Aetna's proposed buyout of Prudential Health Care, which was the subject of a proposed consent decree filed jointly by the U.S. Department of Justice and the Texas Attorney General's Office. U.S. v. Aetna Inc. (N.D. Tex., No. 3–99 CV 1398–H, proposed consent order filed 6/21/99). As a condition of obtaining approval of the merger, the decree requires that Aetna divest certain HMOs operated by a subsidiary in Texas. The government's complaint contended that the proposed merger would have made Aetna the dominant provider of health maintenance organization and HMO-point of service plans in Houston and Dallas, with 63 percent and 42 percent of enrollees in those areas. Is a product market consisting only of HMO and HMO–POS plans defensible? What factual issues might have been raised by defendants had this case gone to trial? What evidence and testimony would the government have relied upon? Review the First Circuit's decision in U.S. Healthcare v. Healthsource, Inc. (page 683 of the casebook) in formulating your responses to these questions. As an alternative theory of harm, the government alleged that the market would reduce competition in the market for physician services. The complaint states, "the proposed acquisition will give Aetna the ability to depress physicians' reimbursement rates in Houston and Dallas, likely leading to a reduction in quantity or degradation in quality of physicians' services." Assuming that physicians in the relevant markets are reimbursed by non-HMO and HMO POS plans (including Medicare and Medicaid) and that such reimbursement constitutes, say three-quarters of total reimbursements in the markets, how might the government prove its theory of competitive harm?

In FTC v. Cardinal Health, Inc., supra, the court carefully analyzed the defendants' rebuttal claims that ease of entry into the wholesale drug distribution market should obviate competitive concerns. The court found that, despite a few examples of successful entry by new drug wholesalers, the defendants had failed to demonstrate that significant and effective entry was likely given various barriers that had impeded or slowed new competitors' effectiveness in the market. 12 F. Supp. 2d at 56–59. The court also rejected the defendants' claim that powerful buyers would likely offset the defendants' market power. Id. at 59–60.

Insert on page 715 immediately after note 9:

Note on Physician Mergers

Rapid consolidation among providers has focused antitrust attention on physician mergers. In the only case thus far decided by the courts, HTI Health Services v. Quorum Health Group, 960 F.Supp. 1104 (S.D.Miss.1997), the district court refused to enjoin a merger of the two largest physician clinics in Vicksburg, Mississippi with one of two hospitals in town. Notably, the court held that plaintiff had properly alleged four distinct physician service markets: primary care, general surgery, urology, and otolaryngology; in addition, it accepted a primary care sub-market for pediatrics. However, the court rejected plaintiff's argument that a distinct market for managed care purchasers could be established based on discounting practices. The case is notable for its treatment of the competitive implications of the merger in these markets notwithstanding the extremely high market shares held by the parties. For example, with respect to urology, the court noted there were only two urologists in the market and concluded that it was inconceivable that Congress had intended for the Clayton Act to prohibit the two physicians from practicing together under the same roof suggesting that the market was a "natural monopoly." 960 F. Supp at 1128. With respect to primary care services in which the merged entity would control between 58% and 70% of the market (which it defined to include general practitioners, family practitioners and internists, but not ob/gyns), the court emphasized that the absence of barriers to entry effectively obviated concerns about the defendant's potential exercise of market power. Id. at 1133. In this connection, the court emphasized that the plaintiff hospital (Columbia/HCA) had a highly successful record in recruiting new physicians into the market to serve its facility.

The antitrust enforcement agencies have also reviewed several physician mergers. Because these investigations involved acquisitions of groups practicing in certain specialty areas, analysis of market definition and entry were critical. For example, in examining a proposed merger between a group of cardiovascular thoracic surgeons and a group of vascular surgeons, the Justice Department analyzed the specific vascular procedures that the two groups performed and defined the relevant product markets based on sixty or more overlapping procedures performed by these specialists. In clearing the merger, the Department emphasized the fact that payers needed to include only a very few peripheral vascular surgeons (the relevant market) in a managed care network and that there were sufficient independent providers of such services who were not a part of the merging groups to obviate competitive concerns raised by the high market shares of the merging parties. In addition, it noted that sponsored entry or expansion by existing competing groups would defeat attempts to raise prices. Letter from Joel I. Klein, Assistant Attorney General, Antitrust Division, U.S. Department of Justice to Bob D. Tucker (Re: CVT Surgical Center and Vascular Surgery Associates) (Apr. 16, 1997). By contrast, in another business review letter, the Department indicated that there was a substantial likelihood that it would challenge a proposed merger of two physician groups of board certified gastroenterologists in Allentown, Pennsylvania. Letter from Joel I. Klein, Assistant Attorney General, Antitrust Division, U.S. Department of Justice to Donald H. Lipson (Gastroenterology Associates Limited, et al.) (July 7, 1997). The Department concluded that although there was some overlap in the procedures performed by gastroenterologists and other physician specialties, gastroenterologists could probably collectively raise prices because managed care organizations required gastroenterologists on their panels as a "critical selling point." The Department also concluded that the service market was highly localized because of patients' "psychological barriers" to traveling even a small distance for treatment.

Note on Virtual Mergers

In recent years, many hospitals have entered into agreements with other hospitals to substantially integrate their operations and governance without undertaking a full-blown acquisition or merger. They do this through various contractual arrangements, including strategic alliances and joint operating agreements, pursuant to which control of the hospitals is typically ceded to a single board or other entity. These affiliations often involve at least one nonprofit or religiously affiliated hospital that is reluctant to give up its own identity or autonomy in a merger. A critical issue in these arrangements is whether the hospitals will be treated as a single entity for antitrust purposes. If it is not, the affiliated hospitals are viewed as separate firms and their joint actions on pricing and other competitive variables may constitute per se violations of Section 1 of the Sherman Act. If, on the other hand, the affiliation is deemed to create a single entity, traditional merger analysis under Section 7 of the Clayton Act is applied. The most pertinent case law involves arrangements between parent and subsidiary corporations in which the courts have questioned whether single entity status is appropriate. In Copperweld Corp. v. Independence Tube Corp., 467 U.S. 752 (1984), the Supreme Court held that a parent corporation and its wholly-owned subsidiary constituted a single entity. Therefore the parent and subsidiary were incapable as a matter of law of conspiring under the Sherman Act. The Court emphasized that the parent-subsidiary relationship is distinguished by a complete unity of the entity's purposes and interests and also by the ability of the parent corporation to exercise its control to assure that the aligned interests are pursued. Application of these principles in the case of virtual mergers between hospitals entails a close factual examination of the specific control arrangements among the affiliated hospitals. The relevant questions would include whether one hospital retains veto power over significant transactions, the role of each hospital's board in choosing or replacing board members, the entity's individual control over strategic decisionmaking, budgets and contracting, and the parties' rights of termination. See generally Roxanne C. Busey, Antitrust Aspects of "Virtual Mergers" and Affiliations, Remarks before the American Health Lawyers Association Annual Meeting, July 1, 1998. The Attorney General of the State of New York has challenged the joint activities of one affiliation of competing hospitals as a per se price fixing and market allocation scheme. In its complaint, the State emphasized the lack of financial integration between the hospitals and other indicia of separateness to argue that the Copperweld doctrine would not apply. Toby G. Singer, Challenge in Poughkeepsie is First To "Virtual Mergers" in Health Care, 7 Health L. Rep. (BNA) 525, Mar. 26, 1998.

Chapter 11

HEALTH CARE COST AND ACCESS:
THE POLICY CONTEXT

Insert at page 718, above Section I:

Note: Recent Developments in Health Care Cost and Access

Since the 3rd edition of Health Law was published in 1997, the problems of access and cost control have gotten worse. There are now over 43 million uninsured Americans—one in six Americans and 10 million more than in 1989. The number of uninsured is growing at a rate of 100,000 a month, and in some states in the South and West, one in four persons is uninsured. This decline in insurance coverage has persisted despite strong economic growth.

Most of the uninsured are employed, and many are offered insurance through their employer. Between the mid–1980s and mid–1990s, however, the percentage of employers who paid the full cost of employee insurance policies declined from two thirds to one third, while the worker's share of premiums on average increased from 13% to 22%. In the face of higher premium costs, the proportion of workers who decline employer-sponsored health insurance has increased from one tenth in the mid–1980s to one quarter today. Though the decline in employment-related insurance seems to have stabilized in the past couple of years, the dramatic drop in the number of Medicaid recipients following welfare-reform (see Chapter 14 below) has continued to drive growth in the uninsured population. See O. Carrasquillo, et al., Going Bare: Trends in Health Insurance Coverage, 1989 Through 1996, 89 Am. J. Pub. Health 36 (1999). See also, Kenneth E. Thorpe and Curtis S. Florence, Why are Workers Uninsured? Employer–Sponsored Health Insurance in 1997, Health Aff., Mar./Apr. 1999 at 213.

For much of the mid–1990s, growth in the cost of medical care was held in check. Indeed, private health insurance premiums increased only .5% in 1996 and only about 2% in 1995 and 1997. Total health care costs grew at a slightly higher rate, driven by increases in spending for public programs, but public spending slowed dramatically in 1998 due to declining Medicaid enrollments and cost-control measures taken in the 1997 Balanced Budget Act, just as private spending increased. Experts predict that private insurance premiums will rise between 6% and 12% in 1999, as one time savings attributable to managed care are exhausted and insurers attempt to recoup losses suffered in the mid–1990s. Moreover, legislation and public opinion are forcing managed care organizations to back off of some of their most stringent cost control measures, allowing costs to rise again. Costs have risen most dramatically in recent years in the prescription drug sector, where cost increases have continued at the 13%–14% level.

If insurance costs increase in the next few years, as predicted, this will undoubtedly lead to further growth in the uninsured population as more employers and employees drop health insurance. Cost increases may also lead employers to switch from defined benefit to defined contribution health plans, leaving employees to absorb the increased premiums. See generally Shelia Smith, et al, The Next Ten Years of Health Spending: What does the Future Hold? 17 Health Aff., Sept./Oct. 1998 at 128; Paul B. Ginsberg and Jon R. Gabel, Tracking Health Care Costs: What's New in 1998? 17 Health Aff., Sept./Oct. 1998 at 141.

Insert at page 730:

Note: Recent Developments Regarding Health Reform

None of the three approaches to cost control discussed in the book has emerged as a clearly preferred policy alternative at the end of the decade. As many predicted, the MSA experiment put in place by HIPAA has failed dramatically. As of the end of 1997, only 42,000 persons had established MSAs, only about 16,000 of whom were previously uninsured. Sales seem to have slowed further in 1998. Although 54 insurers offered the plans when the experiment began, only 48 remained in the market at the end of 1997, and most had sold fewer than 1000 policies, with one insurer accounting for more than half of the policies. MSA plans are most often offered to highly-paid professionals, farmers and ranchers, partnership firms and association groups. No plans have stepped forward to offer MSAs to Medicare recipients under the 1997 Balanced Budget Act, which created the possibility of Medicare MSA plans. However elegant the theoretical arguments may be that support MSAs, almost nobody wants to purchase insurance that leaves the insured responsible for virtually all health care costs. See GAO, Medical Savings Accounts: Results from Surveys of Insurers (GAO/HEHS–99–34, 1998).

Since the death of the Clinton plan, there has been little discussion of managed competition as a strategy for reforming the national health care system as a whole. A number of states are collecting comparative health plan data, and Florida maintains its community health purchasing alliances for small businesses. However, the greatest interest in managed competition has been for public, not private, insurance programs. The Bipartisan Commission on the Future of Medicare considered and narrowly rejected a recommendation that Medicare be changed to a managed competition program, as discussed in Chapter 14 below.

There is also no significant political support currently for a comprehensive national health or social insurance programs. Nevertheless, the proportion of health care financed by public programs continues to expand steadily. While the public sector paid for only 40.5% of health care in 1990, by 1996 it funded 46.4%. A number of states, notably Hawaii, Minnesota, Oregon, Washington, and Tennessee, have expanded Medicaid coverage or created special programs for uninsured families. The most dramatic program expansion in the recent past has come in the Children's Health Insurance Program, established by the 1997 Balanced Budget Act (Pub.L. 105–33, § 4901). As of the end of the first year of the program, 828,000 previously uninsured children were enrolled in the program. About half of the states have implemented the CHIP program by expanding Medicaid coverage for children, the other half have established new programs or combined Medicaid expansion with new programs. The CHIP expansion, however, has been largely offset by declines in Medicaid coverage of families following the end of the Aid to Families with Dependent Children program. 675,000 persons, including 400,000 children, have lost health insurance because of welfare reform as of this writing.

Congress' other major recent effort to expand insurance coverage, the Health Insurance Portability and Accountability Act of 1996 (described at pages 824–833 in the text) has probably made it easier for some persons to maintain insurability while changing jobs, but has not had an easily measurable effect on the numbers of the uninsured. This is true for several reasons. First, many of the reforms found in HIPAA had already been adopted by a number of states, and thus HIPAA had little effect in these states. Second, HIPAA's guaranteed access to individual coverage for persons losing group coverage only applies in states that do not have an "alternative mechanism" to provide coverage, and two-thirds of the states have relied on high-risk pools and other preexisting mechanisms to essentially opt out of HIPAA. Third, and perhaps most important, HIPAA does nothing to guaranty affordability, as opposed to accessibility, of individual policies. A GAO study found that insurers were charging rates 140%—600% above their normal rates for HIPAA individual policies. Moreover, insurers seem to have adopted strategies, at least initially, aimed at avoiding HIPAA insureds, such as not offering commissions to agents who sold HIPAA policies. In sum, incremental regulatory solutions do not seem to be the best approach to expanding insurance coverage, though they may "fix" discrete and limited problems. See GAO, Health Insurance Standards: New Federal Law Creates Challenges for Consumers, Insurers, Regulators (GAO/HEHS–98–67, 1998); Robert Kuttner, The Kassebaum–Kennedy Bill—The Limits of Incrementalism, 337 New Eng. J. Med. 64 (1997).

The most politically feasible approach to the problem of the uninsured may be to offer tax relief, in the form of tax deductions or credits, to those who purchase private insurance. Amendments to the tax law in the Health Insurance Portability and Accountability Act of 1996, as further amended in 1997, extended the tax deduction long offered to employees to the self-employed, but under a phase-in that does not reach 100% deductibility until 2007. Also, the legislation does nothing to help those who are uninsured but not self-employed. Proposals currently before Congress would extend and speed up the implementation of these deductions. Deductions, of course, help wealthy taxpayers in higher brackets more than poorer taxpayers, and do nothing for taxpayers whose income is too small to pay taxes at all.

Alternatively a current proposal by Dick Armey, the House Majority Leader, would offer families a tax credit of $1000 per year per adult and $500 per child up to $3000 per year to purchase insurance. The tax credit would be refundable, and thus help poor as well as wealthy taxpayers. A similar proposal has been put forward by the National Center for Policy Analysis, and is available at their website, www.ncpa.org. Under the NCPA proposal, unclaimed credits would be allocated to the states in block grants to assist low income uninsureds. Representative Thomas and others in the House are also pushing tax credit proposals that would de-link health insurance from the workplace.

The tax credits offered by these proposals, however, are not nearly enough to purchase health insurance in many markets. Moreover, unless insurance underwriting practices are regulated, insurance may become affordable to the healthy, but remain unaffordable to the sick, even with the help of the credit. Tax credits could undermine our current employment-based system if employers decide to simply let their employees take the credit and fend for themselves. At this writing, in the summer of 1999, some tax relief to support the purchase of private insurance seems the most approach to the problem of the uninsured with the most political plausibility.

Chapter 12

ACCESS TO HEALTH CARE: THE OBLIGATION TO PROVIDE CARE

Insert at page 770, before Notes and Questions:

ROBERTS v. GALEN OF VIRGINIA, INC.

Supreme Court of the United States, 1999.
525 U.S. 249.

PER CURIAM.

The Emergency Medical Treatment and Active Labor Act, [ ] [EMTALA] places obligations of screening and stabilization upon hospitals and emergency rooms who receive patients suffering from an "emergency medical condition." The Court of Appeals held that in order to recover in a suit alleging a violation of § 1395dd(b), a plaintiff must prove that the hospital acted with an improper motive in failing to stabilize her. Finding no support for such a requirement in the text of the statute, we reverse.

* * *

Petitioner Wanda Johnson was run over by a truck in May 1992, and was rushed to respondent's hospital ... * * * Johnson had been severely injured and had suffered serious injuries to her brain, spine, right leg, and pelvis. After about six weeks' stay at Humana, during which time Johnson's health remained in a volatile state, respondent's agents arranged for her transfer to the Crestview Health Care Facility ... * * * Johnson was transferred to Crestview on July 24, 1992, but upon arrival at that facility, her condition deteriorated significantly. Johnson was taken to the Midwest Medical Center ... where she remained for many months and incurred substantial medical expenses as a result of her deterioration. * * * Plaintiff Jane Roberts, Johnson's guardian, then filed this federal action under § 1395dd(d) of EMTALA, alleging violations of § 1395dd(b) of the Act.

The District Court granted summary judgment for respondents on the grounds that the plaintiffs had failed to show that " 'either the medical opinion that Johnson was stable or the decision to authorize her transfer was caused by an improper motive.' "The Court of Appeals affirmed, holding that in order to state a claim in an EMTALA suit alleging a violation of § 1395dd(b)'s stabilization requirement, a plaintiff must show that the hospital's inappropriate stabilization resulted from an improper motive such as one involving the indigency, race, or sex of the patient. [ ] In order to decide whether [ ] EMTALA imposes such a requirement, we granted certiorari, [ ] and now reverse.

[T]he Court of Appeals' holding—that proof of improper motive was necessary for recovery under § 1395dd(b)'s stabilization requirement—extended earlier Circuit precedent deciding that the "appropriate medical screening" duty under § 1395dd(a) also required proof of an improper motive. See Cleland v. Bronson Health Care Group, Inc., 917 F.2d 266 . . . The Court of Appeals in Cleland was concerned that Congress' use of the word "appropriate" in § 1395dd(a) might be interpreted incorrectly to permit federal liability under EMTALA for any violation covered by state malpractice law. [ ] Accordingly, rather than interpret EMTALA so as to cover "at a minimum, the full panoply of state malpractice law, and at a maximum, . . . a guarantee of a successful result" in medical treatment, the Court of Appeals read § 1395dd(a)'s "appropriate medical screening" duty as requiring a plaintiff to show an improper reason why he or she received "less than standard attention [upon arrival] . . . at the emergency room." [ ]

[U]nlike the provision of EMTALA at issue in Cleland, § 1395dd(a), the provision at issue in this case, § 1395dd(b), contains no requirement of appropriateness. Subsection (b)(1)(A) of EMTALA requires instead the provision of "such further medical examination and such treatment as may be required to stabilize the medical condition." [ ] The question of the correctness of the Cleland Court's reading of § 1395dd(a)'s "appropriate medical screening" requirement is not before us, and we express no opinion on it here. But there is no question that the text of § 1395dd(b) does not require an "appropriate" stabilization, nor can it reasonably be read to require an improper motive . . . * * * [W]e . . . hold that § 1395dd(b) contains no express or implied "improper motive" requirement.

> 1. We note, however, that Cleland's interpretation of subsection (a) of EMTALA is in conflict with the law of other circuits which do not read subsection (a) as imposing an improper motive requirement. [ ]

* * * Accordingly, we reverse the Court of Appeals' holding that the District Court's grant of summary judgment was proper, and remand the case for further proceedings consistent with this opinion. * * *

Question

1. The Supreme Court was asked a very narrow question about the litigation by Ms. Johnson's guardian. It provided a very brief and narrow answer, relying on the presence/absence of the word "appropriate". As you read the brief statement of facts, what other issues would be raised in the litigation over Ms. Johnson's treatment?

Insert at page 777, before Note, Title VI and Racial Discrimination in Health Care:

BRAGDON v. ABBOTT

Supreme Court of the United States, 1998.
524 U.S. 624.

KENNEDY, J., delivered the opinion of the Court, in which STEVENS, SOUTER, GINSBURG, and BREYER, JJ., joined. STEVENS, J., filed a concurring opinion, in which BREYER, J., joined. GINSBURG, J., filed a concurring opinion. REHNQUIST, C. J., filed an opinion concurring in the judgment in part and dissenting in part, in which SCALIA and THOMAS, JJ., joined, and in Part II of which O'CONNOR, J., joined. O'CONNOR, J., filed an opinion concurring in the judgment in part and dissenting in part.

We address in this case the application of the Americans with Disabilities Act of 1990 (ADA), [ ] to persons infected with the human immunodeficiency virus (HIV). We granted certiorari to review, first, whether HIV infection is a disability under the ADA when the infection has not yet progressed to the so-called symptomatic phase; and, second, whether the Court of Appeals, in affirming a grant of summary judgment, cited sufficient material in the record to determine, as a matter of law, that respondent's infection with HIV posed no direct threat to the health and safety of her treating dentist.

* * *

I

Respondent Sidney Abbott has been infected with HIV since 1986. When the incidents we recite occurred, her infection had not manifested its most serious symptoms. On September 16, 1994, she went to the office of petitioner Randon Bragdon in Bangor, Maine, for a dental appointment. She disclosed her HIV infection on the patient registration form. Petitioner completed a dental examination, discovered a cavity, and informed respondent of his policy against filling cavities of HIV-infected patients. He offered to perform the work at a hospital with no added fee for his services, though respondent would be responsible for the cost of using the hospital's facilities. Respondent declined.

Respondent sued petitioner under * * * § 302 of the ADA [ ] alleging discrimination on the basis of her disability. * * * Section 302 of the ADA provides:

"No individual shall be discriminated against on the basis of disability in the full and equal enjoyment of the goods, services, facilities, privileges, advantages, or accommodations of any place of public accommodation by any person who ... operates a place of public accommodation." [ ]

The term "public accommodation" is defined to include the "professional office of a health care provider." [ ]

A later subsection qualifies the mandate not to discriminate. It provides:

"Nothing in this subchapter shall require an entity to permit an individual to participate in or benefit from the goods, services, facilities, privileges, advantages and accommodations of such entity where such individual poses a direct threat to the health or safety of others." [ ]

* * * The District Court ruled in favor of the plaintiffs, holding that respondent's HIV infection satisfied the ADA's definition of disability. [ ] * * *

The Court of Appeals affirmed. It held respondent's HIV infection was a disability under the ADA, even though her infection had not yet progressed to the symptomatic stage. [ ] The Court of Appeals also agreed that treating the respondent in petitioner's office would not have posed a direct threat to the health and safety of others. [ ] * * *

II

We first review the ruling that respondent's HIV infection constituted a disability under the ADA. The statute defines disability as:

"(A) a physical or mental impairment that substantially limits one or more of the major life activities of such individual;

"(B) a record of such an impairment; or

"(C) being regarded as having such impairment." [ ]

We hold respondent's HIV infection was a disability under subsection (A) of the definitional section of the statute. In light of this conclusion, we need not consider the applicability of subsections (B) or (C).

Our consideration of subsection (A) of the definition proceeds in three steps. First, we consider whether respondent's HIV infection was a physical impairment. Second, we identify the life activity upon which respondent relies (reproduction and child bearing) and determine whether it constitutes a major life activity under the ADA. Third, tying the two statutory phrases together, we ask whether the impairment substantially limited the major life activity. * * *

A

The ADA's definition of disability is drawn almost verbatim from the definition of "handicapped individual" included in the Rehabilitation Act of 1973 [ ] and the definition of "handicap" contained in the Fair Housing Amendments Act of 1988. [ ] Congress' repetition of a well-established term carries the implication that Congress intended the term to be construed in accordance with pre-existing regulatory interpretations. [ ] In this case, Congress did more than suggest this construction; it adopted a specific statutory provision in the ADA directing as follows:

"Except as otherwise provided in this chapter, nothing in this chapter shall be construed to apply a lesser standard than the standards applied under title V of the Rehabilitation Act of 1973 [ ] or the regulations issued by Federal agencies pursuant to such title."

[ ]

The directive requires us to construe the ADA to grant at least as much protection as provided by the regulations implementing the Rehabilitation Act.

1

The first step in the inquiry under subsection (A) requires us to determine whether respondent's condition constituted a physical impairment. The Department of Health, Education and Welfare (HEW) issued the first regulations interpreting the Rehabilitation Act in 1977. * * * The HEW regulations, which appear without change in the current regulations issued by the Department of Health and Human Services, define "physical or mental impairment" to mean:

"(A) any physiological disorder or condition, cosmetic disfigurement, or anatomical loss affecting one or more of the following body systems: neurological; musculoskeletal; special sense organs; respiratory, including speech organs; cardiovascular; reproductive, digestive, genito-urinary; hemic and lymphatic; skin; and endocrine; or

"(B) any mental or psychological disorder, such as mental retardation, organic brain syndrome, emotional or mental illness, and specific learning disabilities." [ ]

In issuing these regulations, HEW decided against including a list of disorders constituting physical or mental impairments, out of concern that any specific enumeration might not be comprehensive. [ ] * * *

* * *

HIV infection is not included in the list of specific disorders constituting physical impairments, in part because HIV was not identified as the cause of AIDS until 1983. [ ] HIV infection does fall well within the general definition set forth by the regulations, however.

The disease follows a predictable and, as of today, an unalterable course. Once a person is infected with HIV, the virus invades different cells in the blood and in body tissues. Certain white blood cells, known as helper T-lymphocytes or CD4+ cells, are particularly vulnerable to HIV. The virus attaches to the CD4 receptor site of the target cell and fuses its membrane to the cell's membrane. HIV is a retrovirus, which means it uses an enzyme to convert its own genetic material into a form indistinguishable from the genetic material of the target cell. The virus' genetic material migrates to the cell's nucleus and becomes integrated with the cell's chromosomes. Once integrated, the virus can use the cell's own genetic machinery to replicate itself. Additional copies of the virus are released into the body and infect other cells in turn. [ ]

The virus eventually kills the infected host cell. CD4+ cells play a critical role in coordinating the body's immune response system, and the decline in their number causes corresponding deterioration of the body's ability to fight infections from many sources. Tracking the infected individual's CD4+ cell count is one of the most accurate measures of the course of the disease. [ ]

The initial stage of HIV infection is known as acute or primary HIV infection. In a typical case, this stage lasts three months. The virus concentrates in the blood. The assault on the immune system is immediate. The victim suffers from a sudden and serious decline in the number of white blood cells. There is no latency period. Mononucleosis-like symptoms often emerge between six days and six weeks after infection, at times accompanied by fever, headache, enlargement of the lymph nodes (lymphadenopathy), muscle pain (myalgia), rash, lethargy, gastrointestinal disorders, and neurological disorders. Usually these symptoms abate within 14 to 21 days. HIV antibodies appear in the bloodstream within 3 weeks; circulating HIV can be detected within 10 weeks. [ ]

After the symptoms associated with the initial stage subside, the disease enters what is referred to sometimes as its asymptomatic phase. The term is a misnomer, in some respects, for clinical features persist throughout, including lymphadenopathy, dermatological disorders, oral lesions, and bacterial infections. Although it varies with each individual, in most instances this stage lasts from 7 to 11 years. * * * [ ] It was once thought the virus became inactive during this period, but it is now known that the relative lack of symptoms is attributable to the virus' migration from the circulatory system into the lymph nodes. [ ] * * * The virus, however, thrives in the lymph nodes, which, as a vital point of the body's immune response system, represents an ideal environment for the infection of other CD4+ cells. [ ]

A person is regarded as having AIDS when his or her CD4+ count drops below 200 cells/mm3 of blood or when CD4+ cells comprise less than 14% of his or her total lymphocytes. [ ] During this stage, the clinical conditions most often associated with HIV, such as pneumocystis carninii pneumonia, Kaposi's sarcoma, and non-Hodgkins lymphoma, tend to appear. In addition, the general systemic disorders present during all stages of the disease, such as fever, weight loss, fatigue, lesions, nausea, and diarrhea, tend to worsen. In most cases, once the patient's CD4+ count drops below 10 cells/mm3, death soon follows. [ ]

In light of the immediacy with which the virus begins to damage the infected person's white blood cells and the severity of the disease, we hold it is an impairment from the moment of infection. As noted earlier, infection with HIV causes immediate abnormalities in a person's blood, and the infected person's white cell count continues to drop throughout the course of the disease, even when the attack is concentrated in the lymph nodes. In light of these facts, HIV infection must be regarded as a physiological disorder with a constant and detrimental effect on the infected person's hemic and lymphatic systems from the moment of infection. HIV infection satisfies the statutory and regulatory definition of a physical impairment during every stage of the disease.

2

The statute is not operative, and the definition not satisfied, unless the impairment affects a major life activity. Respondent's claim throughout this case has been that the HIV infection placed a substantial limitation on her ability to reproduce and to bear children.

[ ]Given the pervasive, and invariably fatal, course of the disease, its effect on major life activities of many sorts might have been relevant to our inquiry. * * * In light of these submissions, it may seem legalistic to circumscribe our discussion to the activity of reproduction. We have little doubt that had different parties brought the suit they would have maintained that an HIV infection imposes substantial limitations on other major life activities. * * * We ask, then, whether reproduction is a major life activity.

We have little difficulty concluding that it is. As the Court of Appeals held, "[t]he plain meaning of the word 'major' denotes comparative importance" and "suggest[s] that the touchstone for determining an activity's inclusion under the statutory rubric is its significance." [ ] Reproduction falls well within the phrase "major life activity." Reproduction and the sexual dynamics surrounding it are central to the life process itself.

While petitioner concedes the importance of reproduction, he claims that Congress intended the ADA only to cover those aspects of a person's life which have a public, economic, or daily character. [ ] Nothing in the definition suggests that activities without a public, economic, or daily dimension may somehow be regarded as so unimportant or insignificant as to fall outside the meaning of the word "major." * * *

As we have noted, the ADA must be construed to be consistent with regulations issued to implement the Rehabilitation Act. [ ] Rather than enunciating a general principle for determining what is and is not a major life activity, the Rehabilitation Act regulations instead provide a representative list, defining term to include "functions such as caring for one's self, performing manual tasks, walking, seeing, hearing, speaking, breathing, learning, and working." [ ] As the use of the term "such as" confirms, the list is illustrative, not exhaustive.

* * * [T]he Rehabilitation Act regulations support the inclusion of reproduction as a major life activity, since reproduction could not be regarded as any less important than working and learning. * * * [W]e agree with the Court of Appeals' determination that reproduction is a major life activity for the purposes of the ADA.

3

The final element of the disability definition in subsection (A) is whether respondent's physical impairment was a substantial limit on the major life activity she asserts. The Rehabilitation Act regulations provide no additional guidance. [ ]

Our evaluation of the medical evidence leads us to conclude that respondent's infection substantially limited her ability to reproduce in two independent ways. First, a woman infected with HIV who tries to conceive a child imposes on the man a significant risk of becoming infected. * * * [ ]

Second, an infected woman risks infecting her child during gestation and childbirth, i.e., perinatal transmission. Petitioner concedes that women infected with HIV face about a 25% risk of transmitting the virus to their children. [ ] Published reports available in 1994 confirm the accuracy of this statistic. [ ]

Petitioner points to evidence in the record suggesting that antiretroviral therapy can lower the risk of perinatal transmission to about 8%. App. 53; see also Connor, supra, at 1176 (8.3%). [ ] * * * We need not resolve this dispute in order to decide this case, however. It cannot be said as a matter of law that an 8% risk of transmitting a dread and fatal disease to one's child does not represent a substantial limitation on reproduction.

The Act addresses substantial limitations on major life activities, not utter inabilities. Conception and childbirth are not impossible for an HIV victim but, without doubt, are dangerous to the public health. This meets the definition of a substantial limitation. The decision to reproduce carries economic and legal consequences as well. There are added costs for antiretroviral therapy, supplemental insurance, and long-term health care for the child who must be examined and, tragic to think, treated for the infection. The laws of some States, moreover, forbid persons infected with HIV from having sex with others, regardless of consent. [ ]

In the end, the disability definition does not turn on personal choice. When significant limitations result from the impairment, the definition is met even if the difficulties are not insurmountable. For the statistical and other reasons we have cited, of course, the limitations on reproduction may be insurmountable here. * * * We agree with the District Court and the Court of Appeals that no triable issue of fact impedes a ruling on the question of statutory coverage. Respondent's HIV infection is a physical impairment which substantially limits a major life activity, as the ADA defines it. In view of our holding, we need not address the second question presented, i.e., whether HIV infection is a per se disability under the ADA.

B

Our holding is confirmed by a consistent course of agency interpretation before and after enactment of the ADA. Every agency to consider the issue under the Rehabilitation Act found statutory coverage for persons with asymptomatic HIV. * * *

* * *

Every court which addressed the issue before the ADA was enacted in July 1990, moreover, concluded that asymptomatic HIV infection satisfied the Rehabilitation Act's definition of a handicap. [ ] We are aware of no instance prior to the enactment of the ADA in which a court or agency ruled that HIV infection was not a handicap under the Rehabilitation Act.

Had Congress done nothing more than copy the Rehabilitation Act definition into the ADA, its action would indicate the new statute should be construed in light of this unwavering line of administrative and judicial interpretation. All indications are that Congress was well aware of the position taken by OLC when enacting the ADA and intended to give that position its active endorsement. [ ] * * *

We find the uniformity of the administrative and judicial precedent construing the definition significant. When administrative and judicial interpretations have settled the meaning of an existing statutory provision, repetition of the same language in a new statute indicates, as a general matter, the intent to incorporate its administrative and judicial interpretations as well. [ ] The uniform body of administrative and judicial precedent confirms the conclusion we reach today as the most faithful way to effect the congressional design.

C

* * *

We also draw guidance from the views of the agencies authorized to administer other sections of the ADA. [ ] * * * Most categorical of all is EEOC's conclusion that "an individual who has HIV infection (including asymptomatic HIV infection) is an individual with a disability." [ ] In the EEOC's view,

"impairments ... such as HIV infection, are inherently substantially limiting." [ ]

* * *

III

The petition for certiorari presented three other questions for review. The
questions stated:

"3. When deciding under Title III of the ADA whether a private health
care provider must perform invasive procedures on an infectious patient
in his office, should courts defer to the health care provider's professional
judgment, as long as it is reasonable in light of then-current medical
knowledge?

"4. What is the proper standard of judicial review under Title III of the
ADA of a private health care provider's judgment that the performance of
certain invasive procedures in his office would pose a direct threat to the
health or safety of others?

"5. Did petitioner, Randon Bragdon, D. M. D., raise a genuine issue of
fact for trial as to whether he was warranted in his judgment that the
performance of certain invasive procedures on a patient in his office
would have posed a direct threat to the health or safety of others?" [ ]

Of these, we granted certiorari only on question three. The question is
phrased in an awkward way, for it conflates two separate inquiries. In asking
whether it is appropriate to defer to petitioner's judgment, it assumes that
petitioner's assessment of the objective facts was reasonable. The central
premise of the question and the assumption on which it is based merit
separate consideration.

Again, we begin with the statute. Notwithstanding the protection given
respondent by the ADA's definition of disability, petitioner could have refused
to treat her if her infectious condition "pose[d] a direct threat to the health or
safety of others." [ ] The ADA defines a direct threat to be "a significant risk
to the health or safety of others that cannot be eliminated by a modification of
policies, practices, or procedures or by the provision of auxiliary aids or
services." [ ] * * *

The ADA's direct threat provision stems from the recognition in School Bd. of
Nassau Cty. v. Arline [ ] of the importance of prohibiting discrimination
against individuals with disabilities while protecting others from significant
health and safety risks, resulting, for instance, from a contagious disease. In
Arline, the Court reconciled these objectives by construing the Rehabilitation
Act not to require the hiring of a person who posed "a significant risk of
communicating an infectious disease to others." [ ] * * * [A]DA's direct
threat provision codifies Arline. Because few, if any, activities in life are risk
free, Arline and the ADA do not ask whether a risk exists, but whether it is
significant.[ ]

The existence, or nonexistence, of a significant risk must be determined from
the standpoint of the person who refuses the treatment or accommodation,
and the risk assessment must be based on medical or other objective evidence.
[ ] As a health care professional, petitioner had the duty to assess the risk of

infection based on the objective, scientific information available to him and others in his profession. His belief that a significant risk existed, even if maintained in good faith, would not relieve him from liability. To use the words of the question presented, petitioner receives no special deference simply because he is a health care professional. It is true that Arline reserved "the question whether courts should also defer to the reasonable medical judgments of private physicians on which an employer has relied." [ ] At most, this statement reserved the possibility that employers could consult with individual physicians as objective third-party experts. It did not suggest that an individual physician's state of mind could excuse discrimination without regard to the objective reasonableness of his actions.

* * * In assessing the reasonableness of petitioner's actions, the views of public health authorities, such as the U.S. Public Health Service, CDC, and the National Institutes of Health, are of special weight and authority. [ ] The views of these organizations are not conclusive, however. A health care professional who disagrees with the prevailing medical consensus may refute it by citing a credible scientific basis for deviating from the accepted norm. [ ]

* * *

[An] illustration of a correct application of the objective standard is the Court of Appeals' refusal to give weight to the petitioner's offer to treat respondent in a hospital. [ ] Petitioner testified that he believed hospitals had safety measures, such as air filtration, ultraviolet lights, and respirators, which would reduce the risk of HIV transmission. [ ] Petitioner made no showing, however, that any area hospital had these safeguards or even that he had hospital privileges. [ ] His expert also admitted the lack of any scientific basis for the conclusion that these measures would lower the risk of transmission. [ ] Petitioner failed to present any objective, medical evidence showing that treating respondent in a hospital would be safer or more efficient in preventing HIV transmission than treatment in a well-equipped dental office.

We are concerned, however, that the Court of Appeals might have placed mistaken reliance upon two other sources. In ruling no triable issue of fact existed on this point, the Court of Appeals relied on the 1993 CDC Dentistry Guidelines and the 1991 American Dental Association Policy on HIV. [ ] This evidence is not definitive. As noted earlier, the CDC Guidelines recommended certain universal precautions which, in CDC's view, "should reduce the risk of disease transmission in the dental environment." [ ] The Court of Appeals determined that, "[w]hile the guidelines do not state explicitly that no further risk-reduction measures are desirable or that routine dental care for HIV-positive individuals is safe, those two conclusions seem to be implicit in the guidelines' detailed delineation of procedures for office treatment of HIV-positive patients." [ ] In our view, the Guidelines do not necessarily contain implicit assumptions conclusive of the point to be decided. The Guidelines set out CDC's recommendation that the universal precautions are the best way to combat the risk of HIV transmission. They do not assess the level of risk.

Nor can we be certain, on this record, whether the 1991 American Dental Association Policy on HIV carries the weight the Court of Appeals attributed to it. The Policy does provide some evidence of the medical community's objective assessment of the risks posed by treating people infected with HIV in dental offices. It indicates:

"Current scientific and epidemiologic evidence indicates that there is little risk of transmission of infectious diseases through dental treatment if recommended infection control procedures are routinely followed. Patients with HIV infection may be safely treated in private dental offices when appropriate infection control procedures are employed. Such infection control procedures provide protection both for patients and dental personnel." [ ]

We note, however, that the Association is a professional organization, which, although a respected source of information on the dental profession, is not a public health authority. It is not clear the extent to which the Policy was based on the Association's assessment of dentists' ethical and professional duties in addition to its scientific assessment of the risk to which the ADA refers. Efforts to clarify dentists' ethical obligations and to encourage dentists to treat patients with HIV infection with compassion may be commendable, but the question under the statute is one of statistical likelihood, not professional responsibility. Without more information on the manner in which the American Dental Association formulated this Policy, we are unable to determine the Policy's value in evaluating whether petitioner's assessment of the risks was reasonable as a matter of law.

The court considered materials submitted by both parties on the cross motions for summary judgment. The petitioner was required to establish that there existed a genuine issue of material fact. Evidence which was merely colorable or not significantly probative would not have been sufficient. [ ]

We acknowledge the presence of other evidence in the record before the Court of Appeals which, subject to further arguments and examination, might support affirmance of the trial court's ruling. For instance, the record contains substantial testimony from numerous health experts indicating that it is safe to treat patients infected with HIV in dental offices. [ ] We are unable to determine the import of this evidence, however. The record does not disclose whether the expert testimony submitted by respondent turned on evidence available in September 1994. [ ]

There are reasons to doubt whether petitioner advanced evidence sufficient to raise a triable issue of fact on the significance of the risk. Petitioner relied on two principal points: First, he asserted that the use of high-speed drills and surface cooling with water created a risk of airborne HIV transmission. The study on which petitioner relied was inconclusive, however, determining only that "[f]urther work is required to determine whether such a risk exists." [ ] Petitioner's expert witness conceded, moreover, that no evidence suggested the spray could transmit HIV. His opinion on airborne risk was based on the absence of contrary evidence, not on positive data. [ ] Scientific evidence and expert testimony must have a traceable, analytical basis in objective fact before it may be considered on summary judgment. [ ]

* * * [P]etitioner argues that, as of September 1994, CDC had identified seven dental workers with possible occupational transmission of HIV. [ ] These dental workers were exposed to HIV in the course of their employment, but CDC could not determine whether HIV infection had resulted. Id., at 15, n. 3. It is now known that CDC could not ascertain whether the seven dental workers contracted the disease because they did not present themselves for HIV testing at an appropriate time after their initial exposure. [ ] It is not

clear on this record, however, whether this information was available to petitioner in September 1994. If not, the seven cases might have provided some, albeit not necessarily sufficient, support for petitioner's position. Standing alone, we doubt it would meet the objective, scientific basis for finding a significant risk to the petitioner.

Our evaluation of the evidence is constrained by the fact that on these and other points we have not had briefs and arguments directed to the entire record . . . * * *

We conclude the proper course is to give the Court of Appeals the opportunity to determine whether our analysis of some of the studies cited by the parties would change its conclusion that petitioner presented neither objective evidence nor a triable issue of fact on the question of risk . . . * * *

The determination of the Court of Appeals that respondent's HIV infection was a disability under the ADA is affirmed. The judgment is vacated, and the case is remanded for further proceedings consistent with this opinion.

It is so ordered.

Justice STEVENS, with whom Justice BREYER joins, concurring.

* * * I do not believe petitioner has sustained his burden of adducing evidence sufficient to raise a triable issue of fact on the significance of the risk posed by treating respondent in his office. * * * [As to this issue] I join [the Court's] opinion even though I would prefer an outright affirmance. [ ]

Justice GINSBURG, concurring.

* * * No rational legislator, it seems to me apparent, would require nondiscrimination once symptoms become visible but permit discrimination when the disease, though present, is not yet visible. I am therefore satisfied that the statutory and regulatory definitions are well met. * * * [ ]

I further agree, in view of the "importance [of the issue] to health care workers," that it is wise to remand, erring, if at all, on the side of caution. By taking this course, the Court ensures a fully informed determination whether respondent Abbott's disease posed "a significant risk to the health or safety of [petitioner Bragdon] that [could not] be eliminated by a modification of policies, practices, or procedures...." [ ]

Chief Justice REHNQUIST, with whom Justice SCALIA and Justice THOMAS join, and with whom Justice O'CONNOR joins as to Part II, concurring in the judgment in part and dissenting in part.

* * *

Petitioner does not dispute that asymptomatic HIV-positive status is a physical impairment. I therefore assume this to be the case, and proceed to the second and third statutory requirements for "disability."

According to the Court, the next question is "whether reproduction is a major life activity." [ ] That, however, is only half of the relevant question. As mentioned above, the ADA's definition of a "disability" requires that the major life activity at issue be one "of such individual." [ ] The Court truncates the question, perhaps because there is not a shred of record evidence indicating that, prior to becoming infected with HIV, respondent's major life activities included reproduction [ ] (assuming for the moment that reproduction is a major life activity at all). At most, the record indicates that after learning of her HIV status, respondent, whatever her previous inclination, conclusively decided that she would not have children. [ ] There is absolutely no evidence that, absent the HIV, respondent would have had or was even considering having children. Indeed, when asked during her deposition whether her HIV infection had in any way impaired her ability to carry out any of her life functions, respondent answered "No." [ ] It is further telling that in the course of her entire brief to this Court, respondent studiously avoids asserting even once that reproduction is a major life activity to her. To the contrary, she argues that the "major life activity" inquiry should not turn on a particular-ized assessment of the circumstances of this or any other case. [ ]

* * *

But even aside from the facts of this particular case, the Court is simply wrong in concluding as a general matter that reproduction is a "major life activity." * * *

* * *

No one can deny that reproductive decisions are important in a person's life. But so are decisions as to who to marry, where to live, and how to earn one's living. Fundamental importance of this sort is not the common thread linking the statute's listed activities. The common thread is rather that the activities are repetitively performed and essential in the day-to-day existence of a normally functioning individual. They are thus quite different from the series of activities leading to the birth of a child.

* * *

But even if I were to assume that reproduction is a major life activity of respondent, I do not agree that an asymptomatic HIV infection "substantially limits" that activity. The record before us leaves no doubt that those so infected are still entirely able to engage in sexual intercourse, give birth to a child if they become pregnant, and perform the manual tasks necessary to rear a child to maturity. [ ] While individuals infected with HIV may choose not to engage in these activities, there is no support in language, logic, or our case law for the proposition that such voluntary choices constitute a "limit" on one's own life activities.

* * *

Respondent contends that her ability to reproduce is limited because "the fatal nature of HIV infection means that a parent is unlikely to live long enough to raise and nurture the child to adulthood." [ ] * * * Respondent's argument, taken to its logical extreme, would render every individual with a genetic marker for some debilitating disease "disabled" here and now because of some possible future effects.

In my view, therefore, respondent has failed to demonstrate that any of her major life activities were substantially limited by her HIV infection.

II

* * *

I agree with the Court that "the existence, or nonexistence, of a significant risk must be determined from the standpoint of the person who refuses the treatment or accommodation," as of the time that the decision refusing treatment is made. [ ] I disagree with the Court, however, that "[i]n assessing the reasonableness of petitioner's actions, the views of public health authorities ... are of special weight and authority." [ ] Those views are, of course, entitled to a presumption of validity when the actions of those authorities themselves are challenged in court, and even in disputes between private parties where Congress has committed that dispute to adjudication by a public health authority. But in litigation between private parties originating in the federal courts, I am aware of no provision of law or judicial practice that would require or permit courts to give some scientific views more credence than others simply because they have been endorsed by a politically appointed public health authority (such as the Surgeon General). In litigation of this latter sort, which is what we face here, the credentials of the scientists employed by the public health authority, and the soundness of their studies, must stand on their own. The Court cites no authority for its limitation upon the courts' truth-finding function, except the statement in School Bd. of Nassau Cty. v. Arline, [ ] that in making findings regarding the risk of contagion under the Rehabilitation Act, "courts normally should defer to the reasonable medical judgments of public health officials." But there is append-ed to that dictum the following footnote, which makes it very clear that the Court was urging respect for medical judgment, and not necessarily respect for "official" medical judgment over "private" medical judgment: "This case does not present, and we do not address, the question whether courts should also defer to the reasonable medical judgments of private physicians on which an employer has relied." [ ]

Applying these principles here, it is clear to me that petitioner has presented more than enough evidence to avoid summary judgment on the "direct threat" question. * * * Given the "severity of the risk" involved here, i.e., near certain death, and the fact that no public health authority had outlined a protocol for eliminating this risk in the context of routine dental treatment, it seems likely that petitioner can establish that it was objectively reasonable for him to conclude that treating respondent in his office posed a "direct threat" to his safety.

* * *

Notes and Questions

1. Until the Bragdon case, cases concerning HIV have relied heavily on CDC guidelines as an authoritative source on level of risk and necessary precautions. See Notes 3 and 5 on page 490 of the text. Still, courts have been risk averse in HIV cases. What are the advantages and disadvantages of deferring to CDC guidelines and standards as carrying more weight than the opinions of individual experts or individual physicians?

2. The dissenting opinion analyzes risk of infection twice: implicitly in the discussion of the ability to reproduce and explicitly in relation to the risk of transmission to the dentist. Does the dissent treat these risks consistently, or are they simply answering or responding to different legal questions or standards?

3. This case also applies to the situation in which the disabled person is claiming discrimination in employment. Do you see how? See Chapter 7.

4. For an analysis of Bragdon, see Wendy E. Parmet and Daniel J. Jackson, No Longer Disabled: The Legal Impact of the New Social Construction of HIV, 23 Am. J. L. and Med. 7. (1997).

5. Justice Rehnquist's concurring opinion refers to the applicability of the ADA to genetic conditions. See Chapter 16 for further material on genetics and employment discrimination.

Chapter 13

LEGAL OVERSIGHT OF PRIVATE
HEALTH CARE FINANCING

Insert at page 815, at note 4:

A recent study indicates that the percentage of employers who self- insure seems to be dropping, particularly among small employers. M. Susan Marquis and Stephen H. Long, Recent Trends in Self–Insured Employer Health Plans, 18 Health Aff., May–June 1999 at 161. Between 1993 and 1997 the percentage of employers that were self-insured within the sample studied dropped from 19% to 13%, while the percentage of enrollees in self-insured plans dropped from 40% to 33%. Apparently the cost advantages of purchasing health care through HMOs outweigh the advantages available through self-insurance, except perhaps for multistate employers. Self-insured HMOs only accounted for 2% of establishments and 6%–9% of employees studied. If this trend continues, the need for federal regulation of managed care might become less pressing.

Insert at page 815, just above Section B:

During the past two years, regulation of the alleged excesses of managed care has been one of the most popular items on the health policy agenda. Every state legislature is expected to consider managed care legislation in 1999, with about half the states considering external review legislation and about thirty states considering legislation that would make it easier to sue health plans. Twenty-two states have adopted legislation permitting insureds to appeal coverage denials based on medical necessity (and, in some states, on investigational treatment grounds) to outside reviewers. Thirty-five states have adopted "direct access" statutes, permitting plan members to go directly to some types of specialists (most commonly obstetricians and gynecologists) without a primary care gatekeeper referral. Other popular legislative topics include creating or expanding quality standards for managed care, requiring parity for mental and physical health coverage, requiring emergency room access, limiting the use of drug formularies, and protecting the confidentiality of medical records. Virtually all of these statutes, however, are subject to ERISA preemption challenges, like that considered in the following case.

CORPORATE HEALTH INSURANCE INC., ET AL. V. TEXAS DEPARTMENT OF INSURANCE, ET AL.

United States District Court, Southern District of Texas, 1998.
12 F.Supp.2d 597.

GILMORE, DISTRICT JUDGE.

* * *

I. Background

Plaintiffs * * * bring this action against Defendants Texas Department of Insurance (the "Department") * * * seeking declaratory and injunctive relief. Plaintiffs request a declaration that Texas Senate Bill 386, the Health Care Liability Act (the "Act"), codified as Tex. Civ. Prac. & Rem. Code Ann. §§ 88.001–88.003 (West 1998)* * * is preempted by the Employee Retirement Income Security Act of 1974 ("ERISA"), 29 U.S.C.A. § 1001 et seq. and by the Federal Employees Health Benefit Act ("FEHBA"), 5 U.S.C.A. § 8901 et seq. * * *

The Act allows an individual to sue a health insurance carrier, health maintenance organization, or other managed care entity for damages proximately caused by the entity's failure to exercise ordinary care when making a health care treatment decision.[ ] In addition, under the Act, these entities may be held liable for substandard health care treatment decisions made by their employees, agents, or representatives.[ ] The Act also establishes an independent review process for adverse benefit determinations and requires an insured or enrollee to submit his or her claim challenging an adverse benefit determination to a review by an independent review organization if such a review is requested by the managed care entity.[ ] Additional responsibilities for HMOs and further requirements concerning the review of an adverse benefit determination by an independent review organization are also addressed by the Act.[ ]

* * *

V. Insurance Savings Clause

Plaintiffs claim that the Act is preempted by ERISA. Thus, as an initial matter, the Court will examine whether the Act is saved from preemption by ERISA's insurance savings clause.

ERISA provides that "nothing in this title shall be construed to exempt or relieve any person from any law of any State which regulates insurance, banking or securities." 29 U.S.C.A. § 1144(b)(2)(a). The Supreme Court "delineated the requirements that a state statute must meet in order to come within the insurance facet of the savings clause" in Metropolitan Life Ins. Co. v. Massachusetts, 471 U.S. 724 (1985). The Supreme Court * * * took the following conjunctive two-step approach:

First, the [C]ourt determined whether the statute in question fitted the common sense definition of insurance regulation. Second, it looked at three factors: (1)[w]hether the practice (the statute) has the effect of spreading policyholders' risk; (2) whether the practice is an integral part of the policy relationship between the insurer and the insured; and (3) whether the practice is limited to entities within the insurance industry. If the statute fitted the common sense definition of insurance regulation and the court answered "yes" to each of the questions in the three part test, then the statute fell within the savings clause exempting it from ERISA preemption.[ ]

[T]he Court * * * can both start and finish its analysis with the third factor of the Metropolitan Life test: on its face, the Act is obviously not "limited to entities within the insurance industry." Even though the Act lists health insurance carriers as one group covered by its terms, it also specifies that it applies to health maintenance organizations or other managed care entities for a health care plan.[ ] As the Act fails to meet the third factor of the Metropolitan Life test, the Court finds that the statute is not saved from preemption by the insurance exception of Section 514(b) of ERISA.[ ]

VI.   ERISA Preemption

Having determined that the Act is not saved by the insurance savings clause, the Court must next examine whether the Act is preempted by Section 514(a) of ERISA.

* * * Section 514(a) provides that ERISA "shall supersede any and all State laws insofar as they . . . relate to any employee benefit plan. . . ."[ ] Under ERISA preemption analysis, a state law relates to an ERISA plan if it has a connection with or reference to such a plan.[ ]

* * *

B.   "Relates To" Analysis

A state law relates to an ERISA plan "in the normal sense of the phrase if it has a connection with or reference to such a plan." * * * Under this definition, a state law can relate to an ERISA plan even if that law was not specifically designed to affect such plans, and even if its effect is only indirect. If a state law does not expressly concern employee benefit plans, it will be preempted insofar as it applies to benefit plans in particular cases. . . . [ ] "The most obvious class of pre-empted state laws are those that are specifically designed to affect ERISA-governed employee benefits plans."[ ]

In determining whether a state law "relate[s] to" an ERISA plan, the Supreme Court has adopted a pragmatic approach.[ ] In Travelers, the Court stated that it "must go beyond the unhelpful text [of Section 514(a)] and the frustrating difficulty of defining its key term ['relates to'], and look instead to the objectives of the ERISA statute as a guide to the scope of the state law that Congress understood would survive [preemption]."[ ]

* * * [I]n passing Section 514, Congress intended 'to ensure that plans and plan sponsors would be subject to a uniform body of benefits law; the goal was to minimize the administrative and financial burdens of complying with conflicting directives among States or between States and the Federal Government . . . , [and to prevent] the potential for conflict in substantive law . . . requiring the tailoring of plans and employer conduct to the peculiarities of the law of each jurisdiction.'[ ] Therefore, "[t]he basic thrust of . . . [ERISA's] pre-emption clause . . . was to avoid a multiplicity of regulation in order to permit the nationally uniform administration of employee benefit plans."[ ]

Although the text of Section 514(a) is clearly expansive, in so far as it affects all state laws that relate to ERISA plans, the phrase "relate[s] to" does not "extend to the furthest stretch of its indeterminacy[.]"[ ] If that were the case, "then for all practical purposes pre-emption would never run its course" and courts would be required "to read Congress's words of limitation as mere sham, and to read the presumption against preemption out of the law whenever Congress speaks to the matter with generality." * * *

"The historic powers of the State include the regulation of matters of health and safety."[ ] The Act, in this case, regulates the medical decisions of health insurance carriers, health maintenance organizations, and other managed care entities,[ ] and therefore, clearly operates in a field that has been traditionally occupied by the States. * * * Consequently, Plaintiffs "bear the considerable burden of overcoming 'the starting presumption that Congress does not intend to supplant state law.' "[ ]

1. "Reference To"

* * * "[w]here a State's law acts immediately and exclusively upon ERISA plans . . . or where the existence of ERISA plans is essential to the law's operation . . . that 'reference' will result in pre-emption."[ ]

In Travelers, the Supreme Court examined New York statutes that imposed "surcharges on bills of patients whose commercial insurance coverage [wa]s purchased by employee health-care plans governed by ERISA and . . . on HMOs insofar as their membership fees . . . [were] paid by an ERISA plan."[ ] Notably, the surcharge on HMOs was "not an increase in the rates to be paid by an HMO to a hospital, but a direct payment by the HMO to the State's general fund."[ ] The Court held that the "surcharge statutes . . . [could not] be said to make 'reference to' ERISA plans in any manner" because the surcharges were "imposed upon patients and HMOs, regardless of whether the commercial coverage or membership, respectively, [wa]s ultimately secured by an ERISA plan, private purchase, or otherwise[.]"[ ]

Similarly, in this case, the Act imposes a standard of ordinary care directly upon health insurance carriers and health maintenance organizations when making health care treatment decisions, regardless of whether the commercial coverage or membership therein is ultimately secured by an ERISA plan.[ ] The Act also requires managed care entities to exercise ordinary care when making medical decisions.[ ] However, as already mentioned, the Act specifically excludes ERISA plans from the definition of a "managed care entity." * * * Consequently, as in Travelers, the Act cannot be said to make any reference to ERISA plans.

Plaintiffs, however, maintain that preemption is mandated because the Act has an express reference to ERISA plans in several other provisions.[ ] In particular, Plaintiffs seem to argue that the mere inclusion of certain terms that allegedly refer to ERISA plans, such as "plan," "health care plan," "health maintenance organization," and "managed care entity," warrants preemption.* * *

* * *

Contrary to Plaintiffs' contention, in Greater Washington, the Supreme Court did not conclude that the statute referred to ERISA plans simply because it contained certain terminology. Rather, * * * the Court reasoned that the reference to ERISA plans resulted in preemption because the existence of ERISA plans was essential to the statute's operation. Unlike the statute in Greater Washington, the Act is not premised on the existence of an ERISA plan. It merely requires health insurance carriers, HMOs, and other managed care entities to exercise ordinary care when making medical decisions. The Act imposes this standard on these entities without any reference to or reliance on an ERISA plan.

In CIGNA,[ ] the Fifth Circuit held that Louisiana's Any Willing Provider statute was preempted by ERISA because it referred to ERISA-qualified plans. The statute required all licensed providers "who agre[ed] to the terms and conditions of the preferred provider contract" to be accepted as providers in the preferred provider organization ("PPO").[ ] Under the Health Care Cost Control Act, a "preferred provider contract" was defined as "an agreement 'between a provider or providers and a group purchaser or purchasers to provide for alternative rates of payment specified in advance for a defined period of time.' " * * * *

Unlike the statute in CIGNA, the requirement imposed by the Act does not contain a reference to ERISA plans. The Act states that health insurance carriers, HMOs, and other managed care entities have a duty to exercise ordinary care when making health care treatment decisions.[ ] None of these enumerated entities constitute ERISA plans since, by definition, they are not "established or maintained by an employer or by an employee organization . . . for the purpose of providing" health care benefits for employees.[ ]

In this case, the Court finds that, as in Travelers, the existence of an ERISA plan is not essential to the operation of the Act. Furthermore, the Act does not work "immediately and exclusively upon ERISA plans."[ ] Consequently, the Court concludes that the Act "cannot be said to make a 'reference to' ERISA plans in any manner."[ ]

* * *

2. "Connection With"

"A law that does not refer to ERISA plans may yet be pre-empted if it has a 'connection with' ERISA plans."[ ] "To determine whether a state law has the forbidden connection, [the court looks] . . . both to 'the objectives of the ERISA statute as a guide to the scope of the state law that Congress understood would survive,' as well as to the nature of the effect of the state law on ERISA plans."[ ]

Here, Plaintiffs contend that the Act has a "connection with" ERISA plans in several ways. Plaintiffs claim that the Act improperly imposes state law liability on ERISA entities, impermissibly mandates the structure of plan benefits and their administration, unlawfully binds plan administrators to particular choices, and wrongfully creates an alternate enforcement mechanism.[ ]

i. Imposition of State Law Liability

According to Plaintiffs, the "Fifth Circuit has twice held that attempts to impose state law liability on managed care entities in 'connection with' their 'health care treatment decisions' fall within the scope of the preemption clause." * * *

In Corcoran, 965 F.2d at 1331, the Fifth Circuit held that a Louisiana tort action for the wrongful death of an unborn child was preempted by ERISA. In that case, United HealthCare ("United"), the provider of utilization review services to an employee benefit plan, determined that Mrs. Corcoran's hospitalization during the final months of her pregnancy was not necessary despite her doctors' repeated recommendations for complete bed rest.[ ] * * * Contrary to her doctor's requests, United only authorized ten hours per day of home nursing care for Mrs. Corcoran.[ ]

While the nurse was off-duty, the fetus went into distress and died.[ ] Subsequently, the Corcorans brought suit against United for wrongful death, alleging "that their unborn child died as a result of various acts of negligence committed by" the mother's health plan and United.[ ]

United argued that the Corcorans' claims were preempted by ERISA because its "decision [was] made in its capacity as a plan fiduciary [and was] about what benefits were authorized under the [p]lan." * * * Thus, United maintained that, under prevailing ERISA preemption law, the Corcorans could not "sue in tort to redress injuries flowing from decisions about what benefits are to be paid under a plan."[ ]

The Corcorans, on the other hand, contended that their cause of action sought "to recover benefits solely for United's erroneous medical decision that Mrs. Corcoran did not require hospitalization during the last month of her pregnancy." * * *

Unable to agree with either characterization, the Fifth Circuit concluded that United made "medical decisions . . . in the context of making a determination about the availability of benefits under the plan."[ ] The Court reasoned that "United decide[d] 'what the medical plan . . . [would] pay for.' When United's actions [we]re viewed from this perspective, it . . . [became] apparent that the Corcorans [we]re attempting to recover for a tort allegedly committed in the course of handling a benefit determination." * * * the Court concluded that ERISA's preemption of "state-law claims alleging improper handling of benefit claims [wa]s broad enough to cover the cause of action asserted here." * * *

Despite its finding of preemption, the Court acknowledged "the fact that . . . [its] interpretation of the preemption clause . . . [left] a gap in remedies within a statute intended to protect participants in employee benefit plans" and suggested a reevaluation of ERISA. * * *

* * *

In light of the Supreme Court's recent mandate regarding ERISA preemption analysis, perhaps the Fifth Circuit would reach a different decision in Corcoran today. Even so, this Court finds the facts in Corcoran to be distinguishable from the conduct covered by the Act.

The plaintiffs in Corcoran filed suit against their HMO regarding a medical decision made in relation to the denial of certain plan benefits. In this case, a suit brought under the Act would relate to the quality of benefits received from a managed care entity when benefits are actually provided, not denied. The Act imposes a duty of ordinary care upon certain entities when making health care treatment decisions and holds those entities liable for damages proximately caused by a failure to exercise that duty.[ ] Furthermore, the Act clearly states that a "health care treatment decision" is "a determination made when medical services are actually provided by the health care plan and a decision which affects the quality of the diagnosis, care, or treatment provided to the plan's insureds or enrollees."[ ] Thus, Corcoran is factually distinguishable from the instant case.

* * *

[This] suit addressing the quality of care actually received is more akin to the claims asserted by plaintiffs in Dukes v. U.S. Healthcare, Inc., 57 F.3d 350 (3d Cir.1995).

* * *

"[T]he plaintiffs in [Dukes] filed suit in state court against health maintenance organizations ("HMOs") organized by U.S. Healthcare, Inc., claiming damages, under various theories, for injuries arising from the medical malpractice of the HMO-affiliated hospitals and medical personnel." The defendant HMOs removed both cases to federal court based on the "complete preemption doctrine."[92][ ]. The Court held that since plaintiffs' claims fell outside the scope of the ERISA provision granting the right to recover benefits and enforce rights due under terms of the plan or to clarify rights to future benefits then the complete preemption doctrine did not permit removal. Id. In particular, the Court held that "[q]uality control of benefits, such as health care benefits provided here, is a field traditionally occupied by state regulation."[ ] The Court then "interpret[ed] the silence of Congress as reflecting an intent that it remain as such."[ ]

This Court finds the discussion in Dukes to be applicable here.[93] The Court, in Dukes, made a distinction between a claim for the withholding of benefits and a claim about the quality of benefits received. The Court reasoned that "[i]nstead of claiming that the welfare plans in any way withheld some quantum of plan benefits due, the plaintiffs in both cases complain[ed] about the low quality of the medical treatment that they actually received...."[ ] * * *

Also in Dukes, the Court distinguished the Corcoran case based on the dual roles that may be assumed by an HMO.[ ] The Court emphasized that in Corcoran, United "only performed an administrative function inherent in the 'utilization review'" whereas the defendant HMOs in Dukes played two roles—the utilization review role and the role as an arranger for the actual medical treatment for plan participants.[ ] "[U]nlike Corcoran, [in Dukes] there ... [was] no allegation ... that the HMOs denied anyone any benefits

92. The "complete preemption" exception provides that "Congress may so completely pre-empt a particular area that any civil complaint raising this select group of claims is necessarily federal in character."[ ] "The Supreme Court has determined that Congress intended the complete-preemption doctrine to apply to state causes of action which fit within the scope of ERISA's civil-enforcement provisions."[ ]

93. Plaintiffs claim that this Court cannot rely on the discussion in Dukes because it is a removal case.[ ] The Court recognizes that a determination that a claim is not completely preempted under Section 502(a) of ERISA does not necessarily mean that that claim is not preempted under Section 514.[ ] However, the Court finds the Third Circuit's discussion of state regulation of "quality of care" to be quite relevant to the instant case.* * *

that they were due under the plan. Instead, the plaintiffs [in Dukes were] . . . attempting to hold the HMOs liable for their role as the arrangers of their decedents' medical treatment." * * *

Thus, the distinction can be summarized as follows:

Claims challenging the quality of a benefit, as in Dukes, are not preempted by ERISA.[ ] Claims based upon a failure to treat where the failure was the result of a determination that the requested treatment wasn't covered by the plan, however, are preempted by ERISA.[ ]

In this case, the Act addresses the quality of benefits actually provided. ERISA "simply says nothing about the quality of benefits received." * * *

Furthermore, "the Supreme Court has cautioned that '[s]ome state actions may affect employee benefit plans in too tenuous, remote, or peripheral a manner to warrant a finding that the law "relates to" the plan.'" * * * In addition, "ERISA does not preempt state laws that have 'only an indirect economic effect on the relative costs of various health insurance packages' available to ERISA-qualified plans" such as quality standards.[ ] As such, the Court finds that "[q]uality control of benefits, such as the health care benefits provided [by HMOs and other managed care entities], is a field traditionally occupied by state regulation and . . . interprets the silence of Congress as reflecting an intent that it remain such."[ ]

Accordingly, the Court concludes that the Act does not constitute an improper imposition of state law liability on the enumerated entities.

ii. Mandating the Structure and Administration of Plan Benefits

Next, the Court will examine Plaintiffs' argument that the Act has a connection with ERISA plans because it improperly mandates the structure of plan benefits and their administration in violation of clear Supreme Court authority. In Travelers, the Court noted that, given the objectives of ERISA and its preemption clause, Congress intended for ERISA to preempt "state laws that mandate employee benefit structures or their administration." * * * [ ] For example, in Shaw v. Delta Air Lines, Inc., 463 U.S. 85, 97 (1983), the Court held that a New York statute "which prohibit[ed] employers from structuring their employee benefit plans in a particular manner that discriminate[d] on the basis of pregnancy . . . [and another statute] which require[d] employers to pay employees specific benefits . . . clearly 'relate[d] to' benefit plans." ERISA preempted these New York statutes because their "mandates affecting coverage could have been honored only by varying the subjects of a plan's benefits whenever New York law might have applied, or by requiring every plan to provide all beneficiaries with a benefit demanded by New York law if New York law could have been said to require it for any one beneficiary." [ ] Therefore, "absent preemption, benefit plans would have been subjected to conflicting directives from one state to the next."[ ]

Plaintiffs claim that the Act "imposes a 'negligence' standard of review on HMOs and PPOs . . . in contravention of the federally mandated abuse of discretion standard of review of a factual benefit determination under ERISA [,]" and "purports to re-define the standard for 'appropriate and medically necessary' as it pertains to ERISA plans."[ ]

With respect to Plaintiffs' first contention, the Court reiterates its conclusion that a suit may only be brought under the Act that challenges the quality of care received, not a benefit determination. Such a claim would not implicate the abuse of discretion standard required under ERISA for factual benefit determinations.[ ] Whether a claim brought under the Act seeks a review of a plan administrator's factual benefit determination rather than a review of a medical decision should be examined by the Court on a case-by-case basis. At that time, the Court could determine whether or not the particular claim conflicts with the standard of review provided under ERISA.

Plaintiffs also claim that the Act wrongfully purports to redefine the standard for "appropriate and medically necessary" as it pertains to ERISA plans.[ ] Section 88.001(1) of the Texas Civil Practice and Remedies Code, which was added by the Act, defines "appropriate and medically necessary" as "the standard for health care services as determined by physicians and health care providers in accordance with the prevailing practices and standards of the medical profession and community." * * * Since Plaintiffs' health care plans purportedly confer authority upon the plan administrator to make coverage determinations in accordance with the terms of the plan, Plaintiffs argue that the Act's definition of "appropriate and medically necessary" changes "the terms of employee benefit plans and restrict[s] the ability of plans to deny claims based upon medical necessity or other terms defined in the plan."[ ]

* * *

[The court reviews at length the statute's provisions governing review of coverage determinations, including review by an Independent Review Organization, or IRO]

Plaintiffs argue that an administrator's determination as to "whether a claim for benefits is covered under the medical necessity definition contained in the plan implicates an interpretation of a plan's term."[ ] Therefore, Plaintiffs continue, the Act which contains these procedures for an independent review of a benefit determination is preempted because it mandates the structure and administration of benefits.

In response, Defendants maintain that "the IRO is geared solely to corporate determinations of 'medical necessity,' the practice of medicine admittedly being a non-preempted traditional area of state regulation."[ ] Defendants also explain, and Plaintiffs do not dispute, that "[o]nly when AEtna, or another managed care entity, makes adverse determinations that benefits are not medically necessary [do] the IRO provisions [become applicable]."[ ] According to Defendants, "the only possible HMO action that could be called a 'benefit determination' which could ever be grounds for action under the IRO provisions of . . . [the Act] are 'adverse determinations.' Adverse determinations are necessarily limited to 'medical necessity' decisions[.]"[ ]

In Travelers, the Supreme Court provided guidance as to the scope of plan administration that Congress intended to protect from state interference.[ ] The Court discussed earlier decisions which held various state statutes preempted for "mandat[ing] employee benefit structures or their administration." . . . The Court [also] explained that ERISA preempted the statutes at issue in Shaw because they imposed "mandates affecting coverage" which directly affected the benefit structures which ERISA plans could offer. . . .

* * * In each of these cases, the [Supreme] Court was concerned with administrative and structural matters central to the administration of ERISA plans themselves.[ ] The Act's use of independent review process implicates the "limited range of administrative functions which are part of operating an employee benefit plan[,]" namely determining the eligibility of claimants.[ ]

Furthermore, the Act's definition of "appropriate and medically necessary" along with the provisions under Section 88.003 for reviewing an adverse determination by an IRO and the further clarification of the IRO procedure and requirements * * * are akin to the situation addressed by the Fifth Circuit in Corcoran. In Corcoran, the Court recognized that United gave medical advice, but emphasized that such advice was made or given while administering the benefits under the plan.[ ] Consequently, since ERISA preempts state law causes of action alleging the improper handling of benefit claims, the Corcorans' state law claims were preempted by ERISA because part of "United's actions involve[d] benefit determinations."[ ] As in Corcoran, by participating in the separate review process provided for under the Act, an insured or enrollee is seeking a review of a benefit determination. Moreover, under Article 21.58A of the Texas Insurance Code, a utilization review agent must comply with the IRO's determination and must pay for the review.[ ]

Allowing state based procedures for independent review of an adverse benefit determination, like the one at issue here, "would subject plans and plan sponsors to burdens not unlike those that Congress sought to foreclose through ... [Section] 514(a). Particularly disruptive is the potential for conflict in state law.... Such an outcome is fundamentally at odds with the goal of uniformity that Congress sought to implement."[ ]

Consequently, * * * the Court finds that the provisions for an independent review improperly mandate the administration of employee benefits and therefore, have a connection with ERISA plans.[ ] "Congress intended ERISA to preempt state laws[,] [such as the IRO provisions in the Act,] that 'mandate[ ] employee benefit structures or their administration.' "[ ] However, the Court finds that the relevant language * * * addressing the IRO procedure, can be severed from the Act without affecting the other provisions or conflicting with the legislative intent.

* * *

iii.   Binding Employers or Plan Administrators to Particular Choices

The Court agrees with Plaintiffs' next argument that, under existing Fifth Circuit authority, certain provisions in the Act bind employers or plan administrators to particular choices. * * * [T]he Court finds that the Act creates two provisions that bind employers or plan administrators to particular choices* * * Section 88.002(f) provides that:

[a]   health insurance carrier, health maintenance organization, or managed care entity may not remove a physician or health care provider from its plan or refuse to renew the physician or health care provider with its plan for advocating on behalf of an enrollee for appropriate and medically necessary health care for the enrollee.[ ]

Section 88.002(g) states that:

[a] health insurance carrier, health maintenance organization, or managed care entity may not enter into a contract with a physician, hospital, or other health care provider or pharmaceutical company which includes an indemnification or hold harmless clause for the acts or conduct of the health insurance carrier, health maintenance organization, or other managed care entity. * * *

Thus, in the instant case, ERISA plans that choose to offer coverage by either a health insurance carrier, HMO, or other managed care entity are limited by the Act to using an entity of a certain structure—i.e., a structure that does not remove a physician or health care provider from its plan for advocating on behalf of an enrollee for appropriate and medically necessary health care and a structure that does not include a prohibited indemnification or hold harmless clause. * * * By denying health insurance carriers, HMOs, and other managed care entities the right to structure their benefits in a particular manner, the Act effectively requires ERISA plans to purchase benefits of a particular structure when they contract with organizations like Plaintiffs.[ ]

Since these provisions require ERISA plans to purchase benefits of a particular structure they essentially cause the Act to have a "connection with" such plans. However, the Court finds that these provisions may be severed from the remainder of the statute.

iv. Alternate Enforcement Mechanism

Lastly, Plaintiffs argue that the liability sections created by the Act, Sections 88.002(a) and (b) of the Texas Civil Practice and Remedies Code, purport to create an alternate enforcement mechanism.[ ]

State laws that provide "alternate enforcement mechanisms [for employees to obtain ERISA plan benefits] also relate to ERISA plans, triggering preemption."[ ] In this case, the Court has already determined that the liability sections of the Act, namely Sections 88.002(a) and (b) of the Texas Civil Practice and Remedies Code, provide a cause of action for challenging the quality of benefits received. Such a lawsuit would not create an alternate enforcement mechanism for employees to obtain ERISA benefits.[ ] Rather, it would ensure the quality of care that employees actually receive. * * *

Based on the foregoing analysis, the Court holds that Plaintiffs have not met their burden of proving that every claim brought under the Act would be preempted by ERISA. Even though some economic impact may result, a claim concerning the quality of a benefit actually received would remain valid.

* * *

[The Court also held that the liability provisions were not preempted by the Federal Employee Health Benefits Acts insofar as they pertained to FEHBA insurees.]

Notes

1. Part of the confusion inherent in ERISA preemption decisions is attributable to the fact that there are two distinct forms of ERISA preemption. One of these is the, by now familiar, explicit or "ordinary" preemption based on § 514(a) (29 U.S.C. § 1144(a)). Section 514(a) provides that ERISA "supersedes" any state law that "relates to" an employee benefits plan. Section 514(a) preemption is qualified

by § 514(b)(2)(A) (which saves from preemption state laws that regulate banking, investment, and insurance) which is in turn limited by the "deemer" clause of § 514(b)(2)(B), which provides that self-insured employee benefit plans shall not be "deemed" to be insurance plans, thus exempting them from state regulation.

The other form of preemption is based on § 502(a) of ERISA (29 U.S.C. § 1132(a)) which provides for federal court jurisdiction over specified types of claims against ERISA plans. The federal courts have interpreted this section as indicating a Congressional intent to preempt comprehensively the "field" of judicial oversight of employee benefits plans. Based on § 502(a), the courts have permitted ERISA plans to remove into federal court claims that were brought in state courts but could have been brought under § 502(a) in federal court. Removal is permitted under the "complete preemption" exception to the well-pleaded complaint rule. The well-pleaded complaint rule normally permits removal only when federal claims are explicitly raised in the plaintiff's compliant. Under the "complete preemption" exception to this rule (sometimes called "superpreemption") federal jurisdiction is permitted when Congress has so completely preempted an area of law that any claim within it is brought under federal law, and thus removable to federal court. "Complete preemption" is in reality not a preemption doctrine, but rather a rule of federal jurisdiction.

Section 502(a) also plays a second role in ERISA jurisprudence, nullifying state claims and remedies that would take the place of § 502 claims. Thus state tort or contract, or even statutory claims, that could have been brought as a claim for benefits or for breach of fiduciary duty under § 502(a) are preempted by § 502(a). Section 502(a) preemption, like § 514(a) explicit preemption, is not comprehensive. In particular, ERISA does not necessarily preempt state court malpractice cases brought against managed care plans that provide as well as pay for health care. Also claims brought by persons who are not proper plaintiffs under § 502(a), or against persons who are not ERISA fiduciaries, may evade ERISA § 502(a) preemption.

Section 502(a) and § 514(a) preemption are not coextensive. More particularly, just because a claim invokes law that might be preempted as relating to an employee benefits claim does not mean that the claim could be brought under § 502(a), and is thus subject to "complete preemption." Not infrequently federal courts remand claims that could not have been brought at § 502(a) claims to state court for resolution of § 514(a) preemption issues.

The Supreme Court has developed in other areas of the law a body of preemption jurisprudence that has largely been ignored in ERISA jurisprudence. Under this schema, the Court will find "field" preemption when a federal law or regulatory scheme so pervasively or significantly dominates a field as to preclude the enforcement of federal law within it. Second, the Court will find "conflict preemption" when it finds that a federal law is in direct conflict with a state law, i.e., when "it is impossible * * * to comply with both state and federal requirements," or "where a state law stands as an obstacle to accomplishment and execution of the full purposes and objectives of Congress'." English v. General Elec. Co, 496 U.S. 72, 79 (1990) Though this schema has been mentioned in recent Supreme Court ERISA opinions, John Hancock Mutual Life Ins. Co. v. Harris Trust & Savings Bank, 510 U.S. 86 (1993); California Division of Labor Standards Enforcement v. Dillingham Const. Co., 519 U.S. , 117 S.Ct. 832, 843 (Scalia, J. concurring), it has to date received little attention in either the leading Supreme Court or in lower court ERISA decisions. In fact, where ERISA decisions distinguish between field and conflict preemption, they tend to identify conflict preemption with § 514(a) express preemption (referred to in some cases as ordinary preemption), and field preemption with § 502 remedial preemption. See, Copling v. The Container Store, F.3d. (5th Cir. 1999); Giles v. NYLCare Health Plan, 172 F.3d. 332 (5th Cir. 1999), and McClelland v. Gronwaldt, 155 F.3d 507 (5th Cir. 1998).

Much of the best writing explicating ERISA preemption continues to be done by Professor Karen Jordan, who has recently published another article on this topic: The Shifting Preemption Paradigm: Conceptual and Interpretive Issues, 51 Vand. L. Rev. 1149 (1998).

2. The issues of whether state court jurisdiction is completely preempted because a complaint presents a federal claim under ERISA or whether state law is preempted by ERISA because it "relates to" an employee benefits plan continue to be frequently and vigorously litigated. Following the Travelers case, and subsequent Supreme Court ERISA preemption cases not involving health benefits issues, the lower courts have tended to be somewhat less likely to find preemption. Thus cases alleging medical malpractice against managed care organizations are commonly found not to be either completely preempted or preempted. (See supplemental materials to chapters 3 and 4 above.) Some courts have similarly found no preemption in fraud and misrepresentation claims against insurers and their agents (See Mehaffey v. Boston Mutual Life Ins., 31 F.Supp.2d 1329 (M.D.Ala.1998); Stetson v. PFL Insurance, 16 F.Supp.2d 28 (D.Me.1998). Further, some state insurance mandates have been found to be saved from preemption. (See Washington Physicians' Service Assn. v. Gregoire, 147 F.3d 1039 (9th Cir.1998) (law requiring HMOs to cover alternative medicine saved from preemption); Community Health Partners v. Kentucky, 14 F.Supp.2d. 991 (W.D.Ky.1998) (Kentucky any willing provider law saved from preemption). On the other hand, state tort cases challenging benefit denials are still routinely held to be preempted by ERISA (see Parrino v. FHP, Inc., 146 F.3d. 699 (9th Cir. 1998), as are some state laws regulating health plans. See Prudential Insurance v. National Park Med. Ctr., 154 F.3d 812 (8th Cir.1998) (finding that the Arkansas Patient Protection Act, a statute permitting patients access to the doctor of their choice, was preempted by ERISA and not saved from preemption as a law regulating insurance); Murphy v. Community Health Network 712 So.2d 296 (La.App.1998)(Louisiana any willing provider statute preempted).

3. The court in Corporate Life quickly disposed of the argument that the Texas statute might be saved from preemption as a law regulating insurance. The Supreme Court, however, may be moving away from a narrow interpretation of the ERISA savings clause. In UNUM Life Insurance Co. v. Ward, 119 S.Ct. 1380 (1999), the Supreme Court interpreted both the "relate to" requirement and savings clause of ERISA in the context of a disability insurance case. The claimant had filed a claim for ERISA plan disability benefits after the time for filing claims provided in the policy had lapsed. He asserted that 1) he had notified the employer in a timely fashion of his disability, and under California law, the employer was the agent of the insurer, and 2) the claim was valid under the California "notice-prejudice" rule, which provides that an insurer cannot reject a claim as untimely unless it can show that it was prejudiced by the delay. The Ninth Circuit reversed a district court summary judgment for the insurer, holding that the California employer-agency rule did not "relate to" the administration of an ERISA plan, and that the "notice-prejudice" rule was saved from preemption as a state law regulating insurance.

Justice Ginsburg, writing for a unanimous court, affirmed in part and reversed in part. The Court held that the California employer-agency rule did "relate to" the ERISA plan, and was thus subject to ERISA preemption. It also held, however, that the "notice-prejudice rule" was saved from ERISA preemption as a law regulating insurance. The Court held that the "notice-prejudice rule" was a state law governing insurance because it was developed by the California courts in the insurance setting, and only applied in the insurance context. It thus met the "common sense" definition of a rule regulating insurance. The Court further held that the rule regulated the "business of insurance" because it met at least two of the three McCarran–Ferguson criteria for laws regulating insurance. The Court pointedly stated that the McCarran–Ferguson considerations were merely "criteria" and "considerations" to be weighed in applying the savings clause, not hard and fast requirements, all of which must independently be met. The Court also rejected the defendant's argument that the 'notice-prejudice' " rule must be rejected because it conflicted with ERISA, noting that the rule merely complemented rather than contradicted rights and remedies available under ERISA.

The Supreme Court in Unum seems to be continuing its trend towards broadening the scope of state regulation of health insurance plans. The decision offers encouragement to states that are eager to move forward with managed care regulation.

In particular, the Court in footnote 7 stated:

> In the instant case, the Solicitor General, for the United States as amicus curiae, has endeavored to qualify the argument advanced in Pilot Life [that all state causes of action against ERISA insurers were preempted]. * * * the Solicitor General now maintains that the discussion of § 502(a) in Pilot Life "does not in itself require that a state law that 'regulates insurance,' and so comes within the terms of the savings clause, is nevertheless preempted if it provides a state-law cause of action or remedy." [] ("[T]he insurance savings clause, on its face, saves state law conferring causes of action or affecting remedies that regulate insurance, just as it does state mandated-benefits laws."). We need not address the Solicitor General's current argument, for Ward has sued under § 502(a)(1)(B) for benefits due, and seeks only the application of saved state insurance law as a relevant rule of decision in his § 502(a) action.

The opinion thus hints that the Court might be open to state statutes authorizing causes of action against ERISA insurers.

4. Among many articles published in the past two years discussing ERISA's effect on health insurance are Peter D Jacobson & Scott D. Pomfret, Form, Function, and Managed Care Torts: Achieving Fairness and Equity in ERISA Jurisprudence, 35 Hous. L. Rev. 985 (1998); Scott D. Pomfret, Emerging Theories of Liability for Utilization Review under ERISA Health Plans, 35 Hous. L. Rev. 985 (1998); Karen A. Jordon, The Shifting Preemption Paradigm: Conceptual and Interpretive Issues, 51 Vand. L. Rev. 1149 (1998); Howard Shapiro, Rene E. Thorne, Edward F. Harold, ERISA Preemption: To Infinity and Beyond and Back Again? 58 La. L. Rev. 997 (1998); E. Haavi Morreim, Benefits Decisions in ERISA Plans: Diminishing Deference to Fiduciaries and an Emerging Problem for Provider–Sponsored Organizations, 65 Tenn. L. Rev. 511 (1998), and Curtis D. Rooney, The States, Congress, or the Courts: Who Will be First to Reform ERISA Remedies, 7 Annals Health L. 73 (1998).

Insert at page 816 in place of Bechtold v. Physicians Health Plan:

HERDRICH v. PEGRAM

United States Court of Appeals, Seventh Circuit, 1998.
154 F.3d 362.

COFFEY, CIRCUIT JUDGE.

The defendants-appellees, Carle Clinic Association, P.C. ("Carle"), Health Alliance Medical Plans, Inc. ("HAMP"), and Carle Health Insurance Management Co., Inc., operate a pre-paid health insurance plan which provides medical and hospital services. The plaintiff-appellant, Cynthia Herdrich ("Herdrich"), was covered under a plan subscription through her husband's employer, State Farm Insurance Company, an Illinois corporation. In March of 1992, Herdrich's appendix ruptured as the result of alleged improper medical treatment while she was in the care of Dr. Lori Pegram ("Pegram"), a physician who practiced under the plan. On October 21, 1992, Herdrich filed a two-count complaint, alleging medical negligence against the health plan operators. Herdrich later added counts III and IV, alleging state law fraud. The defendants, in response, contended that the Employee Retirement Income Security Act of 1974 ("ERISA"), 29 U.S.C. §§ 1001 et seq., preempted counts III and IV, and successfully removed the case to federal court. They subsequently filed a motion for summary judgment as to counts III and IV. * * * The court granted summary judgment against Herdrich on count IV "to the extent [she] relies on § 502(a)(3)(B) [of ERISA] as a basis for monetary relief, as opposed to equitable relief," and that provision does not provide for extra-contractual damages. While the trial judge denied the defendants' summary judgment motion as to count III, he did conclude ERISA preempted that count, and granted Herdrich "leave to submit an amended Count III which clearly sets forth her basis for proceeding under ERISA, including the applicable civil enforcement provision." On September 1, 1995, Herdrich filed her amended count III in accordance with the court's instructions. In it, she averred that the defendants breached their fiduciary duty to plan beneficiaries by depriving them of proper medical care and retaining the savings resulting therefrom for themselves. [The amended Count III was subsequently dismissed. The plaintiff went to trial on Counts I and II for malpractice, and recovered $35,000]

* * *

II. ISSUES

On appeal, Herdrich contends that the district court erred in dismissing the amended count III of her complaint for failing to sufficiently state a claim for breach of a fiduciary duty under ERISA. * * *. The defendants * * * argue that Herdrich's request for damages is inappropriate insofar as beneficiaries under an ERISA benefits plan may not recover "anything other than the benefits provided expressly in the plan."

III. DISCUSSION

* * *

B.   The Plaintiff Properly Stated a Claim Under ERISA

The defendants next contend that Herdrich has failed to state a cause of action for breach of a fiduciary duty under ERISA. As previously mentioned, the district court dismissed Herdrich's amended count III, finding that even as amended, the complaint did not state a claim upon which relief might be granted.

* * *

In order to properly state a claim for breach of fiduciary duty under ERISA, the plaintiff's complaint must allege facts which set forth: (1) that the defendants are plan fiduciaries; (2) that the defendants breached their fiduciary duties; and (3) that a cognizable loss resulted. See 29 U.S.C. § 1104(a). We are of the opinion that Herdrich's pleadings have more than sufficiently alleged each of these three elements.

1.   Fiduciary Status

As previously explained, the district court adopted the magistrate judge's recommendation that Herdrich's amended count III be dismissed for failure to allege that the defendants were fiduciaries because "none of the defendants is even mentioned in the Subscription Agreement attached to the complaint" and "the plaintiff fails to identify how any of the defendants is involved as a fiduciary to the Plan."[94] We disagree with this determination.

ERISA defines the term "fiduciary" in 29 U.S.C. § 1002(21)(A), which reads, in relevant part:

Except as otherwise provided in subparagraph (B), a person is a fiduciary with respect to a plan to the extent (i) he exercises any discretionary authority or discretionary control respecting management of such plan or exercises any authority of control respecting management or disposition of its assets . . . or (iii) he has any discretionary authority or discretionary responsibility in the administration of such plan.

* * *

Consistent with the expressed intent of Congress, this court has routinely construed the ERISA term, "fiduciary," broadly.[ ] In so doing, we have emphasized the importance of discretionary control and authority in determining who is a plan fiduciary. * * * In the case sub judice, the magistrate, in his report and recommendation, opined that "the plaintiff fails to identify how any of the defendants is involved as a fiduciary to the plan," * * * Herdrich's amended count III * * * alleges, * * *, that the "defendants have the exclusive right to decide all disputed and non-routine claims under the plan." The defendant-physicians managed the Plan, including the doctor referral process, the nature and duration of patient treatment, and the extent to which participants were required to use Carle-owned facilities. In fact, the board of directors consisted exclusively of the Plan physicians who were thus in control of each and every aspect of the HMO's governance, including their

94. During the pleading stage of this suit, the defendants and plaintiff took dramatically different positions from what they now argue on appeal concerning the issue of whether the defendants were plan fiduciaries. That is, Herdrich originally maintained that the defen- dants were not plan fiduciaries, while the defendants insisted that they were. In the parties' respective appellate briefs, however, the defendants contend that they are not fiduciaries of the Plan, whereas the plaintiff claims they are.

own year-end bonuses. And, like in Harris Trust, Herdrich pleaded that the defendants had the exclusive right to decide all disputed and non-routine claims. In our view, this level of control satisfies ERISA's requirement that a fiduciary maintain "discretionary control and authority." We can reasonably infer that Carle and HAMP were plan fiduciaries due to their discretionary authority in deciding disputed claims.

* * *

2. Breach of Fiduciary Duty

Having determined that the defendants are fiduciaries under ERISA, we next consider whether the direct and inferential allegations contained in Herdrich's complaint are sufficient to establish the requisite breach of a fiduciary duty. An ERISA fiduciary must perform his duties in accordance with the standards set forth in 29 U.S.C. § 1104(a)(1), which provides:

[A] fiduciary shall discharge his duties with respect to a plan solely in the interest of the participants and beneficiaries and—(A) for the exclusive purpose of:

(i) providing benefits to participants and their beneficiaries; and

(ii) defraying reasonable expenses of administering the plan;

(B) with the care, skill, prudence, and diligence under the circumstances then prevailing that a prudent man acting in a like capacity and familiar with such matters would use in the conduct of an enterprise of a like character and with like aims. . . .

A fiduciary breaches its duty of care under section 1104(a)(1)(A) whenever it acts to benefit its own interests.[ ] For example, ERISA expressly prohibits fiduciaries from "deal[ing] with the assets of the plan in his own interest or for his own account," or "receiv[ing] any consideration for his own personal account from any party dealing with such plan in connection with a transaction involving the assets of the plan." 29 U.S.C. § 1106(b). The requirement that an ERISA fiduciary act "with an eye single to the interests of the participants and beneficiaries,"[ ], is the most fundamental of his or her duties, and "must be enforced with uncompromising rigidity."[ ] This duty, the violation of which subjects a fiduciary to liability under 29 U.S.C. § 1109,[95] is directed particularly at schemes "tainted by a conflict of interest and thus highly susceptible to self dealing,"[ ], like the one at issue here.

* * *

The Northern District of Illinois, in Ries v. Humana Health Plan, Inc., 1995 WL 669583 (N.D.Ill., 1995), faced facts similar to those at bar. In Ries, the defendant, Humana Health, obligated the participants in its health plan to fully reimburse the plan for the costs associated with his or her treatment if such costs were recovered, by way of settlement or judgment, from the party

---

95. Section 1109(a) of ERISA provides:

Any person who is a fiduciary with respect to a plan who breaches any of the responsibilities, obligations, or duties imposed upon fiduciaries by this subchapter shall be personally liable to make good to such plan any losses to the plan resulting from each such breach, and to restore to such plan any profits of such fiduciary which have been made through use of assets of the plan by the fiduciary, and shall be subject to such other equitable or remedial relief as the court may deem appropriate, including removal of such fiduciary.

(other than the plan) who caused his or her injury or disease.[ ] The plan generally provided coverage for 80 percent of costs, while plan participants were obligated to finance 20 percent. Although Humana routinely collected a full 80 percent reimbursement from participants, Humana was in fact not paying 80 percent of the covered medical expenses, because it covertly arranged to receive a substantial discount for its share of the charges, unbeknownst to the plan participants.[ ] As a result, plan participants were paying more than 20 percent of the amounts received by the hospitals, and Humana was, in effect, recouping an additional bonus for itself by paying less than the 80 percent of the medical expenses, as set forth in the plan. The Ries court ruled that ERISA did not "permit a plan insurer to recoup more from its insureds than it actually pays out on their behalf under the terms of undisclosed discounting arrangements with health care providers."[ ] The court went on to note that the "fiduciary's covert profiteering at the expense of insureds is inconsistent with its duties of acting 'solely in the interest of the participants and beneficiaries.' "[ ]

Drawing parallels to the case under consideration, Herdrich sets forth, in the amended third count of her complaint, the intricacies of the defendants' incentive structure. The Plan dictated that the very same HMO administrators vested with the authority to determine whether health care claims would be paid, and the type, nature, and duration of care to be given, were those physicians who became eligible to receive year-end bonuses as a result of cost-savings. Because the physician/administrators' year-end bonuses were based on the difference between total plan costs (i.e., the costs of providing medical services) and revenues (i.e., payments by plan beneficiaries), an incentive existed for them to limit treatment and, in turn, HMO costs so as to ensure larger bonuses. With a jaundiced eye focused firmly on year-end bonuses, it is not unrealistic to assume that the doctors rendering care under the Plan were swayed to be most frugal when exercising their discretionary authority to the detriment of their membership.

* * * Herdrich's amended count III alleged "a claim for relief" that the incentive scheme, which invited and encouraged plan fiduciaries to place their own interests ahead of the interests of plan beneficiaries, constituted a breach of the administrators' fiduciary duty, and that "[a]s a direct and proximate result of defendants' breach of their fiduciary duties, the Plan has been deprived of those sums comprising the supplemental medical expenses...." If we accept her allegations of a breach and claim of damages as true, as we are required to do, she has established sufficient grounds to defeat the motion to dismiss.

The dissent disagrees with this aspect of today's holding, which it characterizes as concluding that "the mere existence of this asserted conflict * * * without more, gives rise to a cause of action for breach of fiduciary duty under ERISA." * * * Our decision does not stand for the proposition that the existence of incentives automatically gives rise to a breach of fiduciary duty. Rather, we hold that incentives can rise to the level of a breach where, as pleaded here, the fiduciary trust between plan participants and plan fiduciaries no longer exists (i.e., where physicians delay providing necessary treatment to, or withhold administering proper care to, plan beneficiaries for the sole purpose of increasing their bonuses).

* * * [The plaintiff's] amended count III included the following allegation:

a. CARLE owner/physicians are the officers and directors of HAMP and CHIMCO and receive a year-end distribution, based in large part upon, supplemental medical expense payments made to CARLE by HAMP and CHIMCO;

b. Both HAMP and CHIMCO are directed and controlled by CARLE owner/physicians and seek to fund their supplemental medical expense payments to CARLE:

i. by contracting with CARLE owner/physicians to provide the medical services contemplated in the Plan and then having those contracted owner/physicians:

(1) minimize the use of diagnostic tests;

(2) minimize the use of facilities not owned by CARLE; and

(3) minimize the use of emergency and non-emergency consultation and/or referrals to non-contracted physicians.

ii. by administering disputed and non-routine health insurance claims and determining:

(1) which claims are covered under the Plan and to what extent;

(2) what the applicable standard of care is;

(3) whether a course of treatment is experimental;

(4) whether a course of treatment is reasonable and customary; and

(5) whether a medical condition is an emergency.

Thus, Herdrich alleges a "serious flaw" that springs from the authority of physician/owners of Carle to simultaneously control the care of their patients and reap the profits generated by the HMO through the limited use of tests and referrals. Under the terms of ERISA, Herdrich most certainly has raised the specter that the self-dealing physician/owners in this appeal were not acting "solely in the interest of the participants" of the Plan.

The dissent also stresses that ERISA allows fiduciaries to adopt dual loyalties, and that maintaining dual loyalties does not in itself constitute a breach of fiduciary duty. We do not disagree with this contention, for it is well established that dual loyalties are tolerated under ERISA.[ ] Our point is not that a fiduciary may not have dual loyalties; it is that the tolerance of dual loyalties does not extend to the situation like the case before us where a fiduciary jettisons his responsibility to the physical well-being of beneficiaries in favor of "loyalty" to his own financial interests. Tolerance, in other words, has its limits.

* * *

From our reading, the dissent would not mark a border at all. It seems to argue that dual loyalties, and incentive schemes generally, are per se valid almost without limitation, and that only when there is a "breakdown in the market," or some "serious flaw" in the manner in which the incentive arrangement in question is established, can there possibly be a breach of fiduciary duty. Specifically, the dissent notes, without citation to any authority, that "plan sponsors are likely to take their business elsewhere if they perceive that incentives are working to the detriment of beneficiaries or the plan itself, and thus market forces go a long way towards ensuring that incentives do not rise to dangerous or undesirable levels."

To our way of thinking, the dissent's market theory flies in the face of the facts as set forth in the very record before us. On March 7, 1991, Pegram, Herdrich's doctor, discovered a six by eight centimeter "mass" (later determined to be her appendix) in Herdrich's abdomen. Although the mass was inflamed on March 7, Pegram delayed instituting an immediate treatment of Herdrich, and forced her to wait more than one week (eight days) to obtain the accepted diagnostic procedure (ultrasound) used to determine the nature, size and exact location of the mass. Ideally, Herdrich should have had the ultrasound administered with all speed after the inflamed mass was discovered in her abdomen in order that her condition could be diagnosed and treated before deteriorating as it did, but Carle's policy requires plan participants to receive medical care from Carle-staffed facilities in what they classify as "non-emergency" situations. Because Herdrich's treatment was considered to be "non-emergency," she was forced to wait the eight days before undergoing the ultrasound at a Carle facility in Urbana, Illinois. During this unnecessary waiting period, Herdrich's health problems were exacerbated and the situation rapidly turned into an "emergency"—her appendix ruptured, resulting in the onset of peritonitis. In an effort to defray the increased costs associated with the surgery required to drain and cleanse Herdrich's ruptured appendix, Carle insisted that she have the procedure performed at its own Urbana facility, necessitating that Herdrich travel more than fifty miles from her neighborhood hospital in Bloomington, Illinois. The "market forces" the dissent refers to hardly seem to have produced a positive result in this case— Herdrich suffered a life-threatening illness (peritonitis), which necessitated a longer hospital stay and more serious surgery at a greater cost to her and the Plan. And, as discussed below, we are far from alone in our belief that market forces are insufficient to cure the deleterious affects of managed care on the health care industry.

Across the country, health care critics and consumers are complaining that the quality of medical treatment in this nation is rapidly declining, leaving "a fear that the goal of managing care has been replaced by the goal of managing costs."[ ]

An increasing number of Americans believe that dollars are more important than people in the evolving [HMO] system. Whether justified or not, this assumption needs to be taken seriously, according to keepers of the industry's conscience. * * *

To regain trust, HMOs need to be more sensitive to the doctor-patient relationship and remove the physician from direct financial interest in patient care, says [Arthur] Caplan. Instead, doctors should have a predetermined budget and be able to advocate for patients without direct personal gain or loss. * * * Another hot-button issue for HMO members is the fear that a lifesaving experimental procedure will be denied because of its cost. Caplan says the industry should follow the lead of the handful of HMOs that have established outside, independent panels to make final decisions.[ ] * * * The specter of money concerns driving the health care system, says a group of

Massachusetts physicians and nurses, "threaten[s] to transform healing from a covenant into a business contract. * * * Canons of commerce are displacing dictates of healing, trampling our professions' most sacred values. Market medicine treats patients as profit centers."[ ] * * *

* * *

We must remember that doctors, not insurance executives, are qualified experts in determining what is the best course of treatment and therapy for their patients. Trained physicians, and them alone, should be allowed to make care-related decisions (with, of course, input from the patient). Medical care should not be subject to the whim of the new layer of insurance bureaucracy now dictating the most basic, as well as the important, medical policies and procedures from the boardroom. If it is, "the cost cutting of managed health organizations and insurers may undermine what is, for now, the best medical care in the world."[ ]

* * *

Along the same lines as its "market forces" argument, the dissent submits that the defendants' plan "encourag[ed] physicians to use resources more efficiently." Although we agree, at least in principle, with the idea that financial incentives may very well bring about a more effective use of plan assets, we certainly are far from confident that it was at work in this particular case. The Carle health plan at issue was not used as efficiently as it should have been. Indeed, the eight-day delay in medical care, and the onset of peritonitis Herdrich incurred as a result of such delay in diagnosis, subjected her to a life-threatening illness, a longer period of hospitalization and treatment, more extensive, invasive and dangerous surgery, increased hospitalization costs, and a greater ingestion of prescription drugs.

The dissent also somehow contends that "ERISA tolerates some conflict of interest on the part of fiduciaries," and therefore, "allowing a plan sponsor to designate its own agent as a fiduciary reassures the sponsor that, in devoting its assets to the plan, it has not relinquished all ability to ensure that the plan's resources are used wisely."

* * *

In considering our [earlier] decisions * * *, it is important to note that this court has heretofore not been called upon to address the situation where each and every member of the benefit plan's administrative review board were the very owners of the plan, and plan beneficiaries were without a single representative on the board. * * * According to the record before us, the doctors who owned Carle and provided medical care to plan beneficiaries were the very same individuals who served as officers and directors of HAMP, the plan-administrating subsidiary of Carle. As the plaintiff alleged in her complaint, it is more likely than not that an incentive existed for the Carle doctors to abuse the dual loyalties that they observed in administering the Plan by "minimiz[ing] the use of diagnostic tests[,] . . . the use of facilities not owned by CARLE[,] . . . and the use of emergency and non-emergency consultation and/or referrals to non-contracted physicians."

* * * Here the Carle physicians were intimately involved with the financial well-being of the enterprise in that the yearly "kickback" was paid to

Carle physicians only if the annual expenditure made by physicians on benefits was less than total plan receipts. According to the complaint, Carle doctors stood to gain financially when they were able to limit treatments and referrals. Due to the dual-loyalties at work, Carle doctors were faced with an incentive to limit costs so as to guarantee a greater kickback. * * *

In summary, we hold that the language of the plaintiff's complaint is sufficient in alleging that the defendants' incentive system depleted plan resources so as to benefit physicians who, coincidentally, administered the Plan, possibly to the detriment of their patients. The ultimate determination of whether the defendants violated their fiduciary obligations to act solely in the interest of the Plan participants and beneficiaries, see 29 U.S.C. § 1104(a)(1), must be left to the trial court. On the surface, it does not appear to us that it was in the interest of plan participants for the defendants to deplete the Plan's funds by way of year-end bonus payouts. Based on the record we have before us, we hold that the plaintiff has alleged sufficiently a breach of the defendants' fiduciary duty.

3. Loss to Plan

Finally, the defendants argue that Herdrich's claim must be dismissed because she does not allege that she suffered any loss attributable to the defendants' disputed breach. Specifically, they contend that beneficiaries in an ERISA plan may not recover anything other than the benefits provided expressly in the Plan itself. This is a mischaracterization of the law as it stands in this circuit.

ERISA allows any plan beneficiary to sue any plan fiduciary for breach of fiduciary duty. "Any person who is a fiduciary with respect to a plan who breaches any of the responsibilities, obligations, or duties imposed upon fiduciaries by [ERISA] shall be personally liable to make good to such plan any losses to the plan resulting from each such breach...." 29 U.S.C. § 1109(a). Furthermore:

A civil action may be brought—

(3) by a participant, beneficiary, or fiduciary (A) to enjoin any act or practice which violates any provision of [ERISA] or the terms of the plan, or (B) to obtain other appropriate equitable relief (i) to redress such violations or (ii) to enforce any provisions of [ERISA] or the terms of the plan....

Id. at § 1132(a). * * * In such suits, plan beneficiaries have standing to bring an action on behalf of the plan itself to recoup monies expended in violation of ERISA, as the plaintiff has done here. See 29 U.S.C. § 1132(a). "[T]he fiduciary duties set forth in § [1109] run only to the plan, and not to individual beneficiaries." * * * In paragraph 13 of her complaint, Herdrich alleges that as a result of the defendants' actions, the Plan was deprived of the supplemental medical expense payment amounts in controversy. We thus hold that she has alleged with sufficient clarity that the Plan suffered a loss as a result of the defendants' actions.

* * *

REVERSED.

FLAUM, CIRCUIT JUDGE, dissenting.

* * * I fully accept the Majority's conclusion that, taking the allegations of the complaint as true, "an incentive existed for [the defendants] to limit treatment and, in turn, HMO costs so as to ensure larger bonuses."[ ] I disagree with the Majority's holding, however, that the mere existence of this asserted conflict, without more, gives rise to a cause of action for breach of fiduciary duty under ERISA. * * *

As described in the complaint, the defendants occupy two different roles in the health plan. The defendants are the plan's doctors, who provide medical care to the plan beneficiaries, and they are also the plan administrators, who (as fiduciaries) make decisions about what claims and conditions are covered under the plan. The complaint alleges that the defendants have breached their fiduciary duty in two ways. First, according to the complaint, the defendants have hired CARLE owner/physicians (i.e., themselves) to provide medical services under the plan while cutting costs by minimizing the resources expended on each patient. By minimizing these expenditures, the defendants preserve funds to be distributed to themselves as year-end bonuses. Second, the complaint alleges that the defendants have administered disputed and non-routine claims. Again, the implication is that these claims are administered with an eye towards denying these claims to augment the defendants' year-end bonuses. Thus, the complaint alleges a structural incentive to deny care both at the point of delivery (i.e., the treatment decisions affecting patient care) and at the point of entry (i.e., the coverage decisions). In my view, however, merely pointing out the existence of these structural incentives does not suffice to make out a cause of action for breach of fiduciary duty under ERISA.

Consider first the defendants' alleged incentive to deny coverage in disputed and non-routine claims. Based on the allegations in the complaint, there is indeed an incentive to deny claims and thereby maintain large year-end bonuses. Unlike the common law of trusts, however, which is merely the baseline for determining the scope of fiduciary duty under ERISA,[ ] ERISA tolerates some conflict of interest on the part of fiduciaries. Most notably, [ ] ERISA permits an employer or other plan sponsor to have its own "officer, employee, agent, or other representative" serve as trustee or other fiduciary. 29 U.S.C. § 1108(c)(3).[ ] One justification for this departure from the common-law tradition is that allowing a plan sponsor to designate its own agent as a fiduciary reassures the sponsor that, in devoting its assets to the plan, it has not relinquished all ability to ensure that the plan's resources are used wisely. This reassurance in turn encourages more employers and other sponsors to establish benefits plans. See Daniel Fischel & John Langbein, ERISA's Fundamental Contradiction: The Exclusive Benefit Rule, 55 U. Chi. L. Rev. 1105, 112728 (1988). Although the dual loyalty ascribed to the defendants in this case is not identical to the conflict experienced by a fiduciary who is also the sponsor's agent, section 408(c)(3) demonstrates that dual loyalties are not per se unlawful under ERISA.

Moreover, we have recognized in a related context that market forces help reduce the risk that the fiduciary's conflict of interest in making coverage decisions will work to the detriment of the plan and the plan beneficiaries. * * * We have recently expanded on this rationale in finding that no conflict of interest existed when an insurer serving as a plan administrator denied a claim that, if it had been approved, would have been paid out of the insurer's assets:

> [I]t is a poor business decision to resist paying meritorious claims for benefits. Companies ... that sponsor ERISA plans are customers who choose which group insurance policies they will use to fund their plans.... [T]hese employers want to see their employees' claims granted because they want their employees satisfied with their fringe benefits. These corporate employers have the sophistication and bargaining power necessary to take their business elsewhere if an insurer ... consistently denies valid claims. In the long run, this type of practice would harm an insurer by inducing current customers to leave and by damaging its chances of acquiring new customers. Thus, no conflict of interest exists because paying meritorious claims is in [the insurer's] best interest.

Mers v. Marriott Int'l Group Accidental Death & Dismemberment Plan, 144 F.3d 1014, 1020–21 (7th Cir.1998).

The reasoning regarding conflicts of interest in the denial of benefits context applies with equal force to the plaintiff's claim of breach of fiduciary duty. The sponsor of the plaintiff's plan, State Farm, is a sophisticated, experienced player in the market for health benefits. The defendants do have a financial interest in denying coverage, * * * But State Farm has an interest in ensuring that its employees are satisfied with their fringe benefits, and the defendants have an interest in ensuring that State Farm is satisfied with the defendants' performance in delivering health care to the beneficiaries. In this sense, the interests of the administrator align with the interests of the beneficiaries and the sponsor. I recognize, of course, that monitoring of plan administrators by sponsors and beneficiaries is sometimes imperfect, and there is no guarantee that a sponsor will be able to find satisfactory alternatives in the marketplace. The plaintiff's complaint, however, alleges only that an incentive to deny coverage exists, which in my view is not enough to support an inference that market forces have failed in this case to protect the interests of beneficiaries.

The complaint's second allegation of breach of fiduciary duty, alleging an incentive to deny care at the point of delivery, also fails to state a claim upon which relief may be granted. As the Majority points out, such incentives are increasingly common in the age of managed care. Although the Majority identifies the potential pitfalls of managed care plans,[ ] there are also benefits to such plans that nevertheless make them attractive to many sponsors and beneficiaries of ERISA plans.[96] Since many sponsors and benefi-

---

96. The goal of a managed care plan is to deliver health care more cost-effectively by eliminating unnecessary or ineffective treatments and providing necessary care more efficiently. Some plans, like the one addressed in this case, attempt to achieve these goals by introducing incentives that encourage physicians to internalize part of the costs of treatment. * * * Other plans try to achieve efficiency goals by implementing utilization review procedures, in which the treating physician must obtain from the insurer advance approval of patient-care decisions. This method also has its drawbacks, especially when the reviewer lacks the medical expertise of the treating physician. See generally E. Haavi Morreim, Diverse and Perverse Incentives of Managed Care: Bringing Patients into Alignment, 1 Widener L. Symp. J. 89, 91–95 (1996) (describing the variety of cost-containment techniques employed by managed care plans).

Of course, the desirability of these different cost-containment measures from a policy standpoint is not our concern. But in assessing the plaintiff's assertion that incentives alone constitute a breach of fiduciary duty, it is worth noting that some commentators defend

ciaries of managed care plans view financial incentives as a desirable way of conserving the plan's assets by encouraging physicians to use resources more efficiently, merely alleging the existence of financial incentives to limit care cannot suffice to make out a claim of breach of fiduciary duty.

The complaint could be read to imply, however, that the defendants' incentives to limit care are so high that they work to the detriment of the plan and plan beneficiaries. When health plans provide physicians with incentives to internalize costs and maximize efficiency, as appears to be the case here, there is a serious concern that patient care will suffer if the incentives to limit care are set too high. * * * If the complaint is indeed asserting that the incentives in this case are excessive, then the plaintiffs in effect are inviting the court to make its own determination about appropriate incentive levels in managed care.

In reversing the dismissal of the plaintiff's complaint, the Majority appears to accept this invitation. In my view, however, judicial efforts to determine permissible levels of financial incentives through the vehicle of ERISA's fiduciary rules are unnecessary and ill-advised. No standards for conducting such an inquiry exist. Such a move would preempt legislative and regulatory efforts in this area and could seriously disrupt the ability of plan sponsors and beneficiaries to manage plan assets by agreeing to incentives that encourage cost-conscious medical decisionmaking. The Majority's decision provides little guidance for the district court on remand, and I fear that the decision today could lead, both in this case and in the future, to untethered judicial assessments of permissible incentive levels in health care plans.

Although I cannot join the Majority's decision in this case, I share the Majority's concern about the possibility of incentives that may harm plan beneficiaries, and I believe that courts have a role in ensuring that incentives are implemented in accordance with the fiduciary duties imposed by ERISA. In my judgment, this role is triggered when the market fails to ensure that the interests of sponsors, administrators, and beneficiaries are in alignment. As noted above, plan sponsors are likely to take their business elsewhere if they perceive that incentives are working to the detriment of beneficiaries or the plan itself, and thus market forces go a long way towards ensuring that incentives do not rise to dangerous or undesirable levels. In order for the market to function in this context, however, sponsors and beneficiaries need information about the financial incentives that are in place. Thus, I would follow the Eighth Circuit's lead in holding that the failure to disclose financial incentives is a breach of fiduciary duty under ERISA. See Shea v. Esensten, 107 F.3d 625 (8th Cir.1997).

Until the Majority's expansion of liability in today's case, Shea stood at the frontier in terms of imposing liability under ERISA on health plans that

the use of financial incentives as a superior alternative to utilization review by insurers. By removing the insurer as an intermediary in patient care decisions, financial incentives can give physicians greater clinical autonomy (provided that the incentives are set at an appropriate level) and may lead to better decisions about how to reduce costs while maintaining

quality. See Frances H. Miller, Capitation & Physician Autonomy: Master of the Universe or Just Another Prisoner's Dilemma? 6 Health Matrix 89, 97–99 (1996); David Orentlicher, Paying Physicians More to Do Less: Financial Incentives to Limit Care, 30 U.Rich.L.Rev. 155, 173–77 (1996).

seek to control costs by providing financial incentives to limit patient care. The Shea decision has proven to be controversial. [ ]

Even when disclosures have been made, I would not rule out the possibility that the imposition of incentives to limit care could support a claim of breach of fiduciary duty when there is a serious flaw in the manner in which the incentive arrangement is established or a significant limitation on the ability of plan sponsors to obtain alternative arrangements in the market. Such a claim would have to make some allegation, which the plaintiffs in the instant case do not, pointing to special circumstances suggesting a breakdown in the market or in the negotiating process that led to the imposition of incentives. The complaint in this case, however, contains no allegation of nondisclosure, and it fails to make any allegations suggesting that the financial incentives to limit care are anything but the result of the bargain fairly struck between the plan's sponsor, administrator, and beneficiaries. I would affirm the decision below dismissing the complaint.

A request for a rehearing en banc was denied by the Seventh Circuit in the Herdrich case. The dissent to this denial by Judge Easterbook adds another perspective on this case:

HERDRICH v. PEGRAM

170 F.3d 683 (Seventh Circuit, March 8, 1999).

EASTERBROOK, CIRCUIT JUDGE, with whom POSNER, CHIEF JUDGE, and FLAUM and DIANE P. WOOD, CIRCUIT JUDGES, join, dissenting from the denial of rehearing en banc.

Physicians employed by Carle Clinic Association, a health maintenance organization (HMO), failed to diagnose Cynthia Herdrich's appendicitis before her appendix ruptured. Peritonitis ensued, and Herdrich has recovered $35,-000 in damages for medical malpractice. She wants more, contending that Carle is a "fiduciary" under ERISA because her husband's employer State Farm Insurance Companies provided Carle's plan as a fringe benefit (making it a "welfare benefit plan" under ERISA), and that the divided loyalties at the core of an HMO structure are forbidden by ERISA. Like other HMO systems, Carle collects in advance for a period of care. The less medical services cost, the more an HMO's owners (here, Carle's physicians) have left as profit at the end of the period. According to the panel, this violates 29 U.S.C. § 1104(a)(1)(A).

Like any business, Carle seeks to hold down its costs. Like most other HMOs, Carle does this through devices that have come to be called "managed care." For example, subscribers must receive their medical care from Carle's own physicians if that is at all possible. Herdrich contends that this rule is responsible for her peritonitis: after finding an inflamed mass in her abdomen, a Carle physician scheduled her for an ultrasound examination eight days later at a Carle facility in Urbana, Illinois, rather than arranging for a local hospital in Bloomington to perform that examination immediately. That delay, the jury found in the malpractice case, led to the peritonitis.

When participants in an HMO plan sought to apply the "fraud" label to the money-saving incentive that characterizes the HMO form of organization, we replied that the details of HMO incentives need not be specifically explained to participants in ERISA plans. Anderson v. Humana, Inc., 24 F.3d 889 (7th Cir.1994). The HMO structure differs substantially from traditional fee-for-service medicine in giving the HMO an incentive to skimp on care once an illness is discovered. It is equally true that the HMO system creates an inducement to keep the subscribers healthy as long as possible. An HMO makes its profit from healthy subscribers and thus provides ample preventive and diagnostic care, while many fee-for-service physicians make their living from sick or injured persons. If the HMO creates an incentive to provide too little care once a subscriber becomes seriously ill, the fee-for-service system coupled with insurance provides an incentive to furnish excessive care, for third parties foot the bill. A choice between prepaid and fee-for-service systems is accordingly difficult to make in principle.

What I find troubling about the panel opinion, and why I believe this case should be reheard en banc, is that the panel has condemned HMO and managed-care systems on medical grounds, [] and used its view of good medical practice as the basis of a conclusion that the HMO structure violates ERISA. According to the panel, market forces do not constrain the pernicious incentives that HMOs adopt, and it is accordingly necessary to throw the weight of the law behind traditional fee-for-service medicine. * * * [S]uppose that HMOs and other managed-care systems are inferior to available alternatives. Why does ERISA authorize a court to prescribe its view of the best system?

The answer, according to the panel, is that ERISA requires plan administrators to act as fiduciaries, while the HMO structure puts physicians at (financial) odds with their patients. HMOs are of course not unique in this regard; insurers likewise seek to minimize their outlays for medical care and employ managed-care devices to promote thrift. But I am willing to suppose that Carle did not act as Herdrich's "fiduciary" would have. It did not have to.

Under ERISA,

> a person is a fiduciary with respect to a plan to the extent (i) he exercises any discretionary authority or discretionary control respecting management of such plan or exercises any authority or control respecting management or disposition of its assets, (ii) he renders investment advice for a fee or other compensation, direct or indirect, with respect to any moneys or other property of such plan, or has any authority or responsibility to do so, or (iii) he has any discretionary authority or discretionary responsibility in the administration of such plan.

29 U.S.C. § 1002(21)(A). Carle does not manage the State Farm plan or control its assets, so the panel emphasized sub-(iii), concluding that Carle has "discretionary authority or discretionary responsibility in the administration of such plan." [] Discretionary authority is obvious; but does Carle exercise discretion "in the administration of [the] plan", or only in the provision of medical services? This is a fundamental divide, for fiduciary status under ERISA is not an all-or-none affair. A person is a fiduciary only "to the extent" that he does one of the listed things * * * A surgeon exercises a great deal of discretion when deciding how (if at all) to perform an operation, but the fact that an ERISA welfare benefit plan pays for the medical procedure does not make the surgeon a "fiduciary" of the patient and convert all medical-

malpractice claims to federal common law under ERISA in the process. What is true at the level of a medical professional is true at the level of a medical practice group such as Carle. Unless the group exercises, not discretion in the abstract, but discretion "in the administration of [the] plan", it is not a fiduciary under ERISA. Lori Pegram, a physician employed by Carle, scheduled Herdrich for an ultrasound examination in Urbana on one day rather than in Bloomington on another; that does not sound like an exercise of discretion "in the administration of [the] plan". Similarly Carle's decision to establish one set of cost-saving incentives rather than another is not an exercise of discretion "in the administration of [the] plan"; it is an exercise of managerial discretion in the administration of Carle's business.

Perhaps it would be possible to read "in the administration of [the] plan" broadly in order to catch all discretionary elements of the HMO structure, but why should courts do this? In order to wipe out HMOs and foreclose the possibility that plan sponsors will choose that structure (or that participants will select it from among options the plan offers)? The panel's opinion sounds very much like this is the objective: its lengthy condemnation of managed care, [] otherwise is hard to understand. But ERISA does not tie the plan sponsor's hands on issues of plan design. An employer is free to offer an HMO as an option without objection on fiduciary-duty grounds. * * * If it is lawful under ERISA for an employer to offer an HMO as a welfare benefit, then it must be lawful for the HMO itself to administer a managed-care system. * * * What the panel has held comes to the same thing—though by a different route—as saying that welfare-benefit plans have a fiduciary duty not to adopt HMO or other managed-care options. If alternatives such as fee-for-service medicine are more expensive, then plan sponsors will be inclined to offer less medical coverage, and participants may be worse off. Clearly the panel thinks that they will be better off, and perhaps they will be. But ERISA allows plan sponsors and participants to choose for themselves. An employer is entitled to offer the combination of fringe benefits that it is willing to pay for; it need not offer the best available medical (or other) services. * * *

If Carle described to State Farm the cost-reduction incentives used by its plan, and State Farm knowingly chose Carle over other providers, then we have a simple plan-design issue. It would defeat the employer's right to specify the benefits conferred by a plan if the dissatisfied employee could turn around and sue the person who delivered those benefits. The only proper question in a suit against the supplier is whether that person did what he promised. Nothing in the panel's opinion suggests that Carle Clinic pulled a fast one on State Farm. Fiduciary duties are vital when contracts are incomplete, but when a contract fully specifies proper behavior, then even a full-fledged trustee need not (indeed, must not) depart from the contractual provisions that the settlor established.[] Carle followed its contract with State Farm and with its subscribers; that is all ERISA requires.

* * *

Perhaps this issue boils down to a matter of characterization. If one conceives of particular medical services as the "benefits" under the plan, then Carle serves as the gatekeeper to those benefits, and handling claims for medical benefits defined by a plan is a fiduciary role under ERISA. [] But if instead one conceives of the CarleCare HMO system as the benefit promised by the ERISA plan, then Carle is not a "fiduciary." It is just the supplier of medical care, like the surgeon discussed above. Which characterization is best? Herdrich does not allege that State Farm hired Carle to administer a medical plan that offers defined medical procedures as benefits; she alleges, rather, that the benefit State Farm offered is the CarleCare HMO system. And, for reasons I have already discussed, to the extent there is uncertainty about the right way to characterize Carle's role, the court should prefer the characterization that preserves plan sponsors' (and participants') freedom of choice. That means treating the Carle HMO as the benefit, rather than treating Carle as the administrator of the ERISA plan. If the HMO system is the benefit, then Carle is not acting as a fiduciary.

The choice between these characterizations is important—more than enough to justify convening the full court. Most medical care these days is furnished under ERISA plans. Most contemporary welfare benefit plans provide for managed care, through HMOs or other devices, at least as an option. The panel's opinion thus implies that the principal organizational forms through which medical care is delivered today are unlawful. If this conclusion is correct, then the cost-saving achieved by managed care must be abandoned, and the cost of medical care will rise, perhaps substantially.

I recognize that my colleagues in the majority of the panel have expressed their holding as a conclusion about this specific complaint and have written that cost-reduction incentives are not necessarily automatic violations of fiduciary duty. [] But a holding such as this is impossible to cabin, for the plan attacked in this case is an ordinary HMO. Drawing parallels to the case under consideration, Herdrich sets forth, in the amended third count of her complaint, the intricacies of the defendants' incentive structure. The Plan dictated that the very same HMO administrators vested with the authority to determine whether health care claims would be paid, and the type, nature, and duration of care to be given, were those physicians who became eligible to receive year-end bonuses as a result of cost-savings. Because the physician/administrators' year-end bonuses were based on the difference between total plan costs (i.e., the costs of providing medical services) and revenues (i.e., payments by plan beneficiaries), an incentive existed for them to limit treatment and, in turn, HMO costs so as to ensure larger bonuses. With a jaundiced eye focused firmly on year-end bonuses, it is not unrealistic to assume that the doctors rendering care under the Plan were swayed to be most frugal when exercising their discretionary authority to the detriment of their membership. [] If Carle's setup violates ERISA, then all managed care does so, because the allegations in the complaint narrate mundane features of health maintenance organizations. Limiting care to specific locations, limiting referrals to specialists, and using capitation fees (with the possibility of profit from cost-reducing strategies), and reaping for the HMO's owners the benefits of reduced health-care expenditures, are the principal features of HMOs and "preferred provider organizations." Unlike some other HMOs, Carle is owned by its physicians, but I do not think that this makes a legal (or practical) difference. Physicians own much of the stock of HMOs organized as corporations or receive some of its profits as bonuses or salary increments; and no matter the HMO's internal organization, the benefit to a particular physician from a particular treatment decision is minuscule. The effect of holding down costs can be large in the aggregate, but this is so whether the HMO is organized as a corporation or as a partnership. Indeed, it is so whether the organization is an HMO or a law firm. Lawyers owe fiduciary duties to their clients. Can it be that the incentive given by the partnership's reward structure to substitute the services of associates for those of the partners creates a conflict of interest that invariably violates those duties? If the answer is "no" for law firms (and that must be the right answer), it is "no" for HMOs, in stock or partnership form.

Even if all of this is wrong, however, the panel's opinion puts all managed-care systems at risk and commits the court to a long (and I should think unhappy) course of distinguishing "good" managed-care systems from "bad" ones. Assessments of this kind belong to plan sponsors and participants, not to judges. Federal law both recognizes and regulates HMOs. See 42 U.S.C. § 300e. It seems to me unwise and improper for a court to use ERISA to impress a different view of desirable medical care on employers and HMOs alike.

Notes

1.   Breach of fiduciary duty might also give rise to common law tort claims. See Chapter 6 above.

2.   Litigation under ERISA for denial of benefits has continued to flourish since the publication of the 3rd Edition. The Courts commonly apply a two step analysis to these claims, first reviewing whether the administrator has correctly interpreted the terms of the plan, and second whether the administrator's interpretation of the plan is an abuse of discretion, if the plan administrator is given discretion to make coverage decisions. (See McLaughlin v. General Am. Life Ins., 1998 WL 736689 (E.D.La.1998). In making the second determination, the courts consider whether the administrator faces a conflict of interest in making the benefit determination but approaches to this issue vary dramatically, with courts at one extreme assuming that an insurer or self-insured company faces a conflict almost by definition, since approval of any particular claim reduces its profits (See Killian v. Healthsource, 152 F.3d 514 (6th Cir.1998); McGraw v. Prudential Ins. Co. 137 F.3d 1253 (10th Cir. 1998); courts at the other extreme finding that conflicts should rarely be found, since any one claim has a negligible effect on the profit margins of plans, but routine denial of claims will give a plan a bad reputation and make it less competitive (See Farley v. Arkansas Blue Cross and Blue Shield, 147 F.3d 774 (8th Cir.1998); and courts in the middle attempting to determine whether there is anything in the particular case that indicates that a conflict of interest drove the particular decision.(See Friends Hosp. v. Metra-Health Serv. Corp., 1998 WL 321264 (E.D.Pa.1998); Elsroth v. Consolidate Edison Co., 10 F.Supp.2d 427 (S.D.N.Y.1998); Peruzzi v. Summa Medical Plan, 137 F.3d 431 (6th Cir.1998).

Insert at page 821 in place of note 2:

In September of 1998 the Department of Labor issued proposed regulations to update its ERISA claims procedure rule, which had been promulgated originally a quarter century ago, before managed care. The proposed rule apparently represents an attempt by the Clinton Administration to implement a managed care consumer bill of rights through regulatory action.

PART 2560—RULES AND REGULATIONS FOR ADMINISTRATION AND ENFORCEMENT

§ 2560.503–1 Claims procedure.

(a) In accordance with the authority of sections 503 and 505 of the Employee Retirement Income Security Act of 1974,[ ] this section sets forth minimum requirements for employee benefit plan procedures pertaining to claims for benefits by participants and beneficiaries (hereinafter referred to as claimants) or their representatives. * * *

(b) Every employee benefit plan shall establish and maintain reasonable procedures governing the filing of benefit claims, notification of benefit determinations, and appeal of adverse benefit determinations (hereinafter collectively referred to as claims procedures). The claims procedures for a plan will be deemed to be reasonable only if:

(1) The claims procedures comply with the requirements of paragraphs (c), (d), (e), (f), (g), and (h) of this section, as appropriate;

(2) A description of all claims procedures (including, in the case of group health plan services or benefits, procedures for obtaining preauthorizations, approvals, or utilization review decisions) and the applicable time frames is included as part of a summary plan description * * *;

(3) The claims procedures do not contain any provision, and are not administered in a way, that requires a claimant to submit an adverse benefit determination to arbitration or to file more than one appeal of an adverse benefit determination prior to bringing a civil action under section 502(a) of the Act;

(4) The claims procedures do not contain any provision, and are not administered in a way, that unduly inhibits or hampers the initiation or processing of claims for benefits. For example, a provision or practice that requires payment of a fee or costs as a condition to making a claim or to appealing an adverse benefit determination would unduly inhibit the initiation and processing of claims for benefits. Also, the denial of a claim for failure to obtain a preauthorization under circumstances that would make obtaining such preauthorization impossible or where application of the preauthorization process could seriously jeopardize the life or health of the claimant (e.g., the claimant is unconscious and has no representative or is in extremely serious need of immediate care at the time medical treatment is required) would constitute a practice that unduly inhibits the initiation and processing of a claim;

(5) The claims procedures do not foreclose or limit the ability of a representative to act on behalf of the claimant; and

(6) The claims procedures provide that, in the event that a claimant or a representative of a claimant makes a benefit request that fails to comply with the requirements of the plan's procedures for making a claim, the plan administrator shall notify the claimant of such failure and of the plan's procedures governing the making of a claim. The plan administrator shall provide this notification within a reasonable period of time appropriate to the circumstances, taking into account any pertinent medical exigencies, not to exceed 5 days (24 hours in the case of a benefit request involving urgent care) following receipt of the benefit request by the plan. The benefit request shall

be deemed to have been received by the plan when the claimant or representative makes a communication reasonably calculated to bring the request to the attention of persons responsible for benefit claim decisions. [Including:]* * *

(i) In the case of a single employer plan, either the organizational unit customarily in charge of employee benefits matters for the employer or any officer of the employer;

(ii) In the case of a plan to which more than one employer contributes or which is established or maintained by an employee organization, the joint board, * * * (or any member of any such board, * * *) responsible for establishing or maintaining the plan or the person or the organizational unit customarily in charge of employee benefit matters;

(iii) In the case of a plan the benefits of which are provided or administered by an insurance company, insurance service, third-party contract administrator, health maintenance organization, or similar entity, the person or organizational unit with the authority to pre-approve, approve, or deny benefits under the plan or any officer of the insurance company, insurance service, third-party contract administrator, health maintenance organization, or similar entity.

* * *

(7) The claims procedures provide that, in the case of a claim involving urgent care within the meaning of paragraph (j)(1), for an expedited process pursuant to which—

(i) A request for an expedited determination may be submitted orally or in writing by the claimant or the claimant's representative; and

(ii) All necessary information, including the plan's benefit determination, shall be transmitted between the plan and the claimant by telephone, facsimile or other similarly expeditious method.

(c) Claim for benefits. For purposes of this section, a claim for benefits is a request for a plan benefit or benefits, made by a claimant or by a representative of a claimant, that complies with a plan's reasonable procedure for making benefit claims. In the case of a group health plan, a claim for benefits includes a request for a coverage determination, for preauthorization or approval of a plan benefit or for a utilization review determination in accordance with the terms of the plan.

(d) Notification of benefit determination.

* * *

(2) In the case of a group health plan, the plan administrator shall notify a claimant of the plan's benefit determination in accordance with paragraph (d)(2)(i), (d)(2)(ii), or (d)(2)(iii) of this section, as appropriate.

(i) In the case of a claim involving urgent care, within the meaning of paragraph (j)(1) of this section, the plan administrator shall notify the claimant, in accordance with paragraph (e) of this section, of the plan's benefit determination as soon as possible, taking into account the medical exigencies of the case, after receipt of the claim by the plan, but not later than 72 hours after receipt of the claim by the plan, unless the claimant (or the representative of the claimant) fails to provide sufficient information to determine whether, or to what extent, benefits are covered or payable under the plan. * * *

(ii) If a group health plan has approved a benefit or service to be provided for a specified or indefinite period of time, any reduction or termination of such benefit or service (other than by plan amendment or termination) before the end of such period shall constitute an adverse benefit determination within the meaning of paragraph (j)(2) of this section. To the extent that such an adverse benefit determination denies a claim involving urgent care, as defined in paragraph (j)(1) of this section, the plan administrator shall provide notice of the adverse benefit determination, in accordance with paragraph (e) of this section, at a time sufficiently in advance of the reduction or termination to allow the claimant (or a representative of the claimant) to appeal and obtain a determination on review of that adverse benefit determination before the benefit is reduced or terminated.

(iii) In the case of a claim that does not involve urgent care, the plan administrator shall notify the claimant, in accordance with paragraph (e) of this section, of the plan's benefit determination within a reasonable period of time appropriate to the circumstances, taking into account any pertinent medical circumstances, but not later than 15 days after receipt of the claim by the plan, unless the claimant (or the claimant's representative) has failed to submit sufficient information to determine whether, or to what extent, benefits are covered or payable under the plan. * * *

(e) Manner and content of notification of benefit determination. (1) Except as provided in paragraph (e)(2) of this section, the plan administrator shall provide a claimant with written or electronic notification of the plan's benefit determination.* * * In the case of an adverse benefit determination, within the meaning of paragraph (j)(2) of this section, the notification shall set forth, in a manner calculated to be understood by the claimant:

(i) The specific reasons for the adverse determination;

(ii) Reference to the specific plan provisions (including any internal rules, guidelines, protocols, criteria, etc.) on which the determination is based;

(iii) A description of any additional material or information necessary for the claimant to complete the claim and an explanation of why such material or information is necessary;

(iv) A description of the plan's review procedures and the time limits applicable to such procedures, including a statement of the claimant's right to bring a civil action under section 502(a) of the Act following an adverse benefit determination on review; and

(v) In the case of an adverse benefit determination by a group health plan involving a claim for urgent care, a description of the expedited review process applicable to such claims.

(2) In the case of an adverse benefit determination by a group health plan involving a claim for urgent care, the information described in paragraph (e)(1) of this section, may be provided to the claimant orally within the time frame prescribed in paragraph (d)(2)(i) of this section, provided that a written or electronic notification in accordance with paragraph (e)(1) of this section, is furnished to the claimant not later than 3 days after the oral notification.

(f) Appeal of adverse benefit determinations.

(1). Every employee benefit plan shall establish and maintain a procedure by which a claimant shall have a reasonable opportunity to appeal an adverse benefit determination, within the meaning of paragraph (j)(2) of this section, to an appropriate named fiduciary of the plan, and under which there will be a full and fair review of the claim and the adverse benefit determination.

(2) A claims procedure will not be deemed to provide a claimant with a reasonable opportunity for a full and fair review of a claim and adverse benefit determination unless:

(i) In the case of all plans, the claims procedure—

(A) Provides claimants a reasonable period of time, related to the nature of the benefit which is the subject of the claim and the attendant circumstances within which to appeal the determination. * * *

(B) Provides claimants the opportunity to submit written comments, documents, records, and other information relating to the claim for benefits;

(C) Provides that a claimant shall be provided, upon request, reasonable access to, and copies of, all documents, records, and other information relevant to the claimant's claim for benefits, without regard to whether such documents, records, and information were considered or relied upon in making the adverse benefit determination that is the subject of the appeal.

(D) Provides for a review that:

(1) Does not afford deference to the initial adverse benefit determination, and

(2) Takes into account all comments, documents, records, and other information submitted by the claimant (or the claimant's representative) relating to the claim, without regard to whether such information was submitted or considered in the initial benefit determination; and

(E) Provides for review by an appropriate named fiduciary of the plan who is neither:

(1) The party who made the adverse benefit determination that is the subject of the appeal, nor

(2) The subordinate of such party.

(ii) In the case of a group health plan, the claims procedure—

(A) Provides that, in deciding appeals of any adverse benefit determination involving a medical judgment, including determinations with regard to whether a particular treatment, drug, or other item is experimental, investigational, or not medically necessary or appropriate, the appropriate named fiduciary shall consult with a health care professional, as defined in paragraph (j)(5) of this section, who has appropriate training and experience in the field of medicine involved in the medical judgment;

(B) Provides that the health care professional engaged for purposes of a consultation under paragraph (f)(2)(ii)(A) of this section shall be independent of any health care professional who participated in the initial adverse benefit determination; and

(C) Provides in the case of a claim involving urgent care, within the meaning of paragraph (j)(1) of this section, for an expedited review process pursuant to which—

(1) A request for an expedited appeal of an adverse benefit determination may be submitted orally or in writing by the claimant or the claimant's representative; and

(2) All necessary information, including the plan's benefit determination on review, shall be transmitted between the plan and the claimant by telephone, facsimile, or other available similarly expeditious method.

(g) Notification of benefit determination on review.

* * *

(2) In the case of a group health plan—

(i) The plan administrator shall notify the claimant, in accordance with paragraph (h) of this section, of the plan's benefit determination on review within a reasonable period of time appropriate to the circumstances, taking into account any pertinent medical circumstances, but not later than 30 days after receipt by the plan of the claimant's request for review of an adverse benefit determination, unless the claim involves urgent care.

(ii) If a claim involves urgent care, the plan administrator shall notify the claimant of the plan's benefit determination on review as soon as possible, taking into account the medical exigencies of the case, after receipt by the plan of the request for review, but not later than 72 hours after receipt of the claimant's request for review of an adverse benefit determination.

* * *

(h) Manner and content of notification of benefit determination on review. The plan administrator shall provide a claimant with written or electronic notification of a plan's benefit determination on review. * * * In the case of an adverse benefit determination, * * * the notification must set forth, in a manner calculated to be understood by the claimant:

(1) The specific reasons for the adverse determination;

(2) Reference to the specific plan provisions (including any internal rules, guidelines, protocols, criteria, etc.) on which the benefit determination is based;

(3) A statement that the claimant is entitled to receive, upon request, reasonable access to, and copies of, all documents and records relevant to the claimant's claim for benefits, without regard to whether such records were considered or relied upon in making the adverse benefit determination on review, including any reports, and the identities, of any experts whose advice was obtained; and

(4) A statement of the claimant's right to bring a civil action under section 502(a) of the Act following an adverse benefit determination on review.

(i) In the case of the failure of a plan to establish or follow claims procedures consistent with the requirements of this section, a claimant shall be deemed to have exhausted the administrative remedies available under the plan and shall be entitled to pursue any available remedies under section 502(a) of the Act on the basis that the plan has failed to provide a reasonable claims procedure that would yield a decision on the merits of the claim.

(j) Definitions. For purposes of this section—

(1) (i) A claim involving urgent care is any claim for medical care or treatment with respect to which the application of the time periods for making non-urgent care determinations—

(A) Could seriously jeopardize the life or health of the claimant or the ability of the claimant to regain maximum function, or,

(B) In the opinion of a physician with knowledge of the claimant's medical condition, would subject the claimant to severe pain that cannot be adequately managed without the care or treatment that is subject of the claim.

(ii) * * * [W]hether a claim is a "claim involving urgent care" within the meaning of paragraph (j)(1)(i)(A) of this section is to be determined by an individual acting on behalf of the plan applying the judgment of a reasonable individual who is not a trained health professional.

(iii) Any claim that a physician with knowledge of the claimant's medical condition determines is a "claim involving urgent care" * * * shall be treated as a "claim involving urgent care" for purposes of this section.

(2) The term adverse benefit determination means any of the following: a denial, reduction, or termination of, or a failure to provide or make payment (in whole or in part) for, a benefit, including a denial, reduction, or termination of, or a failure to provide or make payment (in whole or in part) for, a benefit resulting from the application of any utilization review directed at cost containment, as well as a failure to cover an item of service for which benefits are otherwise provided because it is determined to be experimental or investigational or not medically necessary or appropriate.

* * *

(5) The term health care professional means a physician or other health care professional licensed, accredited, or certified to perform specified health services consistent with State law.

* * *

Note

The proposed ERISA regulations have proved quite controversial, and by early 1999 had generated over 600 comments as well as Congressional criticism. Insurance companies employers, and managed care organizations generally disapprove of the proposed rules, claiming that the time deadlines set out in the rules are too strict, that the rules' definition of "urgent care" is too broad, that the rules' ban on multilevel reviews would eliminate the opportunity many employees now have to obtain an employer review of plan action, that the rules give claimants too early access to the courts, and that the disclosure provisions of the rules would prove burdensome. Some unions are also critical of the rules' ban on arbitration, which often proves an effective tool for settling disputes. Consumer and professional groups are on the whole supportive of the rules, indeed some urge that the rules be made stronger. What provisions of the rules, if any, would you suggest need strengthening, or, conversely, are too restrictive? Are these rules more or less protective of beneficiaries than are state managed care laws in your state?

Insert on page 833 at the end of note 4:

In Geissal v. Moore Medical Corporation, 524 U.S. 74 (1998), the Supreme Court decided that a qualified COBRA beneficiary could elect COBRA coverage, even though he was already covered as a dependent under his spouse's insurance at the time he applied for COBRA continuation benefits.

Insert on page 834, just above Note on Discrimination:

Note on Federal Managed Care Regulation

As noted above, state managed care legislation cannot touch self-insured ERISA plans, and can only affect insured ERISA plans to the extent that the state law "regulates insurance." To deal comprehensively with perceived managed care abuses, therefore, federal legislation will be necessary. In 1997, the President's Advisory Commission on Consumer Protection and Quality in the Health Care Industry proposed a Consumer Bill of Rights and Responsibilities. Managed care legislation was perhaps the most hotly debated health policy issue at the federal level during 1998, with separate legislation proposed by Congressional Democrats, House Republicans and Senate Republicans, in addition to several bills with at least nominal bipartisan support.

There was substantial overlap among the bills, with most guaranteeing coverage for emergency care, banning "gag clauses," providing direct access to obstetrician-gynecologists and pediatricians, requiring broader disclosure of information on health plan policies, and establishing internal and external appeal procedures for coverage denials. The Republican alternatives were on the whole more limited, extending most protections only to the 48 million Americans in self-insured ERISA plans to avoid interfering with state regulation and limiting external appeals to denials involving more than $1000. Republican plans also included several hearty perennials of Republican health policy, like expanding access to Medical Savings Accounts and limiting malpractice plaintiff's rights. The major disputes, on which the legislation ultimately foundered, involved Democratic attempts to give plan members the right to sue health plans for injuries caused by health plan denials and to give health care professionals, rather than insurers, the right to define medical necessity.

The 1998 Congressional proposals for managed care regulation were vigorously opposed by insurers and managed care organizations, and supported by the American Medical Association, which was particularly interested in the medical necessity issue. In the end, a Republican bill narrowly passed the House, but was not adopted in the Senate. At this writing, federal managed care regulation remains contentious in the 1999 Legislative Session, with debate focusing on the extent of plan liability for coverage decisions that result in patient injury and on whether health plans or physicians should have final say on whether care is necessary.

What explains the consensus on appeal and access provisions, and the controversy on the liability and definition of medical necessity issues? What effect would adoption of managed care reforms have on the cost of health insurance? What effect would an increase in cost have on access to health insurance?

There has been a torrent of law journal articles addressing managed care regulation proposals, including symposia in 19 J. Legal Med. (September 1998); 23 J. Health Pol., Pol'y and L. (August 1998); 65 Tenn. L. Rev. (Winter 1998); 7 Ann. Health L. (1998); 28 Cumberland Law Review (1997–1998); 43 Vill. L. Rev. (1998); 15 Health Aff. (Nov/Dec. 1997); and free-standing articles by Peter Jacobson & Scott Pomfret, 35 Hous. L. Rev. 985 (1998); Wendy Mariner, 15 J. Contemp. Health L. & Pol'y 1 (1998); Jose Gonzales, 35 Hous. L. Rev. 715 (1998); Tracy Miller, 26 J.L.Med & Ethics 89 (1998); Eleanor Kinney, 10 Health L. 17 (1998); & Margaret Farrell, 23 Am.J.L. & Med. 251 (1997), among others.

Insert at page 835:

Since the 3rd Edition was published, there has been a steady increase in the volume of ADA litigation involving access to health insurance. The following case concerns a long-term disability rather than a health insurance policy, but the issues raised are identical to those at stake in the health insurance setting.

WINSLOW v. IDS LIFE INSURANCE CO.

United States District Court, Minnesota, 1998.
29 F.Supp.2d 557.

DAVIS, DISTRICT JUDGE.

Susan M. Winslow filed this action for declaratory and injunctive relief and for damages under the Americans with Disabilities Act ("ADA"), 42 U.S.C. § 12101 et seq., and the Minnesota Human Rights Act ("MHRA"), Minn.Stat. § 363.01 et seq. when she applied for and was denied long-term disability insurance by IDS Life Insurance Co. due to her current history of treatment for a mental health condition. The matter is before the Court on Defendant's motion for summary judgment which, for the foregoing reasons, is denied in part and granted in part.

BACKGROUND

On approximately October 27, 1994, Plaintiff Susan Winslow applied to IDS Life Insurance Co. for standard long-term disability insurance or, in the alternative, long-term disability insurance with a rider excluding coverage for periods of disability due to her mental health condition. Plaintiff indicated on her application that she had been treated for mental illness—dysthymia or mild depression[97]—within the past year and was currently taking Zoloft, an anti-depressant. IDS refused both requests for insurance based on its policy of automatically denying long-term disability insurance to applicants who report having received treatment for a mental or nervous condition, regardless of seriousness, within the twelve months prior to application. IDS policy allows such applicants to be reconsidered for long-term disability insurance after a year has passed since their last treatment for a mental or nervous condition. IDS asserts that its above-stated policy is based on industry-wide claims experience and actuarial data that indicates that the highest number of payments are made for depression-related claims. Plaintiff notes, however,

97. Dysthymia is a mental condition characterized by mild, chronic depression that is   treatable with medication and counseling * * *

that the IDS policy differs from that in the Paul Revere Underwriting Manual—a manual used by IDS in making other underwriting decisions—which does not require automatic rejection of applicants with current histories of mental or nervous conditions, such as Plaintiff's dysthymia, but instead provides for a long-term disability insurance policy with a longer exclusion period.[ ]

Plaintiff received notice of the denial of her long-term disability insurance application in November 1994 and requested reconsideration. In her request for reconsideration Plaintiff asserted to IDS that she had never been hospitalized or missed work due to her mental health condition and provided corroborative letters from two psychiatrists from whom she had received treatment, affirming that Plaintiff suffered only mild symptoms, which did not manifest themselves in work situations. Plaintiff also submitted to IDS letters of support from former and current employers praising her work performance. IDS received Plaintiff's additional documents, and after internal discussions, agreed that denial of Plaintiff's application was appropriate.

DISCUSSION

* * *

II.   Disability Under the ADA

In order to defeat summary judgment plaintiff Winslow must demonstrate that she is a person with a disability as defined by the ADA and therefore a plaintiff covered by the ADA. The ADA defines "disability" as "(A) a physical or mental impairment that substantially limits one or more of the major life activities of such individual; (B) a record of such an impairment; or (C) being regarded as having such an impairment." 42 U.S.C. § 12102(2)(A)-(C). Winslow does not argue that she meets criteria (A) or (B) of the ADA definition. Instead, Plaintiff asserts that IDS regarded her as disabled and treated her as having "a physical or mental impairment that substantially limits one or more of the major life activities," in this case, her future ability to work.[ ]

The relevant Equal Employment Opportunity Commission ("EEOC") regulations define "regarded as having an impairment" as:

(i) having a physical or mental impairment that does not substantially limit major life activities but that is treated by a private entity as constituting such a limitation; (ii) having a physical or mental impairment that substantially limits major life activities only as a result of the attitudes of others toward such impairment; (iii) having none of the impairments defined in . . . [above] but treated by a private entity as having such an impairment.[ ] 28 C.F.R. § 1630.2(1)-(3)). Both the ADA and EEOC regulations establish that a plaintiff, such as Winslow, whose claim asserts only that she was regarded by a defendant as having a substantially limiting impairment, need not prove that she in fact suffered such impairment. As a result, although both parties present conflicting views as to whether Winslow's dysthymia falls within the ADA definition of "impairment," this Court need not reach the question and requires only that Plaintiff demonstrate that she was "regarded as having such an impairment" by IDS, as she so asserts.

Plaintiff claims that the "major life activity" that Defendant perceives as "substantially limited" by her dysthymia is her future ability to work. It is undisputed that work is a "major life activity," which if substantially limited or regarded as substantially limited by a significant impairment qualifies a person as disabled under the ADA.[ ] 29 C.F.R. § 1630.2(i))[ ]

This Court finds, as a matter of law, that when IDS denied Plaintiff Winslow's application for long-term disability insurance based on her depression and anxiety, diagnosed as dysthymia, IDS implicitly considered her to be "impaired" and likely unable to perform "either a class of jobs or a broad range of jobs in various classes" in the future. * * *

Defendant asserts that even if Plaintiff can show that IDS regarded her as likely to suffer a substantially limiting impairment in the future, she has failed to show that IDS regarded her as disabled at the time it denied her application for long-term disability insurance as required by the statutory language of the ADA, which contains no future tense. See 42 U.S.C. § 12102(2)(C) ("regarded as having such an impairment")(emphasis added).* * *

In Doukas v. Metropolitan Life Insurance Company, 1997 WL 833134 (D.N.H.), the court held that "the distinction between present and future limitations [in the ADA] is not dispositive."[ ] In Doukas, Plaintiff Susan Doukas applied for and was denied mortgage disability insurance by MetLife. MetLife based its denial on information in Doukas' application indicating that she had been diagnosed with and was being treated for bipolar disorder and was therefore likely to become totally disabled from work in the future. MetLife moved for summary judgment on the grounds that Doukas did not fall within the ADA definition of disabled because she was not regarded as currently disabled and incapable of working but rather as presenting a future risk of disability. The court denied MetLife's motion, finding that "the 'regarded as' definition of disability seeks to eradicate discrimination based on prejudice or irrational fear. Fear, almost by definition, refers not to actual present conditions, but to anticipated future consequences."[ ] Courts have noted that the perception of impairment is included by Congress within the definition of disabled to combat the effects of " 'archaic attitudes,' erroneous perceptions, and myths that work to the disadvantage of persons with or regarded as having disabilities." * * *

* * * This Court finds the reasoning set forth in Doukas persuasive and holds that the purpose of the ADA requires that ADA protection extend to cover perception of possible future disability.

III.   Applicability of the ADA to Insurance Policies

Title III of the ADA provides:

No individual shall be discriminated against on the basis of disability in the full and equal enjoyment of the goods, services, facilities, privileges, advantages, or accommodations of any place of public accommodation by any person who owns, leases (or leases to), or operates a place of public accommodation.

42 U.S.C. § 12182(a). Section 12181(7) provides an illustrative list of entities considered public accommodations for the purposes of Title III. See

Parker v. Metropolitan Life Ins. Co., 121 F.3d 1006, 1010 (6th Cir.1997); Carparts Distribution Center, Inc. v. Automotive Wholesaler's Association of New England, Inc., 37 F.3d 12, 19 (1st Cir.1994). The issue before this Court is whether "public accommodations" are limited to actual physical structures or whether Title III of the ADA prohibits more than physical impediments to public accommodations for the disabled.

This issue is one of first impression for the Eighth Circuit and has been decided only by the First and Sixth Circuits, which split on the matter, and a smattering of district courts, some of which have followed the First Circuit in Carparts and others of which have adopted the reasoning of the Sixth Circuit in Parker.

In Parker, the Sixth Circuit reviewed the regulations applicable to Title III of the ADA to interpret "places" of public accommodation and found that a "place," as defined by 28 C.F.R. § 36.104, is "a facility, operated by a private entity, whose operations affect commerce and fall within at least one of the twelve 'public accommodation' categories."[ ] A "facility," in turn, is defined by 28 C.F.R. § 36.104 as "all or any portion of buildings, structures, sites, complexes, equipment, rolling stock or other conveyances, roads, walks, passageways, parking lots, or other real or personal property, including the site where the building, property, structure, or equipment is located." Parker, 121 F.3d at 1011. The court concluded that the plain meaning of the statutory language and the applicable regulations is that places of public accommodation are limited to physical places open to public access.[ ]

In Carparts, the First Circuit reached the opposite conclusion, determining that "public accommodations" are not limited to actual physical structures. Kotev v. First Colony Life Insurance Company, 927 F.Supp. 1316 (C.D.Cal.1996) followed the Carparts holding and addressed the issue at greater length. Kotev noted that the limited interpretation of "public accommodation" adopted by the Parker court would contravene the broadly stated purpose of the ADA to "provide a clear and comprehensive national mandate for the elimination of discrimination against individuals with disabilities … and invoke the sweep of congressional authority … in order to address the major areas of discrimination faced day-to-day by people with disabilities."[ ]

"Disability" under the ADA includes both physical and mental impairments as well as those with records of or regarded as having such impairments. See 42 U.S.C. § 12102(2)(A)-(C). By restricting "public accommodations" to include only physical structures, the protection under the ADA for individuals with mental disabilities would be virtually negated, absent circumstances in which a physical structure denied access to the mentally impaired.[ ]

Especially relevant to the present case is ADA statutory language that would be rendered irrelevant if Title III were held to apply only to physical access to public accommodations:

(i) the imposition or application of eligibility criteria that screen out or tend to screen out an individual with a disability or any class of individuals with disabilities from fully and equally enjoying any goods, services, facilities, privileges, advantages, or accommodations, unless such criteria can be shown to be necessary …

(ii) a failure to make reasonable modifications in policies, practices, or procedures, when such modifications are necessary to afford such goods, services, facilities, privileges, advantages, or accommodations to individuals with disabilities ...

(iii) a failure to take such steps as may be necessary to ensure that no individual with a disability is excluded, denied services, segregated or otherwise treated differently than other individuals because of the absence.

42 U.S.C. § 12182(b)(2)(A)(i-iii)[ ] Also rendered superfluous by such a narrow interpretation would be the Title III provision for injunctive relief set forth in 42 U.S.C. § 12188(a)(2) that "shall also include requiring the ... modification of policy."

Further supporting the conclusion reached by Kotev and a growing number of district courts—that ADA Title III applies to the provision of insurance policies—is the "Safe Harbor" provision of Title III, specifically addressing insurance. * * * The Safe Harbor provision states, in relevant part:

Subchapters I through III of this chapter and Title IV of this Act shall not be construed to prohibit or restrict-

(1) an insurer, hospital or medical service company, health maintenance organization, or any agent, or entity that administers benefit plans, or similar organizations from underwriting risks, classifying risks, or administering such risks that are based on or not inconsistent with State law;

. . .

Paragraphs (1), (2), and (3) shall not be used as a subterfuge to evade the purposes of subchapter[s] I and III of this chapter. 42 U.S.C. § 12201(c). Courts have concluded, and this Court agrees, that the Safe Harbor provision would be superfluous if "insurers could never be liable under Title III for conduct such as discriminatory denial of insurance coverage."[ ]

* * * The DOJ [in its legislative history of the ADA also] interprets Title III as prohibiting "differential treatment of individuals with disabilities in insurance offered by public accommodations unless the differences are justified."

* * *

Based on the legislative history, the DOJ interpretation of Title III of the ADA, and the reasoning adopted by a growing number of district courts, this Court finds that Title III of the ADA is applicable to insurance policies and not limited to access to actual physical structures.

A.   The McCarran–Ferguson Act

Defendant argues that the McCarran–Ferguson Act, 15 U.S.C. § 1012 et seq., precludes application of the ADA to insurance policies because Title III is not intended to regulate the business of private insurance carriers. The McCarran–Ferguson Act provides, in relevant part:

No Act of Congress shall be construed to invalidate, impair or supersede any law enacted by any State for the purpose of regulating the business of insurance ... unless such Act specifically related to the business of insurance.

15 U.S.C. § 1012(b)[ ]. The McCarran–Ferguson Act bars the application of a federal statute if:

(1) the statute does not specifically relate to the business of insurance; (2) a state statute has been enacted for the purpose of regulating the business of insurance; and (3) the federal statute would invalidate, impair, or supersede the state statute.

* * *

This Court identifies two fundamental provisions of the ADA that specifically relate to the business of insurance. The Court finds that the "subterfuge" provision of the ADA, see supra, 42 U.S.C. § 12201(c), which prohibits the use of the Safe Harbor provision to evade the purpose of Title III of the ADA is a statutory provision specifically related to the business of insurance. * * * The Court also interprets the inclusion of an "insurance office" as an entity considered a public accommodation for the purposes of Title III of the ADA, see 42 U.S.C. § 12181(7)(F), as an explicit indication that the ADA is intended to specifically relate to the business of insurance.

* * *

The McCarran–Ferguson Act is a form of inverse preemption, so principles defining when state remedies conflict with ... federal law are pertinent in deciding when federal rules " 'invalidate, impair, or supersede' state rules."[ ] * * * "[D]uplication is not conflict '[however] and * * * as a general rule,' state and federal rules that are substantively identical but differ in penalty do not conflict with or displace each other," * * * This court * * * holds that the McCarran–Ferguson Act does not "invalidate, impair, or supersede" the relevant Minnesota statutes and does not bar plaintiff's ADA claims.

IV. The Safe Harbor Provision

As indicated above, the ADA provides a Safe Harbor provision for insurance providers under the ADA. See supra, 42 U.S.C. § 12201(c). Under the Safe Harbor provision, the risk underwriting engaged in by insurance companies must be based on or not inconsistent with state law.[ ] The subterfuge provision, see supra 42 U.S.C. § 12201(c), provides, however, that even if an insurer's practices are consistent with applicable state law, they can still violate the ADA if plaintiff demonstrates that the insurance policies are a subterfuge to evade the purpose of the ADA.[ ] Thus, the Court must perform a two-part analysis to determine whether the IDS policies in question violate the Safe Harbor provision of the ADA: (1) is the eligibility criteria employed by IDS based on and consistent with state law; and (2) is the eligibility criteria a subterfuge to evade the purposes of the ADA.

Minn.Stat. § 72A.20 provides in relevant part:

Subd. 9. Making or permitting any unfair discrimination between individuals of the same class and of essentially the same hazard in the amount of premium, policy fees, or rates charged for any policy or contract of accident or health insurance or in the benefits payable thereunder, or in any terms or conditions of such contract, or in any other manner whatever, or in making or permitting the rejection of an individual's application for accident or health insurance coverage, as well as the determination of the rate class for such individual, on the basis of a disability, shall constitute an unfair method of competition and an unfair and deceptive act or practice, unless the claims experience and actuarial projections and other data establish significant and substantial differences in class rates because of the disability.

Subd. 19. No life or health insurance company doing business in this state shall engage in any selection or underwriting process unless the insurance company establishes beforehand substantial data, actuarial projections, or claims experience which support the underwriting standards used by the insurance company. * * *

Minn.Stat. § 72A.20, subd. 9, 19.

IDS categorically denies long-term disability insurance to any applicant who has been treated for a mental health condition within the past year, allowing the applicant to be reconsidered after one year has passed since the last treatment. To comply with Minnesota law, IDS must justify such eligibility criteria with claims experience, actuarial projections, or other data to "establish significant and substantial differences in class rates because of the disability."[ ]

IDS asserts that it has presented such justification for its eligibility criteria and therefore does not violate state law. The Court acknowledges that IDS presents specific industry data based on claims experience and actuarial projections that show a dramatic increase in payments on long-term disability insurance claims due to mental health and nervous disorders. Plaintiff counters that while Defendant establishes that claims for disability due to mental or nervous conditions have increased since 1989, Defendant fails to demonstrate that individuals receiving treatment for mental or nervous conditions at or near the time of application for insurance are more likely to file claims under their long-term disability insurance. Furthermore, Plaintiff notes that the Paul Revere Underwriting Manual includes various impairments, such as dysthymia, and establishes procedures for processing applications from individuals with such impairments without recommending total denial of insurance for such applicants. Implicit in Plaintiff's observation is a challenge to the "substantial" actuarial data and claims experience presented by Defendant and their applicability to Plaintiff's situation. Thus, Plaintiff claims that a genuine issue of material fact exists as to whether IDS' long-term disability insurance eligibility criteria conforms to sound actuarial principles, claims experience, or substantial data as required by Minnesota state law. The Court agrees and denies summary judgment on the matter.

Defendant also asserts that it is entitled to Safe Harbor protection under Title III of the ADA because its eligibility criteria are not a subterfuge. See supra, 42 U.S.C. § 12201(c). The issue of subterfuge arises only if it is determined that Defendant's practices are based on or not inconsistent with Minnesota law. As this Court has determined that a genuine issue of material fact exists as to whether IDS eligibility criteria violates Minnesota law, the Court need not pass on the issue as to whether the criteria is a subterfuge of the ADA.

V.   Disability–Based Distinction Under the ADA

Plaintiff asserts that the IDS policy of denying long-term disability insurance to all applicants having received mental health treatment within the past year is founded on a disability-based distinction violative of the ADA. Courts have found that broad-based distinctions that distinguish between mental and physical health conditions do not qualify as illicit disability-based distinctions under the ADA because the ADA is only applicable to discrimination against disabled persons compared to non-disabled persons, not discrimination among the disabled.[ ] Furthermore, the EEOC, Interim Enforcement Guidance on the Application of the Americans with Disabilities Act of 1990 to Disability–Based Distinctions in Employer Provided Health Insurance ("EEOC Interim Guidance"), establishes the following:

Some employer provided health insurance plans ... [distinguish] between the benefits provided for the treatment of physical conditions on the one hand, and the benefits provided for the treatment of "mental/nervous" conditions on the other ... Such broad distinctions, which apply to the treatment of a multitude of dissimilar conditions and which constrain individuals both with and without disabilities, are not distinctions based on disability.[ ] EEOC Interim Guidance, (June 8, 1993), reprinted in Fair. Empl.Prac.Man. 405:7115, 7118(BNA).

The aforementioned cases and the EEOC Interim Guidance, however, address disability-based discrimination among the disabled that affects the quality and extent of coverage offered to one class of disabled as compared to another and do not address the categorical denial of access to insurance coverage to a class of disabled individuals. When courts have addressed the exclusion of a class of disabled from an insurance plan, they have found such exclusions violative of the ADA.[ ]

Legislative history of Title III of the ADA further supports the proposition that while disability-based distinctions in an insurance policy's terms are permissible under the ADA, a policy to deny insurance coverage categorically to mentally disabled is unacceptable:

[W]hile a plan which limits certain kinds of coverage based on classification of risk would be allowed under this section, the plan may not refuse to insure, or refuse to continue to insure, or limit the amount, extent, or kind of coverage available to an individual, or charge a different rate for the same coverage solely because of a physical or mental impairment except where the refusal, limitation, or rate differential is based on sound actuarial principles or is related to actual or reasonably anticipated experience.... S.Rep. No. 116, 101st Cong. 1st Sess. (1989)[ ] see also H.R.Rep. No. 101–485, pt. 2, at 136–137 (1990),[ ] This Court finds that as Defendant's policy of denying long-term disability insurance to those treated for mental conditions within the past year denies said individuals access to insurance coverage, the policy is founded on a disability-based discrimination violative of the ADA.

VI. Minnesota Human Rights Act

[The court also found that IDS denial violated the Minnesota Human Rights Act, which is similar to the ADA, but concluded that punitive damages were not available under that Act, because the defendant's conduct did not demonstrate "willful indifference" to the plaintiff's rights.]

Note

The meaning of "subterfuge" under the 501(c) of the ADA has proved to be a contentious issue. The Third, Eighth and D.C. Circuits have followed the Supreme

Court's Decision in Public Employees Retirement System of Ohio v. Betts, 492 U.S. 158 (1989) (which interpreted the word "subterfuge" in the context of the Age Discrimination in Employment Act) in construing "subterfuge" very restrictively to mean that the allegedly discriminatory provision must have been "intended to serve the purpose of discriminating in some non-fringe-benefit aspect of the employment relation." The EEOC and other courts, looking to the legislative history of the ADA, conclude that a disability-based distinction may be a subterfuge if it is neither justified by legitimate actuarial date nor necessary to assure the financial soundness of the plan. See Ruth Colker & Bonnie Poitras Tucker, The Law of Disability Discrimination, 2d. 618–646 (1998).

Chapter 14

PUBLIC HEALTH CARE PROGRAMS: MEDICARE AND MEDICAID

Insert at page 857 in place of the Report and Recommendations to Congress:

Perhaps the most important development with respect to Medicare in the past year was the creation of the Medicare + Choice program in the Balanced Budget Act of 1997. The following report from the Medicare Payment Advisory Commission, an entity created by the BBA through the merger of the former Physician Payment Review Commission and Prospective Payment Advisory Commission, describes the new program and problems that it has encountered in implementation.

MEDICARE PAYMENT ADVISORY COMMISSION

The Medicare + Choice Program: Taking Stock After One Year
Testimony to Subcommittee on Health and Environment Committee
on Commerce United States House of Representatives
Gail R. Wilensky, Chair

* * * In August one year ago, the Balanced Budget Act (BBA) of 1997 created Medicare + Choice, a new program intended to give Medicare beneficiaries new choices of private health plans, slow the growth in Medicare spending, and better target the program's resources. The new program takes effect January 1, 1999, although many provisions will not kick in until January 1, 2000.

* * *

My testimony today describes the Medicare + Choice program, discusses the steps HCFA has taken in implementing it, and reports MedPAC's advice to the HCFA Administrator regarding the steps taken to date. I will also discuss the Commission's reaction to developments in the Medicare managed care market.

* * *

The Medicare + Choice program replaces the existing section 1876 risk contracting program and permits participation by a wide variety of private health plans. Under the new program, beneficiaries will be able to choose—in areas where they are offered—among a variety of coordinated care plans, including health maintenance organizations (HMOs) with or without a point-of-service option, preferred provider organizations (PPOs), and provider-sponsored organizations (PSOs). In addition, beneficiaries may enroll in private fee-for-service plans, and high-deductible plans offered in conjunction with a medical savings account (MSA).

The BBA modified the framework in which private health plans participate in Medicare, changing the responsibilities of both HCFA and participating plans. Notable among these changes is HCFA's new obligation to help beneficiaries make informed choices by routinely providing them comparative information about quality, access, financial liability, satisfaction, and financial stability for all plans serving their area. Participating plans are required to report detailed information to enable HCFA to undertake this responsibility and to facilitate program quality assurance. The BBA also established the framework for the Medicare + Choice quality assurance program, which features requirements for quality improvement activities and external quality review that differ by plan type.

The BBA also made significant changes in the way health plans are paid,

* * *

Until 1998, Medicare's payments to private health plans in a county were based on the average payments made on behalf of beneficiaries in its traditional fee-for-service program in that county. Under the Medicare + Choice program, payment rates are no longer based solely on local fee-for-service spending. Instead, base payment rates for each county are calculated as the higher of:

- a blend of an area-specific (county) rate and a national rate;

- a minimum or floor rate; or

- a rate reflecting a minimum update of the county's rate from the previous year.

The blended rate is designed to shift payment gradually away from local county rates, which reflect wide variation in fee-for-service costs and use of services, toward a national average rate. Blending will generally reduce payment rates in counties where payment rates have historically been higher than the national average rate, and will increase rates in counties where payments have been lower. Other things being equal, this should stimulate plan participation and beneficiary enrollment in areas where payments rise and dampen enrollment growth—and perhaps plan participation as well—in areas where payments fall.

MedPAC's Comments on HCFA's Proposals
for the Medicare + Choice Program

[HCFA published an interim final Medicare + Choice Rule on June, 1, 1998 at 63 Fed. Reg. 34968 (42 C.F.R. Part 422) to which these comments respond. This Rule was modified by a final rule published Feb. 17, 1999 at 64 Fed. Reg. 7968.]

* * *

Information for Beneficiaries. Medicare + Choice organizations will be required to provide certain information to their enrollees upon enrollment and annually thereafter. Routinely disclosed information must be provided in a clear, accurate, and standardized format and describe the plan's service area, benefits, number and mix of providers, coverage arrangements for out-of-area and emergency care, supplemental benefits and related premiums, prior authorization rules, procedures for filing grievances and appeals, disenrollment rights and procedures, and quality assurance program.

Recognizing that comparative information is critical both to empower beneficiaries and to support program oversight, MedPAC supports the information disclosure requirements established in the BBA and reiterated in the rule. However, as HCFA begins to develop specific reporting requirements, it should take care to weigh the informational value of each item against the costs borne by plans and providers in reporting it. Further, HCFA should carefully coordinate the information requirements it imposes on its plans with the encounter data standards it establishes to support risk adjustment of payments.* * *

Quality Assurance. As directed by the BBA, the rule requires participating plans to have an ongoing quality assessment and performance improvement program. All plans will be required to maintain information systems to collect, integrate, and analyze the data needed to assess and improve quality. They will also have to ensure the reliability and completeness of data collected from providers. Coordinated care plans—but not MSA plans or private fee-for-service plans—will be obliged to achieve minimum performance standards established by HCFA. Coordinated care plans and network MSA plans must also conduct projects to demonstrate sustained improvement in significant clinical and nonclinical aspects of care.

Implementation of these quality standards will pose formidable challenges. Yet to be addressed are issues such as:

- how to set standards without unduly restricting innovation and competition;

- whether quality measures can be identified that would permit meaningful comparisons across different types of plans and between those plans and traditional Medicare;

- how to adjust for important differences in enrolled populations when reporting performance measures; and

- how to reduce opportunities for manipulating the system at junctures such as choice of quality improvement project.

MedPAC is also concerned that the quality assurance system set forth in the rule will pose significant barriers to participation for all but the most tightly managed coordinated care plans. For example, plans with large, loosely organized networks may face challenges reporting certain types of quality measures or influencing practice behavior.* * *

Payments to Medicare+Choice Organizations. As with other topics addressed by the rule, the regulations concerning payment closely follow the BBA. In several areas, though, HCFA has used general program administration authority to define payment policies that are more prescriptive than was the case in the section 1876 risk contracting program.

Uniform Benefits and Plan Service Area Policy. Medicare's payment rates can vary considerably, even among counties within a single metropolitan area. Under the old risk program, plans could offer different benefit and premium combinations in different counties within their service areas to reflect differences in Medicare's payment rates. * * * After [1999], however, plans must provide uniform benefits at a uniform price to all enrollees across their entire service areas.

One way plans could continue to offer coverage across areas with diverse payment levels would be to divide their service areas into smaller units and match their benefit packages to the payment rates. But the preamble to the rule suggests that after 1999, plans will meet resistance in the plan approval process if they do this. Further, the rule requires service areas to stand alone in terms of meeting network access requirements. If plans could not meet these requirements, Medicare + Choice organizations might decide not to serve these counties at all. The Commission is concerned that beneficiaries in low-payment counties may have decreased access to Medicare + Choice plans as a result.

* * *

Adjusted Community Rate Proposal Calculation. The rule revises the adjusted community rate (ACR) proposal, essentially changing it from an actuarial estimate of costs to a report of actual costs incurred, with allowable adjustments. Administrative costs will be separated from additional revenues, which include profits, contribution to surplus, risk margins, and contributions to risk reserves.

MedPAC supports efforts to improve the ACR by making it better reflect actual costs. However, an ACR based on reported costs will probably require plans to provide more benefits and give them less financial slack to make up for unanticipated fluctuations in costs or payments, or errors and biases in accounting systems. HCFA should therefore monitor the impact of changes to the ACR and revisit policies regarding the benefit stabilization fund (a fund into which plans may contribute surplus payments to allow the provision of stable benefit packages over time).

In addition, the Commission advises examination of alternatives to the ACR for ensuring good value from private fee-for-service and MSA plans. * * *

Risk Adjustment. Risk adjustment is the process of setting capitation rates that reflect health status, paying plans more to care for ill beneficiaries than for healthy ones. Through 1999, monthly payments to private health plans under Medicare will continue to be based on the current risk adjustment method, under which payment to a plan for a particular enrollee is the product of the base payment amount for the county and the enrollee's risk score. Until this year, the base payment reflected 95 percent of the amount Medicare would expect to spend on behalf of an average beneficiary in the traditional fee-for-service program in that county. * * * The risk score, which is assigned on the basis of an enrollee's age, sex, eligibility for Medicaid, and whether or not the enrollee is institutionalized, reflects expected spending for that enrollee compared with spending for the average Medicare beneficiary in the traditional fee-for-service program.

Medicare's existing method of risk adjustment is widely acknowledged to be inadequate because its components account for very little of the variation in beneficiaries' health and use of health care services. As a result, program spending has been higher than it would have been had payments more closely matched the cost of caring for the relatively healthier people who enrolled in managed care. Inadequate risk adjustment leads to health plans having gains and losses unrelated to their efficiency in delivering care, and may also affect access to care for beneficiaries with high-cost health conditions.

The BBA provided a specific mandate and timetable for improving risk adjustment in the Medicare program, directing the Secretary to develop and implement a new risk adjustment methodology by January 1, 2000. * * *

In its September notice, HCFA proposed to implement a risk adjustment system based on enrollees' demographic characteristics and expected relative health status. Initially, health status would be measured using principal inpatient diagnostic cost groups (PIPDCGS), and principal diagnoses associated with any hospital stays that occurred during the preceding year. * * * Some time after 2002, the agency would incorporate information from encounter data from additional sites of care for the purposes of risk adjustment.

Effect of Risk Adjustment on Payments. The new risk adjustment method will change payments to health plans both individually and in the aggregate. Payments to individual plans are likely to change because the new system will be much more sensitive to differences in health status among beneficiaries, so that the average risk score for plans' enrollees may vary substantially. In addition, aggregate payments to plans are likely to decline because the relative healthiness of enrollees—which has not been captured by the current risk adjustment system—will be captured, to some extent, under the new system.

* * *

Next Moves

While the Medicare + Choice provisions of the BBA greatly expanded the array of plans eligible to participate in Medicare, only three non-HMO plans had sought to do so as of late August. And over the past few months, a number of plans have announced their intention to withdraw from or scale back their operations in particular Medicare markets. While some of these withdrawals are related to developments in the broader health insurance market, many plans have cited low Medicare payment rates and concerns about the costs of meeting the standards of the Medicare + Choice program as the reason for their actions.

These developments have raised questions in the minds of policy makers about whether the promise of the Medicare + Choice program will be realized and whether action is needed to boost payment rates to avoid future withdrawals, to modify certain regulatory requirements, or to mitigate the effects of risk adjustment. While these are clearly important questions, we are not yet in a position to give definitive answers to them. Two general considerations are relevant, however.

First, we note that in passing the BBA, Congress intended to slow the growth in payments to private plans and to-make payments more equitable across counties-through blending-and across plans-through risk adjustment.

By their very nature, these policies will change payment rates in ways that lead plans to retrench in some areas and to take advantage of opportunities newly available to them in other areas. The passage of time will help us determine whether this is taking place. Sudden changes in local markets are clearly a concern, however, and enrollment and plan participation should be closely monitored to guard against disruptions in beneficiaries' health care.

Second, circumstances during this transition year are unique. * * * Next year should provide better evidence of whether plans will participate in the program and how beneficiaries will react to their new choices.

Note

As the excerpt notes, experience under the first year following the BBA was not encouraging for those who advocate changing Medicare to a managed care-based program. During the fall of 1998, over forty HMOs insuring 440,000 beneficiaries had pulled out of Medicare. Though many of these beneficiaries changed to other HMOs, and some new managed care organizations entered into Medicare contracts, the dramatic growth in Medicare managed care hoped for by Congress has yet to occur.

The National Bipartisan Commission on the Future of Medicare established by the 1997 BBA to craft a bipartisan proposal for Medicare reform completed its work in March of 1999 without a final recommendation. The chair of the Commission, Senator John Breaux, had presented the following proposal, which received the support of ten of the seventeen members of the Commission. Because the Commission's rules only permitted it to make a recommendation with the support of eleven members, the Commission was unable to make a final recommendation to Congress. Senator Breaux, and Representative Thomas, the Ranking Minority Member of the Commission, intend to introduce the recommendation in Congress. A response to the proposal from an eminent group of health policy scholars follows the proposal:

National Bipartisan Commission on the Future of Medicare
BUILDING A BETTER MEDICARE FOR TODAY AND TOMORROW

* * *

We believe a premium support system is necessary to enable Medicare beneficiaries to obtain secure, dependable, comprehensive high quality health care coverage comparable to what most workers have today. We believe modeling a system on the one Members of Congress use to obtain health care coverage for themselves and their families is appropriate. This proposal, while based on that system, is different in several important ways in order to better meet the unique health care needs of seniors and individuals with disabilities. Our proposal would allow beneficiaries to choose from among competing comprehensive health plans in a system based on a blend of existing government protections and market-based competition. Unlike today's Medicare program, our proposal ensures that low income seniors would have comprehensive health care coverage.

Because the implementation of a premium support system will take a number of years, we recommend immediate improvements to the current Medicare program. In Section 11 we outline the incremental improvements to enhance the beneficiaries' security and quality of care now. We recommend immediate federal funding of pharmaceutical coverage through Medicaid for seniors up to 135% of poverty ($10,568 for an individual and $13,334 for a couple). This would also expand beneficiary participation in currently available subsidies for premiums and cost-sharing.

In reviewing * * * this proposal, it is important to keep in mind the different government roles in the premium support system and in current law. We believe the guarantee our society makes to every senior is to ensure that they can obtain the highest quality health care, and that their health care coverage not be allowed to fall behind that available to people in their working years. We believe that our society's commitment to seniors, the Medicare entitlement, can be made more secure only by focusing the government's powers on ensuring comprehensive coverage at an affordable price rather than continuing the inefficiency, inequity, and inadequacy of the current Medicare program.

I. PREMIUM SUPPORT SYSTEM TO PROVIDE COMPREHENSIVE COVERAGE

The Medicare Board

A Medicare Board should be established to oversee and negotiate with private plans and the government-run fee-for-service plan. Some examples of the Board's role are: direct and oversee periodic open enrollment periods; provide comparative information to beneficiaries regarding the plans in their areas; transmit information about beneficiaries' plan selections and corresponding premium obligations to the Social Security Administration to permit premium collection as occurs today with Medicare Part B premiums; enforce financial and quality standards; review and approve benefit packages and service areas to ensure against the adverse selection that could be created through benefit design, delineation of service areas or other techniques; negotiate premiums with all health plans; and compute payments to plans (including risk and geographic adjustment).

* * *

Ensuring Plan Performance and Dependability

All plans (private plans and the government-run FFS plan) would compete in the premium support system; all plans would have Board-approved benefit designs and premiums. The Board would ensure that the benefits provided under all plans are self-funded and self-sustaining, determining whether plan premium submissions meet strict tests for actuarial soundness, assessing the adequacy of reserves, and monitoring their performance capacity.

Management of Government-run Fee-for-service in Premium Support

The government plan would have to be self-funded and self-sustaining and meet the same requirements applied to all private plans, including whether its premium submissions meet strict tests for actuarial soundness, the adequacy of reserves, and performance capacity.

Cost containment measures would be necessary. The provisions of the Balanced Budget Act of 1997 should be extended, or comparable savings achieved. In any region where the price control structure of the government run plan is not competitive, the government-run fee-for-service plan could operate on the basis of contracts negotiated with local providers on price and performance, just as is the case with private plans. The government plan would be run through contractors as it is today; contractors in one region would be able to bid in other regions; the Board should have powers to assure that the government-run plan would not distort local markets.

Benefits Package

A standard benefits package would be specified in law. This benefits package would consist of all services covered under the existing Medicare statute. Plans would be able to offer additional benefits beyond the core package and plans would be able to vary cost sharing, including copay and deductible levels, subject to Board approval. Benefits would be updated through the annual negotiations process between plans and the Board, although the Board would not have the power to expand the standard benefit package without Congressional approval. Health plans would establish rules and procedures to assure delivery of benefits in a manner consistent with prevailing private standards and procedures offered to employer groups and other major purchasers.

The Medicare Board would approve benefit offerings and could allow variation within a limited range, for example not more than 10% of the actuarial value of the standard package, provided the Board was satisfied that the overall valuation of the package would be consistent with statutory objectives and would not lead to adverse or unfavorable risk selection problems in the Medicare market.

Outpatient prescription drug coverage and stop-loss protection

Private plans would be required to offer a high option that includes at least Medicare covered services plus coverage for outpatient prescription drugs and stop-loss protection. Plans would be able to vary copay and deductible structures. Minimum drug benefits for high option plans would be based on an actuarial valuation. High option and standard option plans each would be required to be self-funded and self-sustaining.

The government-run fee-for-service plan would be required to offer high option (including outpatient prescription drugs and stop-loss) in addition to standard option plans. The Medicare Board approval process would be the same as for private plans. High option and standard option plans would be required to be separately self-funded and self-sustaining. Government contracts would be based on prices commonly available in the market, without recourse to price controls or rebates.

Coverage would be provided through high option plans[for low-income beneficiaries]. The federal government would pay 100% of the premiums of the high option plans at or below 85% of the national weighted average premium of all high option plans for all eligible individuals up to 135% of poverty * * * on a fully federally funded basis. In areas where all high option plans cost more than this 85% threshold, the percentage will be determined locally to ensure that all low-income beneficiaries have access to high option plans. This financial support does not limit these beneficiaries' choice of plans nor restrict plans' design with regard to cost-sharing or other flexibility authorized by the Board. States would maintain their current level of effort, but the federal government would pay 100% of additional costs for these individuals.

* * *

Premium Formula Basics

On average, beneficiaries would be expected to pay 12 percent of the total cost of standard option plans. For plans that cost at or less than 85 percent of the national weighted average plan price, there would be no beneficiary premium. For plans with prices above the national weighted average, beneficiaries' premiums would include all costs above the national weighted average.

Only the cost of the standard package would count toward the computation of the national weighted average premium. Plans with a high option, whether private plans or government-run would separately identify the incremental costs of benefits beyond the standard package in their submissions to the Board, and the government contribution would be calculated without regard to the costs of these additional benefits.

The government-run fee-for-service plan would be treated the same as private plans.

* * *

Guaranteed premium levels where competition develops more slowly

In areas where no competition to the government-run fee-for-service plan exists, beneficiaries' obligations would be no greater than 12 percent of the FFS premium or the national weighted average, whichever is lower. The Medicare Board should periodically review those areas with a fixed percentage premium to ensure that the fixed percentage premium is not anti-competitive.

Medicare's Special Payments in a Premium Support System

Congress should examine all non-insurance functions, special payments and subsidies to determine whether they should be funded through the Trust fund or from another source. For example, payments for Direct Medical Education (DME) would be financed and distributed independent of a Medicare premium support system. Since the Part A and Part B trust funds would be combined and the traditionally separate funding sources of payroll taxes and general revenues would be blurred, Congress should provide a separate mechanism for continued funding through either a mandatory entitlement or multi-year discretionary appropriation program. On the other hand, Indirect Medical Education (IME) presents a unique problem since it is difficult to identify the actual statistical difference in costs between teaching and non-teaching hospitals. Therefore, for now Congress should continue to fund IME from the Trust Fund as an adjustment to hospital payments.

* * *

[Senator Breaux's proposal also recommended immediately providing outpatient prescription drug coverage under Medicare for beneficiaries with incomes up to 135% of poverty, improving access to outpatient prescription drugs through Medigap policies, combining Parts A and B, combining and lowering the A & B deductible, extending copayment requirements, and conforming the Medicare eligibility age to that of Social Security. Finally, the proposal recommended that the artificiality of the notion of a Medicare Trust fund be recognized, and that the financial stability of the Medicare be evaluated in terms of its demand on general revenue funds rather than in terms of the Part A trust fund.]

THE BREAUX PLAN: WHY IT'S THE WRONG MEDICINE FOR MEDICARE

Jonathan Oberlander, Jacob Hacker, Mark Goldberg, Theodore Marmor.
(Used by permission).

* * *

* * * Although Social Security currently tops the domestic policy agenda, Medicare actually faces a more uncertain budgetary outlook, because its costs are driven by medical inflation as well as demographic change. President Clinton has proposed to improve Medicare's finances by reserving 12 percent of the projected budget surplus to shore up the program—an idea resisted by Republican leaders in Congress, who wish to use the funds for tax cuts instead. A national discussion of how to improve and strengthen Medicare is therefore necessary, unavoidable, and even welcome. What is not welcome is the reform proposal that Senator Breaux and a majority of the Medicare Commission endorsed: a radical transformation of Medicare that would sacrifice the inclusive character of the program in pursuit of chimerical cost savings through private health plan competition.

The centerpiece of the Breaux plan is a proposal to transform Medicare into a "premium support" or voucher program. The federal government would replace current Medicare insurance with a fixed financial contribution that beneficiaries would use toward the purchase of insurance from a dizzying array of private plans, including Preferred Provider Organizations (PPOs), fee-for-service insurers, and HMOs. The traditional Medicare program would also remain an option. If beneficiaries chose a health plan that cost more than the amount of the federal voucher, they would have to pay the difference out of pocket. The theory here is that health plans would compete for enrollees by improving their efficiency and lowering their costs. Advocates expect, and hope, that introducing vouchers would encourage many beneficiaries to leave traditional Medicare for lower-cost managed care plans.

If the Commission's Medicare "premium support" plan sounds familiar, it should. The Breaux proposal bears a striking resemblance to the "managed competition" plan proposed by President Clinton in 1993. Ironically, the same coalition of Republicans and conservative Democrats that helped defeat the Clinton plan are now promoting managed competition for Medicare. And while this coalition strongly objected to the Clinton plan, they have voiced few qualms about pushing elderly and disabled Medicare enrollees into a competitive insurance market, despite evidence that these groups have nothing like the disposable income necessary to shop around in a competitive market and that chronically-ill seniors are at risk for inadequate medical care in HMOs. What was recently wrong for the entire population has strangely been deemed appropriate for the most vulnerable groups in society.

Senator Breaux's voucher solution for Medicare rests on four flawed assumptions: that Medicare faces a demographic crisis that requires immediate enactment of a radical solution; that vouchers will save substantial amounts of money for Medicare; that a competitive health market will enhance the choices and improve the medical care of Medicare beneficiaries; and that social insurance is no longer the appropriate means of ensuring health security for America's elderly and disabled.

Myth 1: Demographic Realities Demand Radical Reform

Perhaps the most fundamental flaw in the Breaux plan is its misdiagnosis of the problem. Put simply, the Bipartisan Commission's starting point is that there is demographic imperative to restructure Medicare. * * *

This definition of the problem in Medicare suffers from two basic difficulties. The first is the odd assumption that having more of the nation's population in Medicare is somehow a sign of program failure. Medicare's enrollment will undoubtedly grow in the coming decades, and with that growth will surely come higher levels of program spending. Yet this is hardly an indictment of Medicare. Rather, we should be thankful that we have a public program that helps shield not only the elderly, but also their children, from the potentially catastrophic costs of medical care.

The second problem is that long-term forecasts of health spending—which in the case of Medicare stretch 75 years into the future—are notoriously unreliable and provide a poor basis for public policy. No public program can, or should be, fully funded now for 2075. And while increased enrollment due to population aging will raise Medicare costs, how much those costs rise depends not simply on demography but crucially, on health costs per Medicare beneficiary. Incremental policy measures to raise revenues and slow down those costs can generate substantial savings over time and thereby moderate the fiscal expense of an aging population.

Finally, the Commission's enthusiasm for radical change might have been further tempered had they seriously examined the experiences of other industrial democracies. Many European nations have older populations than the United States and have an age structure that this country will not reach for another two decades. Yet of all these "older" countries spend substantially less on medical care than the United States. That is possible because all of these nations have universal health systems that control costs through budgeting and regulation of payments to medical care providers. Not one of the countries that have been successful in moderating the health care costs associated with an aging population has done so through vouchers. Vouchers are not the only solution to controlling the medical care costs of an aging population. In fact, they are the only unproven policy course.

Myth 2: Managed Competition Guarantees Big Savings

The Breaux plan projects substantial savings from competition among private insurance plans. The question is, with what justification? After all, during the past year, health care inflation in the private sector has surged, and the managed care industry has been beset by financial losses. * * * The Bipartisan Commission is jumping on a bandwagon that already shows signs of breaking down.

Meanwhile, Medicare costs rose by only 1.5% in 1998, slowed by regulatory controls on payments to medical providers. And program costs are now projected to grow less rapidly in coming years than health spending in the private sector, which was precisely the dominant pattern of the 1980s. It simply makes no sense for the federal government to imitate the faltering cost control strategies of the private sector, when its own Medicare regulatory policies are proving more effective.

The claim that managed competition would produce substantial savings in Medicare is no more than a leap of faith. And if that faith is not rewarded, and private plans do not hold their costs down as much as projected, the premium support scheme can save money only by shifting costs to Medicare beneficiaries, most of whom could ill afford the new expense. Seventy-five percent of Medicare beneficiaries have incomes below $25,000, and Medicare now covers only about half of the elderly's medical care costs. Placing the main burden of rising Medicare costs on the elderly and disabled is hardly a reasonable solution to the program's financial troubles.

Myth 3: Vouchers Mean Choice

Voucher advocates claim that the Breaux plan will enhance choice for Medicare beneficiaries by broadening their access to the private insurance market. This is nonsense. The Commission plan would actually lead to a substantial loss of choice, because the "premium support" plan is essentially a Trojan Horse for moving Medicare beneficiaries out of traditional Medicare and into managed care plans. Under a voucher system, private insurers will compete aggressively to avoid enrolling the most expensive and sickest Medicare patients. Traditional Medicare would thus be left with a sicker population, and the costs of the program would inevitably rise. As it did, the vulnerable beneficiaries remaining in Medicare would be left with a true Hobson's choice: pay more or leave traditional Medicare.

Moreover, the "enhanced choices" promised by voucher advocates are, in reality, likely to result in widespread confusion among elderly beneficiaries. Medicare enrollees reportedly are already having trouble deciphering the market changes introduced by the 1997 Balanced Budget Act. A voucher plan would only increase that confusion while making the consequences of choosing the wrong health plan even greater.

The reality is that voucher advocates are not really interested in expanding meaningful choice. Their priority is creating financial pressures for enrollees to leave traditional Medicare. * * * The Breaux plan, then, would cause many Medicare beneficiaries to lose access to the one insurance program—traditional Medicare—that guarantees them free choice of physician.

Myth 4: Social Insurance is Outdated

* * * Since its enactment in 1965, the aspiration of Medicare has been that all elderly, regardless of their income before or after retirement, would participate in the same insurance program. To be sure, this commitment to universalism and social insurance has not been fully realized. But, by fragmenting the Medicare program into a series of private insurance plans, Breaux's voucher approach moves Medicare farther from the goal and, indeed, repudiates the norm of universalism itself. In a voucher system, beneficiaries are likely to segment into different health insurance plans on the basis of their wealth and health status. Inequality in health care among the elderly

would worsen. And the political constituency for Medicare would be divided as enrollment in private insurance advances. And with that, the program's philosophical commitment to collective responsibility for financing medical care and social insurance would be substantially replaced by an ethos of individualism.

* * *

Notes

1. See, supporting the concept of premium support, Matthew Miller, Premium Idea, 220 New Republic, Apr. 12, 1999, at 24; Gail R. Wilensky and Joseph P. Newhouse, Medicare: What's Right? What's Wrong? What's Next?, 18 Health Aff., Jan./Feb. 1999 at 92.

2. Recent decreases in the growth of Medicare spending may make reform less pressing. During FY 1998 the rate of growth in Medicare expenditures was the slowest in history, and during the first half of FY 1999 program spending actually fell $2.6 billion. The cost-cutting measures of the BBA, supplemented by aggressive fraud and abuse enforcement, seem to be having an effect.

3. In the summer of 1999, President Clinton weighed in with his own proposal for reforming Medicare. The centerpiece of the proposal would be the creation of a new Medicare Part D, prescription drug benefit. Beneficiaries who elected the drug benefit, would pay a premium initially set at about $24 a month, rising to $44 a month when the benefit was fully phased in in 2008. The program would pay half of up to $2000 in drug costs (rising to $5000). with no deductible. Low income recipients (under 135% of poverty level) would pay no premium, and premiums would be subsidized for beneficiaries with incomes up to 150% of poverty level. Medicare beneficiaries would obtain a 10% discount on purchased drugs, similar to that offered to may private pharmacy benefit plans. The plan would also create a "competitive defined benefit" managed care program, allowing beneficiaries to choose lower cost managed care plans, and pocket 75% of the savings. Clinton's proposal would eliminate copayments and deductibles for preventive services, but would add a 20% copayment for laboratory services, and index the Part B deductible for inflation. It would extend BBA spending constraints, but ease up on some BBA cuts. Clinton again proposed allowing 62–65 year olds to buy into Medicare at an enhanced premium rate. Clinton proposed to fund the plan in part by diverting 15% of the estimated budget surplus over the next 15 years to Medicare. Though the Clinton administration had earlier suggested means testing as an approach to cutting Medicare costs and expanding benefits, Clinton's final proposal did not include means testing. Pundits opined that Medicare was too juicy a political issue for any major reforms to take place prior to the 2000 elections.

Insert at page 864 before Section III:

As Medicare reform discussions increasingly focus on privatizing Medicare, the question of the extent to which private organizations that administer public programs are bound by constitutional constraints becomes increasingly pressing. The following case is the most important recent case addressing this issue.

GRIJALVA, ET AL. v. SHALALA

United States Court of Appeals, Ninth Circuit, 1998.
152 F.3d 1115.

WIGGINS, CIRCUIT JUDGE:

Medicare beneficiaries enrolled in health maintenance organizations ("HMOs") in Arizona sued the Secretary of Health and Human Services ("Secretary"). Their suit alleged a failure to enforce due process requirements and a failure to monitor HMO denials of medical services to enrolled Medicare beneficiaries. The district court granted Plaintiffs summary judgment, holding that HMO denials of medical services to Medicare beneficiaries constitute state action and that the regulations issued by the Secretary fail to provide due process. The district court issued an injunction mandating certain procedural protections for Medicare beneficiaries enrolled in HMOs. The Secretary appeals. We affirm.

I. Background

Congress passed the Medicare Act, Title XVIII of the Social Security Act,[ ], in 1965 to provide a federal health insurance program for the elderly and the disabled. Today, a Medicare beneficiary can receive Medicare services in two different ways. The first is to receive Medicare on a fee-for-service basis. Under this option, the beneficiary goes to a health care provider for the necessary covered services; either the provider or the beneficiary will be reimbursed by the government for the cost of the services. The second, newer option is to enroll in an HMO or other eligible organization.[ ]

In 1982, Congress authorized the Secretary to enter into "risk-sharing" contracts with HMOs. See [42 U.S.C.] § 1395mm. Under these contracts, HMOs provide to enrolled Medicare beneficiaries all the Medicare services provided in the statute,[ ], in exchange for a monthly flat payment from the Secretary,[ ].

The Medicare statute establishes in § 1395mm(c) procedural protections for those beneficiaries that enroll in HMOs. Among these, the HMO must "provide meaningful procedures for hearing and resolving grievances between the organization ... and members enrolled...." § 1395mm(c)(5)(A). HMO members must also have certain appeal rights:

> A member enrolled with an eligible organization under this section who is dissatisfied by reason of his failure to receive any health service to which he believes he is entitled and at no greater charge than he believes he is required to pay is entitled, if the amount in controversy is $100 or more, to a hearing before the Secretary * * * , and in any such hearing the Secretary shall make the eligible organization a party. If the amount in controversy is $1,000 or more, the individual or eligible organization shall, upon notifying the other party, be entitled to judicial review of the Secretary's final decision * * * § 1395mm(c)(5)(B).

The Secretary created additional appeal protections in subsequent regulations. §§ 417.600—417.638. Under § 417.604, each HMO must establish appeal procedures and ensure that beneficiaries receive written information about the appeal and grievance procedures.[ ] If the HMO makes an "organization determination"[ ] adverse to the enrollee, "it must notify the enrollee of the determination within 60 days of receiving the enrollee's request for payment for services."[ ] An example of an adverse organization determination is an HMO's decision that certain medical services are not covered by Medicare. The notice to the beneficiary must "[s]tate the specific reasons for the determination" and inform the enrollee of his or her "right to a reconsideration." * * *

If the enrollee is dissatisfied with an adverse determination, a request for reconsideration may be filed within 60 days from the date of the notice. Within 60 days of the request, the HMO may make a decision fully favorable to the enrollee.[ ] If it decides to make a decision that partially or completely affirms the adverse determination, it must explain its decision in writing and forward the case to the Health Care Financing Administration ("HCFA").[ ] If the enrollee is dissatisfied with the result of the reconsideration, and the amount remaining in controversy is $100 or more, the enrollee has a right to a hearing before an administrative law judge ("ALJ").[ ] The enrollee can appeal that hearing decision to the Appeals Council and then to the district court.[ ]

The Secretary possesses a number of sanctions to ensure HMO compliance with the Medicare statute and the Secretary's regulations. First, the Secretary "may not enter into a contract ... with an [HMO] unless it meets the [statutory] requirements * * * that require the HMO, inter alia, to provide all Medicare services to eligible enrollees, to have particular open enrollment periods, to provide enrollees annually with information on their rights, including appeal rights, to provide covered services 'with reasonable promptness,' " to provide the aforementioned procedural protections, and not to exceed certain limits on rates charged to beneficiaries and the Secretary.[ ].

Second, the Secretary may terminate any contract with an HMO if she determines that the HMO has not met the terms of the contract or has not satisfied the statutory or regulatory requirements.[ ] If the Secretary determines that an HMO has failed to provide necessary covered services to an enrollee and that failure has adversely affected the individual, the Secretary may seek civil money penalties, suspend enrollment, or suspend payment to the HMO.[ ]

In 1993, five Medicare beneficiaries enrolled in an Arizona HMO sued the Secretary. Among other claims, Plaintiffs alleged that the Secretary "has failed and refused to take effective action to implement beneficiaries' notice and appeal rights when they are denied health care services by their HMOs," and "has failed and refused to provide Medicare beneficiaries enrolled in HMOs with a procedure of obtaining review of HMO denial decisions contemporaneously with the denial decisions." In a decision not on appeal, the district court certified a nationwide plaintiff class.

In October 1996, the district court granted partial summary judgment to Plaintiffs on the claims described above.[ ] The court held that the "organization determinations" made by HMOs constitute state action, triggering constitutional due process requirements.[ ] The court also held that the regulations promulgated by the Secretary regarding adverse determinations by HMOs fail to provide sufficient due process to enrollees under Mathews v. Eldridge, 424 U.S. 319 (1976).[ ] In particular, the district court found that the notices issued by HMOs failed to provide adequate notice: they were often illegible, failed to specify the reason for the denial, and failed to inform the beneficiary that he or she had the right to present additional evidence to the HMO.[ ] Therefore, "[s]ubsequent due process, available in the administrative review phase of the appeal, comes too late in many cases...."[ ] * * *

The district court found that the Secretary violated § 1395mm(c)(1) by entering into a contract with any HMO that failed to provide timely notice for any and all denials of service. The court held that the notice must be legible (at least 12–point type), state clearly the reason for the denial, inform the enrollee of all appeal rights, explain hearing rights and procedures, and provide "instruction on how to obtain supporting evidence, including medical records and supporting affidavits from the attending physician."[ ] The district court also held that any hearing must be "informal, in-person communication with the decisionmaker," available upon request for all service denials, and timely.[ ] The district court also required expedited hearings for "acute care service denials."[ ]

* * *

III.   Discussion

A.   State Action Doctrine

The Secretary appeals the district court's holding that HMO denials of medical services to enrolled Medicare beneficiaries constitute state [i.e. federal] action and therefore invoke constitutional due process protections.

The actions of private parties are not subject to the requirements of constitutional due process unless they can fairly be considered government action.[ ] We use the same standards to attribute the actions of private actors to the federal government under the Fifth Amendment as we do to attribute private actions to state governments under the Fourteenth Amendment.[ ]

* * * In order to show that a private action is in fact state action, the plaintiff must show that " 'there is a sufficiently close nexus between the State and the challenged action of the regulated entity so that the action of the latter may be fairly treated as that of the State itself.' "[ ] The government's regulation of the private actor is insufficient alone to show federal action.[ ] Government action exists if there is a symbiotic relationship with a high degree of interdependence between the private and public parties such that they are "joint participant[s] in the challenged activity."[ ] Government action exists if the challenged private action occurs under government compulsion.[ ] The government must do more, however, than merely acquiesce in the challenged action.[ ] * * *

In this case, the question is whether the challenged action—HMO denials of services to Medicare beneficiaries with inadequate notice—may fairly be treated as that of the federal government. We agree with the district court's cogent analysis and conclusion that, in the circumstances of the Secretary's regulation of and delegation of Medicare coverage decisions to HMOs, HMO denials of services to Medicare beneficiaries with inadequate notice constitute federal action.

We find that HMOs and the federal government are essentially engaged as joint participants to provide Medicare services such that the actions of

HMOs in denying medical services to Medicare beneficiaries and in failing to provide adequate notice may fairly be attributed to the federal government. The Secretary extensively regulates the provision of Medicare services by HMOs. HMOs are required, by the Medicare statute and their contracts with the Secretary, to comply with all federal laws and regulations. The Secretary is required to ensure, inter alia, that HMOs provide adequate notice and meaningful appeal procedures to beneficiaries. The Secretary pays HMOs for each enrolled Medicare beneficiary (regardless of the services provided). The federal government has created the legal framework—the standards and enforcement mechanisms—within which HMOs make adverse determinations, issue notices, and guarantee appeal rights. Medicare beneficiaries enrolled in HMOs may appeal an HMO's adverse determination to the Secretary, who has the power to overturn the HMO's decision. Each of these factors alone might not be sufficient to establish federal action. Together they show federal action.[ ] See Catanzano v. Dowling, 60 F.3d 113, 117–120 (2d Cir.1995) (similar analysis in Medicaid context); J.K. v. Dillenberg, 836 F.Supp. 694, 697–99 (D.Ariz.1993) (same).

The Secretary argues that the Supreme Court case of Blum v. Yaretsky, 457 U.S. 991 (1982), mandates a finding that HMO adverse determinations are not state action. We disagree.

In Blum, the Supreme Court held that nursing home decisions made by doctors and administrators to transfer patients to other facilities, thereby terminating their Medicaid benefits, did not constitute state action. The Court held that the decisions at issue in the case turned "on medical judgment made by private parties according to professional standards that are not established by the State."[ ] Because state officials did not have the power to approve or disapprove the nursing home decisions, but just altered the level of Medicaid benefits accordingly, the Court held that the decisions were not state action.[ ]

Unlike the nursing home doctors and administrators in Blum, the HMOs in this case are not making decisions to which the government merely responds. HMOs are following congressional and regulatory orders and are making decisions as a governmental proxy—they are deciding that Medicare does not cover certain medical services. In Blum, by contrast, the nursing homes decided that certain medical services were no longer medically necessary. While such an inquiry may occur in HMO service denials, the decisions in the case at hand are more accurately described as coverage decisions— interpretations of the Medicare statute—rather than merely medical judgments (particularly when no reason for the denial is given other than that the service does not meet "Medicare guidelines ... based upon [the HMO's] understanding and interpretation of Medicare ... coverage policies and guidelines," to quote a typical notice provided by Plaintiffs).

* * * [T]he government cannot avoid the due process requirements of the Constitution merely by delegating its duty to determine Medicare coverage to private entities. [ ]

We hold, therefore, that, when denying medical services to enrolled Medicare beneficiaries, HMOs are federal actors.

B.   Due Process and Mathews v. Eldridge

The parties agree that the balancing test used by the Supreme Court in Mathews v. Eldridge, 424 U.S. 319 (1976), applies to determine the necessary procedural protections to ensure that due process is provided to Medicare beneficiaries enrolled in HMOs.

In Mathews v. Eldridge, the Supreme Court considered the sufficiency of the procedures by which Social Security disability benefits were terminated.[ ] The Supreme Court held that constitutional due process is flexible, demanding particular protections depending on the situation.[ ] The requirements of due process in a particular situation depend on an analysis of three factors:

First, the private interest that will be affected by the official action; second, the risk of an erroneous deprivation of such interest through the procedures used, and the probable value, if any, of additional or substitute procedural safeguards; and finally, the Government's interest, including the functions involved and the fiscal and administrative burdens that the additional or substitute procedural requirements would entail.[ ] * * *

1. Private Interest at Stake

The district court held that the private interest at stake from an HMO's initial denial of Medicare coverage is the potential that medical care will be precluded altogether. The court held that this interest is a substantial private interest in additional protections such as timely and effective notice of service denials. We agree.

* * *

* * * An HMO's denial of coverage is an initial refusal to provide any medical services. The mere fact that the enrollee may be able to go elsewhere and pay for the services herself is of little comfort to an elderly, poor patient— particularly one who is ill and whose skilled nursing care has been terminated without a specific reason or description of how to appeal.

The Secretary argues that the district court erred by "adjudicating a complex procedural scheme as falling short of basic standards of fairness, without conducting the sort of detailed inquiry needed." * * * The Secretary also argues that the district court's finding that the interests of Medicare HMO enrollees are "especially" great because they may not receive immediate medical care is erroneous because some beneficiaries can seek those services elsewhere (and then seek reimbursement from the HMO) or disenroll from the HMO. The Secretary's arguments fail. Although, in some cases, the effect of service denial may be remedied easily after the fact, the potential for irreparable damage is surely great when it comes to denial of medical services (particularly denial without notice of any reason for the denial)* * *. In many, if not most, cases, the denial of coverage may result in total failure to receive the services.

* * *

Other courts have found on similar facts that a significant private interest is at stake that weighs in favor of additional protections. See, e.g., Kraemer v. Heckler, 737 F.2d 214, 222 (2d Cir.1984) ("In applying the balancing test, the private interest at stake [in the termination of Medicare coverage] should be weighed more heavily than in Eldridge because of the astronomical nature of medical costs.");[ ] The interest of the HMO enrollees in medical services weighs in favor of additional procedural protections beyond that offered by the Secretary's original regulations.

2. Risk of Erroneous Deprivation

The district court also held that factor two weighed in favor of greater procedural protections for Medicare beneficiaries enrolled in HMOs. * * * The court held that the notices failed to provide adequate explanation for the denials.[ ] We agree. This failure creates a high risk of erroneous deprivation of medical care to Medicare beneficiaries. The appeal rights and other procedural protections available to Medicare beneficiaries are meaningless if the beneficiaries are unaware of the reason for service denial and therefore cannot argue against the denial.[ ] Therefore, inadequate notice creates the risk of erroneous deprivation by undermining the appeal process.

The Secretary attacks the district court's analysis of this factor by arguing that the court simply identified an "arguable problem" faced by enrollees—inadequate notice—rather than address whether that problem actually results in deprivations. The Secretary argues that the district court "simply assumed that the perceived failures of notice resulted in fewer appeals, and that more appeals would diminish erroneous deprivations." The Secretary fails to recognize the real problem: Inadequate notice renders the existence of an appeal process meaningless. Moreover, the question established by Eldridge is not whether the inadequate notices actually resulted in erroneous deprivations, but whether the inadequate notices created an unjustifiably high risk of erroneous deprivation. Because due process has at its foundation the notion of adequate notice, the risk of erroneous deprivation caused by ineffective notices points towards the need for added procedural protections for Medicare beneficiaries enrolled in HMOs.

3. The Government's Interest

The Secretary argues that the district court paid only cursory attention to this factor, dismissing the government's concerns. The Secretary argues that the procedures sought by plaintiffs would impose a large burden on HMOs, which would accordingly affect the benefits received by enrollees.

* * * The Secretary has failed to show that the added procedural protections sought by Plaintiffs would result in significant additional costs to the government. Unlike the plaintiff in Eldridge, Plaintiffs do not seek a hearing prior to every denial, which would greatly increase costs. Adequate notices do not impose a burden on HMOs that outweighs the beneficiaries' need for them.[ ] The Secretary fails to advance any convincing argument that an additional burden on the government outweighs the effects of the other factors such that additional procedural safeguards are not necessary.

Taken together, the Eldridge factors point to a need for additional procedural protections for Medicare beneficiaries enrolled in HMOs, in particular for adequate notice of service denials, including the specific reason for the denial and an explanation of appeal rights, and expedited review for critical care denials. We therefore affirm the district court's holdings on Eldridge.

C. The Scope of the Injunction

The Secretary challenges the scope of the injunction issued by the district court. * * *

The Secretary argues that the district court abused its discretion by prohibiting the Secretary from entering into new contracts with HMOs that fail to provide the procedural protections mandated by the court. The Secretary argues that Congress provided the Secretary with a wide range of enforcement mechanisms, and that the district court could not require the Secretary to use the harshest mechanism. This argument fails. The Medicare Act mandated that the Secretary "may not enter into a contract ... with an [HMO] unless it meets the requirements of [§ 1395mm(c)] and [§ 1395mm(e)]."[ ] Under its clear meaning, this provision is not permissive; to the contrary, it is mandatory. The district court did not err or abuse its discretion.

The Secretary notes that, since the district court's summary judgment and injunction in favor of Plaintiffs, she has promulgated new regulations providing additional procedural protections for Medicare beneficiaries enrolled in HMOs. She asks us to review and modify the district court's injunction accordingly. Finding it unnecessary to do so, we decline her invitation. The district court has continuing jurisdiction over the modification of the injunction.[ ] The Secretary may move in the district court for a modification of its injunction.

* * *

Note

On May 3, 1999, the Supreme Court vacated and remanded this decision for further consideration in light of its decision in American Manufacturers Mutual Insurance Company v. Sullivan, 119 S.Ct. 977 (1999), and in light of the BBA and implementing regulations. American Manufacturers had held that the decision of a private insurer participating in a state workers' compensation program to withhold payment and seek utilization review was not state action subject to the due process clause. Arguably the role of a managed care organization administering Medicare benefits is quite different from that of a private insurer participating in a state mandated workers' compensation program, but the issue will undoubtedly result in further litigation.

Insert at page 870 at the end of Section A:

The Balanced Budget Act of 1997 created a new Children's Health Insurance program to expand coverage of uninsured children. The program provides almost $40 billion in federal matching funds over a ten-year period to states that provide child health care assistance to certain targeted low income children, or that expand Medicaid coverage of these children. As of early 1999, all but one state had established an approved program, about half through Medicaid expansions and the other half through new state programs or combined new programs and Medicaid expansions. The program had resulted in coverage of over 800,000 uninsured children. At the same time, however, implementation of the 1996 welfare reform legislation seems to be shrinking the number of Medicaid recipients dramatically. The following report describes this phenomenon.

Issue Paper. Participation in Welfare and Medicaid Enrollment
Mark Greenberg,
Kaiser Commission on Medicaid and the Uninsured: Washington,
DC. September 1998, used by permission

The number of families receiving cash assistance through Aid to Families with Dependent Children (AFDC) or Temporary Assistance to Needy Families (TANF) programs has decreased dramatically in recent years. From March 1994 to March 1998, caseloads fell by 35%, declining from 5 million to 3.2 million families. Recent data also indicates that there has been a decline in Medicaid enrollment. Although the decline is small in comparison to the TANF decline, it is striking at a time of continuing expansions of Medicaid eligibility. Moreover, Medicaid enrollment data corresponding to the period of the greatest TANF caseload declines is not yet available.

AFDC/TANF caseloads began to fall in 1994, but most of the decline has occurred since enactment of the Personal Responsibility and Work Opportunity Reconciliation Act (PRWORA) of 1996. From August 1996 to March 1998, the number of families receiving assistance dropped by 27%. Medicaid enrollment of children under 15 years also fell from 15.5 million in 1995 to 15.1 million in 1996; the number of adults aged 21–44 dropped from 8.6 million to 8.2 million over the same period. Overall, the number of Medicaid beneficiaries declined slightly (from 36.3 million to 36.1 million from 1995–1996), with preliminary indications of a further decline in 1997.

Is the AFDC/TANF caseload decline contributing to a reduction in Medicaid participation? If so, how? Although there is no conclusive analysis of the factors contributing to this reduction, one important piece of evidence comes from a set of recent state studies of families no longer receiving AFDC/TANF. These studies consistently find that Medicaid enrollment falls after families leave AFDC/TANF. If the drop in Medicaid participation was because families were leaving AFDC/TANF due to employment and receiving employment-based health care coverage, the decline might not be a point of concern, but this is often not the case. The reduction in Medicaid enrollment when families leave AFDC/TANF significantly exceeds the numbers receiving employment-based health care coverage.

The TANF exit studies do not analyze the reasons for the drop in Medicaid enrollment and it remains unclear how much of the drop might be attributable to family members no longer being eligible, to failure to identify eligible families, lack of awareness of the availability of continuing benefits, agency errors, or other factors. What does seem clear, however, is that the drop in enrollment is substantial and needs state attention to ensure that eligible families do not lose Medicaid assistance.

* * *

A.   Background: The relationship between AFDC, TANF, and Medicaid

* * *

Prior to the passage of the 1996 welfare law, PRWORA, AFDC recipients were automatically eligible for Medicaid. When a family left AFDC, federal law required the state to continue the family's Medicaid until the state determined whether family members qualified for Medicaid on another basis. In recent years, it became increasingly likely that at least the younger children in the family would remain eligible for Medicaid on independent grounds, e.g., children under six with incomes below 133% of poverty, children born after September 30, 1983 with family incomes below 100% of poverty, children covered through optional state expansions. For parents and older children, however, the principal basis for continued eligibility was through transitional Medicaid, which provided up to twelve months of Medicaid eligibility for family members leaving AFDC due to employment or four months of eligibility for those leaving AFDC due to increased collection of child or spousal support.

* * *

The 1996 welfare law created Temporary Assistance to Needy Families and "delinked" Medicaid from family cash assistance. Thus, TANF recipients are not automatically eligible for Medicaid. As noted above, many children and some parents will be eligible for Medicaid on independent grounds. However, if a family member does not qualify for Medicaid on other grounds, the state must determine whether the family member is eligible for Medicaid based on a new category known as Section 1931 eligibility.

Generally, Section 1931 provides that a family member will qualify for Medicaid if he or she meets the income, resource, and family composition rules that applied to the state's AFDC Program on July 16, 1996. States were provided with a limited ability to modify these rules, including a provision which allows states, in effect, to liberalize their treatment of income and resources.

* * *

There is still a transitional Medicaid category under the new law, but eligibility is not based on losing TANF. Rather, it is based on losing Section 1931 eligibility, i.e., a family member losing Section 1931 Medicaid due to employment may qualify for up to twelve months of transitional Medicaid, and a family member losing Section 1931 Medicaid due to increased collection of child or spousal support may continue to qualify for Medicaid for an additional four months.

Under TANF, a state has broad discretion to impose sanctions or terminate family assistance for reasons of the state's choosing, e.g., failure to attend school, failure to immunize children, etc. However, under the law, the only TANF sanction that could affect Medicaid eligibility is a work-related sanction. A state can choose to terminate the Medicaid of an adult (or minor child head of household) for a refusal to work, but may not extend the Medicaid sanction to other family members. According to preliminary information, fifteen states had elected this option as of January 1997.

B.   AFDC/TANF Exits and Health Care Coverage: Recent Evidence from State Studies

* * *

2.   Findings from State Exit Studies Concerning Medicaid Consequences of Loss of AFDC/TANF

* * *

• When families cease receiving AFDC/TANF, Medicaid enrollment goes down. The magnitude of the decline varies between studies, but often, one-third or more of children and most adults in families that have exited are no longer reported to be receiving Medicaid when exiters are surveyed some number of months after leaving.

● Most families entering employment after having received AFDC/TANF do not have employment-based health care coverage. Typically, among families who are employed, the share reporting employment-based coverage is 25% or less.

* * *

In addition to the state exit studies, another source of evidence about the impacts of loss of cash assistance can be found in the set of evaluations of the impacts of welfare-work initiatives. Several program evaluations contain data which may suggest that one unintended consequence of state efforts to increase employment among families receiving assistance could be a decline in health care coverage:

* * *

3. Findings from State Benefit Termination/Sanction Studies Concerning Medicaid Consequences of Loss of AFDC/TANF

Another set of studies focus specifically on families losing assistance due to sanctions. As noted, until fairly recently, state sanction policies only terminated assistance to the parent rather than to the entire family when a single parent failed to comply with program requirements, but in the last years of AFDC, states began to make use of full-family terminations, and under TANF, such policies have become widespread. The use of full-family terminations has raised many questions about the impacts of such policies on the well-being of parents and children, though to date, there are only a handful of studies that expressly look at the impacts of such terminations.

When a sanction occurs, it is possible that the parent's Medicaid coverage is being terminated as a matter of sanction policy, but under the law applicable both before and after TANF, the imposition of the penalty on the parent should not have affected the childrens' Medicaid coverage.

One of the first indications that loss of cash assistance might be associated with loss of Medicaid came in a review issued by the General Accounting Office of early state experiences with benefit terminations.* * * Three states with early experiences were Massachusetts, Iowa, and Wisconsin. In each of these three states, the level of Medicaid coverage fell substantially after benefit termination. Surveys conducted in the range of two to five months after termination of benefits showed:

● in Massachusetts, the share of families in which at least one family member received Medicaid fell from 100% to 58.5%;

● in Wisconsin, the share of families in which at least one family member received Medicaid fell from 100% to 53.5%;

● in Iowa, the share of families in which at least one family member received Medicaid fell from 86.3% to 54.4%.

* * *

C. Why would exiters lose Medicaid?

The exit/sanction studies make clear that a substantial share of children and parents leaving AFDC/TANF lose Medicaid, either immediately or in a short period of time. * * *

Some of the possible reasons for the drop in Medicaid enrollment after leaving AFDC/TANF are:

• Family members may no longer be eligible. This is less likely to be the explanation for younger children, though it may explain some of the drop for parents and older children.

* * *

• Family members may not seek transitional Medicaid because they do not know about it. * * *

• States may not code families as leaving assistance due to employment although that is the reason for the exit. * * *

• State procedures may erroneously terminate Medicaid or not provide for an effective mechanism to determine continuing eligibility. * * *

• Parents may be discouraged or confused after loss of TANF assistance. Several researchers who were involved in conducting exit studies raised the possibility that after TANF assistance was terminated, families might fail to provide needed information for Medicaid redeterminations or choose not to do so because they wanted no further contact with the state or might even be confused as to whether Medicaid for family members had been terminated.

* * *

The TANF exit studies underscore the importance of using Section 1931 to broaden Medicaid eligibility for working poor families. Without such a broadening of eligibility, it seems likely that one consequence of TANF implementation will be fewer families receiving TANF, more families engaged in employment, and yet reduced health care coverage for poor parents and children.

Add at page 871, following paragraph 3, the following:

In Olmstead v. L.C., S.Ct. (June 22, 1999), Justice Ginsburg, writing for a majority of the Court concluded that, under Title II of the Americans with Disabilities Act of 1990 (ADA), and implementing regulations requiring public entities to administer "programs in the most integrated setting appropriate to the needs of qualified individuals with disabilities." 28 CFR § 35.130(d), the state of Georgia was obligated to care for persons with mental disabilities in community-based programs rather than state institutions, when the state's treatment professionals had concluded that community placement was appropriate, the transfer from institutional care to a less restrictive setting was not opposed by the affected individual, and the placement could reasonably be accommodated, taking into account the resources available to the State and the needs of others with mental disabilities. The Court noted specifically that since 1981, Medicaid had provided funding for state-run home and community-based care through a waiver program, and did not favor institutional over community-based treatment.

Justice Ginsburg, joined by Justice O'Connor, Justice Souter, and Justice Breyer, concluded in Part III—B of the opinion that the State's responsibility to provide community-based treatment to qualified persons with disabilities, was not unlimited. The State should be allowed to show that, in the allocation of available resources, immediate relief for the plaintiffs would be inequitable, given the State's responsibility to care for a large and diverse population of persons with mental disabilities. The opinion further stated that the ADA did not obligate the state to eliminate institutions for the mentally disabled, which might be appropriate for some patients. The opinion approved a rationing approach to allocation of places in community-based facilities. Ginsburg stated that, if the State were to demonstrate that it had a comprehensive, effectively working plan for placing qualified persons with mental disabilities in less restrictive settings, and a waiting list that moved at a reasonable pace not controlled by the State's endeavors to keep its institutions fully populated, persons at the top of the community-based treatment waiting list should not be displaced by individuals lower down simply because they had sued under the ADA.

Add at pages 878–883:

The Balanced Budget Act of 1997 did not block-grant Medicaid, as had been attempted in 1995, but did gave the states considerably more flexibility in running Medicaid programs while significantly limiting the ability of providers to sue states for alleged inadequate provider payments.

First, the BBA made it much simpler for states to move to Medicaid managed care. It made it easier for states to obtain new or retain existing § 1115 waivers to implement managed care. Twenty states are now operating all or most of their Medicaid programs under § 1115 waivers. It also created a new § 1932 (42 U.S.C.A. § 1396u–2) permitting states to convert their Medicaid programs to managed care programs without going through the waiver process if certain requirements are met. Among the most important of these are requirements that in most instances recipients be offered a choice of two or more managed care options and that Medicaid beneficiaries have the option of disenrolling for cause at any time, and within 90 days or enrollment and once every 12 months thereafter without cause. The law also contains a number of beneficiary protections, including mandatory access to emergency services and requirements for grievance procedures, quality assurance processes, and protections against marketing abuses.

The BBA also repealed the Boren Amendment, the primary vehicle through which providers had challenged nursing facility and hospital rates for almost two decades. The law adopted in its place imposes no substantive obligations on the states with respect to hospital and nursing facility payments, rather simply requiring the states to publish proposed rates, the methodologies through which they were adopted, and the justifications for them; give the public a reasonable opportunity to review and comment on the rates; and then publish final rates. 42 U.S.C.A. § 1396a(a)(13).

The repeal of the Boren Amendment may not totally end all litigation challenging state Medicaid provider rates, however. Challenges may still be possible under 42 U.S.C.A. § 1396a(a)(30)(A), which requires that state plans must "assure that payments are consistent with efficiency, economy, and quality of care and are sufficient to enlist enough providers so that care and services are available under the plan at least to the extent that such care and services are available to the general population in the geographic area." A provider suit challenging California hospital outpatient Medicaid rates was recently permitted to proceed under this provision, Orthopaedic Hospital v. Belshe, 103 F.3d 1491 (9th Cir.1997), cert. denied, 118 S.Ct. 684 (1998), but a similar claim was rejected by a Florida district court, which found that providers had no enforceable rights under the provision. Florida Pharmacy Ass'n v. Cook, 17 F.Supp.2d 1293 (N.D.Fla.1998). The courts are split as to whether § 1396a(a)(30)(A) also imposes on the states any procedural requirements, such as a mandated study or investigation of rate adequacy. Compare Arkansas Med. Soc'y Inc. v. Reynolds, 6 F.3d 519 (8th Cir.1993) and Orthopedic Hospital, supra (finding such requirements), with Rite Aid of Pa., Inc. v. Houstoun, 171 F.3d 842 (3d Cir.1999), and Methodist Hosps., Inc. v. Sullivan, 91 F.3d 1026 (7th Cir.1996) (finding no such requirements).

Chapter 15

HUMAN REPRODUCTION AND BIRTH

On page 923, add to note 2, Consent and Notification Requirements:

One new state legislative attempt to get around constitutional limitations on spousal consent is to permit the abortion without such consent but to provide for civil liability on those physicians who perform them without that consent. This approach was found to be indistinguishable from requiring spousal consent, and thus unconstitutional, by at least one court. Planned Parenthood of Southern Arizona v. Woods, 982 F.Supp. 1369, 1380 (D.Ariz.1997).

On page 923, add to note 3, Regulation of Medical Procedures:

Several additional courts have acted to strike down limitations on "partial birth" abortions because they place an undue burden on a woman's right to an abortion, at least under some circumstances. See Richmond Medical Center for Women v. Gilmore, 11 F. Supp.2d 795 (E.D.Va.1998), Carhart v. Stenberg, 11 F. Supp. 2d 1099 (D.Neb.1998), Planned Parenthood of Greater Iowa v. Miller, 1 F.Supp.2d 958 (D.Iowa 1998), Hope Clinic v. Ryan, 995 F.Supp. 847 (N.D.Ill.1998), and Planned Parenthood of Southern Arizona v. Woods, 982 F.Supp. 1369 (D.Ariz. 1997). In Planned Parenthood v. Verniero, 41 F.Supp.2d 478 (D.N.J.1998), a ban on "partial birth" abortions was held unconstitutionally void for vagueness because of the uncertainty of the meaning of such terms as "partially vaginally delivery" and "substantial portion." About half of the states with bans on "partial birth" abortions are under no judicial restraint and continue to enforce legislative limitations on that form of abortion.

On page 925, at the end of note 9, add:

Essentially the same legislation has been introduced in Congress. In 1998 the House passed the Child Custody Protection Act, which would make it a crime for any adult to take a girl across a state line for the purpose of obtaining an abortion that would require parental consent in the home state of the child. The support for this legislation, like support for other abortion related legislation, lost some of its strength when Congressional and public attention turned to the impeachment proceedings in late 1998 and early 1999.

At the bottom of page 926, at the end of the Note: "The Freedom of Access to Clinic Entrances Act of 1994," add:

Both the Freedom of Access to Clinic Entrances Act and RICO were implicated in early 1999 when an Oregon federal court jury returned a verdict in excess of $107 million against twelve individuals, the American Coalition of Life Activists and the Advocates for Life Ministries, for maintaining a web site that threatened those who performed abortions. The site, called "The Nuremberg Files," listed physicians who performed abortions, drew lines through those who had been murdered, and listed those who had been wounded by would-be assassins in gray. The defendants also published old west style "wanted" posters with the names and pictures of physicians who performed abortions. The defendants claimed a first amendment right to publish the web site and the wanted posters, and some first amendment analysts were concerned about the potentially chilling effect of such a large judgment on the publication of unpopular political views. The defendants also claimed that they had transferred their assets to be able to avoid paying any part of the judgment, although their unsubtle approach to the transfer is likely to hinder its legal success. See Sam Howe Verhook, Creators of Anti–Abortion Web Site Told to Pay Millions, New York Times, February 3, 1999, A–9.

In another case that raised the first amendment rights of those opposed to abortion, the United States Supreme Court denied certiorari in Christ's Bride Ministries v. SEPTA, 148 F.3d 242 (3d Cir.), cert. denied 119 S.Ct. 797 (1999). In that case, the Third Circuit had determined that the Philadelphia area agency that operated public busses and subways could not deny advertising space to a group that wished to place signs that said, "Women who choose abortion suffer more and deadlier breast cancer." The agency had accepted other abortion-related advertising, and, thus, had created an open forum on abortion related issues.

On page 927, at the end of the Note: "The Blurry Distinction Between Contraception and Abortion," add:

RU–486 continues to face a rocky road to distribution in the United States. Riders to prohibit the FDA from approving the drug were attached to several bills in Congress in 1998. Despite strong support in the House, none actually made it into law. Marketing problems have also plagued those who want to see mifepristone generally available, although some have predicted it will be available on the retail market soon. See Marc Kaufman, Abortion Pill Inches Closer to Production: American Markateers Hopeful the Drug Will be Available by the End of the Year, Washington Post, March 23, 1999, Z–7.

On page 931, at the end of section 4, "Sterilization," add:

Recently courts and legislatures have considered interventions that are designed to provide sterilization or some form of castration as criminal punishments (or "treatment" for those disposed to criminal conduct). In State v. Kline, 963 P.2d 697 (Or.App.1998) the Oregon Court of Appeals found that a criminal defendant's right to procreate was not unconstitutionally abridged when he was ordered not to have children upon his conviction for mistreatment of children. For a discussion of "chemical castration" provisions that apply to convicted sex offenders, see William Winslade et al., Castrating Pedophiles Convicted of Sex Offenses Against Children: New Treatment or Old Punishment?, 51 SMU L.Rev. 349 (1998), and Karen Rebish, Nipping the

Problem in the Bud: The Constitutionality of California's Castration Law, 14 N.Y.L. Sch. J. Hum. Rts. 507 (1998). For another review of the California statute—the first to actually require "chemical castration" in some cases—see Recent Legislation: Constitutional Law, 110 Harv. L. Rev. 799 (1997).

On page 954, after note 5, add:

5a. Might there be additional legal problems if a state institution were to limit those who could be provided with assisted conception? What kind of equal protection claims would you expect to be successful? Does the Americans with Disabilities Act require medical institutions to provide treatment for infertility if they provide other necessary medical treatment? Is infertility a disability? See Erickson v. Board of Governors of State Colleges and Universities, 1997 WL 548030 (N.D.Ill.1997) and Bielicki v. Chicago, 1997 WL 260595 (N.D.Ill.1997).

On page 985, at the end of note 5, add:

This issue has also arisen in the context of the child custody portion of a divorce case in which the child was born as a result of artificial insemination of a surrogate mother with the sperm of the husband. The child (fourteen at the time of the divorce) was raised by husband and wife, but the child bore no genetic relationship to the wife. Should the wife be entitled to parental rights upon divorce? Is her position weakened by the fact that she had never attempted to adopt the child? Should the court consider the case like any other custody dispute between biological parents, or should the court treat the case like one between the father and a legal stranger to the child? Should the court apply the best interest test in either case? See Doe v. Doe, 710 A.2d 1297 (Conn.1998).

On page 985, after note 5 (and the addition above), add:

While legal pundits were creating ultimate assisted conception hypotheticals in which the sperm from one person was joined with the ovum of a second and implanted in the womb of a third to be raised by a fourth and fifth, the real case arose in California.

BUZZANCA v. BUZZANCA

California Court of Appeal, 1998
61 Cal.App.4th 1410, 72 Cal.Rptr.2d 280

SILLS, P.J.,

INTRODUCTION

Jaycee was born because Luanne and John Buzzanca agreed to have an embryo genetically unrelated to either of them implanted in a woman—a surrogate—who would carry and give birth to the child for them. After the fertilization, implantation and pregnancy, Luanne and John split up, and the question of who are Jaycee's lawful parents came before the trial court.

Luanne claimed that she and her erstwhile husband were the lawful parents, but John disclaimed any responsibility, financial or otherwise. The woman who gave birth also appeared in the case to make it clear that she made no claim to the child.

The trial court then reached an extraordinary conclusion: Jaycee had no lawful parents. First, the woman who gave birth to Jaycee was not the mother; the court had—astonishingly—already accepted a stipulation that neither she nor her husband were the "biological" parents. Second, Luanne was not the mother. According to the trial court, she could not be the mother because she had neither contributed the egg nor given birth. And John could not be the father, because, not having contributed the sperm, he had no biological relationship with the child. We disagree. Let us get right to the point: Jaycee never would have been born had not Luanne and John both agreed to have a fertilized egg implanted in a surrogate.

The trial judge erred because he assumed that legal motherhood, under the relevant California statutes, could only be established in one of two ways, either by giving birth or by contributing an egg. He failed to consider the substantial and well-settled body of law holding that there are times when fatherhood can be established by conduct apart from giving birth or being genetically related to a child. The typical example is when an infertile husband consents to allowing his wife to be artificially inseminated. * * *

The same rule which makes a husband the lawful father of a child born because of his consent to artificial insemination should be applied here—by the same parity of reasoning that guided our Supreme Court in the first surrogacy case, Johnson v. Calvert [ ]—to both husband and wife. Just as a husband is deemed to be the lawful father of a child unrelated to him when his wife gives birth after artificial insemination, so should a husband and wife be deemed the lawful parents of a child after a surrogate bears a biologically unrelated child on their behalf. In each instance, a child is procreated because a medical procedure was initiated and consented to by intended parents. The only difference is that in this case—unlike artificial insemination—there is no reason to distinguish between husband and wife. We therefore must reverse the trial court's judgment and direct that a new judgment be entered, declaring that both Luanne and John are the lawful parents of Jaycee.

CASE HISTORY

John filed his petition for dissolution of marriage * * * alleging there were no children of the marriage. Luanne filed her response * * *, alleging that the parties were expecting a child by way of surrogate contract. Jaycee was born six days later. * * * In February 1997, the court accepted a stipulation that the woman who agreed to carry the child, and her husband, were not the "biological parents" of the child. At a hearing held in March, based entirely on oral argument and offers of proof, the trial court determined that Luanne was not the lawful mother of the child and therefore John could not be the lawful father or owe any support.

The trial judge said: "So I think what evidence there is, is stipulated to. And I don't think there would be any more. One, there's no genetic tie between Luanne and the child. Two, she is not the gestational mother. Three, she has not adopted the child. That, folks, to me, respectfully, is clear and convincing evidence that she's not the legal mother."

* * * [A] judgment was filed, terminating John's obligation to pay child support, declaring that Luanne was not the legal mother of Jaycee, and declining "to apply any estoppel proposition to the issue of John's responsibility for child support." * * *

In his respondent's brief in this appeal, John tries to intimate—though he stops short of actually saying it—that Jaycee was not born as a result of a surrogacy agreement with his ex-wife. He points to the fact that the actual written surrogacy agreement was signed on August 25, 1994, but the implantation took place a little less than two weeks before, on August 13, 1994. The brief states: "At the time that the implantation took place, no surrogacy contract had been executed by the parties to this action."

Concerned with the implication made in John's respondent's brief, members of this court questioned John's attorney at oral argument about it. It turned out that the intimation in John's brief was a red herring, based merely on the fact that John did not sign a written contract until after implantation. Jaycee was nonetheless born as a result of a surrogacy agreement on the part of both Luanne and John; it was just that the agreement was an oral one prior to implantation. The written surrogacy agreement, John's attorney acknowledged in open court, was the written memorialization of that oral contract.

Members of this panel also pressed John's attorney to state whatever factually based defenses John might have offered if the case had actually been tried. John's attorney had not specifically stated such defenses at the [trial court] hearing; he had only vaguely indicated that "the facts as testified to would be somewhat different than" those which the trial court had "assumed."

Again, there was less than was intimated. John's signature on the written surrogacy agreement was not forged, or anything of the sort. His one trump card, finessed out only after repeated questioning and the importuning of one of our panel to articulate his "best facts," was this: John would offer testimony to the effect that Luanne told him that she would assume all responsibility for the care of any child born. Luanne alone would assume "the burdens of childrearing."

Therefore, even though there was no actual trial in front of the trial court on the matter, this appellate court will assume arguendo that if there had been a trial the judge would have believed John's evidence on the point and concluded that Luanne had indeed promised not to hold John responsible for the child contemplated by their oral surrogacy agreement.

DISCUSSION

The Statute Governing Artificial Insemination Which Makes a Husband the Lawful Father of a Child Unrelated to Him Applies to Both Intended Parents in This Case

Perhaps recognizing the inherent lack of appeal for any result which makes Jaycee a legal orphan, John now contends that the surrogate is Jaycee's legal mother; and further, by virtue of that fact, the surrogate's husband is the legal father. His reasoning goes like this: Under the Uniform Parentage Act, * * * there are only two ways by which a woman can establish legal motherhood, i.e., giving birth or contributing genetically. Because the genetic contributors are not known to the court, the only candidate left is the surrogate who must therefore be deemed the lawful mother. And, as John's counsel commented at oral argument, if the surrogate and her husband cannot support Jaycee, the burden should fall on the taxpayers.

The law doesn't say what John says it says. It doesn't say: "The legal relationship between mother and child shall be established only by either proof of her giving birth or by genetics." The statute says "may," not "shall," and "under this part," not "by genetics." Here is the complete text * * *:

"The parent and child relationship may be established as follows:

(a) Between a child and the natural mother, it may be established by proof of her having given birth to the child, or under this part.

(b) Between a child and the natural father, it may be established under this part.

(c) Between a child and an adoptive parent, it may be established by proof of adoption."

The statute thus contains no direct reference to genetics (i.e., blood tests) at all. The Johnson decision teaches us that genetics is simply subsumed in the words "under this part." In that case, the court held that genetic consanguinity was equally "acceptable" as "proof of maternity" as evidence of giving birth. [ ]

It is important to realize, however, that in construing the words "under this part" to include genetic testing, the high court in Johnson relied on several statutes in the Evidence Code [ ], all of which, by their terms, only applied to paternity. [ ] It was only by a "parity of reasoning" that our high court concluded those statutes which, on their face applied only to men, were also "dispositive of the question of maternity." [ ]

The point bears reiterating: It was only by a parity of reasoning from statutes which, on their face, referred only to paternity that the court in Johnson v. Calvert reached the result it did on the question of maternity. Had the Johnson court reasoned as John now urges us to reason—by narrowly confining the means under the Act by which a woman could establish that she was the lawful mother of a child to texts which on their face applied only to motherhood (as distinct from fatherhood)—the court would have reached the opposite result.

In addition to blood tests there are several other ways the Act allows paternity to be established. Those ways are not necessarily related at all to any biological tie. Thus, under the Act, paternity may be established by:

— marrying, remaining married to, or attempting to marry the child's mother when she gives birth [ ];

— marrying the child's mother after the child's birth and either consenting to being named as the father on the birth certificate [ ].

A man may also be deemed a father under the Act in the case of artificial insemination of his wife, as provided by [the Uniform Parentage Act]. To track the words of the statute: "If, under the supervision of a licensed physician and surgeon and with the consent of her husband, a wife is inseminated artificially with semen donated by a man not her husband, the husband is treated in law as if he were the natural father of a child thereby conceived."

As noted in Johnson, "courts must construe statutes in factual settings not contemplated by the enacting legislature." [ ] So it is, of course, true that application of the artificial insemination statute to a gestational surrogacy case where the genetic donors are unknown to the court may not have been contemplated by the Legislature. Even so, the two kinds of artificial reproduction are exactly analogous in this crucial respect: Both contemplate the procreation of a child by the consent to a medical procedure of someone who intends to raise the child but who otherwise does not have any biological tie.

If a husband who consents to artificial insemination [ ] is "treated in law" as the father of the child by virtue of his consent, there is no reason the result should be any different in the case of a married couple who consent to in vitro fertilization by unknown donors and subsequent implantation into a woman who is, as a surrogate, willing to carry the embryo to term for them. The statute is, after all, the clearest expression of past legislative intent when the Legislature did contemplate a situation where a person who caused a child to come into being had no biological relationship to the child.

Indeed, the establishment of fatherhood and the consequent duty to support when a husband consents to the artificial insemination of his wife is one of the well-established rules in family law. The leading case in the country (so described by a New York family [ ]) is People v. Sorensen, [ ], in which our Supreme Court held that a man could even be criminally liable for failing to pay for the support of a child born to his wife during the marriage as a result of artificial insemination using sperm from an anonymous donor.

One New York family court even went so far as to hold the lesbian partner of a woman who was artificially inseminated responsible for the support of two children where the partner had dressed as a man and the couple had obtained a marriage license and a wedding ceremony had been performed prior to the inseminations. [ ] Echoing the themes of causation and estoppel which underlie the cases, the court noted that the lesbian partner had "by her course of conduct in this case ... brought into the world two innocent children" and should not "be allowed to benefit" from her acts to the detriment of the children and public generally. [ ]

It must also be noted that in applying the artificial insemination statute to a case where a party has caused a child to be brought into the world, the statutory policy is really echoing a more fundamental idea * * * already established in the case law. That idea is often summed up in the legal term "estoppel." Estoppel is an ungainly word from the Middle French (from the word meaning "bung" or "stopper") expressing the law's distaste for inconsistent actions and positions—like consenting to an act which brings a child into existence and then turning around and disclaiming any responsibility.

While the Johnson v. Calvert court was able to predicate its decision on the Act rather than making up the result out of whole cloth, it is also true that California courts, prior to the enactment of the Act, had based certain decisions establishing paternity merely on the common law doctrine of estoppel. * * *

There is no need in the present case to predicate our decision on common law estoppel alone, though the doctrine certainly applies. The estoppel concept, after all, is already inherent in the artificial insemination statute. * * *

John argues that the artificial insemination statute should not be applied because, after all, his wife did not give birth. But for purposes of the statute with its core idea of estoppel, the fact that Luanne did not give birth is irrelevant. The statute contemplates the establishment of lawful fatherhood in a situation where an intended father has no biological relationship to a child who is procreated as a result of the father's (as well as the mother's) consent to a medical procedure.

Luanne is the Lawful Mother of Jaycee, Not the Surrogate, and Not the Unknown Donor of the Egg

In the present case Luanne is situated like a husband in an artificial insemination case whose consent triggers a medical procedure which results in a pregnancy and eventual birth of a child. Her motherhood may therefore be established "under this part," by virtue of that consent. In light of our conclusion, John's argument that the surrogate should be declared the lawful mother disintegrates. The case is now postured like the Johnson v. Calvert case, where motherhood could have been "established" in either of two women under the Act, and the tie broken by noting the intent to parent as expressed in the surrogacy contract. [ ] The only difference is that this case is not even close as between Luanne and the surrogate. Not only was Luanne the clearly intended mother, no bona fide attempt has been made to establish the surrogate as the lawful mother.

We should also add that neither could the woman whose egg was used in the fertilization or implantation make any claim to motherhood, even if she were to come forward at this late date. Again, as between two women who would both be able to establish motherhood under the Act, the Johnson decision would mandate that the tie be broken in favor of the intended parent, in this case, Luanne.

* * *

In the case before us, we are not concerned, as John would have us believe, with a question of the enforceability of the oral and written surrogacy contracts into which he entered with Luanne. This case is not about "transferring" parenthood pursuant to those agreements. We are, rather, concerned with the consequences of those agreements as acts which caused the birth of a child.

The legal paradigm adopted by the trial court, and now urged upon us by John, is one where all forms of artificial reproduction in which intended parents have no biological relationship with the child result in legal parentlessness. It means that, absent adoption, such children will be dependents of the state. One might describe this paradigm as the "adoption default" model: The idea is that by not specifically addressing some permutation of artificial reproduction, the Legislature has, in effect, set the default switch on adoption. The underlying theory seems to be that when intended parents resort to artificial reproduction without biological tie the Legislature wanted them to be screened first through the adoption system. (Thus John, in his brief, argues that a surrogacy contract must be "subject to state oversight.")

The "adoption default" model is, however, inconsistent with both statutory law and the Supreme Court's Johnson decision. As to the statutory law, the Legislature has already made it perfectly clear that public policy (and, we might add, common sense) favors, whenever possible, the establishment of legal parenthood with the concomitant responsibility.

* * *

Very plainly, the Legislature has declared its preference for assigning individual responsibility for the care and maintenance of children; not leaving the task to the taxpayers. That is why it has gone to considerable lengths to ensure that parents will live up to their support obligations. [ ] The adoption default theory flies in the face of that legislative value judgment.

As this court noted in Jaycee B. v. Superior Court [49 Cal. Rptr. 2d 694 (1996)], the Johnson court had occasion, albeit in dicta, to address "pretty much the exact situation before us." The language bears quoting again: "In what we must hope will be the extremely rare situation in which neither the gestator nor the woman who provided the ovum for fertilization is willing to assume custody of the child after birth, a rule recognizing the intending parents as the child's legal, natural parents should best promote certainty and stability. . . ." (Johnson v. Calvert [ ]) This language quite literally describes precisely the case before us now: neither the woman whose ovum was used nor the woman who gave birth have come forward to assume custody of the child after birth.

John now argues that the Supreme Court's statement should be applied only in situations, such as that in the Johnson case, where the intended parents have a genetic tie to the child. The context of the Johnson language, however, reveals a broader purpose, namely, to emphasize the intelligence and utility of a rule that looks to intentions.

* * *

In context, then, the high court's considered dicta is directly applicable to the case at hand. The context was not limited to just Johnson-style contests between women who gave birth and women who contributed ova, but to any situation where a child would not have been born " 'but for the efforts of the intended parents.' "[ ]

Finally, in addition to its contravention of statutorily enunciated public policy and the pronouncement of our high court in Johnson, the adoption default model ignores the role of our dependency statutes in protecting children. Parents are not screened for the procreation of their own children; they are screened for the adoption of other people's children. It is the role of the dependency laws to protect children from neglect and abuse from their own parents. The adoption default model is essentially an exercise in circular reasoning, because it assumes the idea that it seeks to prove; namely, that a child who is born as the result of artificial reproduction is somebody else's child from the beginning.

In the case before us, there is absolutely no dispute that Luanne caused Jaycee's conception and birth by initiating the surrogacy arrangement whereby an embryo was implanted into a woman who agreed to carry the [*1426] baby to term on Luanne's behalf. In applying the artificial insemination statute to a gestational surrogacy case where the genetic donors are unknown, there is, as we have indicated above, no reason to distinguish between husbands and wives. Both are equally situated from the point of view of consenting to an act which brings a child into being. Accordingly, Luanne should have been declared the lawful mother of Jaycee.

John Is the Lawful Father of Jaycee Even If Luanne Did Promise to Assume All Responsibility for Jaycee's Care

The same reasons which impel us to conclude that Luanne is Jaycee's lawful mother also require that John be declared Jaycee's lawful father. Even if the written surrogacy contract had not yet been signed at the time of conception and implantation, those occurrences were nonetheless the direct result of actions taken pursuant to an oral agreement which envisioned that the fertilization, implantation and ensuing pregnancy would go forward. Thus, it is still accurate to say, as we did the first time this case came before us, that for all practical purposes John caused Jaycee's conception every bit as much as if things had been done the old-fashioned way. [ ]

When pressed at oral argument to make an offer of proof as to the "best facts" which John might be able to show if this case were tried, John's attorney raised the point that Luanne had (allegedly, we must add) promised to assume all responsibility for the child and would not hold him responsible for the child's upbringing. However, even if this case were returned for a trial on this point (we assume that Luanne would dispute the allegation) it could make no difference as to John's lawful paternity. It is well established that parents cannot, by agreement, limit or abrogate a child's right to support.

[The court discussed the rule that rendered unenforceable contracts between parents relieving one of them of child support obligations.]

CONCLUSION

Even though neither Luanne nor John are biologically related to Jaycee, they are still her lawful parents given their initiating role as the intended parents in her conception and birth. And, while the absence of a biological connection is what makes this case extraordinary, this court is hardly without statutory basis and legal precedent in so deciding. Indeed, in both the most famous child custody case of all time, [19] and in our Supreme Court's Johnson v. Calvert decision, the court looked to intent to parent as the ultimate basis of its decision.[20] Fortunately, as the Johnson court also noted, intent to parent " 'correlate[s] significantly' "with a child's best interests. [ ] That is far more than can be said for a model of the law that renders a child a legal orphan.

Again we must call on the Legislature to sort out the parental rights and responsibilities of those involved in artificial reproduction. No matter what one thinks of artificial insemination, traditional and gestational surrogacy (in all its permutations), and—as now appears in the not-too-distant future, cloning and even gene splicing—courts are still going to be faced with the problem of determining lawful parentage. A child cannot be ignored. Even if all means of artificial reproduction were outlawed with draconian criminal penalties visited on the doctors and parties involved, courts will still be called upon to decide who the lawful parents really are and who—other than the taxpayers—is obligated to provide maintenance and support for the child. These cases will not go away.

19. See 1 Kings 3: 25–26 (dispute over identity of live child by two single women, each of whom had recently delivered a child but one child had died, resolved by novel evidentiary device designed to ferret out intent to parent).

20. While in each case intent to parent was used as a tie-breaker as between two claimants who either had or claimed a biological connection, it is still undeniable that, when push comes to shove, the court employed a legal idea that was unrelated to any necessary biological connection.

Courts can continue to make decisions on an ad hoc basis without necessarily imposing some grand scheme, looking to the imperfectly designed Uniform Parentage Act and a growing body of case law for guidance in the light of applicable family law principles. Or the Legislature can act to impose a broader order which, even though it might not be perfect on a case-by-case basis, would bring some predictability to those who seek to make use of artificial reproductive techniques. As jurists, we recognize the traditional role of the common (i.e., judge-formulated) law in applying old legal principles to new technology. [ ] However, we still believe it is the Legislature, with its ability to formulate general rules based on input from all its constituencies, which is the more desirable forum for lawmaking.

That said, we must now conclude the business at hand.

(1) The portion of the judgment which declares that Luanne Buzzanca is not the lawful mother of Jaycee is reversed. The matter is remanded with directions to enter a new judgment declaring her the lawful mother. * * *

(2) The judgment is reversed to the extent that it provides that John Buzzanca is not the lawful father of Jaycee. The matter is remanded with directions to enter a new judgment declaring him the lawful father. Consonant with this determination, today's ruling is without prejudice to John in future proceedings as regards child custody and visitation as his relationship with Jaycee may develop.[22] The judgment shall also reflect that the birth certificate shall be amended to reflect John Buzzanca as the lawful father.

(3) To the degree that the judgment makes no provision for child support it is reversed. * * *

Notes on Buzzanca v. Buzzanca

1. The California Supreme Court denied review in the Buzzanca case. Why do you think the court did so? Is it because the Buzzanca case traversed no new legal territory? Is it because the issue arises so infrequently? What other reason might there be to deny review in a case like this?

2. What theory of statutory interpretation is being applied by the California Court of Appeal in this case? What would happen if the California Court of Appeal were to apply the "plain meaning" rule? How does the Court of Appeal deal with the issue that the precisely drafted Uniform Parentage Act, by its terms, applies only to sperm sources, not to sources of ova?

3. The result reached by the Court of Appeal seems compelling; as a matter of policy it is hard to accept the trial court's conclusion that the legal arrangements made in this case would leave Jaycee a legal orphan at birth. On the other hand, the reasoning requires quite an expansion of the principles announced in

22. Luanne has had actual physical custody of Jaycee from the beginning. Obviously, it would be frivolous of John to seek custody of Jaycee right now in light of that fact. However, as the lawful father he certainly must be held to have the right, consistent with Jaycee's best interest, to visitation. Our decision today leaves Luanne and John in exactly the same position as any other divorced couple with a child who has been exclusively cared for by the mother since infancy.

And while it may be true that John's consent to the fertilization, implantation and pregnancy was done as an accommodation to allow Luanne to surmount a formality, who knows what relationship he may develop with Jaycee in the future? Human relationships are not static; things done merely to help one individual overcome a perceived legal obstacle sometimes become much more meaningful. [ ]

Johnson v. Calvert and other precedents upon which the court relied. Was there any other way for the court to reach this same result?

4.   Is there any legal theory that could be applied to conclude that someone other than Luanne and John should be treated as Jaycee's parents? What legal theories would lead to the conclusion that the surrogate (i.e., birth) mother should be treated as Jaycee's mother (and her husband should be treated as Jaycee's father)? What legal theories would lead to the conclusion that the genetic sources (i.e., the sperm and ovum sources) should be treated as Jaycee's parents?

5.   Might the child be better off with more than two parents? Could the various potential claimants (sperm and ovum sources, gestating mother and the Buzzancas, who commissioned the whole process) all be found to have parental obligations? If so, must they all be given parental rights? Do you feel any differently about this now than you did after reading Johnson v. Calvert?

On page 987, at the end of the Note: "Cloning," add:

The National Bioethics Advisory Commission published a comprehensive and thoughtful report on the cloning of human beings in June of 1997. The report includes a useful description of the relevant scientific procedures as well as a fully annotated analysis of the ethical, theological, legal and policy issues. The full text of the report can be found at http://earthops.org/cloning_report.html. The Recommendations are reprinted here:

RECOMMENDATIONS OF THE NATIONAL BIOETHICS ADVISORY COMMISSION (NBAC) WITH REGARD TO CLONING

1997

With the announcement that an apparently quite normal sheep had been born in Scotland as a result of somatic cell nuclear transfer cloning came the realization that, as a society, we must yet again collectively decide whether and how to use what appeared to be a dramatic new technological power. The promise and the peril of this scientific advance was noted immediately around the world, but the prospects of creating human beings through this technique mainly elicited widespread resistance and/or concern. Despite this reaction, the scientific significance of the accomplishment, in terms of improved understanding of cell development and cell differentiation, should not be lost. The challenge to public policy is to support the myriad beneficial applications of this new technology, while simultaneously guarding against its more questionable uses.

Much of the negative reaction to the potential application of such cloning in humans can be attributed to fears about harms to the children who may result, particularly psychological harms associated with a possibly diminished sense of individuality and personal autonomy. Others express concern about a degradation in the quality of parenting and family life. And virtually all people agree that the current risks of physical harm to children associated with somatic cell nuclear transplantation cloning justify a prohibition at this time on such experimentation.

In addition to concerns about specific harms to children, people have frequently expressed fears that a widespread practice of somatic cell nuclear transfer cloning would undermine important social values by opening the door to a form of eugenics or by tempting some to manipulate others as if they were objects instead of persons. Arrayed against these concerns are other important social values, such as protecting personal choice, particularly in matters pertaining to procreation and child rearing, maintaining privacy and the freedom of scientific inquiry, and encouraging the possible development of new biomedical breakthroughs.

As somatic cell nuclear transfer cloning could represent a means of human reproduction for some people, limitations on that choice must be made only when the societal benefits of prohibition clearly outweigh the value of maintaining the private nature of such highly personal decisions. Especially in light of some arguably compelling cases for attempting to clone a human being using somatic cell nuclear transfer, the ethics of policy making must strike a balance between the values society wishes to reflect and issues of privacy and the freedom of individual choice.

To arrive at its recommendations concerning the use of somatic cell nuclear transfer techniques, NBAC also examined long-standing religious traditions that often influence and guide citizens' responses to new technologies. Religious positions on human cloning are pluralistic in their premises, modes of argument, and conclusions. Nevertheless, several major themes are prominent in Jewish, Roman Catholic, Protestant, and Islamic positions, including responsible human dominion over nature, human dignity and destiny, procreation, and family life. Some religious thinkers argue that the use of somatic cell nuclear transfer cloning to create a child would be intrinsically immoral and thus could never be morally justified; they usually propose a ban on such human cloning. Other religious thinkers contend that human cloning to create a child could be morally justified under some circumstances but hold that it should be strictly regulated in order to prevent abuses.

The public policies recommended with respect to the creation of a child using somatic cell nuclear transfer reflect the Commission's best judgments about both the ethics of attempting such an experiment and our view of traditions regarding limitations on individual actions in the name of the common good. At present, the use of this technique to create a child would be a premature experiment that exposes the developing child to unacceptable risks. This in itself is sufficient to justify a prohibition on cloning human beings at this time, even if such efforts were to be characterized as the exercise of a fundamental right to attempt to procreate. More speculative psychological harms to the child, and effects on the moral, religious, and cultural values of society may be enough to justify continued prohibitions in the future, but more time is needed for discussion and evaluation of these concerns.

Beyond the issue of the safety of the procedure, however, NBAC found that concerns relating to the potential psychological harms to children and effects on the moral, religious, and cultural values of society merited further reflection and deliberation. Whether upon such further deliberation our nation will conclude that the use of cloning techniques to create children should be allowed or permanently banned is, for the moment, an open question. Time is an ally in this regard, allowing for the accrual of further data from animal experimentation, enabling an assessment of the prospective safety and efficacy of the procedure in humans, as well as granting a period of fuller national debate on ethical and social concerns. The Commission therefore concluded that there should be imposed a period of time in which no attempt is made to create a child using somatic cell nuclear transfer.

Within this overall framework the Commission came to the following conclusions and recommendations:

I. The Commission concludes that at this time it is morally unacceptable for anyone in the public or private sector, whether in a research or clinical setting, to attempt to create a child using somatic cell nuclear transfer cloning. We have reached a consensus on this point because current scientific information indicates that this technique is not safe to use in humans at this time. Indeed, we believe it would violate important ethical obligations were clinicians or researchers to attempt to create a child using these particular technologies, which are likely to involve unacceptable risks to the fetus and/or potential child. Moreover, in addition to safety concerns, many other serious ethical concerns have been identified, which require much more widespread and careful public deliberation before this technology may be used.

The Commission, therefore, recommends the following for immediate action:

- A continuation of the current moratorium on the use of federal funding in support of any attempt to create a child by somatic cell nuclear transfer.

- An immediate request to all firms, clinicians, investigators, and professional societies in the private and non-federally funded sectors to comply voluntarily with the intent of the federal moratorium. Professional and scientific societies should make clear that any attempt to create a child by somatic cell nuclear transfer and implantation into a woman's body would at this time be an irresponsible, unethical, and unprofessional act.

II. The Commission further recommends that:

- Federal legislation should be enacted to prohibit anyone from attempting, whether in a research or clinical setting, to create a child through somatic cell nuclear transfer cloning. It is critical, however, that such legislation include a sunset clause to ensure that Congress will review the issue after a specified time period (three to five years) in order to decide whether the prohibition continues to be needed. If state legislation is enacted, it should also contain such a sunset provision. Any such legislation or associated regulation also ought to require that at some point prior to the expiration of the sunset period, an appropriate oversight body will evaluate and report on the current status of somatic cell nuclear transfer technology and on the ethical and social issues that its potential use to create human beings would raise in light of public understandings at that time.

III. The Commission also concludes that:

- Any regulatory or legislative actions undertaken to effect the foregoing prohibition on creating a child by somatic cell nuclear transfer should be carefully written so as not to interfere with other important areas of scientific research. In particular, no new regulations are required regarding the cloning of human DNA sequences and cell lines, since neither activity raises the scientific and ethical issues that arise from the attempt to create children through somatic cell nuclear transfer, and these fields of research have already provided important scientific and biomedical advances. Likewise, research on cloning animals by somatic cell nuclear transfer does not raise the issues implicated in attempting to use this technique for human cloning, and its continuation should only be subject to existing regulations regarding the humane use of animals and review by institution-based animal protection committees.

- If a legislative ban is not enacted, or if a legislative ban is ever lifted, clinical use of somatic cell nuclear transfer techniques to create a child should be preceded by research trials that are governed by the twin protections of independent review and informed consent, consistent with existing norms of human subjects protection.

- The United States Government should cooperate with other nations and international organizations to enforce any common aspects of their respective policies on the cloning of human beings.

IV. The Commission also concludes that different ethical and religious perspectives and traditions are divided on many of the important moral issues that surround any attempt to create a child using somatic cell nuclear transfer techniques. Therefore, we recommend that:

- The federal government, and all interested and concerned parties, encourage widespread and continuing deliberation on these issues in order to further our understanding of the ethical and social implications of this technology and to enable society to produce appropriate long-term policies regarding this technology should the time come when present concerns about safety have been addressed.

V. Finally, because scientific knowledge is essential for all citizens to participate in a full and informed fashion in the governance of our complex society, the Commission recommends that:

- Federal departments and agencies concerned with science should cooperate in seeking out and supporting opportunities to provide information and education to the public in the area of genetics, and on other developments in the biomedical sciences, especially where these affect important cultural practices, values, and beliefs.

On page 997, at the end of section b, "Criminal Remedies," add:

Might a fetus be considered a child for purposes of a murder statute that provides for the death penalty when the victim is a child under twelve years of age (but not, in the absence of other enumerated circumstances, when the victim is over twelve)? See State v. Ard, 505 S.E.2d 328 (S.C.1998).

Chapter 17

DEFINING DEATH

On page 1056, add the following note:

4. In 1999 the United States Supreme Court determined that EMTALA does not require that the plaintiff show that the hospital acted on the basis of some improper motive, "such as one involving the indigency, race or sex of the patient" in failing to stabilize or properly transfer a patient in order for statutory liability to attach. Roberts v. Galen of Virginia, 119 S.Ct. 685 (1999)(per curiam). Does this case, which reversed the decision of the Sixth Circuit, lend support to the "plain meaning" approach of the two judge majority in Baby "K"? Would it change the nature of the argument that you would make if you were representing the institution in a case like the Baby "K" case?

Chapter 18

LIFE AND DEATH DECISIONS

On page 1078, add to note 5:

The en banc Ninth Circuit decision in Compassion in Dying v. Washington was reversed by the Supreme Court in Washington v. Glucksberg, 521 U.S. 702 (1997), printed below in the supplement to Chapter 18, section VII (A). As did the Ninth Circuit, the United States Supreme Court cited Cruzan in support of its decision. Which opinion seems truer to the principles enunciated by the Court in Cruzan—the Ninth Circuit majority opinion by Judge Reinhardt (in the casebook, at 316), or the Chief Justice's opinion for a unanimous Supreme Court? What light does the Chief Justice's opinion in Glucksberg shine on the meaning and precedential value of Cruzan?

On page 1117, at the end of section "ii. Family Consent Laws," add:

In In re Schmidt, 699 N.E.2d 1123 (Ill.App.1998) an accident victim's husband and the victim's siblings were locked in battle over who should be appointed to make health care decisions for the patient, who had suffered severe head trauma in an automobile accident and who had been in a coma for several months. The siblings claimed that the husband was estranged from his wife, that he constantly made "dumb blonde" jokes about her and otherwise mistreated her, and that they were more likely to make appropriate decisions for her. The husband claimed that he had a good relationship with his wife, who had been married several times, during the three years of their marriage. His wife's 17–year-old daughter from a prior marriage supported the husband. The husband wished to remove life-sustaining treatment and allow his wife to die; he said that he and his stepdaughter had been engaged in discussions with the patient that made it clear that she would prefer not to live under the circumstances in which she now found herself. The siblings wished to keep their sister alive, which, they were sure, would be her wish under the circumstances. The trial court appointed a guardian ad litem for the patient, who recommended that the husband be appointed guardian. After an evidentiary hearing, the trial court appointed the husband guardian, with authority to consent to the removal of life sustaining medical care.

While the appellate court recognized that the hierarchy of decisionmakers under the Illinois family consent law was deeply rooted in state policy, it also recognized that a court was not bound to follow that hierarchy when appointing a guardian, who had priority over any family member under the statute. As the court pointed out, "[t]he best interest and welfare of the disabled person is the paramount concern in selecting a guardian." 699 N.E.2d at 1128. Still, the appellate court found that the trial court had not abused its discretion in appointing the husband guardian, and that, as guardian, he had the statutory authority to consent to the withdrawal of medical care, even if that withdrawal would result in the death of the patient, if other statutory requirements were followed.

On page 1124, at the end of the Note: "Conroy and Persistent Vegetative State," add:

Wisconsin, too, has chosen to treat patients in persistent vegetative state as different from other patients. A person in persistent vegetative state may have life sustaining treatment removed if it is in the patient's "best interests," even if the patient has never made any statement indicating his or her desires. On the other hand, no surrogate decisionmaker can be granted authority to withhold or withdraw life sustaining medical care from a patient who is not in a persistent vegetative state "unless the ward has executed an advance directive or other statement clearly indicating his or her desires." In re Edna M.F., 563 N.W.2d 485 (Wis.1997). Is the Wisconsin distinction between treatment of those in persistent vegetative state and treatment of those who are not parallel to the distinction made by the New Jersey courts? Perhaps the Wisconsin Supreme Court's decision to apply the presumption that those who are not in persistent vegetative state should be provided life sustaining treatment in the absence of clearly articulated desires was necessary to deal with Edna. In that case, the sister-guardian wished to remove a feeding tube on the basis of the patient's single statement, "I would rather die of cancer than lose my mind," made thirty years earlier. The Court found that this could not count as a "statement clearly indicating ... her desires."

On page 1138, after the O'Connor case, add:

Note on the Application of the O'connor Standard

The O'Connor standard has proven to be more flexible than it might have first appeared; whether evidence is "clear and convincing" may well depend on the values of the judge as well as the strength of the underlying facts. For example, in Matter of Christopher, 675 N.Y.S.2d 807 (Sup.Ct. 1998) the evidence showed that a 79 year old Russian immigrant in a nursing home had made a comment to her son ten years earlier while they were watching a television program on the Claus Von Bulow case. "The screen showed Sonny Von Bulow lying in bed in a coma. [The son] said to his mother, 'It's good to be rich in this country, Mom, because even in her condition she still looks like a model.' His mother replied, 'No,[even] if you was rich, I wouldn't want to be in this condition, never." There was no other evidence of the patient's wishes. The court determined that the evidence was "unequivocal" and that it constituted "clear and convincing evidence that the use of such artificial means to prolong her life is against her wishes * * *." 675 N.Y.S.2d at 809.

On page 1160, at the end of note 6, add:

The United States Supreme Court has found the Religious Freedom Restoration Act to be unconstitutional. City of Boerne v. Flores, 521 U.S. 507 (1997). Many states, however, have passed "little RFRA" statutes that apply to actions of those state governments.

On page 1167, substitute the following for Compassion in Dying v. Washington, or alternatively, read after you read the Ninth Circuit opinions in Compassion in Dying:

WASHINGTON v. GLUCKSBERG

Supreme Court of the United States, 1997.
521 U.S. 702.

REHNQUIST, C. J., delivered the opinion of the Court, in which O'CONNOR, SCALIA, KENNEDY, and THOMAS, JJ., joined. O'CONNOR, J., filed a concurring opinion, in which GINSBURG and BREYER, JJ., joined in part. STEVENS, J., SOUTER, J., GINSBURG, J., and BREYER, J., filed opinions concurring in the judgment.

CHIEF JUSTICE REHNQUIST delivered the opinion of the Court.

The question presented in this case is whether Washington's prohibition against "causing" or "aiding" a suicide offends the Fourteenth Amendment to the United States Constitution. We hold that it does not.

* * *

The plaintiffs assert[ ] "the existence of a liberty interest protected by the Fourteenth Amendment which extends to a personal choice by a mentally competent, terminally ill adult to commit physician-assisted suicide." [ ] Relying primarily on Planned Parenthood v. Casey, [ ] and Cruzan v. Director, Missouri Dept. of Health, [ ] the District Court agreed, [ ] and concluded that Washington's assisted-suicide ban is unconstitutional because it "places an undue burden on the exercise of [that] constitutionally protected liberty interest." [ ] The District Court also decided that the Washington statute violated the Equal Protection Clause's requirement that " 'all persons similarly situated . . . be treated alike.' " [ ]

A panel of the Court of Appeals for the Ninth Circuit reversed, emphasizing that "in the two hundred and five years of our existence no constitutional right to aid in killing oneself has ever been asserted and upheld by a court of final jurisdiction." [ ] The Ninth Circuit reheard the case en banc, reversed the panel's decision, and affirmed the District Court. [ ] Like the District Court, the en banc Court of Appeals emphasized our Casey and Cruzan decisions. [ ] The court also discussed what it described as "historical" and "current societal attitudes" toward suicide and assisted suicide, [ ] and concluded that "the Constitution encompasses a due process liberty interest in controlling the time and manner of one's death—that there is, in short, a constitutionally-recognized 'right to die.' " [ ] After "weighing and then balancing" this interest against Washington's various interests, the court held that the State's assisted-suicide ban was unconstitutional "as applied to terminally ill competent [ ] adults who wish to hasten their deaths with medication prescribed by their physicians." [ ] We granted certiorari [ ] and now reverse.

I

We begin, as we do in all due-process cases, by examining our Nation's history, legal traditions, and practices. [ ] In almost every State—indeed, in almost every western democracy—it is a crime to assist a suicide. The States' assisted-suicide bans are not innovations. Rather, they are longstanding expressions of the States' commitment to the protection and preservation of all human life. [ ] Indeed, opposition to and condemnation of suicide—and, therefore, of assisting suicide—are consistent and enduring themes of our philosophical, legal, and cultural heritages. [ ]

More specifically, for over 700 years, the Anglo–American common-law tradition has punished or otherwise disapproved of both suicide and assisting suicide. * * * [The Chief Justice then reviews the common law of England and the American colonies and states with regards to suicide, from the 13th century to the present.]

* * *

[T]he [Early American] prohibitions against assisting suicide never contained exceptions for those who were near death. Rather, "the life of those to whom life had become a burden—of those who [were] hopelessly diseased or fatally wounded—nay, even the lives of criminals condemned to death, [were] under the protection of law, equally as the lives of those who [were] in the full tide of life's enjoyment, and anxious to continue to live." [ ]

* * *

Though deeply rooted, the States' assisted-suicide bans have in recent years been reexamined and, generally, reaffirmed. Because of advances in medicine and technology, Americans today are increasingly likely to die in institutions, from chronic illnesses. [ ] Public concern and democratic action are therefore sharply focused on how best to protect dignity and independence at the end of life, with the result that there have been many significant changes in state laws and in the attitudes these laws reflect. Many States, for example, now permit "living wills," surrogate health-care decisionmaking, and the withdrawal or refusal of life-sustaining medical treatment. [ ] At the same time, however, voters and legislators continue for the most part to reaffirm their States' prohibitions on assisting suicide.

The Washington statute at issue in this case [ ] was enacted in 1975 as part of a revision of that State's criminal code. Four years later, Washington passed its Natural Death Act, which specifically stated that the "withholding or withdrawal of life-sustaining treatment ... shall not, for any purpose, constitute a suicide" and that "nothing in this chapter shall be construed to condone, authorize, or approve mercy killing...." [ ] In 1991, Washington voters rejected a ballot initiative which, had it passed, would have permitted a form of physician-assisted suicide. Washington then added a provision to the Natural Death Act expressly excluding physician-assisted suicide. [ ]

California voters rejected an assisted-suicide initiative similar to Washington's in 1993. On the other hand, in 1994, voters in Oregon enacted, also through ballot initiative, that State's "Death With Dignity Act," which legalized physician-assisted suicide for competent, terminally ill adults. Since the Oregon vote, many proposals to legalize assisted-suicide have been and continue to be introduced in the States' legislatures, but none has been enacted. And just last year, Iowa and Rhode Island joined the overwhelming majority of States explicitly prohibiting assisted suicide. [ ]

* * *

Attitudes toward suicide itself have changed since [the 13th Century prohibitions on suicide] * * * but our laws have consistently condemned, and continue to prohibit, assisting suicide. Despite changes in medical technology and notwithstanding an increased emphasis on the importance of end-of-life decisionmaking, we have not retreated from this prohibition. Against this backdrop of history, tradition, and practice, we now turn to respondents' constitutional claim.

II

The Due Process Clause guarantees more than fair process, and the "liberty" it protects includes more than the absence of physical restraint. [ ] The Clause also provides heightened protection against government interference with certain fundamental rights and liberty interests. [ ] In a long line of cases, we have held that, in addition to the specific freedoms protected by the Bill of Rights, the "liberty" specially protected by the Due Process Clause includes the rights to marry, [ ]; to have children, [ ]; to direct the education and upbringing of one's children, [ ]; to marital privacy, [ ]; to use contraception, [ ]; to bodily integrity, [ ] and to abortion, [ ]. We have also assumed, and strongly suggested, that the Due Process Clause protects the traditional right to refuse unwanted lifesaving medical treatment. [ ]

But we "have always been reluctant to expand the concept of substantive due process because guideposts for responsible decisionmaking in this unchartered area are scarce and open-ended." [ ] By extending constitutional protection to an asserted right or liberty interest, we, to a great extent, place the matter outside the arena of public debate and legislative action. We must therefore "exercise the utmost care whenever we are asked to break new ground in this field" [ ] lest the liberty protected by the Due Process Clause be subtly transformed into the policy preferences of the members of this Court [ ].

Our established method of substantive-due-process analysis has two primary features: First, we have regularly observed that the Due Process Clause specially protects those fundamental rights and liberties which are, objectively, "deeply rooted in this Nation's history and tradition" [ ] and "implicit in the concept of ordered liberty," such that "neither liberty nor justice would exist if they were sacrificed" [ ]. Second, we have required in substantive-due-process cases a "careful description" of the asserted fundamental liberty interest. [ ] Cruzan, supra, at 277–278. Our Nation's history, legal traditions, and practices thus provide the crucial "guideposts for responsible decisionmaking" [ ] that direct and restrain our exposition of the Due Process Clause. As we stated recently in Flores, the Fourteenth Amendment "forbids the government to infringe . . . 'fundamental' liberty interests at all, no matter what process is provided, unless the infringement is narrowly tailored to serve a compelling state interest." [ ]

* * *

Turning to the claim at issue here, the Court of Appeals stated that "properly analyzed, the first issue to be resolved is whether there is a liberty interest in determining the time and manner of one's death" [ ] or, in other words, "is there a right to die?" [ ]. Similarly, respondents assert a "liberty to choose how to die" and a right to "control of one's final days," [ ] and describe the asserted liberty as "the right to choose a humane, dignified death" [ ] and "the liberty to shape death" [ ]. As noted above, we have a tradition of carefully formulating the interest at stake in substantive-due-process cases. For example, although Cruzan is often described as a "right to die" case [ ] we were, in fact, more precise: we assumed that the Constitution granted competent persons a "constitutionally protected right to refuse life-saving hydration and nutrition." [ ] The Washington statute at issue in this case prohibits "aiding another person to attempt suicide," [ ] and, thus, the question before us is whether the "liberty" specially protected by the Due Process Clause includes a right to commit suicide which itself includes a right to assistance in doing so.

We now inquire whether this asserted right has any place in our Nation's traditions. Here, as discussed above, [ ] we are confronted with a consistent and almost universal tradition that has long rejected the asserted right, and continues explicitly to reject it today, even for terminally ill, mentally competent adults. To hold for respondents, we would have to reverse centuries of legal doctrine and practice, and strike down the considered policy choice of almost every State. [ ]

* * * The question presented in this case * * * is whether the protections of the Due Process Clause include a right to commit suicide with another's assistance. With this "careful description" of respondents' claim in mind, we turn to Casey and Cruzan.

[The Chief Justice next discusses the Cruzan case, where, he says,] "we assumed that the United States Constitution would grant a competent person a constitutionally protected right to refuse lifesaving hydration and nutrition."

* * *

The right assumed in Cruzan, however, was not simply deduced from abstract concepts of personal autonomy. Given the common-law rule that forced medication was a battery, and the long legal tradition protecting the decision to refuse unwanted medical treatment, our assumption was entirely consistent with this Nation's history and constitutional traditions. The decision to commit suicide with the assistance of another may be just as personal and profound as the decision to refuse unwanted medical treatment, but it has never enjoyed similar legal protection. Indeed, the two acts are widely and reasonably regarded as quite distinct. [ ] In Cruzan itself, we recognized that most States outlawed assisted suicide—and even more do today—and we certainly gave no intimation that the right to refuse unwanted medical treatment could be somehow transmuted into a right to assistance in committing suicide. [ ]

Respondents also rely on Casey. There, the Court's opinion concluded that "the essential holding of Roe v. Wade should be retained and once again reaffirmed." [ ] We held, first, that a woman has a right, before her fetus is viable, to an abortion "without undue interference from the State"; second, that States may restrict post-viability abortions, so long as exceptions are made to protect a woman's life and health; and third, that the State has legitimate interests throughout a pregnancy in protecting the health of the woman and the life of the unborn child. [ ] In reaching this conclusion, the opinion discussed in some detail this Court's substantive-due-process tradition of interpreting the Due Process Clause to protect certain fundamental rights and "personal decisions relating to marriage, procreation, contraception, family relationships, child rearing, and education," and noted that many of those rights and liberties "involve the most intimate and personal choices a person may make in a lifetime." [ ]

* * *

That many of the rights and liberties protected by the Due Process Clause sound in personal autonomy does not warrant the sweeping conclusion that any and all important, intimate, and personal decisions are so protected, [ ] and Casey did not suggest otherwise.

The history of the law's treatment of assisted suicide in this country has been and continues to be one of the rejection of nearly all efforts to permit it. That being the case, our decisions lead us to conclude that the asserted "right" to assistance in committing suicide is not a fundamental liberty interest protected by the Due Process Clause. The Constitution also requires, however, that Washington's assisted-suicide ban be rationally related to legitimate government interests. [ ] This requirement is unquestionably met here. As the court below recognized, [ ] Washington's assisted-suicide ban implicates a number of state interests. [ ]

First, Washington has an "unqualified interest in the preservation of human life." * * *

* * * The Court of Appeals also recognized Washington's interest in protecting life, but held that the "weight" of this interest depends on the "medical condition and the wishes of the person whose life is at stake." [ ] Washington, however, has rejected this sliding-scale approach and, through its assisted-suicide ban, insists that all persons' lives, from beginning to end, regardless of physical or mental condition, are under the full protection of the law. [ ] As we have previously affirmed, the States "may properly decline to make judgments about the 'quality' of life that a particular individual may enjoy," [ ] This remains true, as Cruzan makes clear, even for those who are near death.

Relatedly, all admit that suicide is a serious public-health problem, especially among persons in otherwise vulnerable groups. [ ] The State has an interest in preventing suicide, and in studying, identifying, and treating its causes. [ ]

Those who attempt suicide—terminally ill or not—often suffer from depression or other mental disorders. [ ] * * * [B]ecause depression is difficult to diagnose, physicians and medical professionals often fail to respond adequately to seriously ill patients' needs. [ ] Thus, legal physician-assisted suicide could make it more difficult for the State to protect depressed or mentally ill persons, or those who are suffering from untreated pain, from suicidal impulses.

The State also has an interest in protecting the integrity and ethics of the medical profession. * * * [T]he American Medical Association, like many other medical and physicians' groups, has concluded that "physician-assisted suicide is fundamentally incompatible with the physician's role as healer." [ ] And physician-assisted suicide could, it is argued, undermine the trust that is essential to the doctor-patient relationship by blurring the time-honored line between healing and harming. [ ]

Next, the State has an interest in protecting vulnerable groups—including the poor, the elderly, and disabled persons—from abuse, neglect, and mistakes. * * * [One respected state task force] warned that "legalizing physician-assisted suicide would pose profound risks to many individuals who are ill and vulnerable. . . . The risk of harm is greatest for the many individuals in our society whose autonomy and well-being are already compromised by poverty, lack of access to good medical care, advanced age, or membership in a stigmatized social group." [ ] If physician-assisted suicide were permitted, many might resort to it to spare their families the substantial financial burden of end-of-life health-care costs.

The State's interest here goes beyond protecting the vulnerable from coercion; it extends to protecting disabled and terminally ill people from prejudice, negative and inaccurate stereotypes, and "societal indifference." [ ] The State's assisted-suicide ban reflects and reinforces its policy that the lives of terminally ill, disabled, and elderly people must be no less valued than the lives of the young and healthy, and that a seriously disabled person's suicidal impulses should be interpreted and treated the same way as anyone else's. [ ]

Finally, the State may fear that permitting assisted suicide will start it down the path to voluntary and perhaps even involuntary euthanasia. * * *

This concern is * * * supported by evidence about the practice of euthanasia in the Netherlands. The Dutch government's own study revealed that in 1990, there were 2,300 cases of voluntary euthanasia (defined as "the deliberate termination of another's life at his request"), 400 cases of assisted suicide, and more than 1,000 cases of euthanasia without an explicit request. In addition to these latter 1,000 cases, the study found an additional 4,941 cases where physicians administered lethal morphine overdoses without the patients' explicit consent. [ ] This study suggests that, despite the existence of various reporting procedures, euthanasia in the Netherlands has not been limited to competent, terminally ill adults who are enduring physical suffering, and that regulation of the practice may not have prevented abuses in cases involving vulnerable persons, including severely disabled neonates and elderly persons suffering from dementia. [ ]

We need not weigh exactingly the relative strengths of these various interests. They are unquestionably important and legitimate, and Washington's ban on assisted suicide is at least reasonably related to their promotion and protection. We therefore hold that [ ] [the Washington ban on assisting suicide] does not violate the Fourteenth Amendment, either on its face or "as applied to competent, terminally ill adults who wish to hasten their deaths by obtaining medication prescribed by their doctors."[22] [ ]

* * *

22. JUSTICE STEVENS states that "the Court does conceive of respondents' claim as a facial challenge—addressing not the application of the statute to a particular set of plaintiffs before it, but the constitutionality of the statute's categorical prohibition. . . ." [ ] We emphasize that we today reject the Court of Appeals' specific holding that the statute is unconstitutional "as applied" to a particular class. [ ] JUSTICE STEVENS agrees with this holding, [ ] but would not "foreclose the possibility that an individual plaintiff seeking to hasten her death, or a doctor whose assistance was sought, could prevail in a more particular-

Throughout the Nation, Americans are engaged in an earnest and profound debate about the morality, legality, and practicality of physician-assisted suicide. Our holding permits this debate to continue, as it should in a democratic society. The decision of the en banc Court of Appeals is reversed, and the case is remanded for further proceedings consistent with this opinion.

It is so ordered.

JUSTICE O'CONNOR, concurring [in both Glucksberg and Vacco].*

Death will be different for each of us. For many, the last days will be spent in physical pain and perhaps the despair that accompanies physical deterioration and a loss of control of basic bodily and mental functions. Some will seek medication to alleviate that pain and other symptoms.

The Court frames the issue in this case as whether the Due Process Clause of the Constitution protects a "right to commit suicide which itself includes a right to assistance in doing so," [ ] and concludes that our Nation's history, legal traditions, and practices do not support the existence of such a right. I join the Court's opinions because I agree that there is no generalized right to "commit suicide." But respondents urge us to address the narrower question whether a mentally competent person who is experiencing great suffering has a constitutionally cognizable interest in controlling the circumstances of his or her imminent death. I see no need to reach that question in the context of the facial challenges to the New York and Washington laws at issue here. [ ] The parties and amici agree that in these States a patient who is suffering from a terminal illness and who is experiencing great pain has no legal barriers to obtaining medication, from qualified physicians, to alleviate that suffering, even to the point of causing unconsciousness and hastening death. [ ] In this light, even assuming that we would recognize such an interest, I agree that the State's interests in protecting those who are not truly competent or facing imminent death, or those whose decisions to hasten death would not truly be voluntary, are sufficiently weighty to justify a prohibition against physician-assisted suicide. [ ]

Every one of us at some point may be affected by our own or a family member's terminal illness. There is no reason to think the democratic process will not strike the proper balance between the interests of terminally ill, mentally competent individuals who would seek to end their suffering and the State's interests in protecting those who might seek to end life mistakenly or under pressure. As the Court recognizes, States are presently undertaking extensive and serious evaluation of physician-assisted suicide and other related issues. [ ] In such circumstances, "the ... challenging task of crafting appropriate procedures for safeguarding ... liberty interests is entrusted to the 'laboratory' of the States ... in the first instance." [ ]

In sum, there is no need to address the question whether suffering patients have a constitutionally cognizable interest in obtaining relief from

ized challenge," ibid. Our opinion does not absolutely foreclose such a claim. However, given our holding that the Due Process Clause of the Fourteenth Amendment does not provide heightened protection to the asserted liberty interest in ending one's life with a physician's assistance, such a claim would have to

be quite different from the ones advanced by respondents here.

* JUSTICE GINSBURG concurs in the Court's judgments substantially for the reasons stated in this opinion. JUSTICE BREYER joins this opinion except insofar as it joins the opinions of the Court.

the suffering that they may experience in the last days of their lives. There is no dispute that dying patients in Washington and New York can obtain palliative care, even when doing so would hasten their deaths. The difficulty in defining terminal illness and the risk that a dying patient's request for assistance in ending his or her life might not be truly voluntary justifies the prohibitions on assisted suicide we uphold here.

JUSTICE STEVENS, concurring in the judgments [in both Glucksberg and Vacco].

The Court ends its opinion with the important observation that our holding today is fully consistent with a continuation of the vigorous debate about the "morality, legality, and practicality of physician-assisted suicide" in a democratic society. [ ] I write separately to make it clear that there is also room for further debate about the limits that the Constitution places on the power of the States to punish the practice.

I

The morality, legality, and practicality of capital punishment have been the subject of debate for many years. In 1976, this Court upheld the constitutionality of the practice in cases coming to us from Georgia, Florida, and Texas. In those cases we concluded that a State does have the power to place a lesser value on some lives than on others; there is no absolute requirement that a State treat all human life as having an equal right to preservation. Because the state legislatures had sufficiently narrowed the category of lives that the State could terminate, and had enacted special procedures to ensure that the defendant belonged in that limited category, we concluded that the statutes were not unconstitutional on their face. In later cases coming to us from each of those States, however, we found that some applications of the statutes were unconstitutional.

Today, the Court decides that Washington's statute prohibiting assisted suicide is not invalid "on its face," that is to say, in all or most cases in which it might be applied. That holding, however, does not foreclose the possibility that some applications of the statute might well be invalid.

* * *

History and tradition provide ample support for refusing to recognize an open-ended constitutional right to commit suicide. Much more than the State's paternalistic interest in protecting the individual from the irrevocable consequences of an ill-advised decision motivated by temporary concerns is at stake. There is truth in John Donne's observation that "No man is an island." The State has an interest in preserving and fostering the benefits that every human being may provide to the community—a community that thrives on the exchange of ideas, expressions of affection, shared memories and humorous incidents as well as on the material contributions that its members create and support. The value to others of a person's life is far too precious to allow the individual to claim a constitutional entitlement to complete autonomy in making a decision to end that life. Thus, I fully agree with the Court that the "liberty" protected by the Due Process Clause does not include a categorical "right to commit suicide which itself includes a right to assistance in doing so." [ ]

But just as our conclusion that capital punishment is not always unconstitutional did not preclude later decisions holding that it is sometimes impermissibly cruel, so is it equally clear that a decision upholding a general statutory prohibition of assisted suicide does not mean that every possible application of the statute would be valid. A State, like Washington, that has authorized the death penalty and thereby has concluded that the sanctity of human life does not require that it always be preserved, must acknowledge that there are situations in which an interest in hastening death is legitimate. Indeed, not only is that interest sometimes legitimate, I am also convinced that there are times when it is entitled to constitutional protection.

II

In Cruzan [ ] the Court assumed that the interest in liberty protected by the Fourteenth Amendment encompassed the right of a terminally ill patient to direct the withdrawal of life-sustaining treatment. As the Court correctly observes today, that assumption "was not simply deduced from abstract concepts of personal autonomy." [ ] Instead, it was supported by the common-law tradition protecting the individual's general right to refuse unwanted medical treatment. [ ] We have recognized, however, that this common-law right to refuse treatment is neither absolute nor always sufficiently weighty to overcome valid countervailing state interests. * * *

Cruzan, however, was not the normal case. Given the irreversible nature of her illness and the progressive character of her suffering, Nancy Cruzan's interest in refusing medical care was incidental to her more basic interest in controlling the manner and timing of her death. In finding that her best interests would be served by cutting off the nourishment that kept her alive, the trial court did more than simply vindicate Cruzan's interest in refusing medical treatment; the court, in essence, authorized affirmative conduct that would hasten her death. When this Court reviewed the case and upheld Missouri's requirement that there be clear and convincing evidence establishing Nancy Cruzan's intent to have life-sustaining nourishment withdrawn, it made two important assumptions: (1) that there was a "liberty interest" in refusing unwanted treatment protected by the Due Process Clause; and (2) that this liberty interest did not "end the inquiry" because it might be outweighed by relevant state interests. [ ] I agree with both of those assumptions, but I insist that the source of Nancy Cruzan's right to refuse treatment was not just a common-law rule. Rather, this right is an aspect of a far broader and more basic concept of freedom that is even older than the common law. This freedom embraces, not merely a person's right to refuse a particular kind of unwanted treatment, but also her interest in dignity, and in determining the character of the memories that will survive long after her death. In recognizing that the State's interests did not outweigh Nancy Cruzan's liberty interest in refusing medical treatment, Cruzan rested not simply on the common-law right to refuse medical treatment, but—at least implicitly—on the even more fundamental right to make this "deeply personal decision," [ ].

* * *

While I agree with the Court that Cruzan does not decide the issue presented by these cases, Cruzan did give recognition, not just to vague, unbridled notions of autonomy, but to the more specific interest in making decisions about how to confront an imminent death. Although there is no absolute right to physician-assisted suicide, Cruzan makes it clear that some individuals who no longer have the option of deciding whether to live or to die because they are already on the threshold of death have a constitutionally protected interest that may outweigh the State's interest in preserving life at all costs. The liberty interest at stake in a case like this differs from, and is stronger than, both the common-law right to refuse medical treatment and the unbridled interest in deciding whether to live or die. It is an interest in deciding how, rather than whether, a critical threshold shall be crossed.

III

The state interests supporting a general rule banning the practice of physician-assisted suicide do not have the same force in all cases. First and foremost of these interests is the " 'unqualified interest in the preservation of human life' " [ ].

Many terminally ill people find their lives meaningful even if filled with pain or dependence on others. Some find value in living through suffering; some have an abiding desire to witness particular events in their families' lives; many believe it a sin to hasten death. Individuals of different religious faiths make different judgments and choices about whether to live on under such circumstances. There are those who will want to continue aggressive treatment; those who would prefer terminal sedation; and those who will seek withdrawal from life-support systems and death by gradual starvation and dehydration. Although as a general matter the State's interest in the contributions each person may make to society outweighs the person's interest in ending her life, this interest does not have the same force for a terminally ill patient faced not with the choice of whether to live, only of how to die. * * *

Similarly, the State's legitimate interests in preventing suicide, protecting the vulnerable from coercion and abuse, and preventing euthanasia are less significant in this context. I agree that the State has a compelling interest in preventing persons from committing suicide because of depression, or coercion by third parties. But the State's legitimate interest in preventing abuse does not apply to an individual who is not victimized by abuse, who is not suffering from depression, and who makes a rational and voluntary decision to seek assistance in dying.

* * *

The final major interest asserted by the State is its interest in preserving the traditional integrity of the medical profession. The fear is that a rule permitting physicians to assist in suicide is inconsistent with the perception that they serve their patients solely as healers. But for some patients, it would be a physician's refusal to dispense medication to ease their suffering and make their death tolerable and dignified that would be inconsistent with the healing role * * * . Furthermore, because physicians are already involved in making decisions that hasten the death of terminally ill patients—through termination of life support, withholding of medical treatment, and terminal sedation—there is in fact significant tension between the traditional view of the physician's role and the actual practice in a growing number of cases.

As [one state task force] recognized, a State's prohibition of assisted suicide is justified by the fact that the " 'ideal' " case in which "patients would be screened for depression and offered treatment, effective pain medication would be available, and all patients would have a supportive committed family and doctor" is not the usual case. [ ] Although, as the Court concludes today, these potential harms are sufficient to support the State's general public policy against assisted suicide, they will not always outweigh the individual liberty interest of a particular patient. Unlike the Court of Appeals, I would not say as a categorical matter that these state interests are invalid as to the entire class of terminally ill, mentally competent patients. I do not, however, foreclose the possibility that an individual plaintiff seeking to hasten her death, or a doctor whose assistance was sought, could prevail in a more particularized challenge. Future cases will determine whether such a challenge may succeed.

IV

In New York, a doctor must respect a competent person's decision to refuse or to discontinue medical treatment even though death will thereby ensue, but the same doctor would be guilty of a felony if she provided her patient assistance in committing suicide. Today we hold that the Equal Protection Clause is not violated by the resulting disparate treatment of two classes of terminally ill people who may have the same interest in hastening death. I agree that the distinction between permitting death to ensue from an underlying fatal disease and causing it to occur by the administration of medication or other means provides a constitutionally sufficient basis for the State's classification. Unlike the Court, however, [ ] I am not persuaded that in all cases there will in fact be a significant difference between the intent of the physicians, the patients or the families in the two situations.

There may be little distinction between the intent of a terminally-ill patient who decides to remove her life-support and one who seeks the assistance of a doctor in ending her life; in both situations, the patient is seeking to hasten a certain, impending death. The doctor's intent might also be the same in prescribing lethal medication as it is in terminating life support. A doctor who fails to administer medical treatment to one who is dying from a disease could be doing so with an intent to harm or kill that patient. Conversely, a doctor who prescribes lethal medication does not necessarily intend the patient's death—rather that doctor may seek simply to ease the patient's suffering and to comply with her wishes. The illusory character of any differences in intent or causation is confirmed by the fact that the American Medical Association unequivocally endorses the practice of terminal sedation—the administration of sufficient dosages of pain-killing medication to terminally ill patients to protect them from excruciating pain even when it is clear that the time of death will be advanced. The purpose of terminal sedation is to ease the suffering of the patient and comply with her wishes, and the actual cause of death is the administration of heavy doses of lethal sedatives. This same intent and causation may exist when a doctor complies with a patient's request for lethal medication to hasten her death.

Thus, although the differences the majority notes in causation and intent between terminating life-support and assisting in suicide support the Court's rejection of the respondents' facial challenge, these distinctions may be inapplicable to particular terminally ill patients and their doctors. Our holding today in Vacco v. Quill that the Equal Protection Clause is not violated by New York's classification, just like our holding in Washington v. Glucksberg that the Washington statute is not invalid on its face, does not foreclose the possibility that some applications of the New York statute may impose an intolerable intrusion on the patient's freedom.

There remains room for vigorous debate about the outcome of particular cases that are not necessarily resolved by the opinions announced today. How such cases may be decided will depend on their specific facts. In my judgment, however, it is clear that the so-called "unqualified interest in the preservation of human life," [ ] is not itself sufficient to outweigh the interest in liberty that may justify the only possible means of preserving a dying patient's dignity and alleviating her intolerable suffering.

JUSTICE SOUTER, concurring in the judgment.

* * *

I

* * *

In their brief to this Court, the doctors claim not that they ought to have a right generally to hasten patients' imminent deaths, but only to help patients who have made "personal decisions regarding their own bodies, medical care, and, fundamentally, the future course of their lives," [ ] and who have concluded responsibly and with substantial justification that the brief and anguished remainders of their lives have lost virtually all value to them. Respondents fully embrace the notion that the State must be free to impose reasonable regulations on such physician assistance to ensure that the patients they assist are indeed among the competent and terminally ill and that each has made a free and informed choice in seeking to obtain and use a fatal drug. [ ]

In response, the State argues that the interest asserted by the doctors is beyond constitutional recognition because it has no deep roots in our history and traditions. [ ] But even aside from that, without disputing that the patients here were competent and terminally ill, the State insists that recognizing the legitimacy of doctors' assistance of their patients as contemplated here would entail a number of adverse consequences that the Washington Legislature was entitled to forestall. The nub of this part of the State's argument is not that such patients are constitutionally undeserving of relief on their own account, but that any attempt to confine a right of physician assistance to the circumstances presented by these doctors is likely to fail. [ ]

First, the State argues that the right could not be confined to the terminally ill. * * * Second, the State argues that the right could not be confined to the mentally competent, observing that a person's competence cannot always be assessed with certainty, [ ] and suggesting further that no principled distinction is possible between a competent patient acting independently and a patient acting through a duly appointed and competent surrogate [ ]. Next, according to the State, such a right might entail a right to or at least merge in practice into "other forms of life-ending assistance," such as euthanasia. [ ] Finally, the State believes that a right to physician assistance could not easily be distinguished from a right to assistance from others, such as friends, family, and other health-care workers. [ ] The State thus argues that recognition of the substantive due process right at issue here would jeopardize the lives of others outside the class defined by the doctors' claim, creating risks of irresponsible suicides and euthanasia, whose dangers are concededly within the State's authority to address.

II

When the physicians claim that the Washington law deprives them of a right falling within the scope of liberty that the Fourteenth Amendment guarantees against denial without due process of law, they are not claiming some sort of procedural defect in the process through which the statute has been enacted or is administered. Their claim, rather, is that the State has no substantively adequate justification for barring the assistance sought by the patient and sought to be offered by the physician. Thus, we are dealing with a claim to one of those rights sometimes described as rights of substantive due process and sometimes as unenumerated rights, in view of the breadth and indeterminacy of the "due process" serving as the claim's textual basis. The doctors accordingly arouse the skepticism of those who find the Due Process Clause an unduly vague or oxymoronic warrant for judicial review of substantive state law, just as they also invoke two centuries of American constitutional practice in recognizing unenumerated, substantive limits on governmental action. * * *

* * *

III

[Justice Souter explained that he was adopting Justice Harlan's approach to the Constitutional evaluation and protection of unenumerated rights under the Due Process Clause, as articulated in his dissent in Poe v. Ullman.] My understanding of unenumerated rights in the wake of the Poe dissent and subsequent cases avoids the absolutist failing of many older cases without embracing the opposite pole of equating reasonableness with past practice described at a very specific level. [ ] That understanding begins with a concept of "ordered liberty," [ ] comprising a continuum of rights to be free from "arbitrary impositions and purposeless restraints" [ ].

"Due Process has not been reduced to any formula; its content cannot be determined by reference to any code. The best that can be said is that through the course of this Court's decisions it has represented the balance which our Nation, built upon postulates of respect for the liberty of the individual, has struck between that liberty and the demands of organized society. If the supplying of content to this Constitutional concept has of necessity been a rational process, it certainly has not been one where judges have felt free to roam where unguided speculation might take them. The balance of which I speak is the balance struck by this country, having regard to what history teaches are the traditions from which it developed as well as the traditions from which it broke. That tradition is a living thing. A decision of this Court which radically departs from it could not long survive, while a decision which builds on what has survived is likely to be sound. No formula could serve as a substitute, in this area, for judgment and restraint." [Harlan, J., dissenting in Poe v. Ullman]

* * *

This approach calls for a court to assess the relative "weights" or dignities of the contending interests, and to this extent the judicial method is familiar to the common law. Common law method is subject, however, to two important constraints in the hands of a court engaged in substantive due process review. First, such a court is bound to confine the values that it recognizes to those truly deserving constitutional stature, either to those expressed in constitutional text, or those exemplified by "the traditions from which [the Nation] developed," or revealed by contrast with "the traditions from which it broke." [ ]

The second constraint, again, simply reflects the fact that constitutional review, not judicial lawmaking, is a court's business here. The weighing or valuing of contending interests in this sphere is only the first step, forming the basis for determining whether the statute in question falls inside or outside the zone of what is reasonable in the way it resolves the conflict between the interests of state and individual.

* * *

IV

A

Respondents claim that a patient facing imminent death, who anticipates physical suffering and indignity, and is capable of responsible and voluntary choice, should have a right to a physician's assistance in providing counsel and drugs to be administered by the patient to end life promptly. [ ] They accordingly claim that a physician must have the corresponding right to provide such aid, contrary to the provisions of [the Washington code]. I do not understand the argument to rest on any assumption that rights either to suicide or to assistance in committing it are historically based as such. Respondents, rather, acknowledge the prohibition of each historically, but rely on the fact that to a substantial extent the State has repudiated that history. The result of this, respondents say, is to open the door to claims of such a patient to be accorded one of the options open to those with different, traditionally cognizable claims to autonomy in deciding how their bodies and minds should be treated. They seek the option to obtain the services of a physician to give them the benefit of advice and medical help, which is said to enjoy a tradition so strong and so devoid of specifically countervailing state concern that denial of a physician's help in these circumstances is arbitrary when physicians are generally free to advise and aid those who exercise other rights to bodily autonomy.

1

[Justice Souter reviewed the history of the legal ban on suicide and evaluated respondent's arguments that it has not become part of good, accepted medical practice.]

2

The argument supporting respondents' position * * * progresses through three steps of increasing forcefulness. First, it emphasizes the decriminalization of suicide. Reliance on this fact is sanctioned under the standard that looks not only to the tradition retained, but to society's occasional choices to reject traditions of the legal past. [ ] While the common law prohibited both suicide and aiding a suicide, with the prohibition on aiding largely justified by the primary prohibition on self-inflicted death itself, [ ] the State's rejection of the traditional treatment of the one leaves the criminality of the other open to questioning that previously would not have been appropriate. The second step in the argument is to emphasize that the State's own act of decriminalization gives a freedom of choice much like the individual's option in recognized instances of bodily autonomy. One of these, abortion, is a legal right to choose in spite of the interest a State may legitimately invoke in discouraging the practice, just as suicide is now subject to choice, despite a state interest in discouraging it. The third step is to emphasize that respondents claim a right to assistance not on the basis of some broad principle that would be subject to exceptions if that continuing interest of the State's in discouraging suicide were to be recognized at all. Respondents base their claim on the traditional right to medical care and counsel, subject to the limiting conditions of informed, responsible choice when death is imminent, conditions that support a strong analogy to rights of care in other situations in which medical counsel and assistance have been available as a matter of course. There can be no stronger claim to a physician's assistance than at the time when death is imminent, a moral judgment implied by the State's own recognition of the legitimacy of medical procedures necessarily hastening the moment of impending death.

In my judgment, the importance of the individual interest here, as within that class of "certain interests" demanding careful scrutiny of the State's contrary claim, [ ] cannot be gainsaid. Whether that interest might in some circumstances, or at some time, be seen as "fundamental" to the degree entitled to prevail is not, however, a conclusion that I need draw here, for I am satisfied that the State's interests described in the following section are sufficiently serious to defeat the present claim that its law is arbitrary or purposeless.

B

The State has put forward several interests to justify the Washington law as applied to physicians treating terminally ill patients, even those competent to make responsible choices: protecting life generally [ ] discouraging suicide even if knowing and voluntary [ ] and protecting terminally ill patients from involuntary suicide and euthanasia, both voluntary and nonvoluntary [ ].

It is not necessary to discuss the exact strengths of the first two claims of justification in the present circumstances, for the third is dispositive for me. * * * The State claims interests in protecting patients from mistakenly and involuntarily deciding to end their lives, and in guarding against both voluntary and involuntary euthanasia. Leaving aside any difficulties in coming to a clear concept of imminent death, mistaken decisions may result from inadequate palliative care or a terminal prognosis that turns out to be error;

coercion and abuse may stem from the large medical bills that family members cannot bear or unreimbursed hospitals decline to shoulder. Voluntary and involuntary euthanasia may result once doctors are authorized to prescribe lethal medication in the first instance, for they might find it pointless to distinguish between patients who administer their own fatal drugs and those who wish not to, and their compassion for those who suffer may obscure the distinction between those who ask for death and those who may be unable to request it. The argument is that a progression would occur, obscuring the line between the ill and the dying, and between the responsible and the unduly influenced, until ultimately doctors and perhaps others would abuse a limited freedom to aid suicides by yielding to the impulse to end another's suffering under conditions going beyond the narrow limits the respondents propose. The State thus argues, essentially, that respondents' claim is not as narrow as it sounds, simply because no recognition of the interest they assert could be limited to vindicating those interests and affecting no others. The State says that the claim, in practical effect, would entail consequences that the State could, without doubt, legitimately act to prevent.

* * *

Respondents propose an answer to all this, the answer of state regulation with teeth. Legislation proposed in several States, for example, would authorize physician-assisted suicide but require two qualified physicians to confirm the patient's diagnosis, prognosis, and competence; and would mandate that the patient make repeated requests witnessed by at least two others over a specified time span; and would impose reporting requirements and criminal penalties for various acts of coercion. [ ]

But at least at this moment there are reasons for caution in predicting the effectiveness of the teeth proposed. Respondents' proposals, as it turns out, sound much like the guidelines now in place in the Netherlands, the only place where experience with physician-assisted suicide and euthanasia has yielded empirical evidence about how such regulations might affect actual practice. Dutch physicians must engage in consultation before proceeding, and must decide whether the patient's decision is voluntary, well considered, and stable, whether the request to die is enduring and made more than once, and whether the patient's future will involve unacceptable suffering. [ ] There is, however, a substantial dispute today about what the Dutch experience shows. Some commentators marshall evidence that the Dutch guidelines have in practice failed to protect patients from involuntary euthanasia and have been violated with impunity. [ ] This evidence is contested. [ ] The day may come when we can say with some assurance which side is right, but for now it is the substantiality of the factual disagreement, and the alternatives for resolving it, that matter. They are, for me, dispositive of the due process claim at this time.

* * *

[Justice Souter next discussed the propriety of a legislative, rather than judicial, fact-finding process with regard to current issues surrounding physician assisted death.]

I do not decide here what the significance might be of legislative foot-dragging in ascertaining the facts going to the State's argument that the right in question could not be confined as claimed. Sometimes a court may be bound to act regardless of the institutional preferability of the political branches as forums for addressing constitutional claims. [ ] Now, it is enough to say that our examination of legislative reasonableness should consider the fact that the Legislature of the State of Washington is no more obviously at fault than this Court is in being uncertain about what would happen if respondents prevailed today. We therefore have a clear question about which institution, a legislature or a court, is relatively more competent to deal with an emerging issue as to which facts currently unknown could be dispositive. The answer has to be, for the reasons already stated, that the legislative process is to be preferred.

* * *

The Court should accordingly stay its hand to allow reasonable legislative consideration. While I do not decide for all time that respondents' claim should not be recognized, I acknowledge the legislative institutional competence as the better one to deal with that claim at this time.

JUSTICE GINSBURG, concurring in the judgments [in both Glucksberg and Vacco].

I concur in the Court's judgments in these cases substantially for the reasons stated by JUSTICE O'CONNOR in her concurring opinion.

JUSTICE BREYER, concurring in the judgments [in both Glucksberg and Vacco].

I believe that JUSTICE O'CONNOR's views, which I share, have greater legal significance than the Court's opinion suggests. I join her separate opinion, except insofar as it joins the majority. * * *

I agree with the Court in Vacco v. Quill [ ] that the articulated state interests justify the distinction drawn between physician assisted suicide and withdrawal of life-support. I also agree with the Court that the critical question in both of the cases before us is whether "the 'liberty' specially protected by the Due Process Clause includes a right" of the sort that the respondents assert. [ ] I do not agree, however, with the Court's formulation of that claimed "liberty" interest. The Court describes it as a "right to commit suicide with another's assistance." [ ] But I would not reject the respondents' claim without considering a different formulation, for which our legal tradition may provide greater support. That formulation would use words roughly like a "right to die with dignity." But irrespective of the exact words used, at its core would lie personal control over the manner of death, professional medical assistance, and the avoidance of unnecessary and severe physical suffering—combined.

* * *

I do not believe, however, that this Court need or now should decide whether or a not * * * [a right to die with dignity] is "fundamental." That is because, in my view, the avoidance of severe physical pain (connected with death) would have to comprise an essential part of any successful claim and because * * * the laws before us do not force a dying person to undergo that kind of pain. [ ] Rather, the laws of New York and of Washington do not prohibit doctors from providing patients with drugs sufficient to control pain despite the risk that those drugs themselves will kill. [ ] And under these circumstances the laws of New York and Washington would overcome any remaining significant interests and would be justified, regardless.

* * *

Were the legal circumstances different—for example, were state law to prevent the provision of palliative care, including the administration of drugs as needed to avoid pain at the end of life—then the law's impact upon serious and otherwise unavoidable physical pain (and accompanying death) would be more directly at issue. And as JUSTICE O'CONNOR suggests, the Court might have to revisit its conclusions in these cases.

* * *

VACCO v. QUILL

Supreme Court of the United States, 1997.
521 U.S. 793.

CHIEF JUSTICE REHNQUIST delivered the opinion of the Court.

In New York, as in most States, it is a crime to aid another to commit or attempt suicide, but patients may refuse even lifesaving medical treatment. The question presented by this case is whether New York's prohibition on assisting suicide therefore violates the Equal Protection Clause of the Fourteenth Amendment. We hold that it does not.

* * * Respondents, and three gravely ill patients who have since died, sued the State's Attorney General in the United States District Court. They urged that because New York permits a competent person to refuse life-sustaining medical treatment, and because the refusal of such treatment is "essentially the same thing" as physician-assisted suicide, New York's assisted-suicide ban violates the Equal Protection Clause. [ ]

The District Court disagreed * * *.

The Court of Appeals for the Second Circuit reversed. [ ] The court determined that, despite the assisted-suicide ban's apparent general applicability, "New York law does not treat equally all competent persons who are in the final stages of fatal illness and wish to hasten their deaths," because "those in the final stages of terminal illness who are on life-support systems are allowed to hasten their deaths by directing the removal of such systems; but those who are similarly situated, except for the previous attachment of life-sustaining equipment, are not allowed to hasten death by self-administering prescribed drugs." [ ] The Court of Appeals then examined whether this supposed unequal treatment was rationally related to any legitimate state interests, and concluded that "to the extent that [New York's statutes] prohibit a physician from prescribing medications to be self-administered by a mentally competent, terminally-ill person in the final stages of his terminal illness, they are not rationally related to any legitimate state interest." [ ] We granted certiorari [ ] and now reverse.

The Equal Protection Clause commands that no State shall "deny to any person within its jurisdiction the equal protection of the laws." This provision creates no substantive rights. [ ] Instead, it embodies a general rule that States must treat like cases alike but may treat unlike cases accordingly. [ ] If a legislative classification or distinction "neither burdens a fundamental right nor targets a suspect class, we will uphold [it] so long as it bears a rational relation to some legitimate end." [ ]

New York's statutes outlawing assisting suicide affect and address matters of profound significance to all New Yorkers alike. They neither infringe fundamental rights nor involve suspect classifications. [ ] These laws are therefore entitled to a "strong presumption of validity." [ ]

On their faces, neither New York's ban on assisting suicide nor its statutes permitting patients to refuse medical treatment treat anyone differently than anyone else or draw any distinctions between persons. Everyone, regardless of physical condition, is entitled, if competent, to refuse unwanted lifesaving medical treatment; no one is permitted to assist a suicide. Generally speaking, laws that apply evenhandedly to all "unquestionably comply" with the Equal Protection Clause. [ ]

The Court of Appeals, however, concluded that some terminally ill people—those who are on life-support systems—are treated differently than those who are not, in that the former may "hasten death" by ending treatment, but the latter may not "hasten death" through physician-assisted suicide. [ ] This conclusion depends on the submission that ending or refusing lifesaving medical treatment "is nothing more nor less than assisted suicide." [ ] Unlike the Court of Appeals, we think the distinction between assisting suicide and withdrawing life-sustaining treatment, a distinction widely recognized and endorsed in the medical profession and in our legal traditions, is both important and logical; it is certainly rational. [ ]

The distinction comports with fundamental legal principles of causation and intent. First, when a patient refuses life-sustaining medical treatment, he dies from an underlying fatal disease or pathology; but if a patient ingests lethal medication prescribed by a physician, he is killed by that medication. [ ]

Furthermore, a physician who withdraws, or honors a patient's refusal to begin, life-sustaining medical treatment purposefully intends, or may so intend, only to respect his patient's wishes and "to cease doing useless and futile or degrading things to the patient when [the patient] no longer stands to benefit from them." [ ] The same is true when a doctor provides aggressive palliative care; in some cases, painkilling drugs may hasten a patient's death, but the physician's purpose and intent is, or may be, only to ease his patient's pain. A doctor who assists a suicide, however, "must, necessarily and indubitably, intend primarily that the patient be made dead." [ ] Similarly, a patient who commits suicide with a doctor's aid necessarily has the specific intent to end his or her own life, while a patient who refuses or discontinues treatment might not. [ ]

The law has long used actors' intent or purpose to distinguish between acts that may have the same result. [ ] Put differently, the law distin-
es actions taken "because of" a given end from actions taken "in spite
ieir unintended but foreseen consequences. [ ]

Given these general principles, it is not surprising that many courts, including New York courts, have carefully distinguished refusing life-sustaining treatment from suicide. * * *

Similarly, the overwhelming majority of state legislatures have drawn a clear line between assisting suicide and withdrawing or permitting the refusal of unwanted lifesaving medical treatment by prohibiting the former and permitting the latter. [ ] And "nearly all states expressly disapprove of suicide and assisted suicide either in statutes dealing with durable powers of attorney in health-care situations, or in 'living will' statutes." [ ] Thus, even as the States move to protect and promote patients' dignity at the end of life, they remain opposed to physician-assisted suicide.

* * *

This Court has also recognized, at least implicitly, the distinction between letting a patient die and making that patient die. In Cruzan [ ] we concluded that "the principle that a competent person has a constitutionally protected liberty interest in refusing unwanted medical treatment may be inferred from our prior decisions," and we assumed the existence of such a right for purposes of that case [ ]. But our assumption of a right to refuse treatment was grounded not, as the Court of Appeals supposed, on the proposition that patients have a general and abstract "right to hasten death," [ ] but on well established, traditional rights to bodily integrity and freedom from unwanted touching [ ]. In fact, we observed that "the majority of States in this country have laws imposing criminal penalties on one who assists another to commit suicide." [ ] Cruzan therefore provides no support for the notion that refusing life-sustaining medical treatment is "nothing more nor less than suicide."

For all these reasons, we disagree with respondents' claim that the distinction between refusing lifesaving medical treatment and assisted suicide is "arbitrary" and "irrational."[11] Granted, in some cases, the line between the two may not be clear, but certainty is not required, even were it possible. Logic and contemporary practice support New York's judgment that the two acts are different, and New York may therefore, consistent with the Constitution, treat them differently. By permitting everyone to refuse unwanted medical treatment while prohibiting anyone from assisting a suicide, New York law follows a longstanding and rational distinction.

New York's reasons for recognizing and acting on this distinction— including prohibiting intentional killing and preserving life; preventing suicide; maintaining physicians' role as their patients' healers; protecting vulnerable people from indifference, prejudice, and psychological and financial pressure to end their lives; and avoiding a possible slide towards euthanasia— are discussed in greater detail in our opinion in Glucksberg, ante. These valid

---

11. Respondents also argue that the State irrationally distinguishes between physician-assisted suicide and "terminal sedation," a process respondents characterize as "inducing barbiturate coma and then starving the person to death." [ ] Petitioners insist, however, that " 'although proponents of physician-assisted suicide and euthanasia contend that terminal sedation is covert physician-assisted suicide or euthanasia, the concept of sedating pharmacotherapy is based on informed consent and the principle of double effect.' " [ ] Just as a State may prohibit assisting suicide while permitting patients to refuse unwanted lifesaving treatment, it may permit palliative care related to that refusal, which may have the foreseen but unintended "double effect" of hastening the patient's death. [ ]

and important public interests easily satisfy the constitutional requirement that a legislative classification bear a rational relation to some legitimate end.

The judgment of the Court of Appeals is reversed.

* * *

JUSTICE SOUTER, concurring in the judgment.

Even though I do not conclude that assisted suicide is a fundamental right entitled to recognition at this time, I accord the claims raised by the patients and physicians in this case and Washington v. Glucksberg a high degree of importance, requiring a commensurate justification. [ ] The reasons that lead me to conclude in Glucksberg that the prohibition on assisted suicide is not arbitrary under the due process standard also support the distinction between assistance to suicide, which is banned, and practices such as termination of artificial life support and death-hastening pain medication, which are permitted. I accordingly concur in the judgment of the Court.

* * *

VI. PHYSICIAN ASSISTED DEATH

On page 1188, at the end of note 8, add:

On March 26, 1999 Dr. Kevorkian was convicted of second-degree murder after a very short trial in which he represented himself. While past cases had involved Dr. Kevorkian's use of a suicide machine which was actually operated by his client (patient? victim?), in this case he injected a lethal drug directly into Thomas Youk, a 52 year old man suffering from amyotrophic lateral sclerosis (Lou Gehrig's disease). What is more, he filmed the entire process, which was then showed to a national audience on "60 Minutes," the CBS news show, in November, 1998.

Dr. Keviorkian was originally charged with first-degree murder and assisted suicide. The trial judge ruled that evidence of Mr. Youk's suffering, which would be provided by the testimony of his family members, would be relevant and admissible on the assisted suicide charge, but not on the murder charge. The prosecutor decided to drop the assisted suicide charge to keep out that kind of evidence, which had played so well in Dr. Kevorkian's earlier trials. The jury apparently found no premeditation, making the second degree murder conviction the most serious available. Dr. Kevorkian was also found guilty of delivery of a controlled substance. He has said that he intends to starve himself to death in prison.

Leading supporters of euthanasia were concerned by the conviction. The executive director of the Hemlock Society said, "To call it murder is barbaric. It highlights the necessity to change the law over the country * * * so that a compassionate physician can help a suffering patient die." One leader of a disability group expressed satisfaction that this "serial killer" of the disabled had finally been brought to justice. It is unclear whether the conviction will end Dr. Kevorkian's role as a spokesperson for euthanasia or turn him into a martyr for the cause. For an account of the trial, see Pam Belluck, Dr. Kevorkian is a Murderer, The Jury Finds, New York Times, March 27, 1999, at A–1.

On page 1195, after note 13, add:

14.   Litigation seeking a right to physician assisted death need not be based only on the United States Constitution, it may have a basis in state law as well, especially in states with particularly strong constitutional privacy provisions. In Krischer v. McIver, 697 So.2d 97 (Fla.1997), a terminally ill AIDS patient and his physician sought an injunction against the prosecution of the physician for assisting in his patient's suicide. The Florida Supreme Court rejected a claim that the privacy provision of Article I, section 23 of the Florida Constitution included the right to have a physician assist in one's suicide. The Court announced that a properly drawn statute authorizing physician-assisted suicide would be constitutionally permissible, but that principles of separation of powers left the decision about whether it should be made legal to the legislature. The Chief Justice filed a vigorous dissent, arguing that, " * * *the right of privacy attaches with unusual force at the death bed. * * * What possible interest does society have in saving life when there is nothing of life to save but a final convulsion of agony? The state has no business in this arena." 697 So.2d at 111.

On page 1201, at the end of note 1, add:

Early in 1999 the Oregon Department of Health issued its first annual report, which collected data on those who received lethal prescriptions under the Act during 1998. The Department compared those who received prescriptions under the Act and died during 1998 with two control groups: all Oregonians who died from similar underlying diseases, and a group of matched control patients. The Department also compared the attributed of the physicians who wrote those prescriptions with physicians who cared for the matched controls. The report was published in the New England Journal of Medicine and it is also available in three parts at the following web sites:

http://www.ohd.hr.state.or.us/cdpe/chs/pas/arsystem.htm,

http://www.ohd.hr.state.or.us/cdpe/chs/pas/arresult.htm, and

http://www.ohd.hr.state.or.us/cdpe/chs/pas/ar-disc.htm.

A slightly edited version of the results section of the report is republished here:

Oregon's Death with Dignity Act: The First Year's Experience
1999

Results:

Results of our data collection and comparison studies are presented in two formats. In addition to this report, the results are also presented in a manuscript published in the *New England Journal of Medicine* (Title: "Legalized physician-assisted suicide in Oregon: The first year's experience") on February 18, 1999. These data are published in a peer-reviewed medical journal for two reasons. First, legalized physician-assisted suicide is unique to Oregon. As such, the reporting system implemented by the OHD under the Death with Dignity Act has no precedent. We believe that a new reporting system which is responsible for collecting data on a controversial issue, such as the Death with Dignity Act, should be subject to the scrutiny of peer review in the medical literature. Such critique may lead to future improvements in the way data are collected. Second, the data and analyses presented in these reports will be of interest and used by parties on all sides of this issue. Again, we believe that the methods, results, and analyses that we present can only benefit from the critique offered by the peer review process.

Characteristics of Prescription Recipients

Twenty-three persons who received legal prescriptions for lethal medications in 1998 were reported to the OHD. Of these twenty-three persons, fifteen died after taking their lethal medications, six died from their underlying illness, and two were alive as of January 1, 1999. * * * The median age of the 21 prescription recipients was 69 years and ranged from the third to the tenth decade of life. All 21 patients were white, 11 (52%) were male, and 11 (52%) lived in the Portland Tri-county area. Of the 21 recipients, 20 had been residents of Oregon for longer than 6 months when they received their prescriptions. One patient had moved to Oregon 4 months prior to death to be cared for by family members and not because of legalized assisted suicide. Four of the twenty-one prescription recipients had a psychiatric or psychological consultation and all patients were ultimately determined to be capable in the context of the Death with Dignity Act. All physician reports were in full compliance with the law.

Twenty (95%) of the twenty-one prescription recipients who died in 1998 were prescribed nine grams of a fast-acting barbiturate, either secobarbital or pentobarbital. One patient was prescribed one gram of secobarbital to be taken with an oral narcotic. Most patients also received a number of nonlethal medications to be taken in conjunction with the lethal medications. These included medications to increase stomach emptying and to prevent nausea and vomiting.

The Physician–Assisted Suicide Process

Fifteen prescription recipients chose physician-assisted suicide and died after taking their lethal medications. The median time from medication ingestion to unconsciousness (available for 11 patients) was 5 minutes (range 3–20 minutes). The median time from medication ingestion to death (available for 14 patients) was 26 minutes (range 15 minutes to 11.5 hours). For eight of the 15 persons who chose physician-assisted suicide, the prescribing physician was at the bedside when they took the lethal medications. For 6 of the 15 patients, the physician was also at the bedside when they died. In instances where the physician was not present for the medication ingestion or death, times to unconsciousness and death, as well as reports of complications, were provided to the physician by persons present at the bedside. No complications, such as vomiting or seizures were reported by any physician.

Comparison Studies

We first compared the 15 persons who chose physician-assisted suicide with all deaths in Oregon in 1996, the latest year for which finalized mortality data are available. The 15 persons who chose physician-assisted suicide accounted for 5 of every 10,000 deaths in Oregon, based on the 28,900 deaths that occurred in 1996. The 13 persons with cancer who chose physician-assisted suicide accounted for 19 of every 10,000 cancer deaths, based on the 6,784 persons who died of cancer in Oregon in 1996. Next, we compared the 15 persons who chose physician-assisted suicide with the 5,604 Oregonians who died in 1996 from similar underlying illnesses. Age, race, sex, and Portland Tri-county residence status did not predict participation in physician-assisted suicide [ ]. Twelve of the fifteen persons who chose physician-assisted suicide had at least a high school diploma. Four of these twelve had graduated from college. The proportions of high school and college graduates were similar among persons who chose assisted suicide and the 5,604 controls. In contrast, marital status was associated with participation in physician-assisted suicide. Persons who were divorced and persons who had never married were 6.8 times and 23.7 times, respectively, more likely to choose physician-assisted suicide than persons who were married.

For our second comparison study, the matched case-control study, we identified control patients who had not participated in the Death with Dignity Act but who were similar to the persons who chose physician-assisted suicide with regard to age, underlying illness, and date of death. Using 1998 death certificates, we identified 81 potential control patients who met these criteria. Of these 81 persons, 17 were disqualified from the study because we could not contact the physician who provided end of life care or because we could not identify an end of life care provider. We were able to obtain physician interviews for 64 potential control patients. Of these 64 persons, 21 were disqualified because they would not have been eligible for a prescription for lethal medications under the law: 10 were deemed incapable of making health care decisions by their physicians; 2 were not Oregon residents; 2 could not take oral medications, and for 7 patients, the time between when the physician determined that the patient had less than 6 months to live and death was less than the required 15–day waiting period. Ultimately, we collected data on 43 persons to serve as controls, 3 matched controls for each of 14 persons choosing physician-assisted suicide and 1 matched control for the single remaining person.

Results of the matched case-control study are similar to the comparison with 1996 Oregon deaths just described. Persons who chose physician-assisted suicide and 1998 matched controls did not differ statistically by race, sex, Oregon resident status (greater than 6 months), Portland Tri-county resident status, or education level (Table 3). Although not statistically significant, there was a trend in that persons who chose physician-assisted suicide were more likely to be divorced than controls. Persons who chose physician-assisted suicide were more likely than controls to have never married.

No patients who chose physician-assisted suicide or matched control patients voiced concern to their physician about the financial impact of their illnesses. Both groups contained similar proportions of patients insured through Medicare, Medicaid, or private insurance, or who lacked health insurance. One patient who chose physician-assisted suicide (7 %) and 15 (35 %) controls expressed concern about end of life pain, although this difference was not statistically significant. Patients who chose physician-assisted suicide and controls were equally likely to have been enrolled in hospice, to have had advance medical directives, and to have died at home. The proportion of patients in each group who expressed concerns about being a physical or emotional burden, or about the inability to participate in activities that made life enjoyable, were similar. However, patients who chose physician-assisted suicide were significantly more likely than controls to express concern to their physicians about loss of autonomy, and more likely to express concern about loss of control of bodily functions (e.g., incontinence, vomiting) due to their illness. At death, patients who chose physician-assisted suicide were significantly less likely than controls to be completely disabled and bedridden.

Physician Characteristics

Fourteen physicians wrote prescriptions for lethal medications for the 15 patients who chose physician-assisted suicide. Forty physicians were the end of life providers for the 43 control patients. The two groups of physicians were similar with respect to age, sex, specialty, and years-in-practice, although there was a trend for prescribing physicians to have been older and in practice longer [ ].

For some physicians, the process of participating in physician-assisted suicide had a great emotional impact. In response to general, open-ended inquiries, prescribing physicians offered comments such as, "It was an excruciating thing to do ... it made me rethink life's priorities", "This was really hard on me, especially being there when he took the pills," and "this had a tremendous emotional impact."

Not all Oregon physicians were willing to participate in physician-assisted suicide in 1998. Six patients who chose assisted suicide had requested lethal medications from one or more providers before finding a physician who would begin the prescription process. Physicians for 67% (29/43) of control patients would have refused to write a prescription for lethal medications had the patient asked; physicians for 21% (9/43) of control patients would have provided prescriptions; and physicians for 12% (5/43) of control patients were unsure. Six control patients (14%) had discussed physician-assisted suicide with the physician we interviewed, but none had begun the formal request process.

On page 1201, after note 5, add:

6. Congress has considered this issue, too. Even before the Oregon statute became effective, Congress passed the Assisted Suicide Prevention Restriction Act of 1997, which outlaws the use of federal money to aid physician assisted death, directly or indirectly.

Shortly after the Oregon Death with Dignity Act became effective, some suggested that any physician who prescribed a lethal drug under that statute would be prescribing that drug without a "legitimate medical purpose," and thus would be acting inconsistently with the federal Controlled Substances Act. A physician's violation of the Act could lead to both the loss of prescribing authority and criminal indictment. In June of 1998, after the matter had been pending for some time, the United States Department of Justice published its report concluding that use of controlled substances under the Oregon statute could satisfy the "legitimate medical purpose" requirement of the federal Act. Immediately, members of the House and Senate introduced the Lethal Drug Abuse Prevention Act of 1998, which would have expanded the authority of the Drug Enforcement Agency to investigate lethal use of controlled substances, which could not be used with the intent of causing death. Supporters of physician assisted death joined many of their staunchest opponents and mainstream medical organizations (including the AMA) to oppose the bill because, they said, it would be likely to chill physicians from providing adequate pain relief at the end of life. While the Lethal Drug Abuse Prevention Act did not pass either house in 1998, it was expected to be resurrected in 1999.

Chapter 19

INTERDISCIPLINARY DECISIONMAK-
ING IN HEALTH CARE: IRBS,
ETHICS COMMITTEES, AND
ADVISORY COMMITTEES

I. REGULATION OF RESEARCH UPON
HUMAN SUBJECTS—IRBS

**On page 1206, at the end of "A. Nazi Experimentation and the Develop-
ment of the Nuremberg Code," add:**

The roles of international research organizations, and American researchers doing research abroad, were called into question as a consequence of a
series of perinatal HIV transmission studies done in Africa and Asia in the
mid–1990s. There is a particular need for treatment for HIV-positive pregnant
women in some African and Asian countries, where the HIV infection rate is
far higher than it is in most of the developed world. There are more than a
half million HIV infected babies born each year, most in the developing world.
The United Nations has put a high priority on finding some genuinely feasible
way of dealing with this increasingly pervasive problem.

As a general matter, without treatment between 17% and 25% of pregnant women who are infected with HIV will give birth to an HIV-positive
baby, although that figure may be even higher in the developing world. In the
United States, an HIV-positive mother will be offered therapy with a combination of drugs, including AZT, during her last six months of pregnancy and
intravenous medication during delivery. A c-section is often recommended if
the mother has been taking AZT. The baby then will be treated for six weeks
after birth. This protocol, which decreases the transmission rate to about 8%,
is too expensive (at more than $500) for use in developing countries, where
any use of a needle may also be too risky. As a consequence, the United
Nations AIDS program, along with the United States National Institutes of
Health, the Centers for Disease Control and others, sponsored research in
which mostly impoverished HIV-positive women in poor countries were randomized to a few different relatively inexpensive courses of treatment. Some
women were also randomized to a placebo. While the consent of those who
participated in the study was sought by the investigators, it was not always
provided in writing, and, given the alternative–no treatment at all–some
believe that it was inherently coerced consent. The purpose of the research

282

was to find some less expensive and safe way of treating HIV-positive pregnant women in very poor countries; of course, the beneficiaries of the research could include the HIV-positive pregnant women (and third party health care payers) in the United States and the rest of the developed world, too.

Some criticized the studies as improper research involving human subjects, and attempts to modify the Declaration of Helsinki to accommodate this kind of research were strongly opposed by the Health Research Group of Ralph Nader's Public Citizen and other medical researchers. First, they argued, modification of the Declaration to permit such research would change the current ethical requirement that a new therapeutic intervention be tested against the best current treatment, not against a placebo. They argued that changing this requirement so that the new treatment would need to be tested against the best treatment "that would otherwise be available" to the subjects, not the best treatment, would endanger the poor, who routinely could be offered a second class alternative to the research treatment being tested. As the Health Research Group argued, "[p]articularly in countries like the United States, which does not have universal health coverage, it is inevitable that this principle will ultimately be used to deny uninsured or underinsured persons access to medical care in human experiments." That group also opposed changes in the Declaration of Helsinki that would permit the use of placebos where "the outcome measures are neither death nor disability," that would allow medical journals to publish research that was done in violation of the Declaration if the editors had "consider[ed] carefully" the reasons for the variances, and that would permit informed consent to be oral (rather than written) in cases of "slight risk" or when the medical intervention would not ordinarily require a written document.

Do you think that the research was properly done? Was this appropriate research likely to save hundreds of thousands of lives, or was it another example of the developed world imposing a burden (here, of medical research) on the poor and on people of color? Does it make any difference to your analysis that the research ultimately found that some (but not all) of the shorter, cheaper, less invasive protocols were almost as good (but not quite as good) as the current protocol used in the United States? For the full text of Public Citizen's letter criticizing proposed changes in the Declaration of Helsinki, see http://www.citizen.org/hrg/WHAT'SNEW/1777.htm. For one summary account of the results of the studies, see Lawrence Altman, Spare AIDS Regime Is Found To Reduce Risks to Newborns, New York Times, February 2, 1999, at A–1.

†